BANANA DIPLOMACY

THE MAKING OF
AMERICAN POLICY IN NICARAGUA
1981–1987

ROY GUTMAN

SIMON AND SCHUSTER
New York London Toronto Sydney Tokyo

To my father

Copyright © 1988 by Roy Gutman
All rights reserved
including the right of reproduction
in whole or in part in any form

Published by Simon and Schuster
A Division of Simon & Schuster Inc.
Simon & Schuster Building
Rockefeller Center
1230 Avenue of the Americas
New York, New York 10020
SIMON AND SCHUSTER and colophon are registered
trademarks of Simon & Schuster Inc.

Designed by Kathy Kikkert
Manufactured in the United States of America

10 9 8 7 6 5 4 3 2 1

Library of Congress Cataloging in Publication Data

Gutman, Roy.
   Banana diplomacy: the making of American policy in Nicaragua.
1981–1987 / Roy Gutman.
      p.   cm.
   Includes index.
   ISBN 0-671-60626-3
   1. United States—Foreign relations—Nicaragua.   2. Nicaragua—
Foreign relations—United States.   3. United States—Foreign
relations—1981–   4. Nicaragua—Foreign relations—1979–   I. Title.
E183.8.N5G87   1988
327.7307285—dc19   88-460
                                                                CIP

ACKNOWLEDGMENTS

This book developed out of a series of articles in *Newsday* about U.S. policy in Central America which I coauthored with Susan Page in mid-1983. The editors of *Foreign Policy* encouraged me to expand on one element, U.S. diplomacy in Nicaragua, for an article that appeared a year later under the title "America's Diplomatic Charade." Alan Tonelson, the associate editor, urged me to write the book.

In organizing my research, travel, and writing, I benefited from the advice and assessments of Viron ("Pete") Vaky, former assistant secretary of state for inter-American affairs and one of the capital's most respected diplomats emeritus. Caesar Sereseres of the Rand Corporation and occasionally the State Department suggested themes, challenged assumptions, and critiqued the first draft. Thomas Etzold, a consultant on defense and foreign affairs, subjected the book to his rigorous analysis. Bruce Bagley, formerly of the Johns Hopkins University School for International Studies, suggested sources particularly relating to the Contadora issues.

Others who read the manuscript in various stages, suggested improvements, and caught omissions or errors were Jim Connally, John Felton, Jacobo Goldstein, Jim Klurfeld, Gabriel Marcella, Geoffrey Pyatt, Fernando van Reigersberg, and several others who asked not to be named. They bear no blame for judgments in the book or any remaining mistakes.

My editors, Alice Mayhew and Henry Ferris, insisted that the book retain its focus and steered the project through the hurdles, and my agent, Gail Ross, provided sound advice at several critical moments.

The *Newsday* management—Tony Marro, Les Payne, Jim Klurfeld, Pat Sloyan, and Charlotte Hall—showed the flexibility that allowed me to complete the book while working. A great many colleagues at *Newsday* and other news media supported this endeavor by discussing stories they had written, suggesting sources, and cheering me on. Alan Lepp, an intern at *Foreign Policy*, researched facts for the first draft; journalists Nancy Nusser in Nicaragua and Caitlan Randall

11

in Costa Rica provided solid assistance; Alison Mitchell and Mike Waldman of *Newsday* offered some timely suggestions; and Christine Merkle, the *Newsday* researcher, rescued me from a clinch on several occasions. I also benefited from the Central American Historical Institute at Georgetown University and the collection of Nicaraguan newspapers kept by Alejandro Bolaños's Nicaraguan Information Center in St. Charles, Missouri.

I will not forget Kwon Ho Chun of Staten Island, who noticed the first 100 pages of manuscript lying in the trash on Seventh Avenue in New York where Amtrak's package delivery service had dropped it and, in recognition of either its merits or the need for revisions, returned it to me.

Finally, my wife, Betsy, after encouraging me to start this project, endured three years of sacrificed evenings, weekends, and vacations. Without her patience and support, the book would not have been possible. Even our infant daughter, Caroline, delayed her arrival until a few days beyond her due date, allowing me to complete the second draft.

To all, my deepest thanks.

CONTENTS

CAST OF CHARACTERS*

PRESIDENT
Ronald Reagan, 1981–

SECRETARY OF STATE
Alexander Haig, January 1981–June 1982 (fired)
George Shultz, July 1982–

ASSISTANT SECRETARY FOR INTER-AMERICAN AFFAIRS
John Bushnell (acting), January–June 1981
Thomas Enders, March 1981 (unofficial), June 1981–May 1983 (fired)
Langhorne ("Tony") Motley, July 1983–April 1985
Elliott Abrams, July 1985 (confirmed October)–

DEPUTY ASSISTANT SECRETARY OF STATE FOR INTER-AMERICAN AFFAIRS
Craig Johnstone, July 1983–July 1985
William Walker, July 1985–

SPECIAL U.S. ENVOY IN CHARGE OF CENTRAL AMERICAN NEGOTIATIONS
Richard Stone, April 1983–February 1984 (forced resignation)
Harry Shlaudeman, March 1984–March 1986
Philip Habib, March 1986–August 1987 (forced resignation)
Morris Busby, September 1987–

U.S. AMBASSADOR TO HONDURAS
Jack Binns, October 1980–November 1981
John Negroponte, November 1981–May 1985
John Ferch, August 1985–July 1986 (fired)
Everett Briggs, October 1986–

U.S. AMBASSADOR TO NICARAGUA
Lawrence Pezzullo, June 1979–August 1981
Anthony Quainton, March 1982–April 1984
Harry Bergold, May 1984–July 1987

---

* Unless otherwise indicated, ambassadors and senior officials are shown as occupying posts from the time of their Senate confirmation. Unless fired outright, officials leaving their jobs often stay on until their successors are confirmed. NSC officials are not subject to Senate confirmation.

NATIONAL SECURITY ADVISER

Richard Allen, January 1981–January 1982 (fired)
William Clark, January 1982–October 1983
Robert McFarlane, October 1983–December 1985
Rear Admiral John Poindexter, December 1985–November 1986 (fired)
Frank Carlucci, December 1986–November 1987
Lieutenant General Colin Powell, November 1987–

NSC ACTION OFFICER NOMINALLY IN CHARGE OF NICARAGUA POLICY

Roger Fontaine, January 1981–December 1983
Constantine Menges, October 1983–July 1985 (fired in 1986)
Raymond Burghardt, August 1985–December 1986
José Sorzano, December 1986–August 1987
Jacqueline Tillman, August 1987–

NSC OFFICIAL IN ACTUAL CHARGE OF NICARAGUA POLICY

(no dominant figure) January 1981–Januay 1983
Major (later Lieutenant Colonel) Oliver North, deputy director for politico-military affairs, January 1983–November 1986 (fired)
(no dominant figure) December 1986–November 1987
John D. Negroponte, deputy NSC adviser, December 1987–

COMMANDER U.S. SOUTHERN COMMAND, PANAMA

Lieutenant General Wallace Nutting, October 1979–May 1983
General Paul Gorman, May 1983–March 1985
General John Galvin, March 1985–June 1987
General Frederick Woerner, June 1987–

CIA OFFICIAL IN CHARGE OF OPERATION

Duane ("Dewey") Clarridge, director, operations, Latin America, August 1981–August 1984
Alan Fiers, Central America task force chief, September 1984–

HEAD OF THE HONDURAN ARMED FORCES

General Gustavo Álvarez Martínez, January 1981–March 1984 (ousted by internal military coup)
General Walter López Reyes, April 1984–January 1986 (ousted by internal military coup)
Brigadier General Humberto Regalado Hernández, January 1986–

SENIOR SANDINISTA OFFICIALS

Daniel Ortega Saavedra, coordinator of the junta, 1981–1985; president, January 1985–
Humberto Ortega Saavedra, minister of defense, 1979–
Miguel d'Escoto Brockmann, foreign minister, July 1979–
Victor Hugo Tinoco, vice foreign minister, 1981–

CHRONOLOGY

1981

JANUARY 20:   Ronald Reagan inaugurated as President.

APRIL 1:   Reagan terminates $118 million in U.S. aid to Nicaragua (obtained by Jimmy Carter) despite report of the U.S. ambassador in Managua that Sandinistas had halted transshipment of arms to leftist guerrillas in El Salvador.

APRIL: At a meeting with CIA Director William Casey, Honduran army Colonel Gustavo Álvarez Martínez proposes that the United States back anti-Sandinista insurgents based in Honduras in a plan leading to direct U.S. intervention to oust the government in Managua.

AUGUST: Casey's newly appointed operations director for Latin America, Duane Clarridge, twice visits Honduras to signal U.S. go-ahead for Álvarez proposal.

AUGUST 11–12:   Assistant Secretary of State Thomas Enders discusses a negotiated resolution of differences with the Sandinistas, centering on their military buildup and support for leftist insurgencies.

AUGUST 11:   Nicaraguan Democratic Forces (FDN) formed in Guatemala.

NOVEMBER 16:   Reagan approves proposal to provide $19.95 million in support for contra rebels.

1982

AUGUST 20:   Enders outlines U.S. policy on Nicaragua in San Francisco speech, adding democratization to list of U.S. conditions for normal relations.

DECEMBER 8:   Democratic-controlled House bans covert aid for purpose of overthrowing the Sandinistas.

1983

MAY 27:   Enders fired; Tony Motley appointed to replace him.

JULY–DECEMBER: U.S. military stages unprecedented

16

sea and land exercises in and around Honduras to intimidate Nicaragua, Cuba, and the Salvadoran rebels.

JULY 28:   For the first time since Reagan took office, the House votes down contra aid.

1984

JANUARY–FEBRUARY: CIA mines Nicaraguan harbors.

MARCH 31:   Álvarez ousted in Honduras.

MAY: NSC adviser Robert McFarlane secures Saudi pledge of $1 million a month to contras.

JUNE 1:   Shultz travels to Managua and launches new negotiating round aimed at resolving U.S.–Sandinista differences.

SEPTEMBER 5–6:   U.S. envoy presents U.S. position at Manzanillo.

OCTOBER 10:   Congress suspends U.S. aid to contras.

NOVEMBER 4:   Daniel Ortega elected president in Nicaragua.

NOVEMBER 6:   Reagan reelected in forty-nine-state landslide.

1985

JANUARY 18:   United States announces suspension of Manzanillo talks.

FEBRUARY 11:   Saudi king Fahd pledges another $24 million to contras, for total of $32 million.

APRIL 30:   Motley resigns; replaced by Elliott Abrams.

MAY 1:   U.S. economic embargo against Nicaragua.

JUNE 12:   House approves $28 million in "humanitarian" aid to contras.

JUNE 30–JULY 1:   After meeting contra military leaders in Miami, Oliver North implements plan to raise funds and deliver arms to contras through offshore enterprise managed by Richard Secord.

DECEMBER 6:   North tells Israeli official of plan to divert profits to contras from secret sale of arms to Iran.

1986

JUNE 25:   House approves $100 million, including $70 million in military aid to contras.

OCTOBER 5:   U.S. supply plane shot down over Nicaragua. Crew member Eugene Hasenfus parachutes into captivity.

NOVEMBER 3:   U.S. arms-for-hostages talks with Iran revealed in Beirut magazine.

NOVEMBER 4:   Democrats win control of the Senate.

NOVEMBER 25:   U.S. aid diversion to contras revealed by Attorney General Edwin Meese; Oliver North fired, John Poindexter resigns.

DECEMBER 15:   CIA Director William Casey disabled by stroke.

1987

AUGUST 5:   Wright-Reagan plan for peace presented.

AUGUST 7:   Central American leaders agree to peace plan drafted by Costa Rican president Oscar Arias.

NOVEMBER 5:   Sandinistas announce readiness for indirect talks with contras.

1988

JANUARY 15–16:   At Central American summit, Daniel Ortega agrees to direct talks with contras, lifts state of emergency.

FEBRUARY 3:   House defeats contra funding request, killing the military aid program.

MARCH 11:   Robert McFarlane pleads guilty to misdemeanor charges arising from Iran-Contra affair.

MARCH 16:   John Poindexter, Oliver North, Richard Secord, and Albert Hakim indicted on criminal charges.

MARCH 16:   Reagan dispatches 3,200 troops to Honduras in a "show of force" after a reported Sandinista incursion into Honduras.

MARCH 23:   Sandinista and contra leaders sign tentative cease-fire.

CHAPTER 1

THE PATTERN IS SET

IN JULY 1980, when Republicans gathered in Detroit to nominate Ronald Reagan as their presidential candidate, Nicaragua was not even on the party's agenda. Yet on July 15, barely one year after the Sandinistas had taken power in Managua, Republicans adopted a platform calling for their overthrow. Party experts had not recommended this position. Nor had it been reviewed by the platform committee. The language was inserted by a staff aide to North Carolina Senator Jesse Helms in a back-room maneuver.

On July 8, Representative Jack Kemp of upstate New York, a former professional football quarterback who viewed himself as a prospective president, had been in the chair of the Subcommittee on Foreign Policy and Defense in Room 2040 of the Cobo Hall convention center when the Latin American plank came up. Kemp had little background in foreign affairs and had been discussing his pet plan to revive the gold standard for U.S. currency, when Helms of North Carolina proposed a new section on Nicaragua.

"I'll be glad to take whatever language we can agree on, whatever," said Helms, one of the most conservative members in Congress. "But what I have written is this: 'We deplore the Marxist takeover of Nicaragua and Marxist attempts to destabilize El Salvador and Guatemala. We will never support U.S. assistance to any Marxist government in this hemisphere. In this regard, we deplore the Carter administration's aid program for the Marxist Sandinista government in Nicaragua.' "

The amendment had the virtue of simplicity, condemning President Jimmy Carter's policy of limiting damage to U.S. interests in the same breath as the Sandinista takeover itself. Carter, over Helms's objections, had convinced Congress to approve $125 million in aid to the Sandinistas, and Helms had waged parliamentary warfare to hold up the disbursement.

"If there's any problem with the language, we can work it out," Helms said. "Fine," Kemp replied.

The amendment was then turned over to staff. "Staff" meant John Carbaugh, an aide to Helms and one of the sharpest political operators in Washington. His lobbying for white minority leader Ian Smith during the Rhodesian independence talks in London had prompted a British government complaint. Carbaugh mocked the attitudes of the conservatives whose cause he championed, calling them the "flat earth society." He liked to say that Nicaragua was not a top priority for him, "about number 300 on a list of 300." But it was an area where a nudge at the right moment had impact.

In the course of his "staff" work, a key sentence was added which pledged the Republican party to "support the efforts of the Nicaraguan people to establish a free and independent government."

"I wrote that," said Carbaugh of the phrase several years later. Asked if he intended by it the overthrow of the Sandinistas, he replied: "Sure."

As for the rest of the party, no one seemed aware of the coup. Kemp congratulated Helms, saying that his "enthusiasm in working out the language" had been very helpful, and he praised the "tremendous work" of Helms's aides. Kemp said he had no problems with this "very strong plank." The official transcript indicated that he did not read the most controversial passage aloud. "I think honestly and sincerely we can deplore the fact that the Marxist Sandinistas have taken over Nicaragua. That's a deplorable condition. It's in our backyard. It's the soft underbelly of America," Kemp declared.

And two days later, when the full platform committee approved the wording on Nicaragua without debate, the draft on which they voted made no reference to a pledge to "support the efforts of the Nicaraguan people to establish a free and independent government." The controversial sentence did appear, however, in the final printed version that was handed to delegates and subsequently approved by the convention. Carbaugh said he could not recall exactly how he slipped the sentence in, but said it "may have been added" in the final rewrite.

The plank was all the more controversial because the party's own experts had tried to steer the party clear of the issue. Gordon Sumner, a retired Army lieutenant general, had headed a study group of six conservatives who called themselves the Committee of Santa Fe. "I myself felt strongly about it. But we were faced with a credibility problem. None of us had that great a reputation. We thought if we came out too strong, it would have sounded like a bunch of right-wing nuts." In addition, he said, "I guess we didn't have that good a data base. The Sandinista revolution and government were just getting started when we were writing this." James Theberge, a conservative academic and former ambassador to Nicaragua, headed another study group on Latin America, this one set up expressly by the Republican National Committee. It did not recommend an automatic aid cut-off but conditioned further U.S. aid on the Sandinistas abandoning "their policy of hostility towards the United States."*

Thus on the subject of Nicaragua, the party's own deliberative

---

* The other members of the committee were L. Francis Bouchey, executive vice president of the Council for Inter-American Security, a conservative think tank; Roger Fontaine, then with the Center for Strategic and International Studies, a center-right think tank; David Jordan, professor of government at the University of Virginia; and Lewis Tambs, professor of history at Arizona State University. All except Bouchey went on to influential positions in Latin America in the Reagan administration. Fontaine went to the National Security Council; Jordan, Tambs and Alberto Piedra, who contributed to the report but did not receive credit, all became ambassadors in Latin America; and Sumner became an adviser to the assistant secretary of state for inter-American affairs.

process was supplanted by a political ruse. In adopting Helms's language, the Republican convention transformed Nicaragua from a foreign affairs into a partisan political issue.

Even as the platform was being approved, Carbaugh was working on ways to turn words into fact. Along with a friend from North Carolina named Nat Hamrick, who had had joint business interests with the family of Anastasio Somoza, the ousted Nicaraguan strongman, he escorted an Argentine envoy around the convention hall, introducing him to some of Ronald Reagan's most conservative advisers. The Argentine, a diplomat named Gerardo Schamis, was doing political reconnaissance for General Roberto Viola, the army leader who was to become Argentina's president in March 1981, and both Hamrick and Carbaugh believed that their services led to an active role by Argentina in the Nicaragua conflict.[1]*

It took the better part of 1981 for the Reagan administration to move into confrontation with the Sandinistas. Abandonment of the Carter policy of damage control—variously called "co-optation," "wedge-driving," or "the full-court press"—came about willy-nilly.

Through no direct fault of Ronald Reagan, Central America became a front-burner issue just as he took office. Reagan was at his Pacific Palisades home putting the finishing touches on his speech ten days before his inauguration when leftist guerrillas, hoping to duplicate the success of the Sandinistas in Nicaragua, launched what they called the final offensive in neighboring El Salvador. Their aim was to overthrow yet another pro-American government on the restive isthmus before Reagan came to office.

The Sandinistas cheered on their Salvadoran comrades and, repaying the "solidarity" they had shown the Nicaraguan revolution, assisted in the transshipment of large quantities of weapons to help.

A strong U.S. reaction was predictable, and in his last week in office Jimmy Carter suspended all U.S. economic aid to the Sandi-

---

* Hamrick said he introduced Schamis to William van Cleave, an expert on strategic nuclear policy, and Edwin Meese, a close associate of Reagan's since he was governor of California. Hamrick said he used the opportunity to send a message to Viola that Argentina could play a useful activist role in Central America. Schamis recalled that Hamrick had asked many questions about the Argentine military leaders, with whom Schamis had close ties. But he said "never in my life" had he received or passed messages regarding Central America to Viola. "Nat loves Nicaragua and he loves Somoza," Schamis later said. "I used to tell him he was to the right of Torquemada."

nistas and sent $10 million in arms and equipment and nineteen military technicians to El Salvador.

At the same time, Nicaraguan moderates who had initially backed the Sandinistas had begun having doubts. Some still in the Sandinista-dominated government junta, such as Violeta Chamorro, widow of slain publisher Pedro Joaquín Chamorro, supported the Salvadoran uprising, but others had left the country to form political and military resistance. The most prominent civilian to depart was José Francisco Cardenal, a construction company owner, who had immediately sought to establish a movement to overthrow the Sandinistas after leaving Managua in May 1980.

A critical role in bringing about the confrontation was played by John Carbaugh and his associate Nat Hamrick, who without official sanction of any kind began an intense lobbying campaign both within and outside the government and throughout Latin America to set up a training program for anti-Sandinista rebels. Their drive intensified the day Reagan took office, and the administration allowed the process to run out of control.

A tightly run White House might have blocked such private foreign policy initiatives and reined in the activists who carried them out. But that was not Reagan's style of government. When he came to power, he had spent a dozen years in the political wilderness. Operating intuitively, he had strong ideological preferences and a desire for a rapid defense build-up and a nationalistic flexing of muscles, but no blueprint for foreign policy and little knowledge of or interest in foreign affairs. He also had no predisposition to establish an orderly process for decision-making, preferring to rely on the consensus of his advisers as he had while governor of California. The former movie actor visualized policy in terms of rhetoric. (Reagan shared these traits with the Sandinistas, who had emerged from the Nicaraguan political wilderness to take power on a wave of popular support just eighteen months before him.)

Reagan's foreign policy philosophy was global anticommunism, and it translated into three ambitious policy goals—regaining U.S. military superiority, rolling back Soviet strategic gains in the third world, and preventing further Soviet advances. Merely by spending more money on new nuclear weapons Reagan could affect the military balance; and a heavy investment in intelligence gathering would warn of trouble before it occurred. But rollback was more difficult. To change facts on the ground required sophisticated policies and strategies, a smooth decision-making process, and good coordination of the agencies of government. Reagan, however, organized his administration in a manner that produced policymaking gridlock.

He delegated great authority to the individuals he selected to head State, Defense, and the CIA—Alexander Haig, Caspar Weinberger, and William Casey, respectively—and set up a National Security Council with a smaller and weaker support staff than his predecessors had had. Reagan stayed aloof from the policy process and laid out only general guidelines but no clear lines of authority. He often drew his guidelines from aides who reinforced his ideological predilections but who bore no responsibility for formulating policy. A prime example was Jeane Kirkpatrick, a professor of government at Georgetown University and a neoconservative Democrat, whom Reagan made his United Nations ambassador. The effect of this structure was to heighten disputes among the agencies while weakening the mechanism for resolving them. The problem, one NSC adviser later put it, was that while Reagan wanted "a diversity of views," he did "not enjoy being involved in the resolution of them."[2] In California, when the time came for a decision, Governor Reagan had convened his aides and forced them to find a consensus on terms they could live with. In a federal government trying to cope with complex foreign policy issues, such a system invited indiscipline and competition.

Previous presidents avoided refereeing every dispute among their top cabinet aides by choosing a strong national security adviser or a strong secretary of state. Interagency disputes are endemic in any administration, and even the strongest adviser will not be able to suppress them. But Reagan wanted to avoid the bickering among top aides that characterized the Nixon, Ford, and Carter administrations. His "cabinet-style" government did not end the disputes, but it produced the outward appearance of harmony.

Ideally, the National Security Council, which coordinates the work of State, Defense, and the CIA, should help a president realize as much of his vision as possible by overseeing an orderly process of formulating and implementing policy. In preceding administrations the NSC had been headed by scholars in international affairs, Zbigniew Brzezinski and Henry Kissinger, and an experienced military officer, retired Air Force Lieutenant General Brent Scowcroft. Reagan picked Richard Allen, a foreign policy specialist who carried little weight among the President's own White House advisers, less still with heads of other agencies or their permanent bureaucracies. The new NSC staff were more ideological than their predecessors and eager to promote a conservative view in foreign policy; they suffered from the shortage of talent and experience in foreign affairs in the conservative wing of the Republican party. This applied particularly to the NSC staff dealing with Latin American affairs. Roger Fontaine, an academic, was widely viewed as a weak player in the struggles among the agencies. Alfonso Sapia-Bosch, a CIA analyst, was respected and competent but not a political operator. There was a claque of hawkish, take-charge junior military officers who lacked experience of specific responsibility in real-world politics and diplomacy but who when asked would find ways to get things done; none had responsibility in Latin American affairs at the start.

Allen's office was moved to the basement of the White House West Wing and he reported to Reagan through White House counsellor Edwin Meese, who had been Reagan's legal affairs secretary in Sacramento. The arrangement downgraded the NSC's role and strengthened the "barons," as the cabinet officers are sometimes dubbed, in their feudal domains. Alexander Haig tried in a famous memo after the inauguration to take up all the reins of foreign policy management and create a comprehensive decision-making system. But the memo was not considered for a full year, and clear lines of authority never emerged. Instead, the notion evolved that the State Department should take the lead in coordinating points of view and present the options to Reagan for decision.

Without a strong central authority, raising issues to the presidential level promised stalemate. Yet problems had to be addressed. To circumvent the clumsy mechanism, one bureaucratic remedy for a subcabinet-level official, whether an assistant secretary of state or an NSC aide, was to circumvent the formal structure of sending important decisions to the President and create a secretive informal structure centering on himself and consisting of representatives of the key agencies. The informal grouping would make important decisions and force them through the government from the middle up—that is, by each participant's securing the approval of his boss—rather than from the top down. When the barons sat down together, consensus was much easier to obtain. One danger was that small groups operating in secret from the rest of the government could make big misjudgments. A second was that once the principle was understood, any number could play the game. This led to contending groups, rival policies, and eventually a parallel government.

COMPETING AGENDAS

Richard Allen's inexperienced transition team undertook one major personnel initiative that could have devastated America's career foreign service; in the event, however, the damage was limited to the careers of a few top diplomats.

Early in January, Allen sent word to the State Department that every Carter appointee should clear his desk by Inauguration Day, Tuesday, January 20. But with Haig's help, Undersecretary David Newsom convinced Allen to reconsider. Newsom argued that, unlike those at many agencies, most senior officials at the State Department were career civil servants who had held high positions in previous Republican and Democratic administrations. Newsom proposed to send a list of all high-level appointees so that Allen could single out only those he thought totally unacceptable. Allen agreed.

John Carbaugh, then an aide to Senator Helms, was a member of the transition team for East Asian policy at the State Department, and although he had no specific role in organizing the Bureau of Inter-American Affairs, that is where he had maximum impact. Carbaugh grabbed his turf where he could find it. He insisted that the administration dismiss William Bowdler, the widely respected career foreign service officer who had led the abortive Carter administration effort in 1978 and 1979 to ease Nicaraguan strongman Anastasio Somoza from office; Bowdler had then served for fifteen months as assistant secretary of state for inter-American affairs. To the right, still smarting over their failure to block Carter's "giveaway" of the Panama Canal to Panama in 1978, Bowdler symbolized the betrayal of a longtime U.S. ally. Carbaugh also insisted on the firing of Robert White, the U.S. ambassador to El Salvador, whose views were decidedly liberal. Bowdler received the word from Newsom in a telephone call on the Friday before Inauguration Day. He moved his effects to the administrative offices and told friends he expected a new assignment, but there was none, and he resigned from the foreign service. There was no farewell ceremony or presentation. His

American flag was folded up and sent in the mail. White was fired ten days later. A new team would be assembled to manage policy which had one thing in common: all its members lacked Latin American experience.

For a time, some of those in positions of responsibility tried to throw out the policy with the policymakers. Experienced Central America hands saw José Napoleón Duarte, a Christian Democrat who had just become president of the reformist junta in El Salvador, as the right man to steer El Salvador through a centrist course between the feudal right and the Marxist left. The Salvadoran junta had proposed land reform, and Latin America experts at State encouraged the plan, not for economic reasons but as a device to strip away the political appeal of the leftist guerrillas for landless peasants. However, Allen viewed Duarte as "a mystic." Early in December 1980, when Duarte visited Washington, Allen told him that he "wasn't much impressed with land reform" and "didn't think land reform was such a key to stability." Allen did promise help in dealing with any military threat to the San Salvador government, saying that "Salvador could not be lost to a Sandinista-type revolution. That threat would not come to pass."

Early in January, in words that had a far different effect than that intended, Reagan echoed Allen's viewpoint. "You do not try to fight a civil war and institute reforms at the same time. Get rid of the war. Then go forward with the reforms," he told *Time* magazine.[3] Reagan's remarks played into internal Salvadoran politics by encouraging rightists to resist any reform.

But other conservatives with some Latin American background had other views and the policy eventually picked up where Carter and Bowdler had left off. Before Duarte visited Allen, he had called on Otto Reich, a neoconservative Democrat who was director of the Washington office of the Council of the Americas, an organization for businessmen with interests in Latin America founded by the Rockefellers. Reich had assembled a group of conservatives with a special interest in Latin America, among them Constantine Menges, an academic with government experience and extremely pronounced views,* Jeane Kirkpatrick, and Roger Fontaine, Allen's deputy for Latin American affairs. Duarte delivered a lecture on land reform

---

* It was Menges who first proposed reversing Marxist revolutions by supporting anti-Soviet "freedom fighters."

and appealed through the group for Reagan's support. Eventually the members of the group, all of whom took on senior posts in the administration, brought Duarte and Reagan together.*

Reagan's loose management structure, his abrupt personnel shifts at the State Department, and his uncalculated rhetoric were sure to complicate any efforts to set policy priorities. A further factor was the competing agendas of Reagan's key aides.

Haig was an outsider to the Reagan camp and one of the last cabinet officers named. A former deputy to Henry Kissinger at the NSC and later the Supreme Allied Commander in Europe, Haig was profoundly European in his orientation. He wanted to make his mark with the Reagan inner circle and sought an issue that would be the turning point in the wake of the Carter administration. He saw El Salvador as his vehicle. Instead of seeking government-wide agreement through the cumbersome NSC mechanism, Haig was the first cabinet officer to make policy by impulse. He had a strategic agenda, to "go to the source," meaning Cuba, and he intended through a combination of pressures and incentives to sever the arms pipeline from the Soviet Union to Cuba and from Cuba to Nicaragua and the Salvadoran rebels. A get-tough approach to Castro had support within different sectors of the Republican party. But Haig also had a

---

* Allen's transition headquarters often tripped up, and clearly had little sensitivity toward developments in Nicaragua. An example was its handling of a proposal for a conspiracy to topple the Sandinistas which arrived over the transom. Edmundo Chamorro Rappaccioli, commander of what was described as the military wing of the rebel forces, sent Reagan a letter outlining their plan. "The armed segment of the democratic forces of Nicaragua would need from 30 to 45 days of basic training in a neighboring country, Honduras or Costa Rica, before starting its military operations there," he said. "It is logical to suppose that the armed forces of the Central American countries would have a favorable attitude toward the liberation movement of Nicaragua and would give it their utmost support." José Francisco Cardenal had drafted the letter and in the absence of a direct entrée to the administration had sent it by ordinary post from Costa Rica on December 10. He never got a response. Allen replied on January 6, but his staff clumsily addressed the response to Chamorro in San José, Costa Rica, without a street address or box number. Sandinista sympathizers, perhaps in the main post office, redirected the letter to Managua, where it was published in Barricada, the party daily. In his form-letter response, Allen welcomed Chamorro's "comment on current events in Nicaragua" and "recommendations concerning the future," and blandly asked for some background on the conspirators: "We are pleased to have your thoughts on these vital topics and appreciate knowing something about your organization and your personal background. I will make certain that the relevant policy people are made aware of your ideas and suggestions in this area. Thank you for sharing your thoughts with the President-elect."[4]

personal agenda—to appear firm and tough and be personally in charge of policy—which did not.

One of Bowdler's last actions in office before he was so abruptly removed had been to send Jon Glassman, then a political officer in Mexico, to El Salvador to examine captured guerrilla documents on Cuban and Sandinista aid for the Salvador guerrillas which turned up after the abortive "final offensive." Glassman said he wrote up a cable in Ambassador White's residence and sent it the following Sunday. The sudden paper flow in response to Glassman's report created what is known in Foggy Bottom as a "fire in the in-basket." Haig ordered the urgent preparation of a White Paper laying out the intelligence and sent top deputies to Western Europe and Latin America to present the information in person. But, as the paper had been produced under pressure, its errors, soon discovered by reporters, weakened its impact. Moreover, there was not then or later any agreement as to whether the Salvadoran upheaval was principally a matter of regional significance or, as Haig depicted it, of global significance.

Haig's plan for dealing with Cuba included a contingency for a naval blockade. But the uniformed military hoped to avoid direct confrontation or any action that might lead to another unpopular war and Defense Secretary Caspar Weinberger did everything to thwart Haig's design. Reagan, on the advice of the Joint Chiefs of Staff, rejected the blockade idea.

"Haig went to [high military alert] so fast that it upset some people in the White House," said Lawrence Eagleburger, who was Haig's assistant secretary for European affairs and later undersecretary of state. Events in El Salvador to some extent bore out Haig's case against the Cubans, but he went so hard and heavy in his reaction that top White House aides—among them James Baker, the key political strategist—told Haig to cool the rhetoric and lower his profile. Their agenda was completely different: to push Reagan's economic program of tax cuts and higher military spending through Congress. Haig's rhetoric was raising questions among centrists in Congress whose votes would be necessary to achieve Reaganomics.

Meanwhile, the agenda of the CIA, or at least of Director William Casey, was expansive: to become far more active and effective and to shake off the taint of the past. A veteran of the Office of Strategic Services (OSS)—the World War II precursor to the CIA—Casey had helped organize covert operations against the Nazis in occupied

Europe. He viewed the East-West struggle in simple terms of good and evil, and likened the results of Soviet foreign policy to the Nazi holocaust. Casey, like Reagan, felt personally committed to rolling back Soviet gains in the third world and preventing further leftist takeovers. Casey wanted to make the CIA the primary instrument in this struggle.

"He was a man in a hurry to get things done. I have no doubt he wanted to be secretary of state," said a CIA veteran professional who worked for him his first six months. But Casey concealed his ambitions from Haig and kept his head down that first year. For most of 1981, Casey was under investigation by the Senate Select Intelligence Committee for his business and stock dealings while in private legal practice. Not until December 1 did he get the committee's back-handed endorsement that "no basis has been found for concluding that Mr. Casey is unfit to hold office as Director of Central Intelligence."[5]

Reagan had no qualms about Casey, a contemporary, an ideological soulmate, and the chairman of his 1980 election campaign. He elevated Casey's role by making him a full member of the cabinet as well as intelligence adviser and gave him an office at the Old Executive Office Building next door to the White House.

Casey's institutional base and his ties with the President assured him a role in foreign policy planning. This he capitalized on through his shrewd behind-the-scenes operating style, which was far more congenial to Reagan than Haig's abrasive, "take-charge" approach. Thus, a complete novice in the field in time became a major player in the foreign policy arena.

Jeane Kirkpatrick was another amateur elevated to the status of high authority. Ostensibly, formulating foreign policy is the job of the secretary of state, but Haig had affronted so many of Reagan's inner circle that his advice was often shunned. Kirkpatrick to some extent filled the void. Her popular writings, polemical in tone but containing little original research, reinforced Reagan's predilection for seeing regional problems as part of the East-West struggle. Her attack on Carter's foreign policy in *Commentary* in December 1979 titled "Dictatorships and Double Standards" first brought her to Reagan's attention. In it, she argued that rightist authoritarian states were preferable to leftist totalitarian states, with Nicaragua a prime example. In another wide-ranging attack on Carter policies, titled "U.S. Security and Latin America" in the January 1981 *Commentary*, she warned that leftist takeovers in Nicaragua and Grenada might confront the United States with "the unprecedented need to defend itself against a ring of Soviet bases on and around our southern and eastern borders," and Jimmy Carter was to blame. "What did the Carter Administration do in Nicaragua? *It brought down the Somoza regime,*" she said (italics in original). Kirkpatrick urged the scrapping of Carter's policy on Nicaragua, which she described as a doomed quest to bring democracy, but proposed no alternative. "Once the intellectual debris has been cleared away, it should become possible to construct a Latin American policy that will protect U.S. security interests," she wrote.

Her third contribution to Reagan's mindset was to declare Central America the preeminent foreign policy concern of the United States, an extraordinary shift of strategic priorities. "Now why is Central America and the Caribbean the most important place in the world for us?" she asked in a speech before the Conservative Political Action Conference on March 21, 1981. "The reason, I think, is geopolitical." The spread of Marxism-Leninism would affect U.S. security "in a very direct, immediate kind of way," and America's ability to play "a major role in the politics and security of countries in remote places and even Western Europe . . . depends on our not having to devote the lion's share of our attention and our resources to the defense of ourselves in our own hemisphere." This translated into denying bases to the Soviets. For different reasons, Kirkpatrick and Haig thus had singled out Central America as the focus of U.S. foreign policy attention, but neither had done so in a way that translated readily into sustainable policy.

The problems of conflicting agendas and priorities were compounded by Jesse Helms, who from his base in the Senate Foreign Relations Committee held up confirmation of key policy officials. One reason for the logjam, according to a former associate, was that his aide, John Carbaugh, had his eye on the job of assistant secretary for inter-American affairs. Carbaugh said he wanted to become congressional liaison, but that still left a wide field of contenders. Haig would have been happy to keep on John Bushnell, a career diplomat who was acting assistant secretary, but the White House viewed him as ineffective in presenting policy issues, and rejected him.

Lewis Tambs, a conservative academic who had participated in Sumner's Committee of Santa Fe, told friends that he wanted the job. Helms backed Tambs. However, Haig instead chose Thomas O. Enders, a career foreign service officer who had been educated at Yale and the Sorbonne and whose professional credentials were impressive. When Enders was appointed, Helms then demanded that Tambs be named Enders's principal deputy. Tambs, a history professor at Arizona State University, was an exponent of the Mackinder school of geographical determinism, which held that the struggle for the "heartland" of Europe would determine the fate of the world. The theories of Sir Harold Mackinder, an early twentieth-century British geopolitician, had been adopted in Nazi Germany to justify Hitler's geopolitics. Tambs used these theories to depict the U.S.-Soviet rivalry with a novel twist. In lectures about world affairs, he told audiences that the Soviet leadership, living in more northerly latitudes than the American one, sees the world differently. So Tambs invented upside-down maps to show the world from the Soviet perspective. Enders decided he could do without deputies for the time being, and Tambs settled for an appointment as ambassador to Colombia, and later Costa Rica.

Enders did not appear on the scene at the State Department in an official capacity until April, although he played an active role in the inter-American affairs bureau throughout March. Haig had brought him back from being ambassador to the European Economic Community to work on an economic revitalization program for the Caribbean Basin, what would later be called the Caribbean Basin Initiative, and that work had to be completed. On being named assistant secretary, Enders, a seasoned professional, accepted the recommendation of the Bureau to put a major emphasis on El Salvador. But he also had a personal agenda.

Like so many who would come to dominate U.S. policy in Latin America in the Reagan administration, Enders was a new face in the Bureau, having never served in the region before. But there the similarity ended. Standing six feet eight, scion of a wealthy Hartford, Connecticut, Republican family, and nephew of the Nobel laureate in chemistry John Enders, Tom Enders was one of the "best and the brightest" officers in the foreign service. He had had bitter experience in the Vietnam era dating from the secret bombing of Cambodia and was still reeling from the humiliation and rage he felt about the treatment of his role in the bombing by William Shawcross in the book *Sideshow*. Enders was a complex figure. While he was coordinating the secret bombing, he had also been working to resettle Cambodian refugees. A hawk on foreign policy, he supported civil rights at home. While ambassador to Canada from 1976 to 1979, he had flown to Harvard twice a week to teach a course in government.

Back in Washington, Enders kept his lines open to every political viewpoint. He kept in touch with Sol Linowitz, the lawyer, trouble-shooter for Democratic administrations, and Latin America expert who had helped negotiate the Panama Canal treaties for Carter, and with Robert Leiken, an academic who in time migrated from being a liberal critic to a valued supporter of administration policy. He regularly saw leaders of the Socialist International, which groups Social Democratic parties in Europe and elsewhere, despite its outspoken criticism of Reagan policies.

To cope with political pressures from the right, Enders turned to three conservatives for advice. One was Carbaugh, who at the time of Enders's appointment was still on Helms's staff. Carbaugh, thirty-five at the time, became an unofficial confidant, or so both men have said. "I held him up for months," said Carbaugh of the Enders nomination, "fucked around with him. But Tom was a decent guy. My view is that if a guy has ability, you respect him." Enders would later say he bore no grudge for the hold-up. "Well, who didn't it happen to?" he said. Of Carbaugh he said: "John and I spent a lot of time together on a lot of issues." Enders also said he had asked Carbaugh to go to Central America "a number of times to talk to people who wouldn't be easy to talk to. He was definitely very helpful."

Haig got a different impression of Enders's view of Carbaugh: "He detested the man." At one point, Haig felt that Carbaugh was "meddling so much in an outrageously right-wing way" that he offered him a far-away ambassadorship. Carbaugh tells the story that Haig asked him to go to "Assumption." Did Haig mean the islands? Carbaugh asked. Haig looked at his note card. It was Paraguay, whose capital is Asunción. Carbaugh declined.[6]

A second conservative with a great interest in Latin America and with his own network of ties to arrive at the State Department was Vernon Walters, a retired Army lieutenant general and former deputy director of the CIA. He became a world-roving ambassador-at-large, and while he did not report to Enders, undertook numerous missions to Latin America on his behalf.

Enders's third conservative adviser was Gordon Sumner, who

became a special assistant with the rank of ambassador assigned to
Enders's outer office. Sumner said Haig had asked him "to babysit
Enders but not to step on his poncho," an assertion that Haig denies.
"And I wouldn't have used the word *poncho*." Haig said he held
Sumner in very high regard for his knowledge of security issues, but
his reason for taking him on was political. "It was very evident that
certain elements who had entrée to the White House were going to
be very influential, such as Jesse Helms; therefore it was very
important to keep those points of view in mind and accessible."
Sumner, he noted, was "very conservative."

Although he visited El Salvador in June, shortly after the arrival of
the new U.S. ambassador, Deane Hinton, Sumner traveled less than
Carbaugh did. On at least one occasion, Enders asked Sumner not to
go abroad. It was a few months into the administration. Sumner and
Walters had organized a "war game" exercise at the Pentagon gaming
agency. Sumner and Walters were the controllers, supplying information to the teams working on the scenario, which related to the
possibility of countries falling like dominoes to leftists in Central
America. Others taking part included General David Jones, chairman of the Joint Chiefs of Staff, Casey, Enders, and Ronald Spiers,
then head of the State Department's Bureau of Intelligence and
Research. Sumner was to leave for Argentina and Chile at the end of
the war game, he later recalled, when Enders told him: "Gordon,
you can't make that trip. The situation is so bad, you must stay here.
We've got to get over to the office. There are some things we've got
to do instantly."[7] Enders had no recollection of the war game, and it
may have been his way of "babysitting" Sumner.

From all these strands and personalities and agendas, Enders
established his own priorities. They would take time to fashion and
even longer to enunciate because it was mid-June before he was
confirmed in his job. With political snipers on all sides, a chaotic
decision-making process at the White House, and a real-life crisis
before him in El Salvador, Enders decided to amplify his personal
power by creating a secret structure centering on himself. He
organized a small circle of subcabinet aides into the "Core Group,"
a policymaking body whose membership did not become publicly
known until after his ouster in 1983. From the start, he put his
energies into developing a policy for El Salvador that could be
sustained on the ground, in the region, in Congress, and in the
administration. There was a price to pay. The price was Nicaragua.

CARBAUGH'S FINGERPRINTS

None of Reagan's close advisers had much sympathy for continuing Carter's "damage-limiting" approach to Nicaragua. A first major step toward clearing what Jeane Kirkpatrick had called "intellectual debris" was taken that March when the administration decided to cut off all U.S. aid, including food for peace. The atmosphere quickly soured, and the opportunities for a diplomatic solution narrowed. In the view of at least some high State Department officials, it proved to be the administration's first major mistake.

The episode traced back to the State Department White Paper after the abortive "final offensive" in El Salvador. At that time the State Department and Jon Glassman in particular had been criticized in one major newspaper account for overstating their case and satirized by Garry Trudeau in the political cartoon "Doonesbury," but the allegations *were* based on guerrilla documents. The administration felt that it had irrefutable evidence of a large flow of arms and ammunition from Nicaragua to El Salvador. The question in the very first days of the administration was what to do about it.*

In Managua, Lawrence Pezzullo, the blunt-spoken U.S. ambassador, had an answer: use diplomacy, and condition further U.S. aid on a change in Nicaraguan behavior. Pezzullo, a career foreign service officer, had been the ambassador since June 1979, when he helped usher Somoza out of Nicaragua. He had wide experience in Latin America and a high reputation among fellow U.S. diplomats, and was one of the architects of the damage-limitation policy after the Sandinista takeover in July 1979. The aim had been to avoid a replay of the confrontation that followed Fidel Castro's revolution in Cuba. There, he felt, the U.S. mistake had been to forget that "the people who really mattered were the people who stayed in the country and kept in the game." His scheme had been to strengthen the private sector, the independent news media, and the political parties and to show interest by the United States and the Western world so that government opponents "won't despair and leave." At the same time Pezzullo had wanted to use every available opportunity to influence the nine-man Sandinista directorate as it confronted the realities of

---

* One solution was to send more military aid. Reagan within weeks of taking office increased Carter's aid fivefold. He approved $20 million for arms and equipment, arranged $5 million in loan guarantees, sent three dozen more trainers, and requested $25 million in loan guarantees for additional arms purchases.

power. With Haig's blessing, Pezzullo plunged into this course of action and felt he had succeeded. Nevertheless, on April 1 the administration abruptly cut off all aid to Nicaragua. Thus, the possibility of any diplomatic solution to the U.S.-Nicaragua dispute during Reagan's term in office was probably doomed in the first three months of the administration.

Pezzullo believed that Allen and his deputy for Latin American affairs, Roger Fontaine, forced the aid decision on the State Department. Once again, the action clearly bore Carbaugh's fingerprints, although with uncharacteristic modesty he asserted only that he "apparently" played a role. It was a perplexing move at the time, and the public explanation seemed to support the opposite course. The State Department said there had been "no hard evidence of arms movement through Nicaragua during the past few weeks, and propaganda and some other support activities had been curtailed. We remain concerned, however, that some arms traffic may be continuing and that other support very probably continues."

Pezzullo helped draft that statement but was dissatisfied with the caveat. The only supplies on which the United States had specific information were those transported on the so-called air bridge, which was run by a Cuban with a Nicaraguan counterpart. "They decommissioned the airplanes that were there," Pezzullo said, "released the Costa Rican pilots who were flying, ripped up the whole process. They sent back the Cuban. The whole thing came apart." But the author of the intelligence report to Washington, in Pezzullo's words, had added a "smart little thing that was his comment, not that of a source." What Pezzullo objected to was the statement that it would appear that even though this "apparat" had been dissolved in this instance, other routes would be sought. Pezzullo took exception at the time because no source was given for the statement, and because he felt the word *apparat*—usually reserved for a Soviet-style bureaucratic apparatus—was loaded. His objection caused a "big brouhaha." But the upshot was that an anonymous intelligence operative working from another country, not the U.S. ambassador in Nicaragua, created the historical alibi for a decision that most officials involved in the process saw in retrospect as a major U.S. mistake.*

---

* The rationale was later redrafted to sound more convincing. "In the immediate aftermath of the meetings [between Pezzullo and Nicaraguan officials], U.S. intelligence indicated that arms traffic through established routes, particularly by air, from Nicaragua to El Salvador had slowed if not stopped but that other routes from

Pezzullo, although in Washington for consultation, was excluded from the final decision-making and he returned to Managua discouraged. He had already told Haig and Enders that he planned to leave his post in the summer, and now he fixed a date in his mind. To soften the blow of the U.S. decision, the statement drafted by Pezzullo and Enders suggested that U.S. aid might be reconsidered at a later point; Pezzullo intended to brief the Sandinista leadership in person before the announcement. "That's like ashes in your mouth," he said later. "You can carry a lot of water, but you can't carry that water. There is no water to carry." For Pezzullo, this was the turning point. "We dealt ourselves out of the game for no reason in April 1981, because of small-mindedness on our side." As he began to brief Sergio Ramírez, a member of the junta, about the decision, the news broke from Washington. "So even that they threw away." Pezzullo said to Ramírez: "Look, I'm sorry. That is not the way it was supposed to be."

Looking back, Pezzullo blamed Enders, although with a good deal of sympathy for his situation. "Enders is the kind of guy that will give on something to maintain control of the policy. I might do the same thing," he said. "Within the policy structure he was in, you had to give away the policy to maintain the control. And that," said Pezzullo, "is not worth the effort."

Enders himself also came to view this as a missed opportunity. "By taking this action, we could have made them gun-shy," he said in an interview more than five years later. But in a subsequent interview, he defended the exclusion of Pezzullo from the decision meeting on several grounds. Enders said he was privy to electronic intelligence that was not available to Pezzullo, which showed a sharp drop-off of shipments after Pezzullo's first warning but their reappearance in late February.[8]

Haig said he did not recall having "any horrendous gas pains" about the decision and disputed Pezzullo's claims of success in stopping the arms flow. "I think very highly of Pezzullo. We got along very well. I thought he was performing very well. But his perspective was very narrow in terms of the time he served as ambassador and how policy was formulated at that time. I wouldn't say he succeeded by any stretch of the imagination."

Nicaragua were being sought." That statement was contained in a State Department document prepared for the World Court in September 1985. Pezzullo took strong exception. "That's sophistry. It's deceptive. That's a phony," he said.

Allen defended the decision without hesitation. "The President of the United States, upon my recommendation and that of the Secretary of State, ordered the termination of aid to Nicaragua. The action was fully justified and did not, as some alleged, 'further estrange' the Sandinistas." [9]

But the State and Defense departments immediately began to fear what they had wrought. The U.S. Southern Command in Panama "went into almost wartime posture," said a senior official there at the time. A team of military engineers was sent to Pezzullo's residence and chopped down trees to provide a landing zone for helicopters if he had to be evacuated.

The Sandinistas treated the U.S. decision as a hostile act, but their reaction was nonviolent. Ironically, the U.S. decision induced a rare moment of unity between government and opposition. Alfonso Robelo, a former junta member and now the leading government critic, said the U.S. decision was unwise, unfortunate, and "to be condemned from every viewpoint." He predicted the cut-off "will actually provoke a radicalization that will be hard to reverse." He wanted the United States to provide aid through private channels in place of the cut-off. The Social Christian party, one of the strongest opposition forces, denounced the cut-off as "harmful to the welfare of the Nicaraguan people." The entire staff of La Prensa, 186 strong, signed a letter to Reagan criticizing the cut-off as counterproductive and asking for the immediate restoration of aid. In an editorial, the opposition daily said, "We must insist that the United States grant us that loan." It went on to ask sarcastically, "Why doesn't the USSR lend us what we need? Why doesn't it show its proletarian solidarity with deeds and not just with words? How much has the USSR, our friend, lent us to date?"[10] La Prensa and Robelo proved prescient. Three weeks later, Moscow announced that it was sending 20,000 tons of grain to Nicaragua.

By April, several patterns were evident. Reagan's NSC was incapable of becoming a focus for the decision-making process; most decisions had to be made outside the framework. Assistant Secretary Enders, facing a real crisis in El Salvador and finding himself outflanked on Nicaragua, bowed to political pressures on the latter in order to save his energies for the former. And Nicaragua's internal opposition became a secondary policy consideration.

CHAPTER 2

THE SLIDE INTO CONFRONTATION

THE STORY of the Reagan administration decision to back the anti-Sandinista rebels is a case study of the perils of fighting strategic battles in secret, on the cheap, and by proxy.

After U.S. funds began to flow in late 1981, this would become one of the most hotly debated foreign policy issues in Reagan's term of office. And yet the origin of the commitment to support the resistance is one of the most obscure events in Reagan's presidency.

The groundwork was laid by a variety of groups and individuals, some Nicaraguan, some American, and some Honduran, who operated on parallel tracks. The accounts given by the different actors do not tally in every respect, but the common thread running through all is that the conception and initial steps in the project came from outside the United States government. What is interesting is that similar ideas apparently occurred to separate individuals—that Ar-

39

gentina should train the rebels and that Colonel Enrique Bermúdez
Varela, a former colonel in Somoza's National Guard, should lead
them.

The Nicaraguan activists were of disparate backgrounds ranging
from Luis Pallais Debayle, Anastasio Somoza's cousin, to Francisco
Aguirre, a lifelong opponent of the Somozas. There was also José
Francisco Cardenal, a former moderate who had backed the Sandi-
nistas but who left Nicaragua in May 1980 when he was drafted
without consultation into the government, and Carlos García, a
Nicaraguan businessman and president of the International Baseball
Federation. A key facilitator and sponsor was Gustavo Álvarez
Martínez, the Honduran army officer whose career was about to take
off with American support. Last but far from least were John
Carbaugh and his North Carolina buddy, Nat Hamrick.

No fewer than three of those seven took credit for discovering
Bermúdez and making him the military commander of the movement. However, according to Bermúdez, he was chosen by a group
of former National Guard officers only after other senior officers
turned down the offer. Bermúdez led the only effective rebel force
from its inception, and the story of his organizational efforts illustrates the inherent problems in starting up such an enterprise and
why he became almost inseparable from it.

As Somoza's military attaché in Washington, Bermúdez had been
a spectator from afar during the Sandinista revolution. He played a
bit part when Omar Torrijos, the Panamanian strongman, proposed
that he be named to head the military in spring 1979, a time when
there was still a glimmer of a chance to save the old National Guard,
but Bermúdez declined. The scheme had never had a chance
because it was rejected by Somoza.

Pallais, a close adviser to Anastasio Somoza and facilitator of the
final confused arrangements at his abdication, was undoubtedly one
of the first persons to suggest that Bermúdez form a resistance
movement following Somoza's overthrow in July 1979. Pallais had
fled Nicaragua along with his cousin and arrived in Miami on July 16.
It was in August or September that he recalled telling Bermúdez:
"Enrique, you are the one." Bermúdez replied: "Do you think so?
What claim do you have to say that?" Pallais responded: "You have
no taint. You have never been in any military position to benefit from
Somoza. You have military connections in Washington."

According to one lengthy account of the period, Bermúdez

received several hundred thousand dollars from Pallais early in 1980; another mentions the figure $300,000. Bermúdez disputes both.[1] "That's a superbig lie. No one in the exile group was willing to give $300,000. I haven't received a penny from anybody in Miami."[2] Pallais, asked to explain, said he spent several hundred thousand dollars to help establish the movement and paid for plane tickets, telephones, and other expenses. Pallais said he had almost daily contact with Bermúdez but perhaps did not give him funds directly. "I spent a hell of a lot of money. I provided salaries for people working with Enrique. My office was their office." He added that he was broke now. "I gave my money to the cause."

In the course of three interviews about the origins of the movement, Bermúdez never volunteered that Somoza's cousin had had any role. But when pressed in a fourth interview, he conceded that Pallais had donated airline tickets and helped out when "one of the guys working for us had a need for $50 or $100 to pay the rent."

It was Pallais's idea to get in touch with Tacho, as Somoza was known. He had moved to Paraguay. On the telephone, Somoza declined to make any commitments. But when Pallais went to Asunción sometime around August 1980, Somoza promised $1 million in cash and the income from his tobacco factories in Honduras. For Somoza, this was chicken feed. He told Pallais that his personal fortune was $40 million; Pallais estimated it at roughly $100 million. Somoza was assassinated on September 17, before he could carry out his pledge. Pallais returned to Asunción a short time after his cousin's death together with Federico Mejía, a former National Guard general who went with Bermúdez's blessing. "We were told the one who could give money or could cooperate was [General Alfredo] Stroessner," Bermúdez said. "We sent him [Mejía]."

They met Paraguayan chief of state General Alfredo Stroessner, the longest-serving dictator in the hemisphere. Stroessner had one question: Was the CIA behind the rebels? Pallais said it was not. Stroessner said the rebels would need outside help and promised to raise the matter with the president of Argentina, General Jorge Videla, whom he was seeing a short time later. "We are too small to provide much help. I don't think Chile can do anything. There is too much turmoil in Bolivia. I think the Argentinians can help," Pallais recalled him saying. Stroessner himself gave no further help, according to Bermúdez. "Never, never. Not a single penny."[3]

Bermúdez said the first Nicaraguan to contact him was Carlos García, who was visiting the United States in the summer of 1979. García had been a classmate of Bermúdez in the Nicaraguan military academy from 1948 to 1952 and was one of his closest friends. "He told me many Nicaraguans are worried about the Sandinistas. People think of you as a military man with a good image. We are starting to get organized and we would like to know if you want to participate in a political and armed movement," Bermúdez said. García made the crucial telephone call in December. He said the situation in Nicaragua was "very, very bad," Cubans were everywhere, controlling even organized sports, and the Marxist-Leninist movement was about to take over. "It is time," he told Bermúdez, "to start thinking about Nicaragua."

García brought together about thirty young officers who could not be viewed as backers of Somoza. "This group didn't want any old or well-known Somocista. The only one they accepted was Bermúdez." Bermúdez flew to Miami and met with about ten of the officers, some of whom had already begun a movement they called the September 15 Legion.

"I started to explain my plan," Bermúdez recalled. "I was very pragmatic. I was sure no former members of the Guardia could have any support or any chance. What I proposed was that military officers who were not so well known as close friends or collaborators of Somoza, who had no bad image, comprise the leadership. So we could organize the Nicaraguan people, train them, and direct them in the coming struggle for freedom in Nicaragua."

Bermúdez had been trained as a military engineer and was a career officer in the Guard. Although he had seen urban combat when Somoza sent a token Guard detachment as a peace-keeping force to the Dominican Republic in 1965, he had spent the period of the Sandinista revolution in Washington. Disaffected rivals, such as Cardenal, later accused him of treachery, attempted murder, even genocide. But Sandinista leaders had respect for Bermúdez's professionalism.

Luis Carrión Cruz, one of the nine comandantes and deputy chief of the interior ministry, acknowledged that Bermúdez, unlike some of his associates, had a reputation for being honest, uncorrupted, and industrious. "Another thing is that he has a cleaner image than most National Guard officers," Carrión said. "It wasn't so easy to find someone proficient in the military arts and not so bloodstained.

Bermúdez is like that. He didn't have a very active career during Somoza's most repressive activities in Nicaragua."

One reason for his clean image was that Bermúdez, according to García, was the only colonel in Nicaraguan history never appointed to a command. Bermúdez had been unemployed from the time of the revolution until the end of 1979 and was selling his house in Bethesda. He had been offered a job by Francisco Aguirre but had wound up driving a truck for a magazine distribution firm from January to March 1980. In the space of a few years Bermúdez would go from delivering *Time, Newsweek,* and *People* magazines to appearing in them. He moved his family to Miami in August 1980, renting a twenty-four-foot U-Haul truck with trailer and driving it down.[4]

It was no small undertaking during Carter's fourth year in office to set up a movement to overthrow a government to which the United States was sending aid. García put up $15,000 to assist; he said other Nicaraguan politicians both in and outside the country provided for Bermúdez's expenses. But Bermúdez said the sums he received that year were minuscule. "There were no funds, no resources at all." Soon he lost even this benefactor. García was arrested in Managua in May 1980 and imprisoned until late 1984.

Early in 1980, Bermúdez traveled to Guatemala and set up offices in a rented house. He said he chose Guatemala because it was farther from the front than Honduras and easier to operate in. About the same time, in February or March, a Nicaraguan ex-National Guard officer named Emilio Echaverry had approached Álvarez in Honduras and asked him to help the rebels. Álvarez, then head of FUSEP, the national police, did not know Bermúdez but he knew Echaverry from Argentina, where both had studied at the military academy. Without authorization, Álvarez started to receive military equipment sent from Miami care of the Honduran armed forces and to pass it on to the rebels. The equipment was boots, fatigues, shotguns, revolvers, pistols, ammunition, and medicines. The variety of weapons, including some sporting rifles, suggests that some of it was probably collected door-to-door. Meanwhile, Álvarez went to the Honduran president, Policarpo Paz García, six or seven times before Paz gave the project his grudging approval. "Don't get into trouble," Paz said. "If something goes wrong, I'll have your head."[5]

Another kind of support came about as a result of Cardenal's self-exile from Managua in May 1980. Cardenal, who twenty years earlier had idolized Ché Guevara and joined in an abortive attempt to overthrow Somoza, had been elected a vice-president of the Council of State at Sandinista initiative and without being consulted. He quit rather than serve. In June, after arriving in the United States, he briefed committees of Congress and met conservatives who had posts in the Reagan administration. Among them was retired Lieutenant General Gordon Sumner, who urged him to join forces with the former National Guardsmen. Cardenal, agreeing, helped found the Nicaraguan Democratic Revolutionary Alliance, or ADRIN, within a month. It split, and the initials of Cardenal's faction changed to UDN for Nicaraguan Democratic Union, which had a fighting arm called FARN, or Revolutionary Armed Forces of Nicaragua. This faction would unite with Bermúdez to form the FDN (Nicaraguan Democratic Forces) in August.

Throughout, the relationship of Cardenal's political group to Bermúdez's military structure mirrored the frustration that Nicaragua's domestic political opposition had always felt toward the military, whether toward the military-backed regimes of Somoza or the Sandinistas. It was the frustration of impotence versus the arrogance of power. So long as they were in Miami, the politicians were unable to affect decisions in the field. Even when they moved closer to the front, they had influence only at the margins.

Meanwhile, in mid-1980, Bermúdez had gone to Honduras to meet Jorge Salazar, one of the most prominent opposition leaders within Nicaragua, who was trying to organize an anti-Sandinista insurrection. The topic of discussion, according to Bermúdez, was "what can we do to screw those Sandinistas up." Bermúdez was trying to organize a group but did not have "a single penny. We had no more than goodwill." Salazar was gunned down in November in circumstances suggesting official government involvement, removing a potential civilian ally for Bermúdez's movement from the scene. In time, as Bermúdez built his infrastructure, he would amass enough power so that he could understate his title, calling himself chief of staff instead of commander in chief. But he and the others knew his real position. "I was in total control of the movement." Bermúdez disparaged the successive waves of politicians who would join, try to take control, then leave. "Those guys have been incapable of doing anything. They have been a failure. They try to hide their failure and blame it on other people."[6]

An important reason civilian politicians never played a vital role in the movement traces to its origins. The resistance did not spring up spontaneously inside Nicaragua in response to Sandinista actions but was organized abroad by Guardsmen from the old regime almost without reference to politics. That heritage would later prove hard to shake.

ÁLVAREZ'S VISION

In the summer of 1980, a new actor, who would form close ties with the Honduran military, appeared on the scene. Robert Laurence Schweitzer, major general of the U.S. Army, looked unkempt as usual as he entered the Pentagon. His shoes were scuffed, an unbuttoned epaulet flapped over his collar, and his briefcase overflowed with papers. He was not an invited guest at the briefing in the "tank," the small boardroom used by the Joint Chiefs of Staff. But as he sat listening to his former commanding officer, Lieutenant General Wallace Nutting, he began to see red.

Most of those in the room, including the armed service chiefs, appeared to be drifting off into slumber as Nutting, the head of the U.S. Southern Command in Panama, discussed the deteriorating security situation in Central America after the Sandinista takeover in Nicaragua. There were no questions.

Then Schweitzer stood up dramatically. "I have seven Purple Hearts in my briefcase from fighting in wars where you people didn't know what you were doing. Why don't you have the balls to listen to what Wally is saying?"

General John Vessey, then the Army vice chief of staff, said to Schweitzer: "Come on, Bob, sit down."

He did, but not for long.

To his admirers, Schweitzer was brilliant, brave, and indefatigable, a zealous anti-Communist, a pious Roman Catholic. He had studied for the priesthood at a Jesuit seminary and still attended mass and took communion every day. Critics, among them two U.S. ambassadors then in key Central American posts, viewed him as a lunatic. Even his friends saw him as an unguided missile. Schweitzer had been Nutting's executive officer in Vietnam in 1970–71. While Nutting slept from 11 p.m. to 5 a.m., Schweitzer had been up and about, visiting all his units and getting mixed up in every firefight at night. During ten months in Vietnam, he absorbed so much shrapnel that, legend had it, he would set off airport metal detectors. "He is the type of soldier whom no one knows what to do with in peacetime," said a friend. There being no war, Schweitzer set off on a crusade of his own. In mid-1980, he was director of strategy, plans, and policy in the office of the Army deputy chief of staff for operations and plans.

A short time later, the barrel-chested black-haired general, then fifty-one, was en route to Central America for an on-the-ground assessment. While in Honduras, he met Colonel Gustavo Álvarez Martínez, then still head of the national police and an anti-Communist crusader in his own right. In talks with the Honduran general staff, it came up that Honduras could use ten helicopters to give its small army increased mobility. Schweitzer promised them on the spot. He had no prior authorization.

Back in Washington, Schweitzer turned his very considerable energies onto the bureaucracy to deliver on his promise. To the chagrin of Nutting and his Southern Command in Panama, which was starved for resources and attention, Schweitzer succeeded. The helicopters were in place by October 1980. In Honduras, he had acquired credibility.

In April 1981, "Mike Farmer," the CIA station chief in Tegucigalpa, approached U.S. Ambassador Jack Binns and said Álvarez had requested high-level talks on security cooperation. The Agency backed the idea, and Binns concurred.

Álvarez had a good deal more in mind. He made two calls in Washington. One was on William Casey, newly named head of the Agency, and the second on Schweitzer, now an adviser on the National Security Council. He viewed Casey as a very close friend of Reagan, and Schweitzer as a friend of the Honduran military.

It was there that Álvarez presented his grand scheme for dealing with the Sandinistas. It would utilize the ragtag bands led by officers of Somoza's scattered National Guard whom Álvarez, without official authorization, had been helping during 1980. Álvarez proposed that with covert American help the rebels could be built up into a mass military movement and sent into Nicaragua, where they would create conditions of civil war and eventually provoke the Sandinistas into a grave military blunder, such as an attack on Honduras or Costa Rica. Then the United States would come to the defense of its ally and move on to intervene in Nicaragua. Álvarez had thought it inconceivable that the insurgents could topple the leftist government or accomplish any significant task and proposed to upgrade and equip the Honduran army, which he argued could play a critical role. The bottom line of his proposal was overthrowing the Sandinistas with U.S. help.

Casey, who was joined by his deputy for Latin America, Nestor Sanchez, listened closely but was noncommittal. He told Álvarez he appreciated the plan and would analyze the recommendations carefully and consult with President Reagan.

Schweitzer was enthusiastic. "We'll do it," he said.[7]

His reaction encouraged Álvarez to think that a positive response would soon be on the way. Schweitzer worked behind the scenes to bring it about.

Back in Tegucigalpa, "Mike Farmer," the CIA officer who had escorted Álvarez to Washington, told Binns he had asked for increased military aid and training for his people in counterintelligence and in protective services. "I suppose I was being fed a line," Binns later said.[8]

Schweitzer was one of those who in fighting the Communist conspiracy maintained one of his own—always communicating on trips through what are called "back channels," provided by the CIA as opposed to the State Department. He did not talk to the press. His former commander, Nutting, had indirectly inspired the enterprise, but Schweitzer did not brief him. Nor, apparently, did he tell Secretary of State Haig, a retired general, what he was up to. This may seem odd, because Haig was close to Schweitzer and thought of him as his protégé; Schweitzer had been his special assistant and policy adviser at the Supreme Allied Command of NATO. He saw him as "a remarkable young fellow, very anticommunist but in a sophisticated way." Schweitzer had coached Haig during his difficult Senate confirmation hearings early in 1981.[9]

While a number of high officials may not have been in the picture, accounts of Schweitzer's talk with Álvarez quickly got back to Central America. In Managua, Ambassador Pezzullo heard about the meeting and cabled what he said were very strong objections.

From the fragmented reports, Pezzullo deduced a change in stated U.S. policy. He suspected that Schweitzer was "getting us into a conspiratorial game" with the Hondurans. Pezzullo recalls directing sharp questions to Enders, by then the designated assistant secretary for inter-American affairs. "What the hell are you doing? Are you giving these fellows a green light to come into Nicaragua?" Pezzullo knew only the outline of Álvarez's grand plan. Enders

cabled back the bland reply that Pezzullo had misread the statements: Schweitzer had no authority to say what he said, and his
remarks did not mean what Pezzullo thought they meant. "It was
very broad, very general, a request for U.S. aid on a very large
scale," Enders later said. The notion of supporting the rebels was "on
the periphery." Time, however, would prove Pezzullo's suspicions
right.[10]

Álvarez's visit to Washington was a key event in the formation of
Reagan administration policy toward Nicaragua. Unsolicited, he had
offered a base of operations, the backing of his army, and an
ambitious plan whose goals were readily shared by conservatives in
the administration. But the way he went about it proved to be flawed
in its conception. In visiting only the CIA, Álvarez effectively
selected the Agency to carry out the scheme; but it was an agency
which had little use for "team-playing" with the rest of the government, which had lost many of its covert experts in a wave of firings,
and whose record at organizing government overthrows was mixed.
In winning Schweitzer's endorsement, Álvarez gained the energies
of a dynamic operator in a useful position. But by limiting his
conspiracy to those two, Casey and Schweitzer, he wrongly assumed
that they could deliver the entire U.S. government, where in fact
they represented only one important faction.

Schweitzer and Álvarez had much in common with others who
helped bring about a U.S. commitment to forces seeking the
overthrow of the Sandinistas. They were "can-do" men who could
change the "facts" on the ground if not always the policy decisions in
Washington. They were zealous anticommunists. They liked to work
in complete secrecy. None had direct policy responsibility.

Until he was removed from the NSC post in November 1981 for
making an uncleared speech in which he said the Soviet Union had
acquired military superiority over the United States and was "going to
strike," Schweitzer was supposed to be advising on military and
strategic issues only. But as long as he was at the NSC and even after
he was supposed to have left, Schweitzer played an active role in
bringing about confrontation with the Sandinistas.* Almost daily he
called up Nutting in Panama to offer advice, according to a senior aide
there at the time. "He was one of those who wanted to overthrow the

---

* Schweitzer told friends that for eight months after he was supposedly fired, he
continued working at the NSC, appearing in civilian clothes instead of uniform.

bastards," said a former staffer on the Senate Intelligence Committee who supported Schweitzer's effort. "He helped things along."[11]

For months after Álvarez appeared in Washington, high officials with policy responsibility had serious doubts about a plan that carried the implication of ending with a U.S. intervention. But in August 1981, four months after receiving his proposal, the CIA dispatched an envoy to Honduras to notify Álvarez that the United States shared his goals: the liberation of Nicaragua and replacement of the Sandinistas by an elected government.*

Álvarez had thus offered a secure sanctuary for the rebels as part of an overall plan. But at the time he approached the U.S. government, there was no coherent movement, no consistent source of training, supplies, or guidance. These came into being between April and August 1981 as the initiatives of other outside actors began to bear fruit.

THE ARGENTINE CONNECTION

In mid-1980, three other actors entered the conspiracy: two Americans, Nat Hamrick and John Carbaugh, and a pillar of the Nicaraguan émigré community in the United States, Francisco Aguirre.

Hamrick was the most impassioned, called a playboy-mercenary by FDN leaders and an "amateur" by Gerardo Schamis, his Argentine diplomatic contact. Carbaugh had the political connections, resourcefulness, guile, and determination to get things done. Conventional diplomats saw him as a one-man demolition team. Aguirre was a former Nicaraguan colonel who had left in a dispute with an earlier Somoza—Luis—thirty years earlier. A Washington real estate magnate and publisher of *Diario Las Americas*, a Spanish-language daily newspaper, he was known in the exile community as the "godfather" and, according to Carbaugh, "always wanted to be president of Nicaragua." Urbane, widely traveled, and secretive, he was a mover and shaker—or influence peddler, depending on the perspective—in Washington, with contacts in many agencies of government and many administrations. Craig Johnstone, who became a key strategist for

---

* The administration quickly and generously delivered on the other aspect of Álvarez's deal. Military aid to Honduras more than doubled to $8.9 million in 1981 from the $4.1 million provided in Carter's last year and rose to $31.3 million in 1982, $48.3 million in 1983, and $77.4 million in 1984.[12]

Central American policy at the State Department, described Aguirre as "an operator" on the Nicaraguan scene who "trades on influence." Aguirre carried considerable weight, for he enjoyed the respect of Nicaraguan émigrés, good relations with the Argentine military, and contacts within the Reagan administration.

It was an unlikely trio, none of whom was an elected or appointed U.S. government official. Through bluff, political connections, and a series of smoke signals amplified by mirrors, they would coax or take credit for coaxing Argentina and then the United States into separate decisions in 1981 to back Bermúdez and his force. "It never was the CIA's secret army or secret war," Hamrick boasted. "We gave it to them on a silver platter. It was a fait accompli."

The three disagreed on many basics. Carbaugh, who had befriended and then fallen out with Anastasio Somoza, favored direct U.S. intervention, while Hamrick, who had had a shared business interest with Somoza family members, opposed it. Aguirre felt a U.S. intervention to be inevitable. "A superpower acts when it acts," he would say. Aguirre was willing to deal with any fighting group and was an old friend of the family of Edmundo Chamorro, who headed a small band of fighters and was allied with Cardenal. But Hamrick said he would not provide Aguirre "pieces of the puzzle to put a bunch of socialists in Managua."

They agreed, however, on Bermúdez.

It took about a year from the time the three free-lancers began their project—shortly before the Republican convention in summer 1980—until it bore fruit. Aguirre gave Carbaugh and Hamrick the credit. "They had more of a role as key players in the institutionalization of the movement." He called them "good, red-blooded Americans, people of great courage." Bermúdez too gave credit to Hamrick and Carbaugh. Hamrick, he said, played a "very helpful role" in introducing him around Capitol Hill, and Carbaugh gave moral support at a difficult moment. "The Sandinistas were at the peak of national popularity. People thought to initiate a movement against that was crazy. So when you receive moral support, you are very satisfied."[13]

The period in which the three engaged in their maximum efforts, from January to August 1981, coincided with Enders's last major attempts at conventional diplomacy.

Hamrick, who was thirty-seven when he returned to Nicaragua four months after the revolution, was from Rutherfordton, North Carolina, a small town in the southern part of the state. There are

126 listings for Hamricks in the local telephone book, but none for Nat, Jr., who ran and still runs a mail-order business in reconditioned Chinese Mausers, Boer rifles, and other guns and pistols. Edgar Chamorro, a disaffected rebel leader who was critical of many Americans who advised the movement, spoke fondly of Hamrick as "a playboy type of adventurer, a fast talker, offering a lot of things, very anti-Communist, very well-intentioned."

Before Somoza's overthrow, Hamrick had set up a hardwood exporting business with Luis Ramón Sevilla Somoza, son of the long-time ambassador to Washington, Guillermo Sevilla-Sacasa, and great-nephew of Anastasio. Just two months after the overthrow, Hamrick got a call from a business partner, Roberto E., with the surprising news that it would be possible to resume business. They did two things: first, they organized a rosewood export, and second, according to Hamrick, they set up an intelligence-gathering network for the Defense Intelligence Agency. Hamrick's idea was "to use Sandinista money to overthrow them." He said that of the $500,000 turnover in his business over eighteen months, $150,000 was used for travel, lobbying, and entertainment on behalf of the project.

Hamrick had made his Argentine connection through Anastasio Somoza in 1974. In autumn 1979, an Argentine friend whom he had met through Somoza contacted him and said if a Republican should be elected President, the military government wanted a rapprochement with the United States. A special envoy would be sent to make the initial contacts.

In the event, the envoy was Gerardo Schamis, who had served in Guatemala and Bolivia as ambassador. Hamrick introduced him to Carbaugh in June. Carbaugh made a strong impression. "Nat is only an activist," Schamis said. "But John Carbaugh is serious." In July they were together in Detroit for the Republican convention.

After Reagan's landslide election victory, Carbaugh said Hamrick told him they could get help for Bermúdez from the Argentines, "but we've got to invite Viola here." (General Roberto Viola, the army chief, had been designated by his military associates as the next president.) Carbaugh said he "made it part of our ongoing process" to press for the visit during the transition. The ongoing process, he acknowledged, was "all bluff and bluster." Aguirre also had a strong Argentine connection, according to Bermúdez. "He was a very close friend of Viola and members of the military group."

Hamrick claimed that NSC head Richard Allen agreed to facilitate the Viola visit, then reneged, whereupon Carbaugh, Hamrick, and other Helms staffers descended on senior Reagan aides in an intensive lobbying effort. Allen maintained that he never heard of Hamrick and had his own direct connection with "people competent to speak with the military leadership of Argentina." He added that "no one in the White House reneged and there was no pressure from anyone to get it restored."[14] Harry Shlaudeman, at the time U.S. ambassador to Argentina, said that before Reagan's inauguration he raised the possibility of Viola's coming for the visit, which was routine for an incoming Latin head of state. "There are always guys hanging around, saying they had something to do with it."[15]

Although there is some question as to what role Hamrick and Carbaugh had in the Viola visit, which took place on March 17, 1981, they unhesitatingly claimed credit for its success. Hamrick said that Viola's visit proved that Argentina and the United States had a working relationship.

The key event, according to Hamrick and Aguirre, followed Viola's visit. Early in April 1981, at about the time Álvarez was visiting Washington, they traveled to Buenos Aires, where they called on Viola, who had just been installed in the presidential palace. Aguirre briefed General Alvaro Martínez, the chief of staff, and Hamrick talked with Colonel Mario Davico, deputy in charge of intelligence. Aguirre lent credibility to the enterprise. "I was not fooled by the Sandinistas," he said later. "I had the moral authority. I was exiled by Somoza. I was on no one's payroll."[16] Bermúdez arrived a few days later and saw General Alberto Valín, head of intelligence. By his own account, Bermúdez did some rather fast talking, but to a receptive audience. His pitch combined prophecy, flattery, and an appeal to self-interest. His aim was to "encourage them to, let's say, try to get the United States' support under the table."

"We stated that the Sandinistas were a Marxist-Leninist regime," he recalled, "and would build up a totalitarian government. Nicaragua was becoming at that time a general headquarters of all the leftist and terrorist movements like the Montoneros, Tupamaros, PLO, North Koreans, Japanese" and others. Argentina, Bermúdez went on, "had been very successful against the urban guerrillas in Argentina and had the prestige. So they must do something." The Montoneros, Argentina's leftist guerrilla group, rang a bell because, Bermúdez asserted, they had moved their exile headquarters from Havana to Managua shortly after the Sandinista victory.

The biggest problem was to explain the relationship between Argentina and the United States, a task made more difficult in that none of the visitors had the least official capacity. Bluff helped, and Bermúdez played to the generals' vanity. "We stated to them that even though the United States is a superpower, the political situation couldn't allow them to do something and that at that moment the United States needed friends from Latin America to do something by themselves or through being indirectly a channel of any kind of aid that the United States wanted to do but could not find a way to do it." In short, the United States needed a proxy.

Bermúdez's argument that the United States wanted someone to help "ease the way for their [U.S.] participation" had an added cachet in that it fit in with the facts the Argentines were gathering through their own sources. As Bermúdez observed, "Of course their intelligence officers were in touch constantly with the intelligence departments of the United States."

Aguirre vouched for Bermúdez. "Enrique Bermúdez is a very convincing fellow," he said later. "I believe in his honesty, his integrity, his professional dedication." Aguirre felt that it was appropriate to support Bermúdez at this early stage because he would run a "responsible operation," which was preferable to "having elements of anarchy take over."

The payoff for Bermúdez was twofold: Argentina agreed not only to support his movement, which consisted at the time of sixty men, but also to back his leadership. "I was selected by them. I talked to the man in charge. He said to me: 'Bermúdez, we have studied your background. We trust you. And we are going to support you.' "

Bermúdez saw this as the turning point in U.S. involvement. "They [the Americans] wanted to do something but at that time they didn't know how to do it. And the Argentinians eased the way for United States involvement."

Within a month of the trip to Buenos Aires, Bermúdez received $30,000 in Argentine aid, and Edmundo Chamorro received $50,000. The Bermúdez faction got a second installment a few months later, and training began. The Argentines took three groups of twenty FDN officers to Buenos Aires later that year to be trained in intelligence and gave a small-unit training course in Honduras.

Aguirre had by then become an important point of contact and support in Washington for Bermúdez. "As this started to grow," he recalled, "I always kept in touch with him. When I went to

Washington, I called him; when I came to Miami, I made a call just to give him a salute." On one occasion, Aguirre invited Bermúdez to a party at his house in northwest Washington to introduce him to "very important persons from the new administration."

According to Bermúdez, Aguirre did not provide financial support. However, he said, "I think he was doing some lobbying. He has very good contacts in Washington."[17]

The next event that Carbaugh and Hamrick claim to have orchestrated was a visit by Vernon Walters to Buenos Aires in June 1981. Walters was close to Jesse Helms and Carbaugh, had worked for Aguirre, and was a good friend of Schamis. But there is general agreement that Walters, while a carrier of messages, was never a central actor.

The partners' stories do not completely jibe. Hamrick asserted that "John sent Walters. Walters owed John a favor." But Carbaugh said Aguirre and Hamrick were responsible for the arrangements surrounding the Walters trip. In any case, Walters did not conclude any deals while in Buenos Aires. Ambassador Shlaudeman confirmed this to have been the case and described the visit as "part of the effort to educate people about Central America." Hamrick maintained—or would claim to the Argentines—that the trip itself was the signal of U.S. concurrence in their plan. "The Argentines felt the agreement was informal. The object of the game was a 'fait accompli.' And that occurred when Walters got on the plane in Buenos Aires to come home." Added Hamrick: "Probably even Walters didn't know. But they knew that we sent Walters." Walters in interviews has denied that he had anything to do with setting up the Argentine connection, and Carbaugh asserted that Walters's contribution consisted of "subtle nudges."

The first sign of the Argentine decision was an expanded presence of intelligence officials in mid-1981 in Honduras. According to Jack Binns, then the U.S. ambassador in Tegucigalpa, it was evident by July that the deal had been done. Binns had tracked fifteen Argentine intelligence operatives working under cover. They had applied for visas to visit the United States and had been introduced to the embassy as employees of Nicaraguan businessmen in Honduras. The visas were granted and on a routine check with Buenos Aires, the embassy learned that the fifteen had used Argentine passports under false names to obtain U.S. visas. Binns informed Washington, "but I couldn't get anyone interested."[18]

THE GREEN LIGHT

Argentina had made its commitment; the funds had begun to flow and military training was about to begin. Technically, the insurgency was a going concern, and William Casey at CIA, acting more like a stock market investor with insider knowledge than a deliberative policymaker, wasted no time in buying into it.

Early in August 1981, Casey sent a representative to Honduras on a secret mission to see Álvarez and the outgoing military president of Honduras, General Policarpo Paz García. This was the debut of Duane ("Dewey") Clarridge, whom Casey had named as chief of the Latin American section of the operations directorate of the CIA. Clarridge, who had been station chief in Rome, fancied big cigars and silk safari outfits. He was another "can-do" operator who had successfully helped combat Italy's Red Brigade terrorists. He understood a little Spanish but did not speak it. He had minimal military background and had never served in Latin America. His detractors, and there were many, would call him a "cowboy."

Clarridge told Paz, Álvarez, and other military leaders that President Reagan had personally ordered him to Honduras. He said the United States had agreed to support action against the Sandinista government using the resistance forces and wanted to "liberate" Nicaragua. Clarridge did not accept all the proposals Álvarez had made in April 1981, but the Hondurans felt that it had become clear as they inquired into the details of U.S. thinking that "we were talking about the overthrow of the government," Álvarez later said.

That may have been a fair reading of Clarridge's remarks, but Reagan apparently had not given any formal approval. Richard Allen said later he could not recall having seen "a plan concerning 'a civilian insurrection and civil war.' That would mean that President Reagan, to my knowledge, had approved no such plan." The Core Group was aware of Clarridge's trip. But to say he had gone on the basis of an executive order was "something of an exaggeration," for there was no executive order, according to Enders. At the time, Enders recalled, "we were working on an alternative; we were actively preparing that decision, seeing who would be responsible. It had not been approved by the President and was not to be until November 17, 1981." Haig also said the plan had not been approved at the highest levels. "I can assure you it was not. I would have strenuously and vigorously opposed it. It is the wrong medicine for the wrong disease."[19]

Clarridge's statement, whatever its validity for the U.S. government, was enough for Álvarez to assure sanctuary for the insurgents and their leadership.

The first formal advice of the Argentines and Hondurans and the informal advice of the Americans to the insurgency had been to unite. Álvarez felt that the September 15 Legion needed a new name and image because the Sandinistas were labeling all armed resistance Somocistas. The unity meeting took place on August 11, 1981, in Guatemala. Argentina was represented by a military officer, Bermúdez said. Unlike most unity meetings in the history of guerrilla movements, this one proved to be a footnote. Edmundo Chamorro did not attend because his UDN movement had split and two former deputies came representing the Cardenal faction. Bermúdez said that some of his associates began to question why even to include the UDN. He said he told them, "I don't care what name we call ourselves. We need financial support in order to go ahead. If we don't sign this [the unity proclamation], we won't be able to get support from anybody. So we have to sign this even if they are not the real representatives [of the UDN]."

The document was a paragraph in length. It said only that "we the representatives of the September 15 Legion and UDN agree to join efforts and constitute a single organization that will be called the Nicaraguan Democratic Forces (FDN) in order to fight against the Sandinistas." They signed it in an upstairs recreation room of the rented house in Guatemala City, paid off three months' back rent and telephone bills, closed the office, and moved it and the staff to Honduras. It was Bermúdez who chose the name FDN, from a list of four or five suggested by his aides.*

The extent of the CIA's role in organizing the August 1981 meeting is not known, although Álvarez thought at the time that the CIA helped pay for the arrangements. But Bermúdez said he paid his expenses out of his own pocket. Funds were so tight, in fact, that he got behind on his bills and American Express canceled his credit

---

* The first and only notice of the meeting was carried in Aguirre's *Diario Las Americas* a month after the event. Bermúdez couldn't get any of his "partners" to take credit. "No one of them wanted to sign the public statement. They didn't want the publicity. I signed it." The UDN found an émigré in Miami named Max Vargas to sign in their name.

card. Enders became aware of the events only after they occurred. He had spent that same day in Managua trying to see if a negotiated solution was possible.

Thereafter it remained only for the CIA to cement the U.S. relationship with the Argentine military government.

Later that month, Clarridge returned to Tegucigalpa on a private aircraft, this time with Colonel Mario Davico, the vice-chief of Argentine military intelligence, in tow. They met with Paz, Álvarez, and Colonel Leonides Torres-Arias, chief of Honduran military intelligence. "I bring the greetings of my president," Davico began formally. "Argentina has faith in democracy and has decided to support Honduras and Nicaragua to be free. We are with you. We will do everything we can."

Again, Clarridge used words that led the Honduran military to believe that the United States intended to take action up to a direct intervention.

Clarridge said: "I speak in the name of President Ronald Reagan. We want to support this effort to change the government of Nicaragua. We must change the government of Nicaragua to give the Nicaraguan people the chance to democratically elect its own government."

Torres-Arias replied that Honduras was a friend and ally of the United States but feared that the United States would renege, as it had in Cuba in 1961. "We are concerned about a new Bay of Pigs," he said.

"Believe me, Colonel," Clarridge replied, "there will never be a new Bay of Pigs."[20]

Thus was born what Bermúdez would call the tripartite relationship. He reduced it to an aphorism: "*Los Hondureños van a poner el territorio, los Americanos la plata, los Argentinos la cara.*" (The Hondurans will provide the territory, the Americans the money, and the Argentines the front.)

As far as Honduras and Argentina were concerned, the United States had thereby committed itself to the common cause in August 1981. Not for three months, however, did the administration formally make a decision and inform Congress.

CHAPTER 3

ENDERS TAKES CHARGE

As Álvarez, Clarridge, Carbaugh, Hamrick, and Aguirre worked behind the scenes arranging the U.S. commitment to the armed resistance, Thomas Enders began the task of drafting official Reagan administration policy for Central America. But before he was fully in charge of his bureau, before he was even officially named to the job, U.S. policy toward Nicaragua had taken a turn. Lawrence Pezzullo, the U.S. ambassador in Managua, felt that the internal game was the critical arena in which the United States should strive for impact; that the diplomatic option should be exhausted before being abandoned; that it was premature to launch external military action. But nowhere else in the U.S. government, including the State Department, would anyone fall on his sword to maintain diplomatic leverage with Nicaragua.

There was little obvious gain in pursuing the Carter administration's damage-limitation course, and a good deal of political pressure against it. "The situation was murky at best," Edmund Muskie, secretary of state for the last nine months of the Carter administration, commented some years later. "A happy ending was certainly not clear. I can understand why the new administration did not want to get its feet stuck in our shoes."[1]

Yet there was no viable alternative to the Carter administration policy. In the words of John Carbaugh, "There was just a vacuum." From his perspective, that meant an opportunity.

"Haig and Enders realized they had to throw a bone to the right-wingers," he said. "They can't have the Soviet Union or the Middle East or Western Europe. All are too important. So they've given them Central America."[2]

Not all of Central America; just Nicaragua.

Moreover, there was a real crisis in El Salvador preoccupying Enders and the Bureau of Inter-American Affairs, compared to which Nicaragua was a sideshow. Despite Duarte's presence on the junta, his reform program, and the collapse of the FMLN's January offensive, guerrilla fighters were increasing in strength and ability and taking good advantage of the corruption and ineptitude of the Salvadoran army leadership. At the same time, the right took Reagan's victory and encouraging statements as a license to step up their free-lance vigilante operations known as death squads. And while Haig had sent military trainers to Salvador and there was a broad consensus across the administration on the need to support the Salvadoran government, the combination of death squad activity, the weakness of the civilian government, and the ineptitude of the army made for a tough battle in Congress to obtain resources. A policy was called for that would sustain support at home while guiding El Salvador to a more stable situation; and something had to be done about the Salvadoran military.

Enders had not only to master a new region but also to draft a policy and build a political base in the administration and in Congress. Under pressure to name certified conservatives as key deputies, he kept the slots open, appointing only one principal deputy, Stephen Bosworth, a foreign service officer. Famed as a quick study, Enders found time to learn Spanish and within months of being named was speaking without an interpreter.

His main battle over Salvador policy was within the administration. Drawing from the agendas of liberals, conservatives, aides, and outside experts, Enders crafted a position that he enunciated on July 16, in his first speech following Senate confirmation. At its heart were two propositions: that El Salvador should resolve its internal dispute through democratic elections; and that the United States should provide military aid until a political solution could be achieved.

Enders paid heed to liberals' concern for human rights abuses by the right and endorsed the land reform that Duarte had championed. He read back the rhetoric of conservatives about Cuba's responsibility in equipping and training the Salvadoran rebels; but in the context of the internal political solution he was proposing, it was lip service.

The major contribution he made to the policy was to champion democracy as the goal for El Salvador; after Vietnam, where the same goal had been pronounced and never achieved, this was a daring return to an earlier era in which democratic ideology guided U.S. foreign policy goals in the third world.

Enders recalled having "a hell of a time" getting this package through the U.S. government, in particular free elections. "People said they don't know what will happen. Who'll win. How can we tell?" But that "is why we did it." He argued that a conservative government should go on the offensive and stand up for its values. "We had never done that. When push came to shove, we got behind dictators. That policy had been very wrong."

The clash took the form of battles over the drafts for his July speech. "Tom came up with this word: the cornerstone of our policy for Latin America is free elections," recalled Gordon Sumner. "Frankly, I wasn't all that enamored of the idea. Not that I have any difficulty with free elections per se, but I wasn't sure that that was the proper basis for a policy when we were faced with some very, very serious problems."

Some of those fighting Enders had a hidden political and constitutional agenda, according to Luigi Einaudi, who directed policy planning, a sort of miniature think tank in the inter-American affairs bureau, throughout the Reagan administration. Some high officials, such as Allen, William Clark, his successor at the NSC, and Fred Iklé, the undersecretary of defense, wanted to use the Salvador issue to force a confrontation with Congress. Also arguing this position was James Lucier, a senior aide to Senator Helms. Adapting Reagan's and Allen's line that you must first win the war and then work for democracy, these officials argued that the central aim of the administration was to restore American strength in order to deal with the Soviet Union. Congress was the obstacle. They believed that democratic reforms were unachievable and would lead to defeat. "So the only question was the kind of defeat, a slow gradual one that will put everyone to sleep, or a sharp clear defeat where the guilty parties can be gotten out of the way," Einaudi said. If the administration won, Congress would be reduced to proper subservience, they argued. And if it lost, Congress would be "reviled for losing Central America to the Communists."[3]

Enders rejected the all-or-nothing approach, and instead committed himself to finding a consensus in Congress that would sustain the policy. With the aid of White House allies such as James Baker, who had good lines to Congress, he succeeded. That was one pillar of the policy.

The second pillar was military reform. About a month after Enders's speech, a high-level decision was made to ask Fred Woerner, then an Army brigadier general, to head a U.S.-Salvadoran team to look into the military strategy and the Salvadoran army. The initiative, according to Nutting, "came from us in Southcom"; Duarte, in his recent autobiography, asserts that he originated the idea.[4]

Woerner was one of a rare breed in the military. He was an intellectual, an area specialist fluent in Spanish who commanded the respect of diplomats and fellow officers and willingly went before academic groups and the press. His mission, as defined by the Joint Chiefs of Staff, was to develop a national plan for El Salvador and to have an end product that looked as if the United States had played no role in the drafting.

Woerner formed the seven-man Military Assistance Strategy team on September 4 and convened them at the U.S. embassy in San Salvador to analyze the aim of the exercise. "I locked us in a room for three days," he recalled. "I put up pieces of paper around the walls. We spent thirty hours just brainstorming." Then for two straight months the U.S. and a similar-sized Salvadoran team worked together at the Salvadoran defense ministry to produce a final manuscript. The crash-study approach was that which had been used by Eisenhower and Marshall on the eve of World War II at Fort Leavenworth, and the methodology was time-honored. First, they analyzed the national purpose and interest, the political objective, and the threat. Then they examined military objectives, concepts, and capabilities. Finally, they drew up a list of requirements for different levels of U.S. support. The result was a five-year military national plan.[5]

Although it is still classified and its ultimate impact is therefore hard to gauge, the Woerner report, completed on November 8, is viewed by many who read it as a benchmark in the U.S. military involvement in the Salvador war. The essence of it was to force the Salvadoran army to focus on its long-term problems and think through its strategy, intelligence-gathering, manpower needs, and logistics. This was the Salvadoran army's plan and it cast United States financial aid and training in a supportive role. It addressed some extremely sensitive issues, such as leadership and organization.

These two documents, the July 1981 Enders speech and the Woerner report, helped give U.S.-Salvador policy coherence and purpose. The order in which they appeared was fortuitous—first the political objectives, then the military. U.S. policymaking toward El Salvador, whatever the inspirations that gave rise to it, may one day be seen as a model for responding to friendly governments under leftist guerrilla attack. With the strategy in place, the U.S. ambassador on the scene had the guidelines for using resources provided to him to support agreed-upon goals and for requesting additional resources on the basis of an agreed-upon plan. Leverage and power were centered, appropriately, on the official responsible for implementing the policy.

Nicaragua was, of course, a different case, because it could not be considered a friendly government. But useful comparisons can be made in the two methods of fashioning policy. First, with Nicaragua there was no Woerner report or Enders July speech laying out policy goals toward Nicaragua. In the unending behind-the-scenes tug-of-war over the purposes and methods of U.S. policy, a clear statement of U.S. objectives was impossible. Second, whereas El Salvador strategy was driven from the top, Nicaragua policy bubbled up from the bottom. And, finally, instead of building up the role of the U.S. ambassador in Nicaragua, early Reagan administration decisions had the effect of cutting it down by ignoring his advice and stripping him of resources. Partly because of its origins and partly because of the individuals who promoted it, the making of U.S. policy in Nicaragua was characterized throughout by duplicity, secrecy, and pretense.

Although Casey was quick to endorse the anti-Sandinista movement, available evidence suggests that the original initiative came not from the CIA but from the leaders of the armed resistance, their friends lobbying the administration, and Álvarez. Casey had given an impression of some reluctance in the early stages. "I don't think Casey was an enthusiast of this at all," said Pezzullo, who had visited him in late March. "He was not inclined toward some adventure in Nicaragua." Pezzullo said Casey asked him if there was any way to do business with the Sandinistas. "You've got to get tough with them and stick with issues, but they understand and you can move them," Pezzullo replied. He gave as an example the halt in the arms flow into El Salvador. Casey had two aides in his office and neither contradicted Pezzullo. In fact, one aide said afterward: "I am glad you were as clear as you were with him."

The possibility should not be excluded that Casey was deliberately trying to mislead Pezzullo. "Bill is more of a fox than Larry," was the view of Hamrick, who said he briefed Casey three or four times in the first six months of the administration.[6]* Casey strongly believed in covert operations, big and small, and started more of them than any of his postwar predecessors, according to CIA officials. He was also a man who liked a secret.

Roughly from the time Álvarez called on Casey in April 1981, the question of whether to support the insurgents had been a matter of constant debate. The State Department and the uniformed military had had serious misgivings, but a first sign of wavering appeared when Haig asked Robert McFarlane, then State Department counsellor and later national security adviser, to examine available policy options in Central America. "We were trying to come up with a panorama of options to deal with the Central American problem," Haig said.[7] But McFarlane's report, titled "Taking the War to Nicaragua," focused largely on Haig's favorite target, Cuba, and on ways to block the flow of arms into Cuba and Nicaragua.[8] The effort, which in retrospect appears to have been a delaying tactic, was rejected in the White House and led to the next step, that of Enders's asking the CIA to examine options for a covert operation. The CIA, of course, had the option already prepared.

Enders's formal role as head of the State Department Bureau of Inter-American Affairs led many observers to conclude that he was

---

* "The first time I went over, Casey said to bring a map of the region. He'd been in the office a week and said they had maps of individual countries but not the region," Hamrick said. Although Hamrick made his pitch for a much more militant policy toward the Sandinistas, Casey gave the impression he viewed things in tactical terms. "He wanted just to slow them up so they didn't take El Salvador on his watch."

the driving force behind establishing the clandestine CIA program. And indeed Enders, at the time and since, encouraged this impression. But his stance was more revealing in the context of his modus operandi. In actuality, support for the rebels was hotly disputed and had little or no support among those State Department professionals with whom Enders had relations of mutual respect. A national security issue in dispute ordinarily is taken over by the National Security Council staff and decided by the President; in addition, the NSC by its charter has control over CIA covert operations. But Enders, one of the most skilled bureaucratic in-fighters in government, was determined to maintain what control he could. According to one close observer, he did this by telling the NSC, "You, the NSC, are in charge. I recognize your preeminence over policy. I also recognize you are short of staff, so I'll do the staff work." Then, in the best State Department tradition, he would draw up options, the most attractive-sounding of which was his preference.[9]

Another technique of maintaining control was to use secrecy to exclude unwanted influences, particularly from the conservative political appointees favoring the covert military assistance program. Enders's instrument was the aforementioned "Core Group" of five top officials to review Salvador policy, which he had set up in the spring. Its members were all men who could be trusted to keep secrets. Lieutenant General Paul F. Gorman, who had served as a national intelligence officer with the CIA in the mid-1970s, represented the Joint Chiefs of Staff. Nestor Sanchez, who had retired from the CIA as chief of operations for Latin America to become deputy assistant defense secretary, represented the Pentagon. Alfonso Sapia-Bosch, a Cuban-born CIA analyst, represented the NSC; and Dewey Clarridge, the CIA. As the resistance program grew, the Core Group, including Enders, operated almost entirely in secret and with little paper flow. Sanchez in meetings with reporters would come across as a superhawk, but behind the scenes was a cautious bureaucrat who waited to see which way the wind was blowing before taking a position, according to defense sources. Sapia-Bosch occasionally met reporters but was a supporter of Enders's line, according to Otto Reich, the deputy administrator of AID. Gorman and Clarridge, both can-do men, did not give interviews; Gorman later came into conflict with Clarridge over the latter's management of the contras.

Although Enders controlled the process in Washington, he had no way of knowing exactly what Clarridge was saying and doing on the ground. It seems certain that what Clarridge told the Hondurans early in August 1981 reflected a very liberal interpretation of his instructions. But Clarridge was able to play the same game as Enders and, by making de facto decisions in his bailiwick, to change the policy. In both meetings with Honduran military officials in August, he saw top officials without notifying the U.S. ambassador. And in laying out his thoughts to Álvarez and others, he asked them not to bring this to the attention of Lieutenant General Nutting, the chief U.S. military representative in Latin America.

The idea of keeping the plans secret from the U.S. military commander responsible for the region seems extraordinary in retrospect. CIA officials say it shouldn't. "They're blabbermouths," said one senior official, summing up the Agency's attitude toward the military leadership.

For his part, Nutting, when he finally learned of the scheme, preferred to look the other way. "I'm sure that's true," Nutting commented when asked about Clarridge's opening to Álvarez. "Frankly, the way it was going and the future I saw, I didn't want to have anything to do with it either. I believed then and even more strongly believe now that the wrong people were doing it [carrying out policy]." After Álvarez took over the leadership of the Honduran military, he and Nutting often met, and they and their wives even spent weekends together on Honduras's north coast at the beaches. But Nutting never broached the subject. "Damned if I wanted anything to do with it on that end."[10]

Between May and August 1981, Enders's attitude toward the Sandinistas hardened significantly, according to a visitor to his office. Early in June, the State Department announced that, according to U.S. intelligence, Soviet-built tanks had been secretly shipped to Nicaragua by way of Cuba in the previous five to six weeks. Daniel Ortega said in reply that the reports were "totally unfounded." Haig said he was confident of the accuracy of the intelligence. Besides sowing rancor between Washington and Managua, the dispute produced an immediate demand by Honduras for antitank recoilless rifles and howitzers. A short time later, Enders asserted that Cuba was trying to build an operations base in the country and that there were 600 to 800 Cuban military advisers there. The relationship was deteriorating, and Enders decided that time was running out for testing the diplomatic option with the Sandinistas.

THE MANAGUA TALKS

Pezzullo meanwhile was leaving Managua in August to take up a fellowship at the University of Georgia; no successor had been named and he feared there would be no way to carry on the dialogue with top Sandinista officials.

"They weren't naming another ambassador to take over the baton. I wanted someone to come down from Washington to retain the relationship." He suggested to Enders's deputy, Stephen Bosworth, that he meet the Sandinista leadership. Bosworth said he would think it over. Then, about a week in advance of the scheduled meeting, Enders cabled that he himself was coming. There was no detailed advance planning. "This wasn't a considered thing. This sort of happened," Pezzullo said.

But Enders had been thinking about the idea for some time, as had others. No matter what course of action would follow, there were good reasons to explore the limits of diplomacy. As a Pentagon official put it, "I certainly felt we should make every effort possible so that the audit trail showed we went every step of the way."[11]

Enders later said that the cut-off of U.S. aid to Managua in April helped prompt his decision to travel to Managua to seek a diplomatic settlement. "We were concerned they would read it as negative," he said. "That is one reason for the August trip. There was a concern that there were two [conflicting] messages being sent."

By the time Enders decided on the mission, Carbaugh and Helms had made their peace with him, Carbaugh said. "Enders knew how to work with Helms." Thus, Enders gave Helms an advance look at his strategy and asked for his blessing. "Jesse, I want six months to try to negotiate an agreement with these guys. And after that we'll do whatever you want. Pull out all the stops," Carbaugh quoted him as saying. To which Helms replied: "Well, you can have one year. If you can get them to negotiate in good faith, you can give it a try." Enders was covering a flank. "I didn't want to be accused of hiding something from him," he later explained.[12] The Core Group was also aware of his mission, but a great many others in the administration who thought they should have been, were not. In the event, he had about six weeks for the effort.

The meetings were a turning point in relations with the Sandinistas. One U.S. official said he had never seen anything so dramatic, so direct, and so lacking in subtlety in three decades of negotia-

tions in Latin America.[13] Enders's tone throughout was accusatory
and threatening. He accused the Sandinistas of supplying arms
to the Salvadoran rebels and all but threatened a U.S. military
intervention.

The most heated confrontation was with Bayardo Arce, one of the
hardest of the hard-line comandantes. Enders's demands reduced to
one sentence, according to another American at the table. "You can
do your thing, but do it within your borders, or else we're going to
hurt you."

"All right, come on in," Arce replied. "We'll meet you man to
man. You will kill us, but you will pay for it. You will have to kill us
all to do it." As Arce spoke, two other comandantes, Jaime Wheelock
and Humberto Ortega, sat up, startled.

Another Sandinista official suggested that perhaps someone in a
lower echelon had arranged the arms deliveries without telling the
leadership.

"Patently ridiculous," Enders retorted.

Both sides were at the boiling point. "Your neighbors are scared to
death of you. You've ruined your relationships with your neighbors,"
Enders said.

Arce shot back: "Even the Costa Rican president is on our side."

Enders blew up. "If I were you, I would be ashamed to claim that
thieving crook as a friend."

Arce and his associates bristled. "That's a trumped-up CIA
accusation," Arce said.

Enders came right back. "You know very well that that's not a CIA
accusation. You know very well what you did, you know very well as
we do the role of the Cubans in this whole affair. We have very good
intelligence on it, and we are possessors of the very same facts."
Enders was referring to allegations that Rodrigo Carazo, the Costa
Rican president, had profiteered on gun-running during the Sandinista revolution.*

Both sides left the first day's talks in a depressed mood. Enders

---

* Unbeknown to Enders, the Sandinistas were recording the session and arranged
for a tape of Enders's remarks to be delivered to Carazo. When Enders arrived in San
José the next day, he briefed Ambassador Frank McNeil on the faux pas. "It's
absolutely true," McNeil told Enders about the Carazo allegations. "But we're going
to pay for that one." Enders's deputy, Bosworth, visited Costa Rica a few months
later and Carazo, who was under parliamentary investigation, showed him a verbatim
transcript of the remarks. For about an hour Carazo lambasted Enders and then
turned around and asked Bosworth for $20 million in aid.[14]

spent the entire evening with Nicaraguan business leaders. Then, sometime after midnight, after the guests had left the U.S. embassy, Pezzullo sat down with him and discussed the results. "I think we've got a deal," Pezzullo said. "You made your point." The Sandinistas were "scared to death" about training camps in Florida and elsewhere run by Cuban-Americans and used by some anti-Sandinista opposition—"even though a lot of these things are just kooky stuff"— and about the United States arming Nicaragua's neighbors to the point that they become a security threat. "And I think they're legitimately afraid of an invasion," Pezzullo continued. "They know what happened in the 20s."*

A prime U.S. concern was export of revolution, which Pezzullo said "really has been controlled but I think we can make it stronger." Referring to the threat posed by the militarization of Nicaragua, he argued, "They can't bring in tanks, they can't bring in sophisticated equipment without it having the symbolic security threat effect on their neighbors.

"So you've got a deal," Pezzullo concluded. "The deal is if they will commit themselves to no export of revolution and to limiting the size of their armed force and their weaponry, we would on the other hand be willing to guarantee that we would not invade." The guarantee, he said, could take the form of a pledge to close down exile military training camps in the United States and a mutual security assurance that the United States would not organize Nicaragua's neighbors into an anti-Nicaraguan alliance.

The setting for Enders's final meeting was the clubhouse of a deserted country club outside Managua built just before Somoza's overthrow. Armed guards stood watch outside and within the building, which was closed to the press.

It was there that Enders made his offer to Daniel Ortega. At the time, Ortega was Coordinator of the Junta, a sort of *primus inter*

---

* Indeed history gave the Sandinistas good grounds to fear an intervention; the United States had intervened in Nicaragua on eleven occasions since 1853, more than in any other country in Latin America. It was not indiscriminate meddling, for Nicaragua has had the most unstable political system in Central America, and calling for outside help as a way of settling political disputes has been a way of life. The most unusual intervention was in 1854, when William Walker, a young American journalist, led an invasion force of fifty-seven other Americans, took power, and was recognized by the United States as president. Walker was overthrown two years later, and when he tried to regain power, U.S. forces intervened to remove *him*. U.S. Marines had been stationed in the country almost continuously from 1912 to 1933.

pares among the nine. Ortega is unprepossessing and uncharismatic. His manner is earnest and self-effacing and in conversation he often mumbles. In the highly ideological context of revolutionary Nicaragua, he is often described as a pragmatist. But he is made of steel. A younger brother and most of his closest friends were killed in clashes with Somoza's National Guard. Ortega spent seven years in Somoza's jails. In the periodic hunger strikes staged to demand better prison conditions, guards denied water and ice to the prisoners, and Ortega drank his own urine to stay alive.[15]

The meeting with Ortega ran for an hour and twenty-five minutes, according to a Sandinista transcript of the conversation that was later presented to the International Court of Justice in the Hague. There is no comparable U.S. account because Enders took no aides in with him. Foreign Minister Miguel D'Escoto interpreted.

Enders began by saying that the United States accepted Nicaragua's revolution and its new internal order. "You see your revolution as irreversible, and so do we. We do not share many political and social ideas but acknowledge that the defeat of Somoza is an accomplished fact and we consider it as such and, moreover, a necessary fact."

He summed up the principal problems from the American viewpoint as being the continued flow of military aid to El Salvador and Nicaragua's military build-up, and from the Nicaraguan viewpoint as being the "fear that the United States has taken actions to destabilize and attack the revolution."

Ortega welcomed Enders's visit as a momentous occasion. "And just as the revolution is a reality, the United States is an enormous reality," he said.

"We are revolutionaries. We do not agree with the aggressive and imperialist attitudes of the United States. We cannot accept that you wish to invade us, that you have invaded us, that you have cut the credits." But he said Nicaragua sought better relations with the United States, and did not want an arms race, nor to become what the Reagan administration had termed a "menace to hemispheric security." In order to survive, the revolution had to look for backing wherever it could find it.

Ortega criticized U.S. policy in El Salvador, charging the United States had "worked to strengthen the position of the more conservative sectors in Salvador . . . which had resisted a political solution." In addition, there were now twenty U.S. advisers in Honduras. All this "obliges us to seek means for our defense."

Enders responded that the United States did not desire the restoration of a conservative order in El Salvador unless it came to power in free elections. Washington wanted agrarian reform and social progress.

Enders also said the United States had no objection to a Sandinista policy of nonalignment. "I feel that we have come to a fork in the road," Enders concluded. "I would like to explore together with you the manner in which our future relations will develop. I would like to submit some ideas. On your part, you could take the necessary steps to ensure that the flow of arms to El Salvador is again halted, as in March of this year. We do not seek to involve ourselves in deciding how and with whom this object should be achieved, but we may well monitor the results."

On the all-important security issues, Enders said that it was for each country to decide the number of soldiers and the quantity of arms it should have, but the arms race must be given attention. This position is worth noting, as it shifted radically within weeks after Enders left.

Finally, Enders offered three incentives. To respond to Nicaragua's fear of intervention, Washington would reaffirm its commitment under the Rio treaty—the inter-American collective security accord signed in 1947—not to resort to force or to threaten the use of force whether directly or "by some other means." The administration also would be prepared to give "somewhat closer consideration" to the problem of Nicaraguan political exiles undergoing military training in the United States. "No one sees them there as a real threat against you, but it is obvious that if you see them as a political threat, the problem would be to see how we could respond to this concern." Third, Enders promised to examine immediately the possibility for resuming food aid, development aid, and Peace Corps assistance. He proposed an exchange of proposals by the end of September, stated that "we would expect that measures be taken to stop the flow of arms into El Salvador" within two weeks, and suggested a return visit by the end of September to review progress.

D'Escoto emerged from the room looking pale. "He told us: 'You can forget defending yourselves because we are one hundred times bigger than you are,'" D'Escoto said. But Enders and Ortega seemed to have reached a catharsis. Enders, who is 6'8", reached down to Ortega, who is 5'8", and tucked him under his armpit in an *abrazo*.

Enders headed to the airport and flew to Costa Rica. En route he tried to use the cramped toilet facility on the small C–12. A fellow passenger recalled that he looked "like a tarantula" with one knee and one elbow on the low ceiling. On landing in San José, he gave his judgment on the experience to the pilot: "Your pisser doesn't work."

"It's a long shot, but worth a try," he told Frank McNeil, the U.S. ambassador, as they walked to the diplomatic lounge, where for the next several hours Enders dictated cables.

Enders returned to Washington after midnight and left early the next morning for Brazil. When he got back to Washington again, some days later, he was already under fire. Carbaugh claimed that Helms kept his word about supporting Enders's efforts, but conservatives within the administration, such as Clark, Kirkpatrick, McFarlane, and Casey, were "convinced that Enders was getting caught up in the process." They wanted "harder action."

The initial assault took the form of criticism that Enders had not put sufficient emphasis on democratization in Nicaragua. L. Craig Johnstone, a foreign service official who had taken over the office of Central American affairs in July, said he had to comb the transcripts and cables to find a defense. "A check through the record showed that he did discuss it and that it was clearly spelled out as one of our objectives," Johnstone said. "I guess you wind up with a question of emphasis. And certainly the emphasis to his visit down there was on the military activity, the military build-up, the Soviet-Cuban presence, and their support for insurgency in El Salvador. But the other point [democratization] was certainly not neglected."

Actually, even Pezzullo, who thought Enders had delivered a "very good pitch," regretted that he had not pushed more for internal democratization. "I would have. I was always pushing it when I was talking to them about their internal system being a major concern to people in the United States. They couldn't go around talking about their new society and then be violating human rights, putting people in jail, closing up newspapers, and so on. I made it almost a fetish. They used to get pissed off as hell. I didn't bring an American down there that we didn't make the first stop in *La Prensa*. And I did it just to stick it in their craw."

But Enders focused on security, apparently hoping it would "sell and keep the wolves off," Pezzullo said. In Washington, however, the wolves had different aims in mind when they discussed democracy than the vigorous criticism expressed by Pezzullo. In an

Orwellian twist, "democracy" in Nicaragua, which has not had a democracy in this century, came to stand for overthrow of the regime.[16]

In the view of his critics, Enders's proposition was "imprudent" and lacked "teeth." Robert McFarlane took exception on grounds both of form and substance. McFarlane's philosophical outlook on Central America echoed Jeane Kirkpatrick's; he saw the denial of Soviet access to the Americas as a key goal of policy. "To the extent one has to contend with deterrence on our southern borders, you are diverted from other accounts," he said. Enders had created a bureaucratic problem, he said, by going to Managua without having the content of the exchanges "blessed" by the standard interagency process. Actually Enders had cleared it through his Core Group, by securing the agreement of each member and having him obtain the approval of his boss, but this did not extend to McFarlane, even though Haig had instructed him to explore various military options for Central America. The substantive problem was that Enders's approach would have allowed a Marxist regime to become consolidated. McFarlane favored a "much more demanding standard of performance" by the Sandinistas.[17]

But if Enders had outflanked his opponents, he too had been outflanked. In fact, some days before he arrived in Managua, Clarridge had gone to Honduras to inform Álvarez that the United States would back his plan. On the same day that Enders was negotiating in Managua, Bermúdez and others were in Guatemala organizing the FDN. And a few weeks after Enders's visit, Clarridge visited Honduras again, this time with a senior Argentine military officer in tow to discuss arrangements with Álvarez.

By the time Enders went to Managua, "everybody knew that this was the last gasp before we moved to a far more serious confrontational policy. And we had begun thinking of what that confrontational policy would be," Johnstone said. He added that the August session was a precursor of the confrontation because it was itself designed as a confrontation. "He went down there and said, 'Look out for what's coming. But you've got one last chance.'"

Years later, the Sandinistas recognized that they had missed an opportunity. A foreign ministry official noted: "We were not so pragmatic in those days." Arce commented that "at the time, we didn't think that Enders was very serious. In retrospect, we consider him as the most serious person who spoke with us." But Ortega put the blame squarely on Enders. "I would say the principal problem that we had in the meeting with Enders was his arrogance. Because he was as arrogant as he was tall." Enders put the blame on the other side. The initiative "got kicked in the head pretty quickly by the Sandinistas."[18]

UPPING THE ANTE

What followed was a series of missteps by both sides which soured the atmosphere. Enders began by sending a virtual ultimatum to Managua. "The continued use of Nicaraguan territory to support and funnel arms to insurgent movements in the area will create an insuperable barrier to the development of normal relations," he wrote on August 31. "Unless this support is terminated right now, I don't think that there can be the proposed dialogue, so I will say this has to be a *sine qua non* for any dialogue."[19]

His words smacked of precondition. "We had to win the right to talk with them," commented Julio López Campos, who was in charge of the DRI, the Sandinistas' foreign policy apparatus.[20]

Enders's first draft proposal, dated September 8, 1981, promised vigorous enforcement of laws against paramilitary training on U.S. soil. He said four other draft proposals were on the way. But delivered with the proposal was a formal notice announcing a cancellation of $7 million in credits, the undisbursed portion of a suspended year-old $15 million loan approved during the Carter administration.[21]

A second proposal, dated September 16, sketched out a mutual declaration of nonaggression. Two days later, the Pentagon announced a joint U.S.-Honduran naval and air exercise to run for three days in October. The exercise, called "Halcón Vista" (Falcon View), did not just happen. The idea had been generated by Major General Robert Schweitzer of the NSC, the same man who had originally encouraged Álvarez in his proposal to overthrow the Sandinistas with the help of contras and Honduran and U.S. forces. His timing was "a deliberate attempt to stick it in their eye," said an aide to Nutting. Schweitzer remembered that similarly named exercises had been run in the past and had actively lobbied Nutting and the chairman of the Joint Chiefs of Staff to get them to agree.

In their first response, the Sandinista leadership said on
September 19 that the military exercise would seriously affect
Nicaraguan consideration of all three letters. At the same time,
they sharply criticized U.S. policy in El Salvador for ignoring
political solutions. Ortega asserted in a public statement that
the U.S. exercise would feature an amphibious landing.* In
response, Enders wrote on September 28 that there would be no
amphibious landing and offered to discuss the possibility of
Nicaragua's sending observers. On October 1, a U.S. Army general
was sent to Managua to explain the aims of the maneuvers, which
involved 260 soldiers, six small ships, and several planes. The aide
to Nutting said the offer to the Sandinistas to observe the exercise
was genuine but no one expected them to accept. "But if they did,
all the better. We wanted to impress them." Ortega again criticized
the maneuvers in an address to the UN General Assembly on
October 7.[22]

The September 28 letter effectively ended the exchange. Although
Enders said that he looked forward to seeing Nicaraguan Foreign
Minister D'Escoto in late October, it is hard to see how there could
have been any cause for optimism. Nicaragua had not delivered
any proposals or responses. But, more important, Enders, the
initiator of the August talks and the exchange of drafts, had reached
a dead end in the critical area of security. "We had some difficulty in
defining the arms control questions, and it was not ready until
mid-September," he recalled later. "We ultimately got agreement
on a set of principles that would be very demanding."[23]

The solution soon became the problem; the demands were
extreme. Nicaragua was to recrate its newly acquired Soviet tanks
and ship them back to countries of origin. Craig Johnstone drafted
the proposal and showed it to the Nicaraguan ambassador, Arturo
Cruz, Sr., who found it insulting.

"I was flabbergasted," Cruz later said. "If that was my reaction as
a moderate, think of what the reaction would have been in Managua.
I told them, this sounds like the conditions of a victorious power."
He asked Johnstone to withdraw the paper. Later that day, Johnstone called Cruz and told him to forget the draft. Cruz did just that

---

* D'Escoto mistakenly identified the exercise as "Aventura Oceanica 81" (Ocean
Venture 1981). Actually, that exercise had been held off Puerto Rico and ended
August 20.

and never reported its contents to his foreign ministry, an omission Johnstone later found "curious."[24]*

The U.S. plan would have halted Nicaragua's acquisition of armed or unarmed helicopters and aircraft, armored personnel carriers, howitzers, and armed vehicles but allowed replacements of those already acquired. Nicaragua would have had to get rid of weapons systems not possessed by its neighbors while not being permitted to acquire systems its neighbors had. The plan appears to have been designed with Honduras in mind. Honduras traditionally has had perhaps the best air force in Central America and this would have allowed it to be modernized while limiting Nicaragua's capabilities in the air and on the ground. It also would have limited the Sandinista army to 15,000 to 17,000, the level Ortega said existed at the time, and proposed working down from those levels. It also called for a halt to foreign guerrilla groups. There was no mention in the plan of foreign military advisers.

"It was an attempt to do two things," Enders later commented of the most controversial features. "One, to remove offensive arms that could be used to support significant attacks against [Nicaragua's] neighbors. And second, to ensure re-export and non-re-import. The T-55's had made their first appearance and should be re-exported."[25]

In less than a month, the ante had been upped significantly. In August, Enders had noted to Ortega that the arms race between Honduras and Nicaragua was over armored vehicles. Honduras had the British-made Scorpions, a light armored car, and Nicaragua its newly acquired T-55 tanks. While the United States could suggest some ways to correct imbalances in arms and personnel, each country would have to resolve questions of the quantity of arms and troops it should have, Enders had said in August. By September, the United States proposed to be the arbiter of what weapons each could have and how to get rid of them.

"It was a pretty tough approach, but as part of a negotiating ploy, not too bad," said Walter Stoessel, then undersecretary of state for political affairs. Johnstone called it "a very reasonable proposal" and

---

* "At the time, Cruz was, after all, their ambassador in Washington. And we were expecting that Cruz was acting as an agent of the government of Nicaragua. We probably operated on the assumption that Cruz communicated on the basis of my conversations with him the substance of what it was that we had in mind," Johnstone said.

said "it was actually seen as a test of goodwill on something that was verifiable as much as anything else." Haig said it was never "presented to me as a stumbling block." But Enders saw it as extremely controversial. Exactly who insisted on the point remains unclear, but it emerged from the interagency process. Some military officials at the time thought that Schweitzer worked behind the scenes to put the proposal on the table.

One outspoken defender of the proposal was Nestor Sanchez, the Pentagon's leading civilian expert on Central America. "The Soviets did it with the missiles in Cuba. What we were trying to do was to stop the build-up that developed before it became what it is." Sanchez did not claim authorship of the proposal, but Johnstone said, "If Nestor claims parentage, I wouldn't take it away from him."

Whether or not it was intended to be a negotiating ploy, it was never presented. The negotiations more or less ended at that point.[26]

That tanks in Managua became an insurmountable obstacle in Washington seems odd in retrospect. In the rugged mountain terrain that separates Nicaragua from its neighbors, a tank-led assault would easily be countered on the limited transit routes. The Sandinistas had begun acquiring tanks in late 1980. Hamrick, then engaged in his rosewood export business, had had an employee stationed at Rama who observed the arrival of the tanks and other armored vehicles on flat vessels from Cuba. Hamrick said he reported this to the Defense Intelligence Agency. Pezzullo confirmed that ten or fifteen tanks had been brought to Nicaragua by late 1980 and were kept under wraps, but he had seen the action as meaningless because tanks are "useful equipment in the Middle East but in Central America a tank means nothing." A second shipment had arrived in the spring of 1981.*

Pezzullo had been derisive. "You've brought in a pile of shit," he had told a Sandinista leader. Asked what he was referring to, he replied: "That crap you brought in from Rama and you've got smuggled away here outside the city. Do you know what you're going to do? You're going to build up a commander here who one day is going to take over your capital. Tank commanders are very

---

* The Reagan administration has ignored the earlier shipments in its principal publications, including the graphically illustrated, highly detailed pamphlet *Sandinista Military Build-up,* published by the State and Defense departments in May 1985.

dangerous people." The comandante had agreed that it was a "silly" project. The U.S. intelligence community also was divided on the importance of tanks. From the reporting of some officials "you'd think they were atomic weapons," Pezzullo said. The Sandinistas also made a big to-do. But at the U.S. Southern Command in Panama, military intelligence officials said they viewed the acquisition of tanks and other weapons as "just the usual Soviet arms dump."[27]

Nicaraguan foreign ministry officials and López of the DRI assert that they were unaware of the Washington flap over arms control; Arce claims to have heard of it from congressional sources. In a letter dated October 31, D'Escoto's deputy wrote finis to the chapter. In the first real response to the Enders proposal, Victor Hugo Tinoco said Enders's offer to enforce vigorously U.S. laws against the camps seemed unlikely to achieve immediate results; the U.S. government should proceed immediately to dismantle the training camps. Two months after Enders stated his precondition, the Sandinistas responded with one of their own. Tinoco said that further consideration of the U.S. proposals depended on concrete action on closing down the camps in Florida and on the relaxation of tensions that would be generated by a change in U.S. policy in Central America and the Caribbean. Enders understandably viewed this letter as ending the discussion.

"Looking back, I come to the conclusion that they had a project," said Enders. "They developed it in the years of fighting Somoza. They really intended to go ahead with that project. It was nonnegotiable: the start of a broad movement of revolution in other countries and most other things that have now been done. It was a strategy and forward-looking."

Enders has been criticized by some Latin American experts for his style before the comandantes, which was cold and confrontational. One long-time participant in U.S.-Latin American negotiations commented: "Whatever their faults or virtues, you are talking to guys that have faced death, that have killed and that have exposed themselves. To threaten them is counterproductive. You can't expect them to say, 'OK, you're right, we're scared.' He backed them into a corner. It's an approach that never works."

And another U.S. official said: "Enders humiliated them. Threats would not work. The way to deal with them was to compliment them and face them with facts they could not cope with. Moreover, he didn't have the tools in his hands at the time to carry out the threats. It wasn't coercive diplomacy. It was bullshit diplomacy."

Pezzullo's judgment differs. "I would give him high credit for a first-class job in presenting the case. I think he just couldn't sell it." He blames the "right wing" for "changing the bidding" as the effort proceeded. "No matter what you do, you are always going to get a new approach by the right that will shoot you down. Because all the people in this administration are people who shoot down negotiations rather than people who negotiate."

One factor that doomed the initiative was the lack of continuity at the U.S. mission in Managua. Eight months elapsed between Pezzullo's departure in August 1981 and the arrival of his successor, Anthony Quainton, in March 1982. Besides Pezzullo, the deputy chief of mission and the political counsellor also were being replaced. All this in an embassy regarded as a potential security problem and where no written record was kept beyond a few weeks.

Enders said he regretted Pezzullo's departure. "I tried very hard to keep him on, but he wanted to retire." He said it was particularly difficult to proceed "without an ambassador of the stature of Pezzullo" and that "maybe if he had stayed," things would have worked out differently.

Pezzullo said Enders had not asked him to stay on. "I decided the year before I wanted to leave. Plus, after April 1 [when U.S. aid was suspended], how could you really think you could do anything?"[28]

The August mission would prove costly for Enders in personal terms as well as for long-term U.S. policy in Nicaragua. By traveling solo and in secret, Enders provoked resentment over the style as well as the substance of his approach among the many officials who were left out of the planning. Moreover, Enders failed to accomplish the minimal aim of leaving a clear audit trail to prove that the United States had exhausted peaceful means before turning to stronger measures. The proposals drafted after his trip pointed to ambivalence on the U.S. side, and the fact they were never presented underscored that the initiative had been abandoned hastily and in large part for internal reasons. Finally, with the internal opposition now aroused, it would take three years before the State Department gathered enough strength within the administration to launch another negotiating initiative. Enders stayed in his job through mid-1983, but from this point forward, he was in charge of Nicaragua policy in name only.

CHAPTER
4

THE GAME SHIFTS

To EXPLAIN THE COLLAPSE of the Enders initiative, U.S.
officials later cited the growing internal repression in Nicaragua. In
a secret speech to military officers on August 25, 1981, Defense
Minister Humberto Ortega had defined the Sandinista revolution as
"profoundly antiimperialist, anti-Yankee, and Marxist-Leninist."
Copies of the speech began to circulate in September. *La Prensa*, the
opposition newspaper, was closed down on three occasions in August
and twice in October. And four prominent businessmen who accused
the Sandinistas of leading the country toward communism were
arrested on October 21.[1] "We were starting to see some indications
of regressive tendencies that got strengthened at about that time,"
Enders noted.[2] But the argument was somewhat contrived. Enders
himself had told Ortega that Nicaragua's internal political system was
not a subject for negotiation; in addition, none of the events cited

caused a great political stir in the press or in Washington. In fact, Nicaragua received little attention at the time. To a far greater extent, the focus was on El Salvador. The Sandinistas could argue with equal justice that internal hardening of attitudes in Washington caused them to exercise caution.

The fact is that for internal political reasons neither side was in a position to rush into a quick agreement. As Ambassador Pezzullo summed it up, "Circumstances required a quick victory. There was no way that could have happened."

Also, the Reagan administration had not merely come to "the fork in the road" but, as a result of Dewey Clarridge's two meetings with Álvarez, already had started down the branch leading to confrontation.

Craig Johnstone, Enders's office director for Central America, confirmed this. The decision to support the rebels in actuality "was taken before the Enders visit on the basis of certain expectations which, if they had not come to pass, would have caused revisions."[3] The expectations were that diplomacy would fail.

Enders blamed the Sandinistas for the collapse of the talks because they "kicked away what we thought were the most interesting items for them" and failed to respond with proposals of their own. "Could we have gone back and said: have another look at our papers? We couldn't put any more on the table. They went forward with their project. We thought we would see whether the insurrection would produce conditions for negotiations. Better not to spend any more cartridges on this. The game then shifted."

And the problems began. Enders saw the anti-Sandinista insurrection as a way of "upping the heat on Nicaragua until we could get a negotiated settlement." He acknowledged, however, that an insurrection is "very hard to fine-tune. If people are willing to give their lives, they would have to have a major say in any ultimate deal."

One remarkable feature of the decision to provide aid to the armed resistance was the depth and breadth of misgivings expressed by high officials in the diplomatic, military, and intelligence communities. Foremost among them was the secretary of state, a retired Army general. Enders said Haig opposed the plan because he "thought it wouldn't get very far" and would "divert energies from Cuba, where he wanted to put the squeeze."

Haig's own version was that "in order for covert activity to be effective in this situation, it would have to be of a scope that by its very nature could not remain covert." More specifically, he felt that a limited U.S. commitment like this effort allowed the adversary opportunity for "damage repair" and escalation; that it violated international law and thus jeopardized the U.S. claim to the moral high ground on other issues; and finally, that covert aid in what was a fundamental security issue was a "cop-out."

Enders also was reluctant, according to Haig. "I never got the impression from our discussions that he was an advocate of covert action," the secretary of state said. Enders said he was concerned because "it is a new principle for the U.S. government" to become the primary means of support for a movement that could not be controlled.

William Casey, Clarridge's boss at the Central Intelligence Agency, also intimated that he had reservations. "Many of the considerations that slowed me down, slowed him down," said Enders. They included how a movement once started could be turned off; how to make sure it becomes democratic and not antidemocratic, as well as "the traditional legal arguments that you are virtually declaring war." However, Casey had good operational reasons to press for the decision: his agency would lead and manage the operation, making him a central player in the policymaking process.[4]

One of the most closely argued analyses of possible options came from within the military community. In a classified report produced about three weeks before the administration formally decided to back the rebels, military and political experts assembled by the Army War College for Lieutenant General Wallace Nutting urged the avoidance of direct confrontation with the Sandinistas.

Their reasoning, which reflected views at the top of the Army, was cogent. "Direct confrontation is a useful tool when there is a reasonable possibility that such a confrontation will bring about the desired response. At present it is too early to challenge the Sandinistas. Based on their role in the overthrow of Somoza, the Sandinistas are still supported by a wide spectrum of the Nicaraguan populace. A well-organized opposition has yet to develop inside Nicaragua. Moreover, Somocistas are not likely to gather sufficient support within Nicaragua to manage a successful counterrevolution."

Indeed, a confrontation was likely to set back U.S. goals in every respect by strengthening the anti-American bias of the government and much of the population; reinforcing the interventionist image of the United States in Nicaragua and elsewhere in the hemisphere; uniting Sandinista decision-makers; diminishing the legitimacy of the internal opposition; forcing a closer alignment with Cuba and the Soviet Union; legitimizing the export of revolution for defense against counterrevolutionary forces; and providing the rationale and opportunity for the Sandinistas to clamp down on domestic opposition before it could mature into an effective political force.

These experts advocated covert aid only to ensure the survival of pluralism, to neutralize Cuban activities in the region, and to raise the costs for Sandinista or Cuban intervention in the region.

Rather than resort to force, they advocated using every political means available to hold the Sandinistas accountable for their self-proclaimed objectives. These means included official policy statements, information programs, and persuasion of the international community.

The Army's experts put strong emphasis on the internal opposition by urging the administration to obtain and keep the confidence of democratic sectors of Nicaraguan society while offering the Sandinista leadership alternatives that would permit them to adopt more pragmatic, less ideological approaches to deal with Nicaragua's difficulties.[5] In short, they were urging a revival of Pezzullo's "full-court press."

The recommendations were read among the military leadership, but the report had virtually no impact on policy and today gathers dust deep inside file cabinets in the Defense and State departments. But in discarding expert advice at the start of so controversial a program, the administration set itself up for a much more serious situation down the road. Eventually, this would be defined as a national security concern. Yet the military establishment was not brought into the organization, planning, or implementation of the program. Indeed, Clarridge had told Álvarez specifically not to brief Nutting about the goals of the program.

Major questions remain unanswered. With so much opposition, where was the political support coming from to back the fledgling insurgency? Was there a triggering event? Or a single point of decision? Here are three answers, each containing a piece of the puzzle. John Carbaugh: "There was just a vacuum. There was no strategy." Major General Fred Woerner: "There is a phenomenon within a bureaucracy. If there is a certain vacuum, there is a sucking-along effect." And Craig Johnstone: "If you look at the evolution from the Argentine presence to the presence of an insurgency movement to the last attempts before the United States became directly involved in what was then the Argentine movement, to a modest U.S. involvement—it is a far more fluid process than sort of reaching a critical stage, and then, boom, it all changes."[6]

In other words, the administration more or less drifted into the commitment. Actually, according to Otto Reich, a hard-line group working together behind the scenes helped push Reagan in this direction. These were Casey, Jeane Kirkpatrick, and three of Reagan's California associates: William Clark, then Haig's principal deputy and a long-time Reagan confidant; Edwin Meese, the White House counsellor; and Caspar Weinberger, the secretary of defense. Reagan's weak NSC structure and chaotic decision-making process opened the door for the project. But as Robert McFarlane later noted, there was no framework within which to analyze the proposal. "It is immensely important to recognize just how crucial the absence of such a framework proved to be." As for Reagan, the decision was part of a pattern. A senior NSC aide at the time put it this way: "When an idea comes along that tracks with his thinking, it comes to the top of the stack."[7]

Kirkpatrick denies that she played any role in the decision. "I didn't know anything about it. I was not informed. I was not initially in the NSC. Even when they included me in the NSC, I wasn't included in the NSPG [national security planning group]. I was included in the NSPG not very long after that. But the decision had already been made." Robert McFarlane had a different recollection. "I'm surprised at what Jeane said. She was a part of that."[8]

Before anything became irrevocable, Haig and Enders made a series of last-minute jabs at finding a more conventional approach to containing the Sandinistas. One was the study McFarlane did for Haig of conventional containment, "Taking the War to Nicaragua," which in fact focused on ways to halt arms shipments to Cuba and Nicaragua.

In October, Enders traveled to Venezuela, Colombia, and Chile in what he described as an effort to rally political support for pressures against the Sandinistas. Bayardo Arce, one of the Nicaraguan comandantes who had met with Enders in August, had a different version. He said the Sandinistas were told by some of the governments that Enders was looking for an international intervention force.[9]

Early in November, Haig asked the Pentagon to study military options in relation to Nicaragua; he then told the House Foreign Affairs Committee he could not rule out a naval blockade of Nicaragua.[10] "I think Haig said why not dust off the old military action plan—one hundred things that can be done about Cuba from the 1962 crisis," said one Pentagon official. Haig's suggestion about the blockade never found much support in the Pentagon. "We found it to be greatly to our disadvantage. If the Soviet purpose is not to confront us directly but to divert our assets, a blockade plays right into their hands," the same official said.[11]

Haig's trial balloons about military measures provoked the predictable rhetorical response from around Latin America. The president of Ecuador, the governments of Venezuela, Brazil, and Mexico, the foreign ministers of Argentina and Peru, and finally President Luis Herrera Campíns of Venezuela, while on a visit to Washington, all spoke out. Herrera at a White House dinner on November 17 said his government rejected "any kind of armed intervention" in Central America. In remarks on November 18, he added that Venezuela, the most stable and successful major Latin democracy, supports "a line of nonintervention and respect for the self-determination of nations."

But it was too late; Reagan had already accepted the recommendation to organize and provide covert support for the rebels on November 16, the eve of Herrera's visit. The following day he signed National Security Decision Directive 17, which endorsed the program.

Enders made the presentation before Reagan and the NSC. Prior to the meeting, Haig had objected vehemently to the plan. But by the time it reached the NSC, Enders said Haig "noted some of the downsides" but did not oppose it outright.

"I explicitly set it in a foreign policy framework," Enders said of his presentation. "I didn't think we could make sense of [the program] at a later time unless we made it clear how this fit in with broader foreign policy purposes." The framework was efforts already under way to deal with the war in El Salvador.

The plan, according to a document later obtained by the *Washington Post*, was to "work with foreign governments as appropriate" to conduct "political and paramilitary operations against the Cuban presence and the Cuban-Sandinista support infrastructure in Nicaragua and elsewhere in Central America." Initially, this would involve a $19.95 million program, but more funds and manpower would be needed, according to an accompanying document.

Also proposed was building "popular support in Central America and Nicaragua for an opposition front that would be nationalistic, anti-Cuban and anti-Somoza" and supporting the "opposition front through formation and training of action teams to collect intelligence and engage in paramilitary and political operations in Nicaragua and elsewhere." The plan called for working through "non-Americans to achieve the foregoing," but said that "in some instances CIA might (possibly using U.S. personnel) take unilateral paramilitary action against special Cuban targets."[12]

In terms of the broader foreign policy context—the war in El Salvador—Enders proposed additional economic aid to Central America and support for democratic elections in El Salvador.

On December 1, Reagan signed the intelligence "finding," a written presidential statement required under a 1974 law stating that the covert operation was important to U.S. national security. A few days later, Casey briefed the two congressional intelligence oversight committees on its content.

It was four months from the time Clarridge had given the green light to Álvarez in Honduras to the presentation of the finding before the intelligence oversight committees in Congress. Although Reagan had made a decision on November 16, it did not change the direction of policy, but just provided notification that CIA funds would now be provided for the program. Thus, the decision ratified a process that had begun months earlier. Congress, of course, did not know that the signal had been given long before to Honduras. Nor did Congress know that the goal of overthrowing the Sandinistas was discussed in Clarridge's contacts with Álvarez and implicit in the program approved on November 16. Casey omitted mention of any political dimension in his briefing to the committees.[13]

The briefing by Casey and Enders would cause grief to the administration in the months and years ahead. Casey's finding, drafted at the CIA, was three sentences in length. It said the program was intended to interdict the flow of weapons from Nicaragua to El Salvador, to get Nicaragua to focus inward, and to make the Sandinistas amenable to negotiations.[14] It was an ambitious set of military, political, and diplomatic goals for a force of 500 men. The diplomatic goal, to apply pressure for a negotiated solution, was indeed Enders's sales pitch. The political goal, to make the Sandinistas focus inward, was ill-defined and its success or failure could not easily be measured. But the military goal, interdiction of weapons traffic, was clear-cut, although far-fetched and downright misleading. It was also the only goal of any specificity.

Johnstone viewed the emphasis on interdiction as a "major blunder." "I was absolutely stupefied when I heard how it had been described to Congress," he said. The program could be described as interdiction only in the indirect sense of putting pressure on the Nicaraguans to stop supporting the El Salvador rebels, but "no one thought that we're going to send a group out and capture some guy running across with weapons." Johnstone said that members of Congress were naive not to have asked at the time how "interdiction" would be carried out; some congressmen later would feel genuinely deceived by the briefing. To describe the program in terms of interdiction was "a terribly unfortunate thing" that "cost us dearly down the line."[15]

Its first encounter with Congress foretold rough passage for the program within the administration and on Capitol Hill. The State Department maintained the appearance of dominating the policy process, but the project had been under way well before Enders put his stamp on it and he had no way of guaranteeing that it would be guided by his stated goals. Indeed, the finding reflected a bureaucratic compromise, under which different players backed the program for different reasons. Although the House and Senate intelligence committees acquiesced, Casey's explanations provoked skepticism. Five days after the briefing, Representative Edward Boland of Massachusetts, chairman of the House Select Committee on Intelligence, wrote Casey to express "serious concerns" about the number and tactics of the rebels, whether they would be under U.S. control, and the possibility of military clashes between Nicaragua and Honduras. In spring 1982, the House committee adopted classified language limiting the purpose of the program to interdiction, and this later became law. Because interdiction had never been intended in any literal sense, the administration quickly found itself skirting the law.

A few days after the CIA finding was presented to Congress, foreign ministers of the Organization of American States met on the Caribbean island of St. Lucia. In a speech, Haig attacked the Sandinistas for their military build-up, which he said was a "prelude to a widening war in Central America."

Haig and Enders then sat down for a rancorous ninety-minute exchange with Nicaraguan Foreign Minister D'Escoto. The Nicaraguan complained that Haig was making "interventionist" noises connected with his allegation that Nicaragua intended to import Soviet-built MiG fighter aircraft.

"First of all, it is the sovereign right of any state to use whatever is required to defend its territorial integrity and sovereignty," D'Escoto recalled saying to Haig. "But having said that, let me assure you that we are not in the process of acquiring MiGs, certainly at this time. We are not in the process and we are not even planning their acquisition and we have not made any specific commitment to that either."

Haig replied: "Well, now, you became a prophet. You don't know how true it is what you're saying. Because we will never allow you to get them."

D'Escoto said he sensed the change in U.S. attitude not from Haig's threatening noises but when he read back to Haig some of Enders's comments during the August 1981 Managua talks. "Mr. Haig, while in Nicaragua, Thomas Enders said that you are a country that respects the sovereignty of other states including that of Nicaragua and that your concern was the possibility that we violate norms for international behavior. But that in no way were you concerned—it was none of your business to intrude in our internal sovereign decisions."

Haig looked at Enders, and Enders made an excuse. "No, I didn't precisely say that."[16]

CHAPTER
5

A FORMULA FOR STALEMATE

THE GROUP OF HARD-LINERS who ensured the approval of covert aid for the anti-Sandinista rebels came to be known in different parts of Washington as the "war party." Members of the Joint Chiefs of Staff used the phrase as shorthand for those who were hard-line in all foreign policy areas. In the State Department, the term was employed mostly in connection with Central America. Despite its name, the war party did not want to go to war to overthrow the Sandinistas. It wanted the same result, but at far lower cost and by proxy.

During 1982, the hard-liners, or hard right, developed as an effective power center. Enders fought to keep open the negotiating option with Nicaragua, the prospects for which had improved as a result of political and military developments in El Salvador. But those who wanted the overthrow of the Sandinistas succeeded at this very time in thrusting a new U.S. policy goal for Nicaragua onto the table: internal democratization. Inasmuch as no sovereign government can be expected to negotiate its own replacement except under military occupation, incorporating this change effectively removed the option of a peaceful settlement. Enders did his best to contain the hard-liners by delaying his announcement of the new policy goals and by not supporting expansion of the Honduras-based rebels, the means for these broader ends.

It was a classic Washington power struggle. Each side could block the other.

The hard right was a broad, informal, and shifting group. All professed, and most shared, Reagan's ideology—in particular his anticommunism and his deep distrust of the Soviet Union. But few had hands-on experience of policymaking or implementation; fewer had much knowledge about Latin America, least of all about Central America.

Enders and the Central America specialists at State who backed him up certainly were not soft on communism. But they tried to preserve flexibility in policy that would allow occasional testing of the possibilities for a peaceful solution.

The conceptualizer of the hard right was Jeane Kirkpatrick, the combative UN ambassador who was determined to make Central America an issue at center stage. Kirkpatrick had studied Argentine politics and felt she also had an insight into Central and Latin American issues. More important, her writings and speeches were in tune with Reagan's preconceptions, and he welcomed her advice. But she was ineffective in working through the bureaucracy. Although she had a seat at the cabinet table, her position at the UN did not provide the institutional base needed for impact on day-to-day decisions. Edwin Meese, who had been a close associate from Reagan's California days and was now the White House counsellor, was familiar with the President's thinking and had easy access. William Clark, who was Haig's deputy for the first year, was another confidant. Judge Clark had no background in foreign affairs and few ideas but listened to Kirkpatrick, as did Robert McFarlane, who became Clark's deputy. From January 1982, when he was named to succeed the ineffectual Richard Allen as national security adviser, Clark wielded real power.

Unlike Allen, who was subordinate to Meese, Clark reported directly to Reagan and had a status equal to that of a cabinet-level official. Casey too played a growing role behind the scenes because of the program his agency had just taken over, and in time became the driving force behind the Nicaragua policy. Weinberger was a member of the group by virtue of his closeness to Reagan and his energetic anticommunism.

Well into 1982, Reagan refused to focus on Central America or on any foreign policy issue, but devoted his energies to remaking federal fiscal policy. Clark introduced some order into decision-making but never reexamined covert aid in Nicaragua. In the circumstances, a grab bag of second-tier officials, drawing on the clout of their cabinet-level soulmates, could on occasion make a real difference at the working level. To their adversaries at State, they were known collectively as "the pygmies."

At the CIA, Constantine Menges, a conservative academic who had worked at the Rand Corporation and more recently at the Hudson Institute, became national intelligence officer for Latin America. Physically, Menges was no pygmy. He was tall, balding, bespectacled, and doctrinaire, but in a strange way. One friend called him a "fanatical centrist," who would argue so vehemently for democracy that discussion was impossible. At the State Department, Richard Burt, a former *New York Times* reporter in charge of the Bureau of Politico-Military Affairs, a sort of mini-Pentagon, supported the get-tough attitude toward Nicaragua although he knew little about Central America. On the other hand, Burt became the principal proponent for negotiating arms control with the Soviet Union, an issue on which most of the hard-liners were opposed to him.

In some ways the war party was more like an all-night party than a political cabal; many individuals would wander in and out depending on the issues. The bottom line was global anticommunism and the application Nicaragua.

William Middendorf, a wealthy industrialist and former Navy secretary who had become ambassador to the Organization of American States, was also a charter member. And at the Pentagon, there was Swiss-born academic Fred Iklé, who was Weinberger's undersecretary for policy. His distant manner won him the nickname "Dr. Warmth." Nestor Sanchez, who claims descent from the Spanish conquistadores, had moved to Defense from a career with the CIA to become deputy assistant secretary for western hemisphere matters in the Bureau of International Security Affairs. Sanchez had been deputy chief of station in Guatemala in 1954 when

the CIA mounted its successful coup to topple the Arbenz government. Another activist was Jackie Tillman, Kirkpatrick's former
secretary-researcher at Georgetown University, who helped run
Kirkpatrick's office at the State Department. Tillman, who grew up
in Puerto Rico, was fluent in Spanish and had an undergraduate
degree in sociology from the College of Notre Dame in Baltimore but
no professional qualifications. She struck first-time acquaintances
more as a housewife starting a second career than a participant in the
policy process. Even some Reagan appointees at the State Department thought her to be incapable of formulating or selling policy. "If
she pushes it, people go the other way," one political appointee said
of her. She became deeply involved in publicizing the plight of
Miskito Indians on Nicaragua's Atlantic coast who were resisting
Sandinista attempts to bring them under control. The circle also
included non-executive branch members who supported their way of
thinking, such as Jesse Helms and John Carbaugh.

The "pygmies" lunched and socialized together; acting through
their principals, they came to wield power in decisions on the
Nicaragua issue perhaps more than any other. Lower-level officials
who did not recognize this state of affairs and failed to set up direct
lines of communication with them were headed for trouble. But
anyone who went too far in accepting their authority, be he a military
commander or a U.S. ambassador, could jeopardize his institutional
support base. The tensions generated by this unorthodox power
arrangement appear to have shortened the tenure of top officials at
the State Department, including Enders and his successor, Langhorne Anthony Motley, as well as some of the hard-liners' key
operatives on the scene—the U.S. ambassador to Honduras, John
Negroponte, and Nutting's successor as commander of the Southern
Command, General Paul Gorman.

Oliver Laurence North, an ambitious Marine Corps major, came
to be the main instrument for carrying out the war party's aims.
North had been named to the staff of the National Security Council
in August 1981 to assist in administration efforts to win congressional
approval for the sale of advanced AWACS radar planes to Saudi
Arabia, working with Air Force Major General Richard Secord and
Robert McFarlane.

North was clean-cut and trim in physique and projected an earnest,
boyish, all-American look. He had many qualities in common with
Major General Schweitzer, with whom he overlapped for some

months at the NSC. A hard-line anti-Communist, North came from a religious Roman Catholic background, was hyperactive, indefatigable, and given to working sixteen-hour days no matter what his job. North had sought out front-line duty in Vietnam, proved to be an aggressive platoon commander, and returned from the war with a chestful of decorations. He let others know that he had been shot at in his country's service, and that gave him added luster in the Reagan White House.*

North was an unabashed self-promoter at the White House. "The President was asking the other day what you thought about this topic," one NSC staff aide recalls North saying. His name-dropping had the combined effect of flattering the hearer and building up North. To outside consultants, he sometimes referred to Reagan possessively as "my President."[1]

The atmosphere was intimidating to anyone with doubts about the program. Clark's deputy, Robert McFarlane, thought the United States ought to demonstrate its will to manage a problem in its own hemisphere but that the contras were not the appropriate instrument. Like so many others, he swallowed his reservations. "Where I went wrong," he later said, "was not having the guts to stand up and tell the President that. To tell you the truth, probably the reason I didn't is because if I'd done that, Bill Casey, Jeane Kirkpatrick, and Cap Weinberger would have said I was some kind of Commie, you know."[2]

The most important U.S. official in Central America with respect to Nicaragua through mid-1983 was the U.S. ambassador in Honduras, which, thanks to Álvarez, had become the base for the FDN and thereby the linchpin of U.S. policy. Enders chose John Negroponte, a career officer who had held high posts in the Nixon and Carter administrations—so high that he immediately aroused the suspicion of Senator Jesse Helms and John Carbaugh, who together held up his nomination. Negroponte had to be a chameleon to satisfy the hardliners, but his "action" orientation and his devotion to Reagan's goals endeared him to the war party, although he was never really a member.

After Negroponte took up his post in Tegucigalpa in November 1981, a pattern was perceived by many observers. Most of the

---

* North, according to his military comrades, saw Vietnam as a step to his career ambitions. "He told us right up front that he was a lifer, that he was out to get rank, that war is where you get it. He used to volunteer us for things for more points for his career," his former radio operator told a newspaper interviewer.

principal officials dealing with Central America at the State Department had reputations as hawks; few had any background in Latin affairs, and most had held diplomatic posts in Indochina during the conflict there. Enders chose as his chief aide for Central America L. Craig Johnstone, who had spent a year in Vietnam in the summer of 1965 as an intern dealing with refugee problems, then joined the foreign service and gone back to work on the rural pacification program from 1966 to 1970. In April 1975, as Saigon was falling, he and another foreign service officer, Lionel Rosenblatt, went back to rescue Vietnamese who had worked under them, for which they received a high State Department award.* From 1981 to 1985, under both Enders and Motley, Johnstone was the principal architect of State Department policy on Central America. Johnstone, then forty, had graduated from the University of Maryland and done graduate work there and at Harvard. And in Honduras, Negroponte had as his political counsellor Raymond Burghardt, a friend from his own Vietnam days. It made for a memorable newspaper headline: "The Gang That Blew Vietnam Goes Latin."[4]

The difference was, of course, that Vietnam represented exactly what almost everyone with Vietnam experience wanted to avoid repeating. With regard to El Salvador, the deliberative policy process charted by Enders, Nutting, Fred Woerner, Johnstone, and others made the avoidance of another Vietnam a realistic goal. Not so on Nicaragua. Enders and Johnstone may have seemed hard-line to the general public, but they were not nearly hard enough for the war party. Incrementally, under pressures from the right and without much thought about where it was leading, U.S. policy was reshaped for Nicaragua. Here was the real point of comparison with Vietnam.

The great policy battle of 1982 took place behind the scenes, cloaked by the secrecy of Enders's bureaucratic creation, the Core Group.

Enders's first major policy defeat happened so quietly that it went

---

* Rosenblatt and Johnstone were on the special task force set up to oversee the American withdrawal early in April 1975 and became alarmed when cables from U.S. Ambassador Graham Martin indicated a willingness to overlook the fate of local employees. Rosenblatt decided to go to Saigon and confided in Johnstone, who quickly offered to collaborate. On April 20, a Sunday morning, they both signed out of the State Department on annual leave and bought round-trip tickets from Washington to Saigon. Each paid the $1,700 fare out of his own pocket. Arriving on the last Pan American flight, they spent several days in Saigon, smuggling out about twenty high-risk local employees and their families, at least 200 people, none of whom had exit papers. They then returned to Washington.[3]

unnoticed even by his boss, the secretary of state. The issue was democratization. Enders had deliberately played down the question in his main presentation to the Sandinistas in the Managua talks in August 1981. In December, a fierce battle had gone on behind the scenes over whether Haig, in his St. Lucia speech, should demand changes in Nicaragua's internal system as a condition for coming to terms with the United States. A number of State Department aides had appealed to McFarlane, then State Department counsellor, to intervene on behalf of the new demand. McFarlane concurred. But Haig, on Enders's advice, had turned them down.

A hint that the tide was turning came in a speech by Reagan on February 24 to the Organization of American States in which he referred to a promise cabled to the OAS by the Nicaraguan junta in 1979 to uphold human rights and hold free elections after they came to power. "Two years later, these commitments can be measured by the postponement of elections until 1985, by repression against free trade unions, against the media, minorities, and in defiance of all international civility, by the continued export of arms and subversion to neighboring countries," Reagan said. It was the first appearance of a new theme, which Reagan would embellish in future speeches. He and his speechwriters deliberately overlooked the cautious wording of the original pledge, which spoke of holding "the first free elections of the century."

At the time of his defeat on the issue of Nicaragua's internal politics, which appears to have been in early April, Enders did not utter a word in public. The triumph of the right was signaled in an NSC policy summary that month, which proclaimed that the U.S. goal in Central America was to build stable democracies and prevent the proliferation of "Cuba-model states." Negotiations were not to be pursued seriously. It called for stepped-up efforts to "co-opt" the negotiations issue "to avoid Congressionally mandated negotiations, which would work against our interests." The way to do this was "by demonstrating a reasonable but firm approach to negotiations and compromise on our terms."[5]

"Our terms" translated into no negotiations.

The document stated that National Security Decision Directive 17, which had been approved in November 1981, had authorized "significant covert" activities, but noted that "not all provisions of N.S.D.D. 17 have been implemented." It called for "full implementation thereof."

Indeed, although support of the rebel force was authorized to begin in December 1981 and the first news leaks about its existence occurred in February, U.S. funding did not really commence until spring, according to Johnstone. "You'd have difficulty showing that [the funds] began flowing in December 1981. In fact, I think people thought the process could have been reversed until April of 1982 had there been some remarkable breakthrough" in diplomacy. "Up to that time, it was essentially futzing around. As of then, it became a more serious operation." Some NSC sources have suggested that the delay in funding was caused by foot-dragging by Enders.

The first impact of the new hard-line policy on diplomacy was contained in the secret U.S. negotiating position drawn up at that time. Responding to an initiative by the president of Mexico, Haig had met in early March with Jorge Castañeda, the Mexican foreign minister, and later that month told him that Enders would go to Managua in mid-April for talks about normalization of relations. For reasons that are not entirely clear, the trip was called off. Enders said he had taken advance soundings in Managua and concluded that he would accomplish little by traveling there at that time.[6] Instead, the new U.S. ambassador in Managua, Anthony Quainton, presented a new eight-point plan for negotiations on April 8. The news was in point eight. Noting that the Sandinista party had a short time earlier restated its commitment to political pluralism, Quainton said fulfillment of "this commitment and of the previous commitment of your government before the OAS in 1979 to convoke the first free elections in the country would be *essential elements* of the political context of future relations between our two countries." This was a remarkable demand that ought to have drawn public attention. One reason it did not was that when the State Department briefed reporters in Washington, the wording was softened. Everett Briggs, a deputy to Enders, told the press the commitments to democratization would be "*important determinants* of the political context of our future relations" (emphasis added).[7]*

The new wording signified that Enders had temporarily thrown in

---

* In the area of security, the April proposal was more balanced than the draft that had been prepared after the August 1981 talks. It called for a ban on importing heavy offensive weapons instead of requiring their re-export to countries of origin; it proposed only that foreign military advisers in the region be reduced to low, reasonable levels and that military forces be reduced to appropriate levels needed for defense purposes.

the towel on negotiations, for he knew well, according to close aides, that the proposal would be rejected. "He's a classic diplomat. A classic diplomat tries to deal with things he can control, for which there are clear precedents, not to expand [demands] forever," said Luigi Einaudi, an assistant who advised Enders on long-term strategy.

Quainton, who viewed the U.S. initiative as a mistake, did not leave a copy of the eight points with his two collocutors, Julio López Campos, the foreign policy expert of the ruling Sandinista party, and Victor Hugo Tinoco, the vice minister of foreign affairs, but provided a copy six weeks later on their request. A week after Quainton's oral presentation, the Managua government, expressing a "sincere disposition to begin serious negotiations," sent a list of thirteen points and principles, which were largely compiled from public speeches. The State Department ignored them. On May 7, D'Escoto replied testily to what he said were "threats and arrogant attitudes" contained in the eight points, which he described as an ultimatum. "We regard the inclusion of point eight as an inexcusable position of interference in matters which are of Nicaragua's sole and exclusive competence."

The comandantes were cynical and told Quainton they thought the gambit was aimed at Congress to obtain more support for the covert war.

Haig said he was unaware that the ante had been raised. He was preoccupied with the Argentine-British dispute over the Falklands/ Malvinas Islands and with the Middle East. Had he known, he said, he would have opposed the change because it undercut the basic premise of the U.S. approach to Soviet encroachments in the third world. "Clearly, we don't have a right and the Soviet Union or their proxies do not have a right to insist on a political formula in any developing country. This is a manifestation of the free choice of the people." Haig said he thought that during his absences from Washington, a liaison had formed between Enders and Clark, "and I wasn't really sure what kind of hanky-panky went on."[8]

The policy shift was not disclosed in public until after Haig had resigned under pressure at the end of June. His successor, George Shultz, took over in the midst of the Lebanon crisis and had no interest in, background on, or time for Central America. He had received a memo from Enders saying policy was proceeding well and was under control, according to Enders's colleagues.

Quainton delivered the U.S. reply to D'Escoto's tart letter in July.

It stated that the "tone and content of your response was unhelpful and not conducive to a useful dialogue." While calling for further talks, the letter toughened the eighth point. "The present political climate in Central America makes the fulfillment of these promises [of free elections] imperative."[9]

In August, Managua proposed a meeting at the foreign ministers' level to discuss the combined twenty-one points, but asked that Mexico take part in the negotiations. Washington did not respond until August 20, when Enders delivered a policy speech in San Francisco. In the absence of special envoys, high-level visits, or a forum, this second round of diplomatic exchanges died.[10]

In retrospect, the eight-point April initiative appears to have been doomed from the start, and it is not clear why Enders decided to undertake it. Some aides suggest that he made a deal under which he stayed in formal control as shown by his ability to undertake the negotiating initiative, while the hard right forced a major change in substance. It was probably another instance of what Pezzullo said so bluntly: to maintain the control, Enders had to give away the policy.

Three months after losing the battle, Enders introduced the new position guardedly and in the form of a question in his speech before the Commonwealth Club of San Francisco. First he seemed to make a disclaimer, saying that it was "for Nicaragua to decide what kind of government it has." Then he added: "But we believe we are all entitled to ask what assurance can any of us have that promises of noninterference will be kept if the Nicaraguan state remains the preserve of a small Cuban-advised elite of Marxist-Leninists, disposing of growing military power, and hostile to all forms of social life but those they dominate?"

Enders concluded the speech by calling for reciprocal "action" by Nicaragua and its neighbors on four fronts: the establishment of democratic or at least pluralistic institutions; an end to support for foreign guerrilla movements; a cap on the build-up of heavy arms; and the removal of all outside military and security advisers.

In this manner, Enders articulated for the first time in public what his closest aide said had become a "fundamental element of policy." In "a major change in attitude," Johnstone said, "we elevated democratic pluralism in Nicaragua to be the *sine qua non* of restoring relations."

The four points were internally incompatible. The latter three points, relating to subversion, arms control, and the foreign military presence, could not be negotiated except with the existing Sandinista government. But the first point, proposing to replace Sandinista one-party dominance by a "pluralistic" structure meriting U.S. approval, implied a change of government. Logically, American policy could aim either at replacing the Sandinistas or at negotiating a security accord with them, but not both.

Aides to Enders conceded the contradiction, but asserted that the administration would back down on its demand for democracy if the two countries concluded an iron-clad accord on the security issues. They said the onus was on the Sandinistas to force the decision. In fact, wariness was warranted on the part of the Sandinistas as to whether Enders could deliver the U.S. government. While Enders genuinely may have hoped for an arms control accord with the existing regime, the hard right insisted on the priorities in the order stated. They argued that only democracies can reach an iron-clad agreement on security issues and if the Sandinistas adopted democracy, the security issues would be secondary.[11]

Although the speech signaled an important policy shift, it practically escaped public notice. The structure of secrecy that Enders had built up, his opposition to the shift, and his reluctance to admit defeat combined to prevent public discussion or even recognition of the fact that it had occurred. It was the downside to secrecy. Had there been a public debate in April, the administration would have been hard-pressed to justify such a shift and might have had to back down.

The winners in this secret policy struggle included leaders and followers of the war party. One of the most impassioned champions of the cause was Menges. Others included Kirkpatrick, Jon Glassman, who had researched the controversial State Department White Paper on El Salvador in January 1981, McFarlane, who by this time had moved to the White House to become Clark's deputy, Elliott Abrams, then assistant secretary for human rights at the State Department, and Paul Wolfowitz, head of policy planning. Most were Democrats who called themselves neoconservatives. "It was the triumph of the Jacksonian Democrats over realpolitik," Glassman later commented. He was referring not to Andrew Jackson but to the hard-line anti-Soviet Democratic senator from Washington State, Henry ("Scoop") Jackson, and to Enders's conventional diplomacy based on pursuit of national interests.

The irony was that at the very time the United States was raising its ante, the Sandinistas were lowering theirs. The enormous public turnout for the constituent assembly elections in El Salvador gave the Sandinistas cause to reflect on whether the Salvadoran guerrillas would long remain their "shield" from the United States, as Ortega had purportedly described them in August 1981 to Enders. In addition, economic projections showed that the Nicaraguan economy would soon be developing a hard-currency balance-of-payments gap of $500 million annually that could only be filled from foreign sources. The comandantes were told they faced the decision, but put it off. At this sensitive moment, the U.S. ambassador in Managua had little leverage because he could not offer financial aid as an incentive.

The diplomatic opening was quickly disappearing for a basic reason: once U.S. participation commenced in the anti-Sandinista insurgency, the program took on its own momentum on the ground and, among the press and the hard right, assumed mythical proportions.

Yet it would be wrong to see the outcome of this behind-the-scenes battle as a defeat only for the State Department. The unresolved dispute undercut not only the opportunities for a negotiated settlement but for the proxy war option as well. U.S. allies in the looming confrontation with the Sandinistas, including the government and military establishment of Honduras, the FDN, and the internal opposition in Nicaragua, were left in a state of confusion about the aims of U.S. policy. And so were the Sandinistas. Press leaks about the "secret war" prompted questioning in Congress. The U.S. military leadership expressed serious doubts about where the program was going. Congress publicly debated a covert program. The collision of the two strategies meant that the overwhelming U.S. resources, influence, and leverage that might have been brought to bear on Nicaragua were largely wasted.

Given the "chairman-of-the-board" style in which Reagan preferred to run national security policy, a competition of strategies was not surprising. One former NSC senior official analyzed it simply: "This President makes policy decisions. But he does not initiate strategy decisions." That is, Reagan was prepared to select overall goals but left it to his aides to work out how they should be accomplished. "He almost always gets contradictory advice. In order to give him a single choice, the State and Defense departments try to come up with a common position, even though their positions are incompatible. You can accomplish that by plastering over the differences. But the result is willy-nilly or not well-resolved plans."[12]*

Decision-making by the splitting of differences had the domestic political merit of preserving an outward show of harmony in the cabinet but at the cost of producing incoherent strategy for real-world problems. It was not all that different from the method used by the Sandinista directorate. Pezzullo concluded from close observation that the directorate made its decisions by consensus rather than majority rule, thereby giving hard-liners such as Tomás Borge the veto. "That kind of system will lead to bad decisions. The orthodox position, which is usually the lowest common denominator in thinking, will dominate," Pezzullo said. The same applied in Washington. "If you get a group of orthodox thinkers together in this country, once they start to discuss viable options and one says, 'Dammit, they're Communists,' well, what is at play? Your credentials. Are you going to argue against that? So every time you come up with a decision on Nicaragua, it is stampeded into the most hard-line inflexible thing." Pezzullo saw the Sandinistas' method of decision-making and Reagan's as "symbiotic, mirror images of one another."

Given this approach to the Nicaragua issue, it is hard to see how a positive result could emerge. Many officials wanted overthrow; Enders felt the means were unavailable. "So our problem was all along what is it we were trying to accomplish," commented Lawrence Eagleburger, at the time undersecretary of state for political affairs. Instead of trying to resolve the argument over ends, the

---

* The most clear-cut example was the deployment of U.S. Marines in Lebanon in August 1982, arguably the single biggest foreign policy blunder of Reagan's first term in office. Ambassador Philip Habib wanted the Marines to remain for up to sixty days to oversee the departure of Palestinian fighters and the inauguration of President Gemayel. Shultz concurred. But Weinberger opposed sending troops under any circumstances. Reagan told the aides to find a solution both could live with. So the Marines were sent to Beirut for thirty days. Halfway through those thirty days Weinberger went to Beirut and announced without any prior consultation that the Marines had done their job and would be coming home. He had not cleared his action with Shultz, Habib, the multinational forces, or the Lebanese government. The Marines came home, Gemayel was assassinated, the Israelis entered West Beirut, and the Marines returned, this time for an indefinite time and purpose.

"What was debated was how long they should go for, not the mission," said Wallace Nutting, the commander of the U.S. Southern Command, who likened the Lebanon initiative to Nicaragua policy. In both places, he observed, the administration had failed to examine the internal and external sources of conflict and U.S. interests before setting goals.

government came to a typical bureaucratic compromise. Enders's four points laid out the contradiction at the policy level; in application, the two camps backed covert funding for distinctly different reasons, either overthrow or to build pressure on the Sandinistas for a negotiated solution. Eagleburger said there would have been a "moral dilemma" if the Sandinistas "decided to meet you halfway" in the negotiations. But he noted: "Not that that was ever thought about much."[13]

The process leading to commitment to the covert program also suggested trouble down the road. According to a CIA official who had participated in two of the major U.S. covert operations in Latin America after World War II, the successful ouster of a pro-leftist Guatemalan president in 1954 and the abortive Bay of Pigs in 1961, the criteria for success of a covert operation are fairly well understood. A successful operation is usually initiated by a decision from the top and backed up by a military contingency plan. It must be finite in duration and have a beginning, middle, and end. The best operations are initiated when the representative of a foreign government approaches a U.S. ambassador, who endorses the request and passes it on to Washington.*

The Nicaraguan insurgency project failed all these criteria. It was not initiated by a request from the ambassador on the scene, a State Department policy review, or a decision from the top. Rather, the administration edged its way into the program in response to events on the ground, vigorous promotional efforts by individuals who had no line responsibility, and political pressures from the hard right. The beginning was hazy; there was never a middle or an endgame. As a military operation, it also broke every rule in the book. If there was a rigorous examination as to the means and ends of the project before it began or a careful review of tactics after it started, no high military or State Department official seems aware of it.

In addition to problems with policy and program at the Washing-

---

* David Atlee Phillips, a retired CIA official and author, put stress on the importance of a back-up military contingency plan for a covert operation to overthrow a government. Citing recently declassified documents, he noted that had the Guatemala operation not succeeded within *a week*, a contingency plan called operation "Hard Rock Baker" would have been employed. Ostensibly aimed at evacuating Americans from Guatemala, it would employ U.S. fighter aircraft and fourteen cargo planes carrying in a Marine landing force. By contrast, he said, there was no contingency plan at the Bay of Pigs invasion of Cuba. "We never asked: where is the contingency plan? We convinced ourselves there had to be a contingency plan."[14]

ton end, a sizable misunderstanding developed on the ground in 1982 between the United States and Honduras, its key ally and collaborator in the project. The policy aims that Casey had stated to the intelligence committees in Congress were rather different from those supported by the Honduran leadership. Álvarez mistakenly believed the administration backed his scheme, by which insurgents would provoke the Sandinistas into a major blunder that would lead to a U.S. military intervention. But Álvarez was in a position to ensure that the rebel force's strategy, structure, and tactics developed in accordance with his vision. Washington was divided over the purpose of the insurgency, and the competing forces there never could agree on the strategy, structure, and tactics. They certainly could never have agreed among themselves to Álvarez's scheme.

With so shaky a basis of understanding, it was only a matter of months before the first crisis developed with Álvarez.

ÁLVAREZ WIELDS HIS VETO

The central event of the first half year after U.S. support for the rebels became official policy occurred quite fortuitously. It was the decision by Argentina's military government to invade the British-held Falkland Islands on April 2. The Argentine military leaders apparently felt that their burgeoning relationship with Washington as well as their support for U.S. goals in Central America would ensure U.S. neutrality if not diplomatic support in the Falklands affair. It was a catastrophic misjudgment. Many among the hard right, in particular Kirkpatrick, had cultivated close contacts with the Argentines, but they proved to be no match for the Anglophiles, such as Haig and James Baker. By deciding to back Britain, the administration found itself in a confrontation not only with Argentina but also with Honduras. What followed in short order were two setbacks for U.S. policy. One was an abortive attempt by the State Department to end the Argentine liaison with the FDN. American conservatives, such as John Carbaugh, swung into action to ensure that the Argentines stayed. The second was the prolonged but futile effort by the CIA to enlarge the FDN leadership to include Edén Pastora, the charismatic commander who had fought with the Sandinistas, joined their government, then quit in protest. The story of these two events illustrates why, in the words of Nat Hamrick, this was never the CIA's secret war. The CIA was used by the various players as much as it used them.

To understand the impact of the Falklands/Malvinas War on the contra program, it is first important to sketch out what had become of the tripartite Honduran-Argentine-American relationship since the time it was consummated in August 1981. Honduras had elected its first civilian government in a decade in November 1981. Roberto Suazo Córdova was a country doctor who, a prominent critic noted, had "all the defects that Hondurans are supposed to have—he is a libertine, he lies, he conspires, he is incompetent, he plays cards, he is a reformed alcoholic."[15] Suazo was sworn in as the president of Honduras in January 1982. One of the first actions of his term was the selection by the supreme military council and the parliament, controlled by Suazo's party, of Álvarez to head the Honduran armed forces. In a military service noted for ineptitude and corruption, Álvarez was viewed by his American military counterparts as "Mr. Clean." "He was dynamic, aggressive, and disciplined. He had a clear chain of command. He fit our mold of military leader. He was our candidate," said a U.S. military source. The CIA station chief and defense attaché let their counterparts know their preference, and consequently Álvarez began his five-year term in a very powerful position.[16]

Honduras, the original banana republic, was poor but relatively placid and had long, extensive, and friendly ties with the United States. The new team in power sought to make the most of the deepening American connection. Suazo wanted funds to stabilize and develop an economy dependent on commodity exports; and Álvarez wanted to modernize his army. Negroponte's mission was to keep both on board the Nicaraguan program. Álvarez shared with Suazo his plan to build up the insurgents in order to provoke the Sandinistas into war, and Suazo supported him. Álvarez did not directly inform Negroponte, although presumably Negroponte knew about it. Other than the CIA and Suazo, Álvarez shared the secret only with the Argentines and the FDN leadership.

This delicate relationship was complicated by the nature of U.S. involvement in the rebel movement. Argentina had stepped up its token military presence in Honduras from mid-1981 to fifteen or more men, and in September of that year Oswaldo Ribeiro, an Argentine army colonel, arrived on the scene to take charge of the program. Ribeiro was nicknamed "Balita," or "little bullet," a reference to his compact physique and hard-driving nature. Carbaugh and Hamrick said they knew him well. Carbaugh called him "probably the best strategist on guerrilla warfare in this hemisphere." More important, Álvarez and Ribeiro had studied together in the early 1960s at the Argentine military academy. Álvarez viewed him as experienced, pragmatic, a good planner, and "a real gentleman." The FDN leadership also expressed confidence in him. But Ribeiro did not like the Americans and let them know it, and did his best with Álvarez to keep day-to-day operations under his control. The CIA kept some distance from the FDN soldiers and leadership. Except for top-level coordinating meetings each week with Álvarez, the Argentines formed the interface between the CIA and the rest of the FDN throughout 1982.*

The illusion in Washington that the administration was directing the insurgency was fed by the insurgents' first major action, the dynamiting of two bridges in Nicaragua near the Honduran border on March 14, 1982. Johnstone took responsibility. "The Core Group was responsible for coordinating and passing judgment in advance on whether something would be done or not done," he said with regard to this action.[17] The sabotage was carried out by the FDN at express U.S. request, according to Bermúdez. "When an ally comes and joins you and tells you, 'we are going to give aid to you,' and they suggest it could be a good impact to do this, you are going to comply with their will." Besides, he said, "blowing up a bridge is in any guerrilla military plan." He was not sure whether the costs, which were modest, were paid from U.S. or Argentine funds. (Honduras also helped fill the funding gap, according to Álvarez.)

The impact was immediate. On March 15, Tomás Borge, the interior minister, announced a state of emergency in Nicaragua. The Sandinistas called the rebels "contras," short for contrarevolution-aries in Spanish, and the label stuck.

The CIA told the congressional oversight committees throughout 1982 that the Argentines were just "cut-outs" who acted as a buffer between American personnel and the insurgents. But members of the FDN political leadership say that decisions on timing, training,

---

* According to congressional sources familiar with the program, training was conducted by some Cuban-Americans from Miami who were CIA contract employees, but for the most part were Hondurans, Argentines, and other non-American nationals. U.S. nationals were brought in to set up lesson plans and while they may not have been in the classroom, they would meet the instructors before each class. But the Argentines remained in overall control of strategy and operations.

logistics, and targets were made by the Argentines. The Argentines were also the paymasters.[18]

Argentina's attack on the Falklands/Malvinas on April 2 exposed the underlying power relationships to those responsible for running the contra program. As Haig began his London–Buenos Aires diplomatic shuttle, Negroponte called on Álvarez and said he understood the concern of the Honduran government that the United States was moving toward supporting Britain in the dispute. "I ask you to prevent an action that will take us by surprise," Negroponte told him. Álvarez blew up. "Look, Mr. Ambassador, I am not an adventurer. I am a very responsible man. Even so, the government has to take the decision, not me." He said the United States could ask Argentina to leave the Malvinas but not if it allowed Britain, an extra-continental power, to put a garrison on the American continent. "Where is the Monroe Doctrine?" he said. "Look at the geography. Is South America part of Europe?"

Negroponte's face reddened as Álvarez continued. "And let me ask you something. Who is the next one you betray? Honduras? El Salvador? Guatemala? Costa Rica?" The envoy replied that it was Argentina that had used force. Álvarez shot back: "One hundred years ago, England used force to take the island. Argentina has been claiming sovereignty for 130 years." It was a moment, Álvarez later told associates, when he recalled the aphorism that the United States has "its mind in Washington, its heart in Britain and its feet in Latin America."[19]

After Britain sent its fleet and defeated the Argentines, toppling the Argentine government, many U.S. officials in Washington hoped for a radical change on the ground in Honduras, but the war party was split. Kirkpatrick was the champion of having proxies, in particular Argentines, support U.S. policy aims. Carbaugh, who felt he had helped bring the Argentines in originally, agreed they should stay. But Menges felt that the only worse proxy than the Argentines would have been General Augusto Pinochet of Chile. From the time he arrived at the CIA, Menges campaigned to replace the Argentines in Honduras. (He may not have been aware that even Paraguayan dictator Alfredo Stroessner, when approached by Somoza's cousin, had toyed with the idea of providing assistance.) So Menges, who would later be derided at the Bureau of Inter-American Affairs as "constant menace," in effect made common cause with the State Department.

"From the beginning of our involvement, the Argentine involvement was something that everybody hoped would go away," Johnstone said. "We thought we'd gotten a 'two-fer' at one stage, in the sense that with the clearing up of the Malvinas problem, there would be enough anger on the part of the Argentines that they were going to pull out [of Honduras]. They didn't," and U.S. officials "were at wit's end trying to figure how to end it."

Johnstone believed the Argentines stayed because of their close links with Álvarez. Indeed, Álvarez knew that the Americans wanted the Argentines removed but felt that the Argentines had worked out very well. But this was only part of the reason they stayed. For as the U.S. government conveyed one message regarding the Argentine involvement, conservative interlopers were delivering another.

Cardenal said he got calls from Jackie Tillman, Kirkpatrick's aide, and from Carbaugh and Alberto Piedra, a co-author of the Committee of Santa Fe report and later U.S. ambassador to Guatemala. All three told him they were working to ensure that the Argentines continued their advisory role. Ribeiro phoned from Buenos Aires. "Don't worry, Chicano," Cardenal recalls his saying. "We have made a decision to go all the way in this movement, no matter what problems we are having right now with the United States." Late in April, Cardenal hosted a meeting in his small Miami townhouse with Ribeiro, Carbaugh, and Piedra in which the Americans encouraged Argentina to stay.

Carbaugh also went to Honduras. Because the nature of his travel was not always clear, Carbaugh's visits to Central and South America raised eyebrows in many U.S. embassies. Enders said he had asked Carbaugh to go to Central America a number of times and that Carbaugh was "very helpful." But Enders conceded that "you can never say you know of everything he does." This was a case in point.[20]

At Carbaugh's urging, Senator Helms defended Argentina in the public debate about the Falklands/Malvinas. "Everyone jumped on Helms for supporting the Argentines," Carbaugh recalled. "We had a hidden agenda. It left us in a position of friends who can go back to them." Carbaugh delivered a message to Estaban Takas, the Argentine ambassador in Washington, and Ribeiro in Tegucigalpa which was quite the opposite of the one Johnstone and Enders wanted to send. "I said their only ace in the hole to get back in good stead with the United States" was to maintain their military mission in Honduras, Carbaugh said. Carbaugh accompanied Vernon Walters and Piedra when they called on Álvarez. "They were about to go off the reservation and wanted to talk with someone from Washington who looks official," Carbaugh said.

Enders was informed of Carbaugh's official contacts with Honduran leaders but probably not of his talks with the Argentines. "I don't think we consulted with Enders on that," Carbaugh said.*

Members of the FDN political leadership believe the end result of the Falklands/Malvinas flap was to *strengthen* the role of the Argentine military vis-à-vis the FDN. The Argentines began to speak disparagingly of the "Johnnies" to Cardenal and others and to blame "the SOBs" for failing to deliver on promises. The Argentines maintained their presence through 1984, and it took the CIA well into 1983 to gain effective control over events.

As this episode unfolded, a second with equally great significance for the contras began. This centered on Edén Pastora, the famous Comandante Cero, who turned up in Costa Rica in April 1982 publicly attacking the Sandinistas. Pastora, a man of charisma, wit, and charm and a legend from the time he seized the national parliament in 1978, was the ideal resistance leader to open a Costa Rica-based "southern front." The efforts to use him came to naught, however, owing to a clash between Pastora's own ego and Álvarez's orthodox approach. It was a real setback for Clarridge.

Many contra leaders have long wondered how Pastora first came into contact with the CIA. "Let me tell you this," Bermúdez said, "Pastora was a great achievement for the guy who recruited him." According to Pastora, the "guy" who recruited him was Pastora himself.

Pastora's disenchantment with the revolution had come early, as he watched the leftists take power and exclude him. He had left Nicaragua in July 1981 and spent a month with Panamanian leader Omar Torrijos. After Torrijos's death in an airplane crash, Pastora said he left for "Europe via Cuba." He stopped off in Havana, where Fidel Castro "left me for five months under house arrest."

---

* Haig, when asked about Carbaugh's activities, expressed strong disbelief and said if he had known Carbaugh at any point was representing the U.S. government, he would have resigned from his job long before he did (June 1982). Enders said Carbaugh had traveled to Central America at his behest. "Tom's a hell of a guy, but don't believe everything he says," Carbaugh commented in reply. On most occasions, he said, "I talked Tom into it. . . . To be cynical, Enders was happier to have me down there fiddling around than up here fiddling in the process. It was a question: do they want me on the outside of the tent pissing in or inside of the tent pissing out?"[21]

However, while he was still in Managua in early 1981, Pastora said, the CIA had passed a message to him through a Costa Rican diplomat.

Not long after he left Cuba, Pastora sought out the diplomat, who had by then returned to his home country. Through him, Pastora met up with Dewey Clarridge. Pastora had a plan to present to him.

Clarridge by this time, February 1982, was beginning to make a name for himself in Central America. He was brash and abrasive, as befits a man of action who has a mission, the confidence of his boss, and the resources to carry it out. Moreover, he was neither a linguist nor a scholar. Though he had been station chief in Rome, he had not learned Italian because, he told congressional sources, "all the Italians that are worth something speak English." He understood some Spanish but had never learned to speak it. In CIA stations throughout Central America, his visits were dreaded. He would travel under his semitransparent cover, "Dewey Maroni," and keep station chiefs up all night as he smoked big cigars and drank brandy. He would issue instructions and leave in his wake many questions about whether they had been authorized in Washington or not.

Clarridge flew Pastora to Acapulco and booked him into a hotel room "with my own personal swimming pool, with rose petals floating in the water." In Acapulco, Pastora laid out his plan. He told Clarridge the Reagan administration had a "historic opportunity" to counteract Marxist-Leninist revolutions with democratic revolutions. He had Guatemala in mind and proposed that, as the government there was likely to be toppled by guerrillas, it was essential they be non-Communist guerrillas with democratic ideals. It was not the sort of game plan the Reagan administration had in mind for Guatemala. Pastora said he believed that "Maroni bought the idea from me" but it "seems to me they didn't buy the idea from Maroni."

What exactly Clarridge did with the proposal is not known.*

---

* What is known is that he decided to indulge in some promotion of his "catch," bringing Pastora to Washington to meet Casey twice, in March and May. The meetings with Casey were mainly what is known in the trade as photo opportunities. On both occasions, he said, Casey fell asleep but he was not sure if it was because he was "really tired or didn't want to speak to me." Pastora expressed astonishment that at no point in his two-year relationship with the CIA was he ever debriefed on his background, even on his long ties with Castro. "I understand they are not going to sit down and interrogate me. But I did expect that someone with some intelligence would sit down and dialogue with me, take out what I had in my head." (Government officials say this is because Pastora was being "run" by CIA operations and the analytical division had little input.)

All the same, Clarridge had plans for Pastora. "What he wanted me to do was to criticize the Sandinista regime so the war in the north would be legitimized," Pastora recalled. At the same time, the CIA tried to build bridges between Pastora, whose supporters were gathering in Costa Rica, and Bermúdez. Pastora obliged Clarridge with a public denunciation of the Sandinistas in April, and thus was born a close friendship.

That month Pastora founded the "Sandinista Revolutionary Front" and declared war on the Sandinistas. Casey readily decided to back him, but this created a problem for intelligence professionals in Washington because the activity went well beyond the stated purpose of the original December 1981 finding to curb arms deliveries to the Salvadoran guerrillas. Deputy CIA director Admiral Bobby Inman urged that a new finding be prepared, and Donald Gregg, then head of the NSC intelligence directorate and responsible for all covert action projects, did the drafting in July. It stated that the CIA would provide paramilitary support for forces inside Nicaragua in order to "effect changes in Nicaraguan government policies." But Rear Admiral John Poindexter, then military adviser to Clark, advised him that he saw no need for the finding, and Reagan never approved it.[23]

Cardenal traveled to Costa Rica to see Pastora on four or five occasions, and then went to Washington to have his first meeting with CIA officials. Another person who tried to bring Pastora together with Bermúdez was Luis Pallais, Somoza's cousin.*

In mid-1982, Pallais, then in Miami, received an indirect request from the White House to get the message to Pastora that U.S. funds would be made available for him. He also lobbied Bermúdez, but to no effect. "I told Enrique twenty times: get together with Pastora." He urged Pastora not to continually attack

---

* Pallais had been captured along with 1,500 others when Pastora seized the National Palace in 1978. He had been in the chair as acting president of the Congress when Pastora, clad in a purloined National Guard uniform, burst into the chamber. In the forty-eight-hour takeover, Pallais had gotten to know Pastora. Some would say it was an example of the "Stockholm syndrome," in which hostages identify with their captors. "He came to me and said: 'Luis, I am not a Communist. I am here because I hate Somoza,' " Pallais recalled. He suggested that Pastora make a speech before the assembly, and was floored by the reply: "I am not a very good speaker." Pastora could have shot him, said Pallais, but he was "so honest . . . I would put my arms in the fire for him."

the ex-National Guard members associated with Bermúdez, also to no effect.*

But the combined efforts to unite Pastora and Bermúdez foundered on a different rock: the messianic anticommunism of the armed forces chief of Honduras. In about May of 1982, Clarridge had Pastora visit Honduras to meet Álvarez. They did not hit it off. According to one high U.S. official, Álvarez, who was still angry over the U.S. role in the Falklands/Malvinas affair, started things off on the wrong foot by calling Pastora by his last name instead of "Comandante." "Pastora thought he was really being put down," Johnstone said. "He was infuriated. Like someone calling him 'boy.' After that, it was three months seeing if you could overcome a personal slight."

Pastora denied the story; Álvarez confirmed it. "I don't recognize guerrilla rank," he said. "It's a matter of professionalism." The real issue, both men said, was power. According to Álvarez: "Pastora wanted to be number one in the anti-Sandinista movement. He said to me: 'I am talking in the name of the Nicaraguan people.' " Álvarez said he replied: "Who gives you the right to talk in the name of the people of Nicaragua? I want to be clear. You can't be the number one. The FDN has the right. They paid with blood. You, I only know when you worked with the Sandinistas. If you have real leadership over the Nicaraguan people, I will give you an appropriate right. Show me."

Álvarez said Pastora then demanded that every Guardia officer leave the movement. "I don't believe Pastora has the charisma the gringos want to give him. He has too much ego. Why should we have to surrender to his ego?"

Pastora's version is that Álvarez insisted that only the FDN could have access to Honduran territory and he never sought any unity. "All he thought about was the FDN."[24]

Álvarez may have had good reasons for holding out against U.S. wishes regarding both the Argentine advisers and Pastora, but the effect of his vetoes was to weaken seriously the CIA's potential ability to manage the rebel force. How much that would have benefited the

---

* It is ironic that Pastora, who made a practice of denouncing Somocistas in the FDN, would remain in frequent touch with Somoza's cousin; but Bermúdez, who was directing the "Somocista" force, had broken off ties with Pallais from the time the United States began providing funds. Bermúdez explained that while he would accept private support from those associated with Somoza, he would not allow any public link with them.

movement is moot because Clarridge demonstrated daily that he managed things out of his hip pocket. Clarridge's military background consisted only of Marine Corps basic training, and his poor knowledge of military tactics put off Álvarez as well as U.S. military officials who came in contact with him at the U.S. Southern Command. As Clarridge continued to make promises he could not fulfill, Álvarez was getting upset that no progress was being made toward his military solution for the Sandinistas.

Just how ragged were the beginnings of the project was scarcely known outside the Core Group in Washington. Even they had to depend to a large extent on Clarridge's version of events. And Clarridge seemed to be setting his own guidelines. "I have the impression that Dewey Clarridge was sort of a viceroy, a gauleiter. He was operating on his own one hell of a lot," said Lawrence Eagleburger, the third-ranking State Department official. "Dewey very much had his own agenda. I cannot even vouch for the fact that he and Casey had the same agenda."[25]

Key decisions in U.S. security strategy for Nicaragua were thus subject to local vetoes in Honduras while day-to-day management was ad-libbed by an operator who inspired more concern than confidence in Tegucigalpa and Washington. In the vacuum that developed in Washington as the hard right wrested policy control from Enders, the direction of U.S. diplomatic efforts became increasingly the prisoner of local initiatives.

CASEY BLOWS THE COVER

Honduran president Suazo may have won no prizes for his management of the economy or domestic politics, but his choice of one top aide in January 1982 proved to be exceptional. This was Edgardo Paz Barnica, as foreign minister, a university professor often controversial in his own right but who assembled the most skilled team of foreign policy advisers to be found in Central America. At times, the proposals emerging from the Honduran foreign ministry were not only the most original in the region but set the lead for the United States. The policy formulators began methodically by examining the conflicts surrounding them. Indeed, *all* the conflicts of Central America surrounded them.

The Paz Barnica team decided that the disputes in El Salvador,

Nicaragua, and Guatemala could be solved through internal dialogue, negotiations, and democracy. "We proposed democracy in all of the three countries," said one of Paz Barnica's deputies. "We never worried whether we could achieve it or not. I don't think we ever thought it would become true. We felt we were morally obligated to do this."

In March 1982, scarcely two months after taking office, Paz Barnica delivered the Honduran peace initiative before the OAS. The six points, like so many compilations of this period, touched base on all the obvious security concerns before addressing the most sensitive political issue: democracy. Here it called for a "permanent multilateral dialogue" leading to "securing a pluralist and democratic system." Other goals included arms reduction, removal of most foreign military advisers, verification mechanisms, a halt to arms trafficking, and respect for boundaries.

The underlying problem facing the Honduran civilian policy formulators was that their diplomacy was working at cross-purposes with Álvarez's military activities. The situation there was not unlike that faced by Enders. Paz Barnica expressly told the OAS that "Honduras, its people and its government do not wish, nor will they tolerate having its territory used for destabilizing operations in the region." But, of course, Álvarez had been providing sanctuary and support for such operations for the previous two years.

A second problem with the Honduran approach was that it was overly ambitious. "We were trying to do too much," said a senior aide to Paz Barnica. "Too much on the outside and not enough on the inside [of Honduras]." He blamed this on the lack of experience in foreign affairs. "We know better now what our limitations are."

An example was the "Central American Democratic Community," which the leaders of Honduras, El Salvador, and Costa Rica had decided to form with strong U.S. encouragement at the end of 1981. It had begun before the new Honduran government took office and before any elections in El Salvador. "It was a regional approach. It was precipitate. You can't have a democratic community without democratic governments. It was badly timed and failed," said Paz Barnica's aide.[26]

Yet, despite the shortcomings in this and later regional diplomatic initiatives, the Reagan administration characteristically embraced them and smothered them in the process. In his OAS speech in late February 1982 unveiling the Caribbean Basin Initiative, Reagan said, "We strongly support the Central American Democratic Community."

Subsequently, in his August 20 San Francisco speech, Enders suggested publicly that "perhaps the democratic countries should come together and see whether they cannot formulate a common approach" to dealing with Nicaragua. They came together in October, but by then the effort was futile.

More significantly, about a week after Enders delivered his speech, Álvarez launched his independent approach. Frustrated over U.S. antagonism toward Argentina and the lack of progress in implementing his plan for Nicaragua, he had reacted to what he viewed as a menacing movement of Nicaraguan forces toward the Honduran border and put his forces on a "red alert," the second highest stage of readiness. According to his intelligence, more than 2,000 Sandinista troops had massed and were advancing toward the border. With tanks, artillery, and infantry in the rear, the Nicaraguans, he felt, were in a position to launch an offensive. Álvarez moved six battalions, including artillery, antitank, cavalry, and infantry, into the El Paraiso region near the border and issued orders to destroy "every troop who comes onto our land as well as every piece of his equipment."

U.S. officials were concerned. "Everyone thought he was on the verge of going to war," said an official at the U.S. embassy. Asked what his plans were, Álvarez replied: "Be prepared to go to Managua. This is our chance."

U.S. military sources said they were aware of only a minor movement of about five Sandinista tanks into Somotillo in the border area. American embassy and military officials came down very hard on Álvarez in an attempt to calm the situation. "The Hondurans had to be gently reminded that they were not in the business of trying to foment a regional war, and we were not looking for an excuse to become involved in the region," Johnstone said. The Southern Command provided Álvarez with photographs of Sandinista troop movements from satellites and aircraft, and discouraged him from taking any independent action. "I think we were able to be sufficiently convincing on that score that we probably scared them half to death and probably had the opposite effect," Johnstone said.[27]

Shortly after the incident, Colonel Leonides Torres-Arias, who had been Álvarez's intelligence chief, announced his resignation from the Honduran armed forces and called a press conference in

Mexico to denounce what he called Álvarez's "criminal and bloody campaign" against Nicaragua. Torres-Arias charged that Honduras was getting ready to invade Nicaragua and accused Álvarez of operating death squads against his political opponents and bringing Honduras to the point of civil war. In Tegucigalpa, Torres-Arias was stripped of his rank and property and charged with treason. He ended up in Miami, as would Álvarez.

Compared to the war scare, the October 4 forum "for peace and democracy" in San José, Costa Rica, was anticlimactic. The meeting of the region's democracies, from which Nicaragua and Guatemala had been excluded by design, essentially adopted the Honduran six points of the previous March. Enders provided a commanding presence. And while Honduran representatives put the emphasis on security, Enders emphasized the political aspects. The final wording of the joint declaration said that "truly democratic government institutions . . . as expressed in free elections" were part of "the essential framework that must be established in each state in order to promote regional peace and stability."

"Clearly, it was organized to put Nicaragua in a box," said Francis McNeil, then U.S. ambassador to Costa Rica.

The State Department called the San José declaration a "blueprint for peace in the region," but the initiative foundered when Fernando Volio, the Costa Rican foreign minister, offered to present the final statement in Managua but the Sandinistas refused to receive him. Costa Rica dropped the ball. Honduras, beset by the lack of coordination between military and diplomatic efforts, was unable to pick it up. U.S. diplomatic efforts ground to a halt.

Disputes over policy at home and an incapacity to affect organization on the ground all but foreclosed the administration from using the covert war as an instrument to achieve its aims in the region. Meanwhile, news accounts based on leaked information made the program out to be bigger than it was and helped create a myth of its viability, whereas in fact the contras had not even been tested in battle. The final development of 1982 was that this untested program became the irreplaceable cornerstone of Reagan's Nicaragua policy, a process to which Casey made an important behind-the-scenes contribution.

Initially, the administration pretended to be embarrassed by the leaks, which appeared to come from congressional sources hostile to the covert program. But the pattern changed, and late in the year, in the single most influential news story on the subject, a November 8 cover story in *Newsweek*, Casey himself sat down with the magazine staff and discussed the covert war before the issue went to press.

Both with Congress and the press, Casey had become something of a promoter of the program. He used the number of fighters recruited for the insurgency as the principal indicator of the program's success.

In the course of 1982, the number of rebels as reported to the intelligence committees rose steadily from the 500 for whom funding was sought in December 1981 to 1,100 in May, 1,500 in August, and 4,000 men in December. By February 1983, the Agency reported, the number had gone up to 5,500, including Miskito Indians and forces operating out of Costa Rica and loyal to Pastora; and by May 1983, it was up to 7,000. "People are recruiting themselves," Casey told the House oversight committee. The CIA also took credit for organizing and supplying the attack on the bridges.

Yet the true dimensions of the force on the ground were hard to confirm. Both Casey and Clarridge repeatedly left the oversight committees unsure what the program was or what the numbers meant. But by focusing on numbers, they distracted attention from the real issues such as the rebels' own program. Casey was particularly confusing in his appearances. As an OSS veteran, he understood what was involved in running secret operations, and his personal experience and feeling for what Reagan would or would not approve gave him a basis for making decisions. In congressional appearances he invariably mumbled softly and no one knew if he was informing them or deceiving them. "Even if he told us what he was thinking, we couldn't understand what he said," said one staff aide. Casey, an investor and businessman, had for twenty years been in and out of courts on allegations of defrauding other investors but had always gotten off the hook. A Senate Intelligence Committee investigation of Casey's past activities had concluded he was not "unfit" for the job of CIA director. Casey at times made it hard to be taken seriously. He pronounced the country "Nicawawa," prompting a senior intelligence committee staffer to say, "You can't overthrow the government of a country whose name you can't pronounce."

Clarridge was a different case. Generals appear before the committees in uniform. State Department and CIA officials wear dark pin-striped suits. Clarridge dressed like a zoot-suiter. Sometimes he appeared in a white linen suit, sporting a purple necktie, a purple silk handkerchief, and an off-color shirt of light yellow or blue. He never buttoned his jacket except when he wore a double-breasted suit, of which he owned many. Clarridge slouched in the chair, positioning himself almost sideways. Often he did not look at senators when answering them but cast his eyes to the ceiling. Daniel Patrick Moynihan, the Democrat from New York and vice-chairman of the Senate oversight committee, exploded at least once and called Clarridge rude. Many on the committees assumed Clarridge did it on purpose and with Casey's backing.

If it was an act, they carried it off successfully until late 1982.

What galvanized doubts was the November 8 *Newsweek* cover story titled "America's Secret War. Target: Nicaragua." The cover showed U.S. and Honduran troops airborne and about to jump. Inside were pictures of U.S. "advisers" training Honduran soldiers as well as of Negroponte, Pastora, Clark, Enders, Miskito Indians at a funeral, everyone but FDN troops or leaders. The article quoted an unnamed "insider" as saying that Haig and Enders were the "driving forces" behind the project, while the CIA and Pentagon had "qualms" about it. A box portrayed Negroponte as the "ugly American" who was directing the war by ordering Álvarez around. There was not much news, but it put the story on the map for both the general public and Congress. The impact was in the title and dramatic presentation, which for the first time drew together the strands of a host of news leaks over the previous year. *Newsweek*'s decision to make it a cover and not an inside-page story, according to those who reported it, was influenced by Casey's readiness to confirm key facts. The CIA director, after stating his reluctance to answer questions, met twice with *Newsweek* staff and even agreed to be quoted, although not by name. Casey had a message he wanted to get across. Quoted as "one senior official involved in the decisions," he suggested that the insurgents, who had yet to launch their first major offensive, might topple the Sandinista government. "There are secondary and tertiary consequences which you can't control," he said. Casey also revealed in the interviews that the CIA was running paramilitary operations in at least ten countries. Thus, he not only oversold the contras' potential but suggested they were part of a far broader policy.

Public reaction was sharply negative.

The *Boston Globe*, taking note of the *Newsweek* article, wrote a stinging editorial about the operation. Among those reading the editorial were Representative Edward Boland and his close friend, another Massachusetts Democrat, House Speaker Thomas P. ("Tip") O'Neill. Boland was chairman of the House Select Committee on Intelligence. House and Senate liberals began a move to cut off the covert aid, and Boland took an initiative to head them off that resulted in the first open legislation limiting the operation. In April, Boland's committee had authorized further support for the anti-Sandinista force, but in classified language directed that the program be limited to interdiction of arms to the insurgents in El Salvador. This was already law. Now he drew another phrase from the April authorization, prohibiting the CIA or the Department of Defense from supplying equipment, training, or advice for military activities "for the purpose of overthrowing the government of Nicaragua or provoking a military exchange between Nicaragua and Honduras." The administration, fearing a much harsher alternative offered by Democrat Tom Harkin of Iowa, backed Boland, and his amendment passed 411–0. But in seeking refuge, as it did, in the legalism that the stated U.S. purpose was never to overthrow the Sandinistas, the administration was too clever by half. As soon as the Boland bill was passed, liberal critics would assert that the law was being violated by the covert program. In reality, both sides had ducked the issue.

Robert McFarlane, at the time deputy NSC director, felt that the administration had put itself in a posture of "terribly misleading" Congress and the public. But McFarlane also blamed congressional leaders for giving the White House "a very surreal interpretation" that the amendment was intended to "help out" the administration. Indeed, there was ambivalence about the program in Congress in light of the widely accepted intelligence that most of the arms going to the Salvadoran rebels transited Nicaragua. Many Democrats were willing to support a covert program with the goal of harassing the Sandinistas but not attempting to overthrow the government. Looking back, he would have preferred a six-month "cat-fight" that resulted in an "honest" policy to having to "sneak around" by claiming that cutting off arms flowing into El Salvador would change the Sandinista government. "It's just nuts," McFarlane said of the policy rationale he had to defend.[28]

In Honduras, the *Newsweek* article prompted angry denials and a statement by Suazo promising to crack down on the armed exiles.

Paz Barnica met with Daniel Ortega and signed an agreement to limit arms trafficking.

Within the Core Group, the *Newsweek* assertion that the FDN had been led and staffed by Somocistas touched a sensitive nerve. For months, the CIA had been talking with Cardenal about creating a new civilian leadership, and now, pressured by public discussion, politics, and criticism from within the Core Group of its failure to act, the CIA took action. In short order, it assembled a six-person civilian team and presented it at a press conference in a fancy Fort Lauderdale hotel as the new leadership. Cardenal, who by then had fallen out completely with Bermúdez and the Argentines, was not among them. The remake was completed just in time for the Boland vote. As part of the new image, even the CIA liaison with the civilians changed his name, Cardenal said. He had been "Philip Mason." Henceforth, he would be known as "Tony Feldman." He was the same man.

But the publicity to which Casey contributed had a greater significance than was evident at the time. The contradiction in U.S. policy goals expanded. Options accordingly were reduced. Strategy became more unworkable. And the public debate shifted its focus. For Casey, however, it was a political boon. His program now was irreversible even though, thanks partly to him, it had turned into a crazy "overt-covert" hybrid. The voice of the canny behind-the-scenes operator had been strengthened in policy forums.

The impact on policy was profound. So long as the operation was covert, as it had been, it could be plausibly denied and terminated. However, once U.S. support was known, the administration would be obliged to accommodate the rebels in any solution. Thus, the rebel force, instead of playing a supportive role in achieving U.S. policy goals, had become an end in itself.

Military strategy meanwhile had become almost impossible to develop. No one argued seriously in the councils of government that the insurgents could achieve their goal of a military overthrow; they had hardly begun to fight. But to acknowledge that a military solution was unattainable after they had launched their first offensive would cut the props from under the whole military operation. Not to acknowledge it, on the other hand, would permit the illusion that the rebels might achieve their goals, which now accordingly became U.S. goals, even though the rebels were not under day-to-day U.S. control.

The only strategy that could conceivably deal with this set of contradictions was a domestic public relations drive. Indeed, that had become necessary for a second reason, because the public focus changed. When the insurgency was exposed, the means displaced the end as the focus of the debate. This put Reagan on the defensive and made it harder for him to modify his support.

Without having done a thing, Reagan thereby found himself in an almost untenable position, one in which there was no longer a way to synchronize means and ends. The project went forward by inertia. But it made little sense.

General John Vessey, chairman of the Joint Chiefs of Staff, later pithily summed up the situation to his associates. "Where the policy really went wrong was with the contras going overt. That's when the horse turd dropped in the punch bowl."

In just one year, then, U.S. policy had become riddled with contradictions. Enders had formally stated a goal of normal relations with Nicaragua based on principles that were likely to heighten the confrontation. At the same time, the administration's readiness to continue its covert program overtly suggested that it had decided on a military solution when in fact none was desired or even available. Finally, pluralism in Nicaragua had come to be equated in Washington with the armed overthrow of the Sandinista government by the insurgent force. Reagan decided on nothing, except postponing a decision. It was a formula for stalemate.

As public controversy grew, another sleeping giant awakened, the leadership of the uniformed military services. The Joint Chiefs were brought up to date in a briefing by the CIA and realized then that the policy had undergone a transformation. "It didn't seem to jell with what the purpose of the forces was," said General Edward ("Shy") Meyer, then Army Chief of Staff. The Chiefs rarely weigh into a political debate—they prefer to keep a low profile, providing advice before decisions are made, then accepting and implementing the decisions—but in this case the slow drift in U.S. goals from interdiction to overthrow caused alarm. "That's when you start calling time, when you wonder whether you're being bypassed and whether you're able to perform your constitutional role," Meyer said. When the uniformed military gets disturbed over an issue, "they normally bring it to everybody's attention, very loudly." This does not mean public disclosure or press leaking but, more commonly, conversations with trusted members of Congress. Dependent for their funds and programs on continuing support in Congress, the top brass form liaisons with powerful congressmen that rarely become known in public.

It is not clear how much impact if any the Joint Chiefs' disquiet had in Congress, but it may have added to the rebellious mood in the House. By coincidence of events, the Chiefs' newfound interest in Central America quickly developed into a much bigger role in a situation that was getting out of hand.[29]

CHAPTER
6

TURF WARS

WALLACE NUTTING is tall and square-shouldered, laconic and deliberate in speech. He is "probably the most honest general I have met, totally lacking in guile," says a civilian expert on Latin American military affairs who knows him well. Nutting likes to talk with reporters, scholars, and the general public. For three years, from 1980 to 1982, he tried in vain to arouse interest in his views in official Washington. The commander-in-chief at the Southern Command, responsible for U.S. security interests south of Mexico, believed the tangle of problems afflicting Central America had primarily local roots. The military, he said repeatedly, could contribute to a broad-based policy but could not operate successfully in the absence of one.

Nutting had wanted a total approach, incorporating economic, political, social, psychological, and military programs. He had

121

initiated the use of U.S. military trainers for the Salvadoran army in the last months of the Carter administration and had organized the first exercises with Honduras. In the spring of 1981, in a lengthy cable on U.S. options in Central America, he had proposed one unusual military response to deal with problems emanating from Nicaragua: using special forces on unconventional operations to interdict the flow of arms into El Salvador.

But the war party in Washington wanted to avoid using U.S. forces. They were entranced with the idea of covert aid to the contras, which they claimed would achieve the same purpose. Yet by late 1982 it was apparent something had gone seriously wrong with their scheme, and Nutting decided to dramatize the bad news.

The context for his warning was what he viewed as an across-the-board deterioration in El Salvador. Constituent assembly elections in March of that year had been a public relations success but a political and social disaster; the right had gained strength, halting land reform and paralyzing the political process. Meanwhile, a guerrilla offensive that began in September was knocking off army posts and patrols right and left, destroying public transportation and electric power installations in the eastern third of El Salvador, and crippling an already weak economy. As rumors of a possible rightist coup developed, Deane Hinton, the U.S. ambassador, said right-wing "gorillas" were as much a threat to the country as leftist guerrillas. His remarks caught White House officials by surprise and they anonymously hinted their displeasure. Enders said Hinton's remarks had been cleared and backed him to the hilt. But in face of human rights abuses, the sentiment in Congress was against providing supplemental funds for the El Salvador army. Enders delayed asking for funds to avoid what could have been a losing battle.

Nutting's message was as straightforward as the man himself. "If we continue on our present course," he told the Joint Chiefs of Staff on January 26, 1983, "we are going to lose." He repeated the warning twice. His fellow lieutenant general Paul Gorman invited him to visit the Core Group to give the same briefing the next day. Finally, he put it to William Clark at the NSC. The warning was far more pessimistic than anything coming from the U.S. embassy in San Salvador or from the State Department. But it was timely. In a spectacular feat a few days later, 500 rebel troops captured Berlín, a town in eastern El Salvador.

Judge Clark had been concerned about the ebbing of congressional support and its impact on the region and, about the same time Nutting briefed him, had Reagan send Jeane Kirkpatrick on a tour of the region. Reagan also approved his recommendation to appoint Richard Stone, a former Democratic senator from Florida, to be "special representative for public diplomacy"—a euphemism for using advertising techniques to influence national policy. Nutting's message and the call to arms that Kirkpatrick presented after her trip were catalysts that aroused official Washington, but the ultimate results were hardly what either intended. The war party used the opportunity to go after Enders, and in a few months, he and Hinton were removed from their posts. The U.S. military stepped up its presence in the region and the State Department found that it had been reduced to the margins in the policymaking process in Washington. Conservative ideologues, who wanted a rollback of Soviet-bloc gains in the third world but knew little about Central America, suddenly were riding high at the White House. The pragmatists, those Latin area experts at the State Department who sought a policy that Congress could support over the long term—most likely an accommodation with the Sandinistas—were humiliated. The problem for the conservatives was that in the absence of the State Department, which has the function in government of formulating a framework for policy, they had no idea where they were riding.

DEMISE BY INSTALLMENT

Nutting's perspective on Central America was shared by leaders of the uniformed military, but his presentations apparently lacked the punch or polish to attract wider attention—that is, until he declared, "We are going to lose."[1]*

But his low profile enabled him to do things that even a few months later would seem extraordinary. For most of his four years in Panama, Nutting was able to fly his C-12 through Nicaraguan airspace en route from Panama to Honduras. He overflew the location north of Managua where the Sandinistas kept their Soviet-supplied tanks. Nutting, a tank commander by training, carried out

---

* Nutting said an aide had been telling him for two years that there was no other way to get the attention of official Washington than with such a message. "I waited until in my honest professional judgment I could say that with belief."

his own aerial reconnaissance. Until early 1983, U.S. C-130 cargo flights and helicopters also overflew Nicaragua regularly. He organized one major exercise with Honduras in early 1983, Big Pine I, which moved a Honduran army battalion into Mocorón in south-central Honduras, where there had previously been only a token military presence. That move stirred little controversy because Nutting had organized advance consultations with Anthony Quainton, the U.S. ambassador in Managua, and John Negroponte in Tegucigalpa. Nicaragua had been invited to send an observer, but declined. Quainton recalled that participating units in Big Pine I overflew Nicaragua en route to Honduras. "I think they finally told us we couldn't do that," Nutting said.

Nutting and Kirkpatrick, reporting on the same situation, reached the same overall conclusions, but each was unaware of the other's efforts. Both had become interested in the region after the Sandinista revolution. Each operated in his or her own milieu: Nutting, the professional officer, relied on staff and expert advice and worked through channels. Kirkpatrick, an academic who had the President's ear but no experience in foreign policymaking and no institutional back-up, operated as a loner. The contrast between Nutting's trip to Washington and Kirkpatrick's fact-finding mission was telling. Nutting took the initiative to deliver his warning, one of the most important messages of his career, while Kirkpatrick clearly was unprepared for her February 8–12 fact-finding mission. ("I didn't know that the President was going to ask me to make that trip, frankly," she said.) She went to Panama, Costa Rica, Honduras, El Salvador, and Venezuela and met leaders of the government, trade unions, opposition, private sector, and press, those she called "the leadership core of a society." However, she avoided the military establishments, despite the fact they are at the heart of power in Latin America. "I am not a military specialist and I did not in fact attempt to make judgments about the military situation," she said later. Kirkpatrick did not call on Nutting.*[2]

Nutting's message energized what is sometimes called the permanent government in Washington, those career officials and officers who operate the levers of government no matter who is in the White

---

* "Since then I have taken more interest in the military side," she said three years later. "But as of then, much less."

House. It hit hardest at the Pentagon, where the newly installed chairman of the Joint Chiefs of Staff, General John Vessey, did a review of previous National Security decisions and compiled a check list of all the steps that were to have been taken but were not. He brought these before a National Security planning group meeting, which produced another document, more rounds of interagency meetings, and, eventually, some results. Kirkpatrick for her part stirred the interest of politicians from the President on down. A more sophisticated NSC might have brought Nutting and Kirkpatrick together, at least to compare notes. The two might have made an effective team to brief Congress and the public, although this would have run up against Enders, who maintained tight control on public presentations of policy.

At the same time, El Salvador was not the only thing on the minds of the uniformed military leadership. Of equal or greater concern was Cuba. Since Reagan's inauguration and Haig's vague threat to go "to the source," that is, to cut the Soviet arms pipeline to Cuba, the Soviet Union had undertaken an enormous military resupply of its closest third world ally. This complicated the already difficult planning problem of how to deal with Cuba in time of war.*

In these circumstances, Nutting got the go-ahead to establish a regional military training center in Honduras to train Salvadoran soldiers. He also finally overcame State Department resistance to sending his staff to San Salvador to develop and implement a national military campaign plan. U.S. ambassadors have say over which U.S. officials can visit them, and Hinton had refused to allow Nutting in

---

* Soviet deliveries to Cuba totaled 66,000 tons in 1981, triple the amount of the previous year and the highest quantity since the Cuban missile crisis, a level that continued in 1982. Its combat aircraft rose to 250 from 175. The inventory of MiG-23 fighters, which have a 500 nautical mile combat radius, tripled to 36. Citing these figures, Colonel James L. Cole, Jr., a JCS representative in the interagency consultations on Central America, wrote in mid-1983 that the expansion was "unprecedented" and "alarming." "Soviet presence and Cuban capability now pose a serious threat to U.S. interests, and that threat is growing rapidly." The MiG-23s meant that significant air defense assets would be required to defend southeastern U.S. territory. Speaking a year later, Cole's boss in the interagency process, Colonel James Connally, said the uniformed military's concerns centered on Cuba and extrapolated from there to Nicaragua: "Cuba has become a second-order world power. That power is very significant. It has impact on the ability of the United States to help its allies. Cuba gives us pause. We don't know how we would handle Cuba in time of war. We have worked this problem many times and we simply don't know how. If a second Cuba emerges and is similar to the first, I don't know how we would do it."[3]

except on three or four occasions. (He had also refused country clearance to Negroponte except for one visit, which took place on a weekend.)

Kirkpatrick came back with tough-minded recommendations of her own, including a major push for $60 million in emergency aid to El Salvador, something that Enders had shelved the previous month.

In the crisis atmosphere brought about by the continuing guerrilla offensive and the two doomsayers, Enders immediately came under attack. "He was running a one-man show without a lot of help from the rest of the government," said one high military official. Enders's operating methods had slowly but surely alienated most other power centers in Washington dealing with Central America, and his high profile made him an inevitable target. The question that arose was not "Why is the policy not working?" but "Why is Enders's policy not working?" said a State Department official. "A part of Enders's problem was his remarkable ability to get everyone mad at him because he runs everything out of his hat," said another skilled infighter, Lawrence Eagleburger, then undersecretary of state for political affairs. "He's got three or four different groups going and nobody knows what the other's doing, all largely aimed at his managing the policy as much unconstrained as possible."[4]

Enders had indeed been pursuing his own course. Early in February, he had circulated a working paper on policy toward El Salvador and had flown to Madrid for talks on February 8 with Spanish premier Felipe González Márquez. The paper called for negotiations to end the civil war combined with continued support of Salvadoran military efforts to defeat the guerrillas. A third country, possibly Spain, would act as intermediary. But Enders had not sought Clark's approval for the trip, and in the context of Nutting's alarming briefing just days earlier and the search for a scapegoat, the timing could not have been worse.*

Clark was angry. When John Goshko and Lou Cannon of the *Washington Post* approached him to ask about the aims of the

---

* James Theberge, the conservative academic who had become Reagan's ambassador to Chile, is one of those who cites the Nutting briefing as "a critical factor" that led to "a whole lot of reactions," including the focusing of blame on Enders. Theberge was called back by Clark that spring to examine areas where policy needed to be strengthened.[5]

Enders trip, they turned up a bigger story than expected. Clark, identified only as "an administration official," said he had received Enders's paper advocating a "two-track" policy. "Frankly, there are a lot of us at the White House who think that this is a very bad idea," Clark told them. Kirkpatrick also was said to be less than enthusiastic. Goshko asked Enders for an explanation, but Enders refused. It was a tactical misjudgment, for Enders could easily have cleared up the critical misimpression conveyed by his opponents that he was advocating sharing power with the armed guerrillas. In fact, his idea was to have the Salvadoran government talk with Guillermo Ungo, a Social Democrat, and members of the political wing, who provided the internationally respectable face for the ultra-leftist fighters. Given their military momentum, the fighters probably would have been loath to make concessions, and the proposal would have served U.S. aims by dividing the fighting and political wings and enticing Congress back on board the program.*[6]

To the extent that Enders's real intentions ever became known at the time, they were just a footnote in the coming months. In the context of the guerrilla offensive, the February 10 lead article created an enormous stir. Reagan read about the Enders proposal for the first time and was reported to have exploded.[7] Kirkpatrick, who was in El Salvador on her fact-finding trip the day the article appeared, told reporters that Duarte and other Salvadoran leaders all opposed a negotiated settlement to end the civil war. Ideologues rallied around Kirkpatrick, believing that Enders was ready to sell out. The right began attacking Enders by name; so did some on the left, who assumed that his proposal for negotiations was probably disingenuous, as it no doubt was.†

On her return from Central America, Kirkpatrick made a series of specific proposals in addition to recommending a showdown with Congress over Salvador aid. One was to set up a full-time inter-agency Central America task force to oversee day-to-day policy

---

* A State Department official with good ties to conservatives said Clark had grown so distrustful of Enders that he "deliberately read the worst into the memo. Everybody said to me that the judge didn't understand the memo."

† Enders viewed the attacks as coming from those who wanted a military confrontation in Central America. "When the two-track proposal was drawn up under the direction of the Secretary of State, it was immediately leaked as being a giveaway, which it clearly was not, by people who feared that peaceniks were going to sell out Central America," he said more than two years later.[8]

questions. Clark immediately approved it, and the interagency group began meeting twice daily six and sometimes seven days a week in the State Department operations center, chaired by Enders's assistant, Craig Johnstone.*

Kirkpatrick also called for a "Marshall Plan" of economic assistance for Central America. And fresh from her talks with Venezuelan leaders, she urged the administration to support but not embrace the new Contadora mediating group. Each of her proposals added to the bad blood with Enders. Enders did not welcome anyone's challenging his dominance of the bureaucratic process and had objected to Kirkpatrick's mission in the first place; he felt that Congress would not appropriate the sums needed for a massive Marshall-type economic aid plan and the idea thereby would jeopardize the Caribbean Basin Initiative†; and he did not take Contadora seriously.

Just as Enders followed an independent course, after the Kirkpatrick trip Clark began to pursue his. Enders preferred to adjust policy to the political constraints on the ground and in Congress. Clark wanted to change both, and assembled his own team of trouble-shooters to handle Central American problems. It was not as easy as he thought.

In late February he sent Richard Stone, his newly appointed "special representative for public diplomacy," accompanied only by two NSC officials, Oliver North and Al Sapia-Bosch, to El Salvador to ask that the schedule for presidential elections be moved up to the autumn of 1983. With the aim in mind that this would help sell a reluctant Congress on more military aid for El Salvador, Stone apparently convinced Alvaro Magaña, the provisional president, to go along. But in a classic misfire of amateur diplomacy, he celebrated his success prematurely on the way back to Miami on

---

* Kirkpatrick was represented on the task force by her assistant, Jackie Tillman. In the first weeks of the task force, Tillman's major concern was turning the forthcoming visit of Pope John Paul II to Central America into a public relations plus for the administration. "She would always talk about the Pope and what we have to have the Pope say about the Sandinistas," said another participant. About a week before his trip, trouble-shooter Vernon Walters went to Rome to discuss the forthcoming trip, which as it turned out featured a public confrontation in Managua between John Paul and opponents bused in by Tomás Borge's interior police.[9]

† Enders had personally helped develop the project known as the CBI in 1981. It consisted of a variety of measures to loosen trade restrictions and to encourage the flow of private investment to the chronically poor countries of Central America and the Caribbean.

board the Salvadoran airline TACA, many of whose passengers are apt to understand English, discussing the mission aloud with North. Unknown to them, Mark Feldstein, a reporter for a Tampa television station, had boarded the plane in Belize, an intermediate stop, and sat in the row ahead of them. North boasted about their success and discussed with Stone how well the move would play in Congress. At the end of the flight the reporter introduced himself. Stone turned ashen. He warned Feldstein that to report the story at this time would "jeopardize national security irreparably" and offered the "inside" account if Feldstein would agree to hold it back. As they talked, Stone explained what the trip was about and filled in the context. North told him emotionally: "If you love your country, you won't do this." Feldstein reported the news. The disclosure embarrassed Magaña; the date was repeatedly set back, and the election was finally held in March 1984.[10]*

The same small group of hard-line conservatives—Clark, Kirkpatrick, Weinberger, Casey, and Meese—who had tipped the balance for aid to the contras now gathered forces to press for Enders's removal. It was an unequal struggle. Enders-baiting had become a chorus among conservatives. Reagan political appointees at State held monthly lunches, and in spring 1983 everyone was complaining bitterly about Enders's "total control" over policy.

Kirkpatrick, although she came to be seen as an adversary, denies that she had policy disputes with Enders except for her "Marshall Plan" proposal. She maintains that Enders fell not for policy reasons but because of the conspiratorial way in which he operated; many share her conclusion.† However, in the context of a weak national security structure, with ideologues anxious to take over the policy and with Helms trying to promote his own candidates and preventing Enders from staffing his office properly, Enders may have had little choice. This situation also brought out one of Enders's less attractive but ingrained traits: a penchant for secretiveness.

Another major player and close associate of Reagan's at logger-

---

* Stone took no other trips as special representative for public diplomacy and instead became a member of the Central America task force. When he became roving ambassador in April 1983, he traveled in a government plane.

† Although the "administration official" quoted in the February 10 *Post* article had intimated that Kirkpatrick was one of those concerned about Enders's "two-track" policy, Kirkpatrick defended Enders on the memo. "No official of this government has ever advocated power-sharing as one track except in the context of power-sharing through elections," she said in a July 1983 interview.

heads with Enders was William Casey. "Casey did not like and did not have a lot of use for Enders," for both substantive and ideological reasons, according to Lawrence Eagleburger. Primarily, Enders was "too much nonconfrontational" regarding Nicaragua. Fred Iklé at the Defense Department shared Casey's nervousness about Enders's approach, involving, as it did, diplomatic initiatives. "In part," Eagleburger said, "they misunderstood it because Enders was playing these bureaucratic games and they were afraid he was doing some things he wasn't doing."[11] Meese and Weinberger, whether for ideological or bureaucratic reasons or both, also had little sympathy for Enders.

Unwittingly, Enders may also have undercut his best source of support, Secretary of State George Shultz. Shultz had shown little interest in Central America from the time he succeeded Haig in June 1982, in the midst of the Lebanon crisis. That had suited Enders well at the beginning. In July he had drafted a memo to Shultz to the effect that trends in Central America were running favorably, provided Congress continued supporting aid to El Salvador, and Shultz had then given Enders free rein.[12] But by May 1983, Shultz found himself with egg on his face because of his failure to master the issues.

The story told by a conservative insider is that Shultz, at Enders's request, made a pitch at a cabinet meeting for suspending aid to El Salvador because of human rights abuses. He reportedly said that State had "a strong belief" that a certain first lieutenant, apparently Lieutenant López Sibrián, had been involved in a killing, but the Salvadoran military refused to act and the government could not act. Therefore, he said, aid should be suspended. The concern at the State Department was always that if the administration did not act, Congress might take the matter into its own hands. Kirkpatrick protested that a suspension would be "highly imprudent." Reagan listened, then spoke. "Well, George," he said, "I tell you the truth. I really find it hard to accept that our military policy and our support for the government of El Salvador should depend on the actions or inactions of some obscure lieutenant. Let's forget that and go on to the next item." This did not help Shultz, or Enders, when the showdown came.[13]

Enders's demise occurred in installments. Where Enders had an expressed preference to work within constraints imposed by Congress, rather than challenge it, Clark favored a confrontation with the Hill and, if necessary, the news media over Central America. So when Enders voiced reservations about Clark's proposal to have Reagan speak on Central America before a special session of Congress, a rare event, Clark overrode him. As a compensation, Enders won the battle over the contents of the speech. "That [speech] was one we controlled, wrote, and handled," said a colleague at State. "We beat out alternative drafts till the bitter end."[14]

The speech on April 27, 1983, was one of the most effective policy statements of Reagan's first term. He defined U.S. goals in terms of four "D's": democracy, development, defense, and dialogue. As for Nicaragua, Reagan said: "We do not seek its overthrow. Our interest is to ensure that it does not infect its neighbors through the export of subversion and violence." Although he called it a "dictatorial junta" that should not be protected "from the anger of its own people," he added: "We should, through diplomacy, offer an alternative."

Enders had held out successfully against the drive by the hard right for economic war against the Sandinistas. Now Enders had run out of capital. Clarridge that spring had even put forward a proposal to mine Nicaragua's harbors, but after a debate in the Core Group, "It was then set aside," Enders said.[15]

Enders's last battle was perhaps the most trivial—whether or not to issue a new White Paper on Soviet and Cuban military involvement in Central America. Enders felt that State had been burned twice already by rushing into presentations before all the facts had been verified.*

"At certain times, you have to draw the line," he told staff aides. Clark, however, strongly supported efforts to publicize the Communist military threat.

The publication in question had been inspired by Constan-

---

* Two examples stand out. The first is the original White Paper on arms supplies to El Salvador of February 1981, which was rushed into print and today is remembered not for the content that has been borne out by events but for its flaws. The second occurred in March 1982, when the CIA and Defense Intelligence Agency (DIA) sent their top experts to a State Department briefing with reconnaissance photos, maps, and charts to demonstrate the Sandinista military build-up. The impact was destroyed three days later when a purported Nicaraguan defector captured in El Salvador was presented to the press to confirm Nicaraguan and Cuban involvement in the Salvador war. Orlando José Tardencillas Espinosa told a bemused press conference he had never seen a Nicaraguan or Cuban in El Salvador and had made his previous statements under coercion.

tine Menges and prepared by a CIA-DIA team, and State had done its best to hold it up. On May 20, those who had a hand in the drafting met informally in the Old Executive Office Building to go over the publication. Roger Fontaine, the NSC senior director for Latin America, was nominally in the chair, but Oliver North, whose role had been to get intelligence photos declassified, did most of the talking. Enders had sent Stephen McFarland, the Nicaragua desk officer. The decision was out of the State Department's control, and McFarland was told to approve the document if he thought he could live with its contents.

North cut the debate short. "Judge Clark and the President have decided that the White Paper will be released," he said. "I'll give everyone five minutes. Say your piece." Fontaine, obviously embarrassed, stood up and walked. North, by force of personality, had taken charge. Each spoke. Menges had some last-minute changes. U.S. intelligence had counted thirty-six military bases in Nicaragua. Menges suggested altering the phrase to read "almost forty." After some objections, he backed down slightly. "Let's change that to 'about forty,' " he said. North called for order. "OK. The five minutes are up. Goddammit, we're going to press."

North wanted the Pentagon presses to start rolling immediately. But State refused to provide its seal for the cover. So a Pentagon artist reproduced it. The presses ran all night, and the following week the publication was distributed to the news media.

In the meantime, shortly after North ordered publication, the decision was made to fire Enders. Enders saw the curtain coming down. "Shultz was the last to be convinced I should go. I convinced him I should go or he would lose all control of Central American operations," Enders later said. At his request, Shultz went to see Reagan to ask if he still had confidence in the assistant secretary.

"Well, no," Reagan said.

"Then I guess he should be replaced," Shultz said.

"Yes, I guess he should," Reagan said.

Hours after the publication was handed to reporters on May 27, Shultz announced that Enders had been removed.*

---

* The publication contained no news and attracted little press coverage. The novelty was on the cover. The Pentagon artist had reproduced the wrong seal, using an

Shultz tried to go on the offensive and take charge of the policy but met with rebuff. "The present management situation is a mess and would not work even if the problems were simple," Shultz said in a memo to Reagan after the White House meeting on May 25 at which Enders was fired. He proposed a "simple and straightforward" structure with himself in charge. "You will look to me to carry out your policies. If those policies change, you will tell me. If I am not carrying them out effectively, you will hold me accountable. But we will set up a structure so that I can be your sole delegate with regard to carrying out your policies."

Reagan's policies, as described by Shultz, in essence reduced to Enders's two-track approach. The administration would seek negotiated solutions in El Salvador and with Nicaragua. The goal in El Salvador was to secure rebel participation in elections, not a sharing of power. In Nicaragua, the United States would seek a "reciprocal and verifiable agreement in which the Nicaraguans come to terms with the need for them to mind their own business." The United States would continue supporting the Salvadoran army and the contras in order to achieve these goals.

"These I understand to be your policies," Shultz said. "I support them and I accept the responsibility to carry them out."

Shultz's maneuver was not unlike that which Alexander Haig had attempted at the beginning of the administration, and it suffered a similar fate. Reagan's reply, presumably drafted by Clark, reduced the Department of State to one player in a free-for-all.

"Success in Central America will require the cooperative effort of several departments and agencies. No single agency can do it alone nor should it," Reagan wrote. "Still it is sensible to look to you, as I do, as the lead Cabinet officer, charged with moving aggressively *to develop the options in coordination with Cap, Bill Casey and others and coming to me for decisions*" (emphasis added). He added: "I believe in Cabinet government. It works when the Cabinet officers work together. I look to you and Bill Clark to assure that that happens."

Enders was still at the State Department waiting to take up a new

---

ornate eagle inside a double ring with the insignia Department of State. On publications, State usually uses a stencil of an eagle with no inscription. The cover also stated, inaccurately, that the publication had been released by the Department of State and the Department of Defense. No one at State took up the issue, however; with Enders gone the fight was lost and the matter dropped.

assignment as ambassador to Spain and was "aware" of the White
House rebuff of Shultz. "For a while he was completely margin-
alized," Enders said of Shultz.*[16]

THE POLITICS OF BLAME

Shultz's rebuff was only one factor that made Enders's demise a
watershed. The President had put his prestige at stake, focusing

---

* Shultz had attached a draft decision directive setting up a "restricted interagency
group" (RIG) to address the formulation and execution of policy but stipulating that
the Secretary of State "is responsible for the overall direction, coordination and
supervision of the interdepartmental activities incident thereto." And he sent along
a chart showing the decision process as flowing in a straight solid line down from the
President through Shultz to his assistant for inter-American affairs and finally to the
interagency group. The NSC was sketched in almost as an afterthought between the
top two boxes, suggesting that decisions flowed through it, not from it. The National

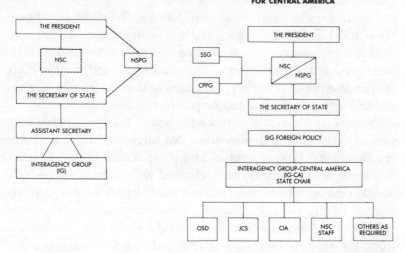

Security planning group, a small, informal grouping of the top national security
advisers including Casey and Weinberger, was shown as a box off to the side
connected by dotted lines with Reagan and Shultz. Shultz's schema contained just six
boxes. Reagan's reply said the current system was working just fine. Attached was a
sketch with twelve boxes clearly interposing the NSC between Reagan and Shultz
and listing even subgroupings run by NSC personnel at a level higher than that of
Secretary of State. One NSC subgroup, called the "standing crisis pre-planning
group," was chaired by Clark's deputy, Robert McFarlane, and run by Oliver North;

public attention on Central America. Important parts of the permanent government, in particular the military establishment, were aroused and ready to act. Policy had been removed from the hands of the "cookie pushers" from the State Department, as one White House official smugly put it. But who had inherited overall charge was not so easy to determine. Enders thought he had been dispatched by those who wanted "an all-out confrontational posture," and it is true that rightists who wanted the confrontation had ousted him. But the Joint Chiefs also felt it was time for a spectacular show of force. They, however, very much regretted the departure of Enders. The military leadership was worried enough about El Salvador and Cuba that they offered to defray the expenses of subsequent military exercises out of their own funds.

Thus, in assessing the crisis and in prescribing a military remedy, there was a temporary alliance between the conservatives, who had ousted Enders, and the military leadership, who controlled the assets. State was the odd party out, for the U.S. embassy in San Salvador had neither raised the alarm nor acted as if there had been a major crisis, and Enders had followed suit.

The balance of forces was subtly changed with respect to America's Central America policy aims. To be sure, the Joint Chiefs still agreed with State that the goal should be a settlement with the Sandinistas and the rightists still favored overthrow; each side had a veto over the other and neither had the upper hand. But in a situation in which there was no unity in the government over the ends of Central America policy, the agency controlling the means ran the policy. Thus, power passed from Enders to the Pentagon. Reagan was not inclined to make a firm decision on policy goals, and so the dispute was put aside. Later in the year, his procrastination would exact a heavy price, for after getting the attention of the Sandinistas, no one could agree on what to do next.

Personalities made a big difference in post-Enders Washington. In contrast to the imperious, cold Eastern establishment man who literally and figuratively looked down on most of them—humorist Art Buchwald called him "Too Tall Tom"—the new group were outwardly very friendly people, like Ronald Reagan himself. The appearance was deceptive. Judge Clark was shy and kind in inter-

---

the other, the special planning group, was the highest level crisis management group and was chaired by Vice-President George Bush.

personal relations, but his instincts were tough. Clark had had it with
the State Department and its "candy-ass approach," said an aide,
who summed up Clark's attitude as "Let's rip their faces off." Oliver
North charmed most people he met, but he got to be known in the
State Department as a "cowboy" looking for action—overbearing,
obstructive, and contemptuous of the uses of diplomacy. Paul
Gorman, with his graying hair, glasses, and friendly smile, looked
more like a grandfather or favorite uncle than an Army general, but
critics and admirers agreed that the brilliant conceptualizer was cold
and abrasive in person.

Clark expected that Enders's successor would be more amenable
to the concerns of hard-liners. Langhorne ("Tony") Motley was
Brazilian-born, had studied at the Citadel, a military academy, spent
ten years in the air force, then become a wealthy Alaska land
developer. Through Republican connections, he had been appointed
Reagan's first ambassador to Brazil. And when the presidential party
passed through on an official visit in early December 1982, Motley's
gung-ho "can-do" style had impressed Reagan and Clark. Equally
important, he made a big impression on William Casey. The CIA
director thought Motley had guts, filed "brilliant reports that
outshone the CIA station's," and was "willing to play rough and
dirty," according to writer Bob Woodward, who interviewed Casey
extensively for his book *Veil*. Motley had dealt directly with Casey in
the spring of 1983 when several Libyan planes heading toward
Nicaragua stopped in Brazil to refuel with a cargo described as
medical supplies. Motley asked Brazilian authorities to stop and
search the planes, and they discovered seventy tons of weapons and
explosives, delivering a propaganda coup for the administration.[17]

Motley had a sense of humor and charm and a street fighter's
instinct in bureaucratic struggles. Not an intellectual or an expert on
Central America, he chose to rely on Johnstone and other career
professionals in shaping policy. He had had no great desire for his
new job—on hearing of his appointment, he quipped, "It is like
seeing your mother-in-law go over the cliff, but in your Cadillac." It
took Motley some months to come up to speed, and he maintained
a low profile until late 1983. In time, he tried to pursue policy as
Enders had envisaged it. In the interim, everyone else got into the
act. The stage was crowded.

From the time of his arrival at the U.S. Southern Command in
May 1983, Paul Gorman eclipsed Negroponte as the major player in

the field. His post was upgraded from three to four stars, giving him more clout than his predecessor had had; he also went in with substantially more resources, a close working knowledge of the Washington bureaucracy, and a commitment of support from the Joint Chiefs. Working through Vessey or Weinberger, or in person, Gorman (and the Pentagon) became a pole of power in the Washington arena that Nutting never had been.

Meanwhile, Casey was pursuing an unusual path in support of his program. Besides overseeing the covert war, he also pushed behind the scenes for a drive to build public support. Early in August, Casey called together a half-dozen PR experts, personally briefed them on Central American issues, then asked for their ideas for generating a nationwide campaign. They proposed a fund-raising drive and better internal government coordination in order to sell Central America as a "new product." Casey insisted that the task not be turned over to the State Department.[18]

With patronage from Casey and Clark, North also became a major player in 1983. North was on a roll. In February, he had made a first foray into amateur diplomacy with Stone. In March, he had been selected for promotion to lieutenant colonel. In May, he had taken charge of the interagency squabble and settled it with a firm decision; he had delivered the coup de grace to Enders and come out as one of the winners in the internal power struggle. As his role grew, he went in for self-promotion. In September, the NSC issued a biography of North that asserted he had a background in special operations, for which there is no service record. The embellishments on an otherwise impressive record seem puzzling but the context in which North suddenly found himself may help explain them.*

---

* The official Marine Corps record showed no reference to involvement in "unconventional warfare operations in Southeast Asia," as North claimed in his biography. And according to his commanding officer at the time, the detachment North commanded in Okinawa was a routine training post, not a "Special Operations Training Detachment" as he had asserted. North also described himself as a "company commander in combat," where the Marine Corps record shows him as a platoon commander in Vietnam.

The riddle of North's past was difficult to sort out because of his ambivalence about publicity. In mid-1985, when the news media began writing about North, the NSC withdrew his biography. Although his associates say North likes to read about himself, he sent word to Marine headquarters that he did not want his personal record or even the citations connected with his combat medals made available to this author, although these are public record. "North feels you cannot possibly be writing

On Enders's demise, the innermost circle of policymakers began to enlarge as agencies that he had excluded vied to join what had been the Core Group. Motley, in an effort to regain control of policy, reorganized the group secretly. Henceforth, it was called the Restricted Interagency Group, or RIG, and its membership was tightened still further, effectively to four or five people. The membership of the RIG reflected the new political reality. Dewey Clarridge represented Casey and the CIA; Vice-Admiral Arthur Moreau, Jr., represented Gorman and the Joint Chiefs; North represented Clark and the NSC; Motley represented Shultz and the State Department; and Nestor Sanchez represented Weinberger. Each was a pole of power. Shultz had wanted the RIG to report to him directly, but because of Reagan's reluctance to delegate responsibility for decision-making to him, its members reported separately to their respective bosses, and only Motley, who chaired the group, reported to the secretary of state. Motley at times appeared to be the weakest, but Sanchez was said to be in an even weaker position. "Nestor would play along but Moreau was the heavy," said one participant.* It was in the RIG that key decisions were made on covert operations and other central policy questions.[19]

For North, his newfound strength within the NSC confirmed the value of his hard-charging style. Leading the pack that had ridden roughshod over Enders in May had not set him back but gained him a coveted seat in the innermost policy council. His self-enhanced credentials allowed him to claim technical expertise in special operations, and he gained new clout with his military superiors. North, the field-grade officer, and Gorman, the four-star general, treated each other like equals.

Most of those in the top positions had in common an inability or unwillingness to articulate in public what they were trying to do. Motley could not sound convincing in his appearances before the press or Congress and often wisecracked his way out of difficult

---

anything positive about the administration and doesn't want to cooperate," a Marine spokesman said.

North's job title was deputy director for politico-military affairs, a position in which he had no staff other than secretaries. His responsibilities were listed as national-level contingency planning, crisis management, and counterterrorism. There was no reference in his biography to language skills or any sign of interest in diplomacy, politics, history, or foreign affairs.

* Moreau was reserved in public appearances but was described by an associate as "very bright" and "very powerful" because he had Vessey's ear.

questions. Clark, whose knowledge of Central America or other foreign affairs topics was limited, avoided give-and-take with the press. North, claiming that terrorists were after him and that "nobody in the press writes good stuff," refused to see most journalists. ("Ollie does have the military mind," said a fellow officer. "He thinks reporters should be cheerleaders.")[20] Moreau was almost a complete unknown. Weinberger's glib and unstudied approach to issues gained him limited credibility in Congress and the media. Vessey, an unpretentious, thoughtful soldier who wanted to protect his close relations with Reagan, made as few public appearances as he could get away with. And Gorman, when approached by reporters, customarily walked away.

Two other figures emerged on the scene who were more willing to articulate U.S. policy, though neither was in the inner policy circle. One was Richard Stone. Clark had Reagan name Stone as special envoy to Central America at the end of April 1983 mainly to appease Clarence Long, the crusty Maryland Democrat who controlled the House purse strings and who had been refusing to support an emergency appropriation to El Salvador of $30 million. Enders had opposed Stone's appointment and Stone kept a low profile as long as Enders was around.* The other was Otto Reich, an assistant administrator at the Agency for International Development, who was named special envoy for public diplomacy to succeed Stone. Reich had been, like so many others on the team, a neoconservative Democrat. Cuban-born, he had campaigned for George McGovern, the liberal Democrat, in the 1972 election but converted to the Republican party by way of the "neoconservative" movement that had attracted Kirkpatrick, Elliott Abrams, and other conservative Democrats. Enders had opposed creating the public diplomacy position, too, arguing that it would create an additional center of power and influence.

Still another center of advice and influence was the White House speechwriting staff, a group that had gained considerably in the shake-up. Enders's departure "was like an infusion of fresh blood" and Clark gave free rein, said Bently Elliott, then director of speechwriting. The speechwriting shop was a repository of

---

* Enders had proposed Francis McNeil, a foreign service officer who was returning from a tour as ambassador to Costa Rica, for the job. The White House rejected the recommendation, and McNeil concurred that it was more appropriate to name a political appointee.

Reagan true-believers, and at times they seemed to be making policy.

But, in fact, highly placed officials who were jockeying to influence policy used the speechwriters to carry their message to their rivals, not to mention the President, the country, and the world. Casey had close ties with Anthony Dolan, a newspaper reporter who had worked on the 1980 campaign, and brought him into the White House and frequently stopped at his office when working nearby at the Old Executive Office Building. There was a constant flow of memos and phone calls back and forth between Casey and Dolan. Out rolled phrases for Reagan's speeches like "a dictatorship of counterfeit revolutionaries" in July 1983. "Under Clark, it was a 'pop,' " Elliott said of those heady days. But the linguistic excesses continued after Clark left, and by 1984 Nicaragua had become "a Communist reign of terror" and "a totalitarian dungeon."[21]

In short, the new policymaking organization, as it developed, was anything but orderly. In place of a simple scheme of Enders dominating and others vying for influence, there was now a multipolar power structure. It was unstable and proved to be accident-prone.

When the new policy team got together to formulate aims, they had no choice but to be fuzzy on the critical issues. Nutting had concluded late in 1982 that the Sandinistas had consolidated their internal position to such an extent that they probably could not be removed except by direct U.S. intervention. A draft National Intelligence Estimate in January 1983 had concluded that the amount of pressure from guerrilla groups needed to change Sandinista policy was only marginally lower than the amount needed to overthrow it. Options were limited. No serious military analyst thought the contras could win on their own and the question was to what use could they be put. With the "covert" war now overt and under fire in Congress, any accommodation with the Sandinistas was open to attack from the right as a betrayal of the contras. The issue was postponed and the problem was papered over.

One of the first actions taken after Enders's removal was the approval in June or July by Reagan of a memorandum forwarded to him by Clark which symbolized the new thrust of Nicaragua policy. The memorandum stated that since the Sandinistas were not going to agree to any sort of diplomatic settlement, and since economic and other pressures were unlikely to have much effect on them, the United States must pursue a policy of "destabilization." According to Norman Bailey, then NSC senior director for strategy and plans, *destabilization* was a code word that meant overthrow. But overthrow was not stated explicitly, and top military officials now say Reagan never endorsed such a goal. Like so many other facets of the Nicaragua policy, "destabilization" meant different things to different people. For the permanent government, who had to implement policy, it meant pressures to modify behavior; for the right, who sought a rollback of Soviet influence, it meant overthrow. The language papered over the very real differences. "That memorandum represented a consensus of the people who counted," Bailey said, referring to the war party. "What they didn't know was that they couldn't mobilize the country behind it."[22]

Mobilizing the country was the problem. Enders had invested enormous energies to obtain just $30 million from Congress for El Salvador, and more funds were needed. Meantime, the program was heading into deep trouble. The right had long believed that Enders's approach of working within congressional constraints was a formula for defeat. Now they seized the opportunity to carry the confrontation to the domestic critics of policy.

"The idea was to put Congress on the spot," explained an NSC staffer assigned to implement the strategy. "Let's play the politics of blame." This meant cornering the Democrats and defining the issue in political terms: Were they ready to take the blame when Central America went "sneakers up"? It meant labeling the Sandinistas as Marxist-Leninists, calling the contras "freedom fighters," and asking Congress to pick sides. It was to provide "cover" for Democrats willing to back the President that Clark, in response to a congressional initiative in late July, organized the Kissinger Commission on Central America, a bipartisan group headed by former Secretary of State Henry Kissinger. The commission did not report its results until January 1984, when it drew attention to the social and economic causes of Central America's problems and recommended support for current administration policy, particularly in El Salvador. But merely setting it up bought time and credit in Congress for the administration's troubled El Salvador policy.[23] Lawrence Eagleburger, representing State, had agreed reluctantly to the creation of the commission in an interagency meeting, but expressed fear that any major new funding recommendations by the commission would compete with existing programs for resources.*

The confrontation was supported by a vigorous public relations campaign. To give the administration position a respectable centrist look, White House support of the trend toward democracy in Latin America was emphasized in public statements and the message that the Sandinistas were subverting El Salvador was rammed home by such devices as news leaks linking the Sandinistas to drug-running, displays of captured arms, and "outreach" briefings for select groups of conservative supporters, who would be invited to organize, write their congressmen, and contribute to causes supporting the President.

Those involved felt the approach succeeded. The terms of the debate changed; Democrats preferred to compromise rather than fight. Some aid was generated for El Salvador, and sentiment did indeed shift on Nicaragua. A *Los Angeles Times* poll in May 1983 found that 37 percent of those polled thought Nicaragua was unfriendly while 47 percent were undecided; but in November 1984, a Lou Harris poll showed that 69 percent of those polled thought Nicaragua was unfriendly.[25]

However, confrontation with Congress is difficult to sustain, for Congress generally does not want confrontation. More often than not, its members prefer to bleed a program slowly until the administration pronounces it dead. The strategy with regard to Nicaragua backfired badly in the short term, for the full House voted down aid to the contras in late July 1983, and the Senate Intelligence Committee forced Casey to scale down his goals. In the medium term, the confrontation may have averted a final cut-off of covert aid but proved inadequate to keep the aid running steadily. In the long

---

* But State quickly took advantage of the bipartisan nature of the project to propose a new drive for aid to El Salvador. A confidential memo to Clark from Shultz's executive secretary Charles Hill dated July 14 said that the administration should use the occasion to revive its request for the full $60 million in reprogrammed funds as well as $50 million in supplemental aid for El Salvador. Such a move would "be viewed by many on the Hill as an appropriate short term quid for the quo of an enthusiastic Administration support for the Commission concept." Once the commission was constituted and had commenced its deliberations, "the time should be appropriate for requests for increased funding over and above the 1984" levels. But Hill warned that dropping "a large bill on the table even before the Commission is underway would be seen by many skeptical members as merely a cynical effort to use the Commission as a fig-leaf to cover a vastly increased U.S. involvement, much of it military, in the region."[24]

term, the strategy polarized the Nicaragua issue and made genuine debate about national security interests next to impossible.

In order to "destabilize" the Sandinistas, whatever meaning one gave the word, a combined diplomatic-military strategy was needed. But the absence of a clear goal made that almost impossible. A selection of measures had been collected from around the now-aroused government. Each major agency had made proposals in the Central America task force, which had produced a list of nineteen action plans before it was disbanded in late April or early May. Missing were an escalation scenario and coordination. Instead, each agency "made its contribution" to the vague overall goal, a State Department official said. The timing of many actions was motivated by "emotion, a drive for vengeance," according to a source close to the events.

The principal plans were contributed by the Joint Chiefs with the aim of creating a significantly enhanced military presence in Central America. The most spectacular action centered on Honduras. In addition to joint U.S.-Honduran land exercises, which were expanded and extended, two aircraft carrier task forces would carry out maneuvers at sea.

In a July 13 memo to Reagan that was stamped top secret, Weinberger laid out twelve exercise plans ranging from aircraft carrier exercises near Grenada and Surinam, both leftist-led countries in the Caribbean, down to jungle warfare training for Honduran troops. It proposed building two airstrips capable of handling C-130 cargo jets in San Lorenzo and Puerto Castilla, Honduras, and installing a radar on Tiger Island in the Gulf of Fonseca. Most of these plans were later implemented. Others were not, such as a proposal to spend $150 million to build an air and naval base at Puerto Castilla and to raise the number of military trainers in El Salvador to 125 from the limit of 55. Weinberger also requested an additional quarter-billion dollars in funds for additional military assistance to Honduras and El Salvador—$168 million in additional funds for 1984 and $120 million for 1985.

Weinberger's memo noted that the Joint Chiefs maintained detailed plans for quarantine and interdiction if other measures failed. But the Joint Chiefs plainly wanted to avoid that. In a secret June 15 memorandum to Fred Iklé, Lieutenant General James Dalton, the director of the JCS joint staff, said a quarantine would demand a tremendous commitment of U.S. resources. To be effective, Dalton estimated, a quarantine would require three carrier battle groups with a total of fifty ships and at least fifty aircraft at a cost of $100 million for a thirty-day period. An effective overt interdiction program would require up to 1,000 personnel and cost up to $300 million the first year and $100 million each subsequent year.[26]

A number of smaller actions were intended to cause direct harm to the Nicaraguan economy, but they were uncoordinated. U.S. sugar imports from Nicaragua were slashed by 90 percent in May for no apparent reason. Announcing the move, the White House said it would reduce the resources available to the Sandinistas "for subversion and extremist violence." The matter was not so simple, for only about half the sugar production was owned by the Nicaraguan government, the rest belonging to the private sector. The principal champion of the move at the State Department was Richard McCormack, a former aide to Jesse Helms who was assistant secretary for economic affairs. Enders, in his swan song, lessened the impact by insisting that the cut not take effect until the new fiscal year began on October 1.

Early in June 1983, the Sandinistas expelled three American diplomats from Managua on the bizarre ground that one had taken part in a plot to kill or incapacitate D'Escoto, the foreign minister, with a drugged bottle of Benedictine. In a draconian response, the administration ordered the expulsion of twenty-one Nicaraguan consular officials and the closure of all six Nicaraguan consulates in the United States. Then the administration vetoed a $2.2 million loan in the Inter-American Development Bank for completing a road-building program in a region of small coffee farms in Nicaragua, even though all forty-two other members voted for it. A Treasury Department official said American policy was to oppose World Bank and IDB loans to Nicaragua until the Sandinistas moved to "revitalize the private sector and . . . improve the efficiency of the public sector."[27]

The CIA, which already had one major program under its supervision, contributed smaller covert programs to the list. One related to "perception management," which in this case referred to the use of electronic radio or other signals to confuse or mislead a targeted population. The idea was to spread the notion that the United States was planning an invasion. The CIA argued that creating hysteria would goad the Sandinista leaders into making silly statements and possibly trigger a provocative military move. When Daniel Ortega or Tomás Borge or another comandante would state publicly that the United States was planning an invasion, U.S.

officials scoffed; but it was a sign that the program was working. The impression that an invasion was under consideration that summer was reinforced by U.S. officials at a variety of levels who made a point of citing previous U.S. interventions.*

And then there were the plans that barely got off the ground. In a move to circumvent congressional limits on spending for the contras, Reagan on July 12 ordered the Defense Department to provide additional support to the CIA in its efforts to aid the contras. The CIA requested $28 million worth of equipment to be transferred to it, including medical supplies and aircraft which the CIA would stockpile and provide if the need arose. But the Pentagon's general counsel ruled later that summer that this would violate a law requiring reimbursement for interagency transfers. In the end, the CIA obtained three surplus Cessna aircraft without cost and at cost received ten night-vision goggles, one night-vision sight, and a Bushmaster cannon.[29]

In the context of conventional diplomacy, escalation without a defined goal would seem mindless. The military moves scared Congress and the public as much as they did the Sandinistas; the economic steps hurt the private sector within Nicaragua as much as the public. Combined, the economic, military, and covert actions also sent the unintended signal to the internal political opposition and the armed opposition fighting the Sandinistas that the United States might come to the rescue, a contingency for which there was no plan. Weinberger, Vessey, Shultz, and a great many others in the administration opposed such a step, and even the right was divided. While Iklé at Defense and others are said to have favored a direct U.S. intervention, Kirkpatrick, North, Sanchez, and most of the war party argued that Nicaraguans, specifically the contras, were the answer, even if they could not topple the Sandinistas. With the question unresolved even among the hard right, it is hard to see how

---

* Nestor Sanchez in an interview with the author on July 19 suggested that intervention under a multilateral framework was a possibility. "Anything we do has to be in cooperation with others," he said. Recalling the direct U.S. intervention in the Dominican Republic in 1965, an action later endorsed indirectly by the Organization of American States, he said: "We have in the past. Look at Santo Domingo. We got involved." Four years later, Sanchez said that the scare talk had been justified in the context of a broader program of building pressures against the Sandinistas. "Let them think that it might happen," he said. "Why let them sit fat and sassy and think that everything's okay? Let them think that they have problems."[28]

a military step could have been taken that would satisfy the aroused expectations of Nicaraguans.

General Vessey felt that the escalation, even if not fully coordinated, might cause the Sandinistas to change their course. The evidence is that he was right.

THE BIG STICK

When General Paul Gorman arrived in Panama in May 1983 to take over the Southern Command, there was no contingency plan for a U.S. military intervention in El Salvador or Nicaragua. One reason was that the Joint Chiefs had not been asked to draft such a plan. But by the time he left in March 1985, Gorman had built one from the ground up. It consisted of the new facts on the ground in Honduras: airstrips capable of handling C-130 cargo planes on either coast of Honduras, radars, and semipermanent military facilities designed for rapid expansion to process thousands of U.S. troops. Whatever official name it had, if any, the infrastructure he created became known as "Portavión Honduras," or Aircraft Carrier Honduras, for to all appearances, Honduras had been turned into an American aircraft carrier. Operationally, according to an aide, Gorman foresaw a U.S. intervention only if the Sandinistas did something exceedingly ill-conceived, such as bringing in foreign forces to fight the insurgents or attacking Honduras frontally to terminate their support of the contras. But the likelihood of such a response was lessened by the new Honduran defense capabilities. "I don't think that so long as the Nicaraguans are confident that the Hondurans can defend themselves they are likely to make a major mistake," another aide said.[30]

The most dramatic show of force was sending the U.S. fleet. The object was to show the region that, despite its problems with Congress, the administration had the capacity to move a substantial amount of power into the region on short notice. Too short, it turned out.

Things quickly went awry, and the build-up of pressures on the Sandinistas that Reagan and his national security aides had approved came instead to be seen as an arbitrary show of force. Weinberger had proposed in his July 13 memo that the naval operations begin shortly after August 1. But Clark jumped the gun on July 15, when he recommended diverting the aircraft carrier *Ranger* and seven support ships to Central America. Reagan gave his approval. His haste was politically disastrous. Clark did not tell Shultz or congressional leaders, and the State Department therefore was unable to inform U.S. allies in the area. Johnstone said that top officials endorsed the plan but he had not had a chance to inform Shultz. "Before anybody had a chance to do anything further, we simply ended up with a fait accompli. We had no idea it was happening. But when I read about it in the newspaper, I sure knew what it was, because we discussed it," he said. This was also how Shultz learned of the carrier's movements. Word then leaked to the press that the carrier's movements were part of a much broader program of military pressures, prompting a *Newsweek* cover on August 1 titled "Gunboat Diplomacy." The uproar in Congress contributed to the first major defeat for the administration in the House, which voted down covert aid 228-195. "It was one of those fiascos because we immediately lost the vote on the contras, which was devastating to us," said Johnstone. Actually, disquiet had been building for months in the Democratic House. In May, the Intelligence Committee, headed by Edward Boland of Massachusetts, had voted along party lines to terminate the program; in June, the Foreign Affairs Committee, headed by Clement Zablocki of Wisconsin, followed suit. Boland argued that the administration was violating his 1982 amendment requiring that funds be used only for the purpose of interdiction of arms and prohibiting covert actions "for the purpose of" overthrowing the Sandinistas or provoking a military conflict between Nicaragua and Honduras. Boland's committee said the activities of the rebels "point not to arms interdiction but to military confrontation" and that the continued funding would be counterproductive to interdiction. The firing of Enders at the end of May, the new confrontational attitude in the White House, and finally the gunboat diplomacy contributed to the outcome. In October, the Senate approved aid for the antigovernment rebels but only after cutting Casey's request in half. Aid continued into 1984, but the House vote apparently alarmed Casey. Four years later, North revealed that about this time Casey had begun discussing with him the need for an independent "off-the-shelf" covert operations capability that would be independently financed and not accountable to Congress.

"It's so easy to move ships around," a Clark aide said later. "The attitude was 'Gee, it sounded like a good idea at the time.' "[31]

Despite its abruptness, the move may have had the desired effect.

Vessey's idea was to create an impression in Managua that the United States could invade and might invade even though the Joint Chiefs very firmly opposed any such course. And, regardless of the vote in Congress, the military preparations did move ahead. The ground exercises, which ordinarily would run a few weeks, extended to six months. The laying of the U.S. military infrastructure was done before the cameras of the international press. More warships cruised along the coasts.

Gorman had the support in his build-up of Álvarez and Suazo, both of whom left no doubt of their desire that the Sandinistas be removed, preferably by direct U.S. intervention. He also had their support for injecting some new direction into Clarridge's erratic management of the contra program. But to convert the psychological advantages of the military build-up into policy gains was virtually impossible; that would have required coordination with the State Department. And State's role had been reduced to that of an observer of the policy process. Shultz had been rebuffed when he tried to take charge of policy in May. In July, he had been embarrassed when American warships suddenly headed for Central America. Then in August came another surprise, when Clark's deputy, Robert McFarlane, went on a three-week trip to Lebanon, Saudi Arabia, Syria, Israel, Jordan, and Egypt; once again, Shultz had not been informed. Finally, Shultz handed in his resignation. "Mr. President, you don't need a guy like me for Secretary of State, if this is the way things are going to be done," he said.*

Reagan asked him to reconsider, and Shultz stayed. But he had become almost irrelevant, along with the policies he tried to articulate.[32]

---

* Shultz did not specify the date of his resignation threat, but I and other reporters covering him had the impression it was in early August 1983.

CHAPTER
7

FORCE WITHOUT
DIPLOMACY

AFTER A YEAR of recruiting, training, and reconnaissance, the FDN launched its first major offensive in February and March 1983. Up to then, it had been engaged in isolated sabotage and cross-border raids. Bermúdez had sent in patrols to test support among peasants and villagers throughout 1982, and, depending on the feedback, some units had gone back to their home regions to establish support bases and an infrastructure. By February 1983, Bermúdez claimed to have 5,500 combatants.*

They moved on foot deep into the central part of the country—the coffee-growing highland region around Matagalpa, the more sparsely

---

* Edgar Chamorro, a member of the FDN political directorate since December 1982, estimated that there were no more than 2,500, but James LeMoyne, then of *Newsweek*, quoted Honduran army estimates that the FDN had 4,000 to 5,000 men inside Nicaragua.

populated province of Boaco, and the agricultural region of Chontales. It took up to forty days to march from the border to these areas north and east of Managua. The FDN forces had as many as 600 men in Puerto Viejo in the mountains north of Tipitapa, about twenty-five miles northeast of Managua. The plan had been worked out among Bermúdez, the Argentine military advisers, and Álvarez, and utilized small-unit tactics. There were attacks on interior ministry posts, state farms, police, officials of government ministries, and state corporations.

As incidents began to occur as much as 200 miles apart, the Sandinista leadership became alarmed and called for a session of the United Nations Security Council. There they accused the United States of mounting an invasion. UN Ambassador Jeane Kirkpatrick replied equally disingenuously that it was a spontaneous insurrection. Finally, Reagan topped them both by calling the fighting a factional conflict between different elements of the coalition that seized power in 1979. American allies refused to back the U.S. position, and the debate ended inconclusively.

At the same time as the FDN move, separate but coordinated attacks were underway against government installations and personnel in northeast Zelaya province by members of Nicaragua's Atlantic coast Indian community. Indian country in Nicaragua is vastly different from the rest of Nicaragua, consisting of lowlands, river inlets, and jungle. Sparsely populated by members of the Miskito, Sumo, and Rama tribes, who speak an English dialect and belong to the Moravian Protestant Church, it had maintained a separate identity under Somoza. The Sandinista leadership, judging from its actions, was divided over whether to grant autonomy or keep the region under control of the interior ministry. Steadman Fagoth Mueller, a young Miskito trained as a biologist, had commanded Indian fighters on the Sandinista side during the civil war and had become the representative of the Indians on the Council of State in 1979. In January 1981, he had presented a plan for Indian autonomy that would have kept control of most of the oil and mining resources. Daniel Ortega had seemed to support it, but Borge was opposed. Fagoth rallied international support for autonomy, was arrested twice by the Sandinistas, then fled the country.

Early in 1982, the Sandinistas took the military route against the Indian community, burning some eighty-one villages; at least 250 people disappeared without trace. Indian groups trained by the

FDN had been hitting government offices, posts, and installations since the end of 1981, but the Indian movement took on a direct relationship with the CIA only at the end of 1982.

"I started to look where was the CIA people," Fagoth said. "I talked with people in Miami and asked. Someone put me in contact with the CIA. I said: 'I want weapons for the young boys.' That was December 21, 1982." In February 1983, the agency gave him $600,000 worth of weapons, a half-million bullets, and 2,000 pairs of boots.[1]

In April 1983, a third front opened, but it was more rhetorical than military. Edén Pastora, operating out of northern Costa Rica, declared war for the second time in a year, this time as the Democratic Revolutionary Alliance (ARDE). He claimed fewer than 500 troops but a few months later said the number had grown to more than 2,000. Pastora, still a national hero in Nicaragua and an authentic revolutionary, probably worried the Sandinistas as much by his political proselytizing and radio broadcasts as by his military exploits.

Underlying the success of the armed offensive was the element of surprise. There were no set-piece battles or organized resistance; the FDN established itself with relative ease. Moreover, their offensive may have been helped by a worsened economic and political climate inside Nicaragua. Alfonso Robelo had gone into exile in May 1982 in Costa Rica; hostilities between the Roman Catholic Church and the Sandinistas had led to a confrontation between Pope John Paul II and Borge's bused-in protesters in March 1983. And the harsh repression against the Atlantic coast Indian population awakened outside interest and eventually led to Sandinista amends.

But the FDN found it difficult to capitalize on the discontent. For one thing, Managua had labeled the military leadership Somocistas, and the name stuck, as did their description of the forces as contrarrevolucionarias, counterrevolutionaries, or "contras" for short. The Core Group had pressed through Clarridge for the FDN to "clean up its act" by ridding itself of some of the most notorious Guardia personnel, such as Ricardo Lau, who was Bermúdez's chief of counterintelligence, and Pedro Pablo Ortíz Centeno, also known as Comandante Suicida, a regional commander who often wrote his own orders and executed his own men. Bermúdez resisted, successfully. By this time he had strengthened his standing with Álvarez through an astute political move. In December 1982, Bermúdez had appointed as his chief of staff Emilio Echaverry, the Guardia officer who had been Álvarez's classmate at the Argentine military academy and had introduced Bermúdez to Álvarez. "We reinforced our ties with the chief of the armed forces" of Honduras, Bermúdez said.

A second reason was the sham FDN political structure that the CIA had created in December. In addition to Bermúdez, its members included Edgar Chamorro, a former Jesuit priest and intellectual living in Miami, who became the FDN's spokesman in Honduras, and, in January, Adolfo Calero, former manager of the Coca-Cola bottling plant in Managua. Bermúdez resented the artificiality of the structure and the fact that Chamorro had been assigned to the directorate by the CIA along with several others of the seven. Chamorro said the same of Calero: that the CIA had brought him out and installed him as head of the directorate. Indeed, U.S. government sources said that Calero had been a CIA asset well before he left Managua. Others in the directorate were Marco A. Zeledón Rosales, an industrialist; Indalecio Rodríguez Alaniz, a former university rector; Lucia Cardenal de Salazar, widow of Jorge Salazar; and Alfonso Callejas Deshon, a former vice-president under Somoza from 1969 to 1972.*

The structure simplified itself in time. Bermúdez allied with Calero and each strengthened the other; Calero provided the public face and Bermúdez had control over the military side. Whatever their many differences, Bermúdez and Chamorro both saw the new structure as a CIA creation designed to influence Congress; another apparent purpose was to give Clarridge a handle for easing the Argentinians out of the operation. Providing political leadership that would inspire support inside Nicaragua seems to have been a distant third.[2]†

---

* The choice of Calero to head the civilian side puzzled even the Sandinistas. "Why not Robelo? He is a much better known figure. He has much more political image, history, and tradition and is much, much more intelligent. Calero is a bit small-minded," commented Luis Carrión Cruz, one of the comandantes. Carrión said he thought Robelo would have accepted such an offer and the reason the CIA chose Calero was that he had collaborated with it "from a long time ago" and was considered trustworthy. The real reason may lie with Bermúdez. "I talked to Adolfo Calero months before he left the country and invited him and some other members of the political parties in Managua to come out and establish the political body of the movement," Bermúdez said.

† But the existence of the FDN directorate enabled the CIA to do things that were hitherto out of the question, such as trying to build a positive public image for the insurrection. U.S. government agencies are banned from spending public funds to

The FDN's first impressive showing in the field coincided with a steady deterioration of the CIA's showing in Washington. In January 1983, Patrick Leahy, a Vermont Democrat on the Senate Intelligence Committee, led a fact-finding mission on a tour of Central America and found it to be an eye-opener. In Honduras, he met General Álvarez, who told him directly, "We're going to be in Managua by Christmas." But staff members discovered that CIA officials on the ground had no idea how this was to come about.

Raymond Doty, a retired Army colonel in charge of operations and logistics for the contras, was, along with the station chief, Don Winters, the principal liaison between the CIA, the FDN, and Álvarez. Doty, an old-timer with paramilitary experience in Laos, explained to Leahy that the plan was to link up with the south by mid-1983. Was the intention to bring down the government? he was asked. "If they fall of their own weight, we don't care," Doty replied. But when pressed on the exact goals and strategy, he professed ignorance. "I don't know. That's not my job," he said. "Ask the boys in Washington."

Clarridge went out of his way to make things difficult for Leahy when the senator and his staff investigated a covert program under which Panama was training Pastora forces. Traveling under his pseudonym, Dewey Maroni, Clarridge arrived in Panama before them and instructed the local CIA chief of station not to discuss the matter with Leahy. After a half-day of stand-off, Clarridge showed up the next morning at the Panama Hilton and, sitting on a double bed in the senator's hotel room, answered Leahy's questions. "I suppose he bracketed us the whole trip," said one aide.

Back in Washington, Leahy reported two conclusions. The Nicaragua program "was growing beyond that which the Committee had initially understood to be its parameters"; and, second, "There was uncertainty in the Executive Branch about U.S. objectives in Nicaragua, particularly in view of the goals avowed by some of the

influence opinion in the United States, but nothing prohibits such expenditures overseas or, in the event of favorable media attention, from publicizing that at home. Beginning in January 1983, the CIA authorized the FDN to hire Woody Kepner Associates, a public relations firm in Miami, to assist with slide presentations and information kits in six languages for use outside the United States as well as recruitment literature and posters that were dropped inside Nicaragua. But the FDN leadership, despite expensive European tours, failed to make much of a splash abroad or at home. Kepner said he was paid about $3 million over two years and he believed other firms were also hired.[3]

forces receiving U.S. support." Leahy also observed an apparent lack of coordination between the covert program and U.S. diplomatic initiatives, "with the program appearing at times to be preceding policy rather than following it."[4] The observation proved prescient in 1983. Diplomacy had taken a back seat to military force.

The few remaining pretenses of covertness fell away when in late March the Agency agreed to allow reporters for the *Washington Post* and *Newsweek* to spend ten days with FDN fighters. Their graphic accounts of the fighting and the goals of the fighters fueled concerns in Congress. Representative Boland declared that the administration appeared to have violated the spirit of the Boland amendment. A House Foreign Affairs subcommittee voted a ban on further aid to the rebels, and in May the House Intelligence Committee voted to end the program.

The reason it survived was Thomas Enders, again in a swan song. With the House heading toward a rejection of the program, only a solid Senate committee vote could sustain it, and Enders staged one of the best performances of his career. Arguing that U.S. diplomacy would not work without the program, he convinced the Senate committee not to ditch the program by a strong majority. "He could talk a dog off a meat truck," commented Senator John Chafee (R.-R.I.) of Enders.[5] It was a performance Enders's successor could not repeat. But the committee asked the administration to produce a new finding that clarified its objectives and motives.

In the meantime, Clarridge, under growing criticism in Washington for having organized an offensive to overthrow the Sandinistas, was under attack from his clients in Honduras for failing to support them adequately. In Washington, he dodged the critics by bluffing about the rapid growth of the movement, using figures for recruits that could be verified only with considerable difficulty by members of the Core Group or the two oversight committees. Meanwhile, in Honduras, Clarridge had promised aerial resupply to support the rebels, which he was unable to produce. As news accounts began to depict the rebels' advances and goals, Clarridge suddenly switched roles and set about slowing the offensive. The CIA told Congress that it had ordered the FDN to "shape up" and become more responsive to instructions or face a funding cut-off by September 1983. What raised concern, according to congressional sources, was an abortive attempt by "Comandante Suicida" to capture the town of Jalapa in northern Nicaragua in May, with heavy loss of life and equipment; in

June, "Suicida" was rumored to have executed as many as thirty contra commandos, prisoners, and civilians out of personal vengeance. But Edgar Chamorro said he had the clear impression the new instructions related more to the CIA's continuing fight with Congress than to FDN actions in the war.[6] Chamorro had the clear impression that the CIA had a fight with Congress. "They had to tell Congress that they control us and could slow us down."

Units began returning from inside Nicaragua. Álvarez was shocked. He went to Washington in June 1983, met with CIA and military officials, and told them the rebel troops were desperate as a result of a supplies cut-off. "When the supplies didn't reach them, they had to take the contras out. Then they had to prepare another operation to send them back in," Álvarez said. "In and back, we lost months. It was a Bay of Pigs in slow motion."

"Speak clearly," he told officials in Washington. "If you don't want to go ahead with the project, tell us. It is our territory."

Gorman got the message. He already had the mandate. So peeved was Álvarez over Clarridge's management that he proposed to Gorman that the Pentagon take over the entire operation. They went over the operation and its flaws as well as Honduras's own military needs.

One of the fundamental problems was structural. Ribeiro stayed on through 1983, and others of the Argentine contingent into 1984, leaving finally a month or so after the new Argentine president, Raúl Alfonsín, took office on December 10; but their influence was being gradually diminished. However, in place of the advisory structure the Argentines had built, Clarridge had created a void. Bermúdez attempted to fill it with his own staff officers. Military history is filled with strongmen who have a grasp of strategy, operations, and logistics and carry on unaided. But Enrique Bermúdez was a desk colonel who had never commanded in the field; he was not Lawrence of Arabia. And the Guardia was not renowned as a fighting force. General Vessey's view was: "If you could have gotten all the talent in the Guardia Nacional, you wouldn't have had a coherent strategy." After all, he said, "they got beaten by the Sandinistas." Álvarez was more charitable, feeling that the FDN had not done badly in the face of the obstacles. In neighboring El Salvador, the guerrilla forces had begun setting up logistics networks, infrastructure, and supply arrangements eight years before they started fighting. The contras, by comparison, had been in existence only about a year before their first major offensive.

In early 1983, Álvarez offered to provide his own staff people to assist in strategy and planning to organize the functioning of a new government. But Clarridge would not hear of it. Gorman, with Weinberger's backing, had then offered the use of special forces to train the contras, and had brought a senior Army special forces officer to Honduras for a meeting with Álvarez and the top CIA officials. "We can help. We will talk with the Pentagon," Gorman said. But Clarridge, with Casey's backing, declined. "The Agency does not believe in team-playing," said a military official at the Southern Command at the time.[7]

By summer 1983, with official Washington now energized and Gorman breathing down his neck, Clarridge churned into action, but with less design than ever. The FDN political and military staff were complaining that they had been stopped in midoffensive and denied the promised air resupply. Clarridge took the offensive. At a day-and-a-half meeting in a safe house in Tegucigalpa early in July, he urged the FDN to send its troops back into Nicaragua. To strengthen the leadership structure, Álvarez and the CIA station chief urged Bermúdez to name a commander of the theater of operations; he agreed to the concept but, with Calero's backing, insisted on naming his own man. Clarridge took the opportunity to cut Bermúdez down a notch by citing Edén Pastora as an example of a charismatic leader, a more effective political organizer, and even a better guerrilla than the FDN leaders, who he said were fighting a conventional war.

Bermúdez felt the attack was part of an attempt to replace him fomented by his critics at the State Department. According to Craig Johnstone, however, that was not the case. "For a guy who had associations with Somoza, Bermúdez was always considered to be probably the most acceptable of the group," said Johnstone. "I have no nits to pick with Bermúdez. When [Ricardo] Lau was part of the organization, I had lots to pick with Lau."[8] Bermúdez's reaction was: "Well, I felt the pressure, and nobody told me this pressure was because of Lau." Clarridge may have been needling him to take the heat off himself.

Clarridge did not have additional resources to offer, so he flattered the leadership, telling them that President Reagan often asked about them. "The President is very interested in your cause," Bermúdez quoted Clarridge as having said. "We brief him regularly. He asks where you are, what you have achieved, where you are going."

Clarridge also gave the contras an intelligence briefing weeks before the general public was made aware in the United States. Cuba had been calling up military reserves, which the CIA felt meant they were sending more of their trained light artillery specialists to Nicaragua. The Sandinista army had acquired mobile field kitchens, suggesting they were preparing to fight a long war. And they had acquired big mortars and howitzers, suggesting they expected prolonged fighting. But Clarridge had little available in compensation. Instead, he let the contras in on another secret project that was part of the package of new pressures on the Sandinistas. This was "to isolate Nicaragua from petroleum." It was the first hint that Clarridge had begun building his own small navy, complete with a mother ship, Piranha speedboats, hired Latino frogmen, and demolition experts. It was one of the most counterproductive projects Clarridge carried out other than the mining of Nicaraguan harbors, which followed directly from it.

Meanwhile, Casey was getting nowhere with Congress. In July the House took up consideration of the Boland-Zablocki amendment, which would halt all aid to the rebels. But the administration was traveling in the opposite direction, projecting that the contras would grow in size to 12,000 to 15,000 from the 8,000 to 10,000 then estimated.[9] Appearing before a closed session of the House, Casey defended the contra program as supporting the U.S. goal of interdicting the weapons flow from Nicaragua to El Salvador, according to a State Department source. That shattered what little credibility he had. It also earned him the contempt of many administration aides trying to sell the program. "Marble-mouthed, full of B.S., barely in control of the facts," said one White House aide who had to pick up the pieces after Casey's presentation.[10]

Other than to resume supplies, Clarridge was able to provide one added resource, a small C-47 aircraft to resupply units inside the country. It was nicknamed "the Rusty Pelican." In comparison with the mother ship, Piranha boats, and hired frogmen that Clarridge was assembling, its worth was little. As for firearms, the FDN asked for more and the CIA came back with a novel solution.

The scene was La Quinta Escuela, a Honduran army training camp northwest of Tegucigalpa used to train the contras; the time late August 1983. Ray Doty, known to the FDN leaders as Colonel Raymond, was telling them about a wonder weapon: World War II bolt-action Mauser rifles—4,000 of them. This was the perfect rifle because it could hit a target from a great distance, Colonel Raymond told the assembled regional and task force commanders. It was not automatic and you could control how many shots you fired; so it would not be wasteful of ammunition. The military commanders replied that it was slow-action, putting them at a disadvantage against the Sandinista army, which had AK-47 submachine guns. Without missing a beat, Doty said this was "the jewel of weapons. It was for real marksmen, for the top of the crop, for veteran soldiers who enjoyed fighting. The FDN leadership did not swallow the line, but some of the rifles were brought in, converted to use the same ammunition as AK-47's, and given to FDN sympathizers. Bermúdez prefers not to discuss the story, obtained from Edgar Chamorro. But he confirmed the incident. "That happened. Maybe they ran out of resources."[11]

September was the month of the U.S. military spectacle. As the FDN and the Miskitos carried out attacks throughout northern Nicaragua, U.S. warships exercised off the coast. The first of thousands of U.S. ground troops began arriving for exercises. Secretary of Defense Caspar Weinberger paid a flying visit to Central America, the highest ranking official of the Reagan administration to tour the region up to that time. Weinberger escorted Salvadoran president Alvaro Magaña on a visit to the newly refurbished battleship *New Jersey*, and the next day ARDE rebels flying in light aircraft bombed Managua airport. Weinberger coyly told reporters he was "not really able to share any information which would be very useful" on the air raid. That same day the FDN claimed it had attacked a vital oil pipeline at Puerto Sandino. Other air attacks followed against oil storage facilities in the port of Corinto.

Early in October, attackers in speedboats fired 50-caliber machine guns and rocket-propelled grenades at the oil tanks, setting five on fire. A second strike ran into trouble when a speedboat got caught in the cross-fire. Helicopters from the mother ship had to be called in to suppress the ground fire and create a diversion. The speedboat team said that was their last mission on the Pacific coast. Clarridge had to come up with a new way of shutting the flow of oil; he later hit upon the idea of mining Nicaraguan harbors, an abortive operation carried out in January and February of 1984. The attacks on Corinto caused more upset in Congress, where the House on October 20 voted again, 227–194, in an authorization bill against further covert aid to the rebels.

As the military spectacle unfolded followed by another political setback, Shultz watched helpless and unable to move toward negotiation as he had proposed in his May 25 memo to Reagan. About all he could do was to take the bureaucratic offensive once again by reaffirming his understanding of the official goals and blocking attempts to alter them. The focus shifted to a behind-the-scenes battle over a new covert action finding which the Senate Intelligence Committee required as a condition for further contra support. Shultz preempted the debate with a September 6 memo to Reagan about advancing U.S. policy goals through regional negotiations. Laying out priorities toward Nicaragua in pragmatic order, he listed first the security concerns about Sandinista support for foreign guerrilla movements, then in fourth place, somewhat vaguely, "respect for human rights and political democracy in all countries, including Nicaragua."

Although the draft finding appears to have been hotly debated between Shultz and Casey at the September 17 meeting of the National Security Planning Group, the goals listed at the top of the finished product were suspiciously like those Shultz had put forward: to curb alleged Nicaraguan security threats and "to bring the Sandinistas into meaningful negotiations and constructive verifiable agreement with their neighbors on peace in the region."[12]

But deeds and words were not synchronized. As U.S. troops and warships maneuvered menacingly around Nicaragua, all was quiet on the U.S. negotiating front. Shultz could state his position on U.S. goals in private and in public, but he could not undertake any initiative on that basis.

DIPLOMACY WITHOUT FORCE

With its goals ill-defined and contradictory and upheaval in its power structure of policymaking, the United States had had no bilateral negotiations under way with the Sandinistas since April 1982, nor any prospect for an early resumption. In the vacuum, the four Latin countries on the periphery of Central America—Colombia, Mexico, Panama, and Venezuela—established a multilateral negotiating forum on Contadora Island in January 1983. It was in this forum that the diplomatic impact of U.S. military pressures on the Sandinistas first began to be registered.

Contadora arose in part from the desire of the four countries to play a role on the regional stage, but the real catalyst was the tensions mounting in the region as U.S. diplomacy sat in idle gear. Álvarez's "Red Alert" of August 1982 coupled with his open threats and drive for a military solution raised fears in the region that Honduras and Nicaragua were on the verge of war. Presidents Luis Herrera Campíns of Venezuela and José López Portillo of Mexico, fearing that Honduras might launch a preemptive strike against Nicaragua and force the United States to intervene, wrote Reagan on September 7 about the "grave situation" that could lead to a region-wide conflict and asked for a "joint exploration" of ways to reduce the tensions. They invited Honduras and Nicaragua in separate letters to hold talks. Meanwhile, Herrera Campíns sent his able ambassador in Washington, Marcial Pérez-Chiriboga, to other Andean pact countries, Peru, Bolivia, and Colombia, as well as Panama to discuss what they could do to respond to the heightened tensions. Reagan did not reply to the letter for nearly a month. His October 4 response ignored the contents of the Venezuelan-Mexican initiative and said the solution to the region's problems was "to achieve democratic pluralism within each nation." Daniel Ortega of Nicaragua agreed to the talks, but Suazo Córdova of Honduras said he preferred to meet in a multilateral forum. [13]

Although instrumental in launching the process, Venezuela took a back seat to Colombia and Mexico once the talks got going.

In Bogotá, a new president had been elected in mid-1982. Belisario Betancur Cuartas had made the mission of his four years in office to disarm Colombia's leftist guerrillas and bring them back into politics. A conservative who had once been a militant rightist, Betancur had been elected as a democratic reformer and populist. He was a "red sheep" for his party on security issues and international affairs and immediately distanced Colombia from the Reagan administration by joining its neighbor Venezuela in the nonaligned movement and pursuing a more independent foreign policy than his predecessors. Betancur was fond of saying that peace is like a drum; when you tap one surface, the entire drum reverberates. So he closely integrated his domestic reconciliation efforts with the search for peace in Central America.

Some of Betancur's philosophy derived from a Colombian novelist who became a close confidant—Gabriel García Márquez, who received the Nobel Prize for Literature shortly after Betancur's inauguration. García Márquez had good ties with Castro, the Sandinista directorate, and Presidents François Mitterrand of France and Felipe González Márquez of Spain. He facilitated Betancur's links with them and his rise as an international figure. García Márquez also offered the proceeds of his Nobel prize to the cause of peace in Central America. Critics say that Betancur's unorthodox approach to the peace process, which relied more on the appearance of agreement than on verification mechanisms, borrowed from the novelist's concept of *realismo mágico,* or magical realism.

Mexico at the beginning of 1983 also had a new president, Miguel de la Madrid Hurtado, and he inherited the broader regional role created by his predecessor, José López Portillo, as well as Mexico's worst economic crisis in fifty years. De la Madrid, a technocrat, developed a close relationship with Reagan and generally kept a low personal profile. However, his foreign ministry, one of the few in Latin America staffed by professionals, did most of the technical arrangements for Contadora. With its own revolutionary history and recollections of armed U.S. interventions and the loss of half its territory to the United States, Mexico took a close and paternal interest in the Sandinista experiment, and backed it up with oil. (Mexico and Venezuela had provided all of Nicaragua's needs from 1980 as part of an oil facility for Central America and the Caribbean; but Venezuela had halted supplies to Nicaragua in August 1982 because it was not being paid. Mexico picked up the slack.)

Panama also had entered a new era following conclusion of the canal treaties between Presidents Jimmy Carter and Omar Torrijos and the death in July 1981 of Torrijos in an airplane crash. Panama, like the other Contadora countries, was looking for a new role to play.

Venezuela, in some ways the best placed of the four countries to act as a mediator, instead assumed a low profile. Although the richest country in South America in terms of per capita income, Venezuela had suffered an economic downturn when oil prices fell; in addition, 1983 was an election year and Herrera tried to avoid undue strains with Venezuela's closest trading and cultural partner, the United States.

All four had good domestic political reasons to try to avert a U.S. military intervention in Central America. But the two most active players, Colombia and Mexico, had little previous interest in or familiarity with Central America or its problems. Colombia's political parties were so inward-looking they had not even been members of the Christian Democratic or Socialist internationals and had had few contacts with politicians of the region. Until the discovery of its oil wealth, Mexico had had no resources to offer and also had focused inwardly. Venezuela, the stablest democracy in South America and a refuge for exiled democratic politicians, had long maintained close ties with Costa Rica; its COPEI party, a Christian Democratic affiliate, had maintained close ties with Duarte of El Salvador, who had spent years of exile in Caracas. Panama enjoyed friendly relations with Costa Rica and Nicaragua and also had the hotel and communications facilities for meetings.

To a certain extent, Contadora came about as a reaction to Enders's stillborn effort to organize the emerging democracies of Central America in a common front at the Costa Rica "Forum for Peace and Democracy" in October 1982. Nicaragua had not been invited and refused an invitation to a follow-up meeting. There the project had died. But the following month, Edgardo Paz Barnica, the foreign minister of Honduras, encountered the Nicaraguan deputy foreign minister at the OAS in Washington and asked why Managua had declined the invitation. "We are not going to participate in any group in which the United States is participating," Victor Hugo Tinoco said. Paz Barnica then approached the foreign ministers of Mexico, Colombia, and Venezuela and suggested they remodel the Costa Rican forum as a purely Latin effort, excluding the United States.[14]

From the first meeting of the four Contadora foreign ministers on January 8 and 9, the process would be characterized by high-minded intentions, improvised agendas, and informal procedure. No minutes were kept; the conversations were informal. "We handled it that way so we could speak openly, so no one would feel pressure and take a stand that might compromise his government," said Juan José Amado of Panama, the host foreign minister. "Economics was one of the basic items in the agenda, but everything pointed to politics. How can we change the attitude of the Sandinistas and make sure they can comply with their promises in 1979 to the OAS? How can we approach Guatemala and work with them?"

So it became a political forum. But as military tensions spurred on their effort, the agenda was transformed again into largely security issues. For a year, nevertheless, the foreign ministers and their deputies conducted meetings without military experts present. Panama and Colombia viewed their inclusion as a necessity and felt that military forces would have to be deployed on borders to monitor arms trafficking. But Mexico, whose military is constitutionally constrained from being sent abroad except in war, vetoed it. Contadora operated like that: any of the four had a veto on procedure. In time, the Contadora countries found that diplomacy without force was every bit as problematic as the course Washington was pursuing, force without diplomacy.

Panama contacted the United States and Cuba after the initial meeting to ask for support. Amado said Enders made it clear he did not favor the project. (An aide to Enders characterized him as "hard-headed enough to understand that people in those countries get carried away by rhetoric and improvisation.") But others at the State Department felt it was a worthwhile effort. Cuba also had divided opinions.

Kirkpatrick, who toured the region in February, came away with a more positive impression. Luis Herrera Campíns, the president of Venezuela, laid out the project to her. "I asked her as a person with much influence to tell Reagan that we don't want him to back Contadora but also not to put any obstacles in the way. Because we knew the problem was a Latin American problem and must be solved by ourselves." He also assured her, according to a State Department official: "Don't worry about the legitimate security interests of the United States. We will take care of them." Kirkpatrick relayed the request and a few days later Reagan sent a message back. "He let me know his thoughts about the political facts in Central America, especially the leftists," Herrera Campíns said. "But he said he sided with a peaceful solution, so he wouldn't put up any obstacles to the Contadora process."[15] Kirkpatrick argued that none of the Contadora countries wanted consolidation of a Communist government in Nicaragua, and this could be of use to Washington.

The four Contadora partners invited the five Central American countries—Guatemala, Costa Rica, El Salvador, Honduras, and Nicaragua—to a first meeting in April. But the Nicaraguan envoy refused to meet the others as a group except over dinner. The only agreement reached was to meet again.

In May, following a tour of Central America by Betancur, the four invited the five for what was billed as a preliminary talk about procedure. All accepted. "Someone locked the doors. We stayed there for sixteen hours," said one participant. They produced an agenda listing the political, security, economic, and social problems as well as the machinery to implement and verify compliance.[16]

On July 17, even as the aircraft carrier *Ranger* steamed toward

Nicaragua's Pacific coast, the four Contadora presidents had a one-day meeting without the Central American countries in Cancún, Mexico. A joint statement called for the nations of Central America to sign ten binding treaty commitments, among them pledges to end hostilities, freeze weapons levels, eliminate foreign advisers, prohibit bases, and negotiate arms reductions. But the presidents dealt circumspectly with political issues, saying only that it was necessary that democracy be strengthened. They made no mention of verification.

Their omissions led to contradictory reactions. The Sandinista directorate quickly welcomed the "positive proposals" from Cancún as "a great push forward," and on July 19 proposed its own six-point agenda and announced it would take part in multilateral negotiations. The Sandinista plan focused exclusively on security issues; it was clearly aimed at expelling the U.S. military presence from the region and ending the contra program. It called for a nonaggression pact between Nicaragua and Honduras, a halt in any form of military aid to either of the combatant forces in El Salvador or to irregular forces anywhere in Central America, a ban on foreign military bases, and a suspension of all military exercises by foreign troops. Honduras, concerned that the presidents had left too much out, drew up its own statement, which it called the "Basis for Peace in Central America," and won the backing of Guatemala, El Salvador, and Costa Rica. The Honduran document took up all the missing elements: democracy, internal reconciliation, and verification.

On July 30, the Sandinistas reverted to their pre-Cancún stance by calling for bilateral negotiations with the United States, Honduras, and Costa Rica. In an indirect sense, the negotiations had begun.

Shortly after the Cancún meeting, Special Envoy Richard Stone left on a tour of the region and delivered a letter from Reagan to the four presidents. It was his second major tour since his appointment at the end of April. Reagan again stressed as a top priority that "democratic institutions be established and strengthened as a means to resolve political differences within the Central American states." Both through Stone and through conventional diplomatic channels, U.S. officials firmly reminded the Latin countries that the principle had to be included. "We talked to all about how the agreements should look," said a State Department official. "This wasn't our document, but of the many parties involved, we were one party that had to be satisfied."[17]

Stone carried the point a step further. As previously mentioned,

Enders, in August 1982, had defined establishment of democratic or at least pluralistic institutions as one of four policy goals in Nicaragua, the others being to end cross-border arms traffic and infiltration, stop arms build-ups, and limit foreign military advisers. But the State Department had avoided setting a rigid priority, aware that if democracy was the primary goal, no resolution was possible except by overthrowing the Sandinistas. Stone, feeling no such inhibition, now defined democratization in Nicaragua as the leading goal, which if solved would take care of all the others. Johnstone called this a strategic blunder by Stone that exceeded instructions and helped lead to his downfall.[18]

Inside Nicaragua, members of the political opposition felt they had been abandoned in the aftermath of the Cancún statement and sought outside allies. It is a commonplace that every opposition leader thinks he should be president of Nicaragua and is unwilling to rally behind anyone else. They were divided on how and whether to cooperate with the Sandinistas, uncertain whether to stay in the country or leave, unclear about what the United States planned to do. But they quickly joined forces to do something about Cancún. Visiting the ambassadors of the four countries, they found a warm welcome in Venezuela, which had always cultivated close ties with them. The result was that President Herrera invited twenty-six of them to Caracas. "We said in effect that peace is achieved through democracy, not the other way around," said Enrique Bolaños Geyer, one of the most conservative businessmen in the group. They presented Herrera with a copy of *their* statement, titled "Basis for Peace in Central America," on August 7. Now there were four documents on the table and one roving U.S. ambassador competing for the attention of the Contadora ministers.[19]

Another country to take up the cause of democracy was Costa Rica, whose own smoothly functioning democracy was the envy of the region. Costa Rica conditioned its continued participation on the issue of democratization.

Thus, when the four Contadora foreign ministers met again on September 8 to draft a statement of objectives, democratization was back on the agenda. The Contadora ministers met in advance but were unable to agree on wording, and the five Central American ministers were about to arrive. So Roderigo Lloreda Caicedo of Colombia took it on himself. "Imagine if they had arrived and we had not had a draft," he said. "I told the others to go to bed. I stayed there typing until 2 A.M. I put the draft under their doors." After some more work, they produced a twenty-one-point document of objectives, which really amounted to a laundry list drawn from four sources—the original ten-point Cancún document, the eight-point Honduran "Basis for Peace," the six points proposed by Nicaragua on July 19, and the internal opposition's August 7 statement.* It contained strong statements on verification and national reconciliation, but the strongest was on democratization. The statement called on all Central American countries "to take measures leading to the establishment, or where appropriate, the improvement, of representative and pluralistic democratic systems that will guarantee the effective participation of the people in decision-making and ensure free access by the diverse tendencies of opinion to honest and periodic elections, based on the full observance of the rights of citizens."[20]

"There wasn't much discussion on that among the Contadora four," Lloreda said. The five Central American ministers took the document back to their respective capitals. To the surprise of everyone, Daniel Ortega accepted it in writing on September 26. Both Venezuelan and Colombian diplomats believe that the U.S. show of force—sending in the fleet and holding joint maneuvers in Honduras—made the difference. "I think American pressures played a role in the sense that the Nicaraguans would try to grasp onto Contadora for protection if something happened," said a Colombian diplomat.[21]

Within a month, however, the Sandinistas reverted to an earlier mode by raising the Central American issue at the U.N. Security Council and by offering the United States a set of bilateral treaties, which Foreign Minister Miguel D'Escoto made public shortly after presenting them. The Reagan administration rejected the proposals as a sham because they had ignored democratization.

Exactly how much American diplomacy contributed to the contents of the twenty-one points is not clear; it appears that the U.S. diplomatic role was more supportive than central.†

The Contadora objectives were announced on September 10 and

---

* There are actually only twenty substantive points, but the statement is often referred to as containing twenty-one by counting a reference to the procedural decision to establish machinery to formalize the objectives in the document.

† Johnstone said the twenty-one points was "a good document," but did not claim U.S. credit for it. "If you look at the formation documents of the Central American democratic community to the San José forum documents to the twenty-one points, you'll find a remarkable consistency," he said. "I don't attribute cause and effect to those things. It's just that the situation called for a certain set of things. Different people arrived at them differently."

formally presented as a United Nations document on October 2. But the reaction of the administration was divided. "State hesitated to support the twenty-one points," a Honduran diplomat said. But "we were very satisfied when we got a statement from the White House saying that Reagan accepted it."[22]

One explanation for this puzzling state of affairs is that Assistant Secretary for Inter-American Affairs Motley was struggling to gain control of Central America policy while White House Special Envoy Stone had the negotiating portfolio.

Stone had his own political base, had developed his own style and his own goals, and, according to State Department officials, had been writing his own instructions. He spoke fair Spanish and had developed a good rapport with many leading political figures, such as Betancur of Colombia and Fernando Andrade Díaz-Durán, the foreign minister of Guatemala, who was steering that country back toward democracy.

But all this put him on a collision course with the turf-conscious Motley, who had the title and responsibility for U.S. policy but found himself only a bit player in making and implementing it. Motley's battles with Stone were fought away from the public eye and involved arcane bureaucratic and policy struggles whose significance did not become clear until long after Motley succeeded in having him fired in February 1984.

The White House reaction to the twenty-one points was an example of a fight that Motley lost. Ironically, neither Motley nor Stone had much use for Contadora, although both paid it lip service. The State Department, although formally welcoming the Contadora effort, had kept its distance from the time Contadora was founded. Professional diplomats in the State Department's inter-American affairs bureau felt uneasy about the improvised process pursued by the ministers. The structure of successful mediation was missing—a central secretariat, a team to devise strategy, or an experienced mediator among the foreign ministers. Instead, in the traditional style of Latin American diplomacy, there was a constant flurry of trips, meetings, and declarations. The twenty-one points, moreover, by including democracy, widened the negotiating agenda to the point where it could easily prove unworkable. To endorse this process and give it credibility might remove the possibility of a U.S. diplomatic initiative to address long-term U.S. concerns, centering on security.

On the other hand, Stone, a politician, was attuned to the views of

Reagan and Clark, and the very features that made Contadora unattractive to the State Department made it alluring to the White House, at least in October 1983. The White House aim was to head off a State Department-led initiative, or for that matter any agreement that would leave the Sandinistas in place. It was relatively easy to embrace the twenty-one points on the assumption that this was a nonnegotiable agenda.*

The way to head off a solution that would leave the Sandinistas in place was to help give the contras a role to play in the process, and it is here that Stone in fact made a special effort. Unlike the State Department, which preferred to keep an arm's length from the FDN leadership, Stone devoted unusual attention to them and, indeed, built his diplomatic strategy around them.

"We considered that Stone was our friend, that he had our interest in mind," commented Adolfo Calero. "He was a promoter for the contras, sort of an ambassador for the contras," said Edgar Chamorro. "It was part of the effort to make the Sandinistas look very, very bad."

However, Motley could not stand Stone and mocked his regular appearances at "photo opportunities." "Stone wanted to strut, not to work," Motley would say.

After completing his first trip in June, which had included stops in all the Contadora countries and every Central American state, Stone had received Calero in Washington. He had briefed him about his tour and, according to a Stone aide, had urged him to offer to negotiate with the Sandinistas. At the end of June, Calero had written Betancur and the Contadora foreign ministers asking them to sponsor a dialogue between the FDN and the Sandinistas to end the fighting. Calero also had gone to see Betancur in person. Chamorro asserts that Calero had drafted his letter and made the trip on the advice of Stone or the CIA. "The Americans said this is 90 percent propaganda," said Chamorro, "to make you appear reasonable and

---

* "Stone didn't have much interest in Contadora," according to Harry Shlaudeman, who in 1984 succeeded him as the U.S. negotiator. Neither, according to Latin foreign ministers, did Shlaudeman. One Contadora foreign minister commented: "I don't recall in two years the Americans ever trying to discuss what was going on in Contadora. You would think they would have." One U.S. official familiar with cable traffic from Shlaudeman's visits says the assertion that he had no interest in Contadora was "absolute nonsense." But others say that Shlaudeman's interest, like Stone's, was strictly "pro forma," and he did not try to engage in the process in any serious way.

civilized and willing to have a cease-fire if the other side is willing to moderate its position."[23]

Through the summer, Stone alternated between the Nicaraguan front and the Salvadoran front, where he portrayed himself as a middleman between the Salvadoran guerrillas and the pro-American government in San Salvador. He met Salvadoran guerrilla leaders in August, but nothing came of the talks.

On trips to Managua, Stone put on a performance that borrowed from the Wizard of Oz. "Usually when he came, an attack took place on a cooperative or a bridge or on electrical towers," said a foreign ministry official. "He would come and say, 'Now there. You have a concrete problem you have to deal with. You have two problems: your neighbors and the contras.' " Stone left the impression that the contras had become the key element in U.S. strategy and that the pressures were orchestrated.

It was probably bluff. "Neither did I ever ask for any such action nor was it coordinated. I was coming often enough that it might have happened by coincidence," Stone later said. "As diplomatic envoy, I was not consulted about what acts would take place. I never knew if anything would happen or where or when." Nevertheless, he welcomed any pressure that enabled him to accomplish something.[24]

But if U.S. military pressures and U.S. diplomacy were not coordinated at a time the United States was waving the big stick, to what purpose was either the diplomacy or the pressure addressed? It is a question with no single answer. NSC officials say the principal aim of Stone's diplomacy was to form a united front against the Sandinistas as part of an overthrow scenario. A Colombian jurist who served on Betancur's internal peace commission recalls that Stone was adamantly insisting that the Sandinista junta were Marxist-Leninists and "there is no possibility of any negotiation with them while they are there."[25]

Stone left a different impression in the State Department. "I think he was one of those who thought that the leopard could change its spots," said Undersecretary of State Lawrence Eagleburger.[26]

CHAPTER 8

OPPORTUNITIES MISSED

FOR A BRIEF PERIOD IN LATE 1983, the leopard really did change in appearance. U.S. military and diplomatic pressures had caught Managua's attention, but the invasion of Grenada on October 25 caused genuine shock. Motley, backed up by Shultz, championed the intervention over the resistance of Weinberger and the Joint Chiefs. Motley assessed it as a target of opportunity: Maurice Bishop, a leftist of Marxist sympathies and a close friend of Castro, had been ousted in a bloody coup by a pro-Soviet faction. The small island was in chaos, and five of Grenada's democratic neighbors asked for a U.S. intervention, offering token forces of their own. The intervention was hastily mounted, swift, and effective. Grenadians cheered their American "liberators," who ostensibly had come to rescue American students at an offshore medical school but stayed to install a new government. For the State Department, Grenada was a turning point in the struggle to regain control of the policy process; Motley became known around State as the "hero of Grenada." The Sandinistas and Fidel Castro both drew the lesson that Cuba could do little to defend other leftist governments if and when the United States committed its forces.

The Sandinistas were already rethinking their commitment to the Salvadoran guerrillas at the time. In late September, Julio López Campos, director of the DRI, the Sandinistas' Department of International Relations, said the guerrillas were unlikely to topple the American-backed government. "We triumphed and they haven't. It will be very difficult for them to win." He blamed disunity among the factions—the leader of one rebel faction had murdered another in Managua in spring 1983—and a deterioration of the international scene, in other words the active engagement of the United States in Central America.[1]

Following U.S. intervention in Grenada, the Sandinistas apparently acted on this assessment. They demanded that the Salvadoran rebel high command leave Nicaragua by November 12, dismantle their support structure, and find another source for their supplies. "The Sandinos have decided to expel us and cut off all logistic support to us," Schafik Jorge Handal, a top rebel commander, complained in a note to Roberto Roca, another commander. In a follow-up letter, Handal, Roca, and the three other top guerrilla leaders criticized the "coercive tactics" and "inappropriate management" of the DRI.[2]

Later, in November, Rubén Zamora and other leaders of the political front of the Salvadoran rebels said they were leaving Managua so that their presence would not "provide an excuse for Reagan to invade." At the same time, Daniel Ortega announced that 1,000 Cuban advisers would leave the country. At home, the comandantes relaxed the censorship of La Prensa and had conciliatory meetings with political, church, and business leaders. On December 1, the Sandinistas submitted a draft treaty to Contadora which included the agreed-upon Contadora language calling for free and regular elections in each country, the expulsion of all foreign military advisers in the region, and a freeze on all arms. For the first time, they also expressed a readiness to discuss weapons limitations and reductions in the size of their army, which, at 25,000, was the biggest in Central America.

A week later, the Sandinistas announced that presidential elections would be held in 1985. This was the high-water mark of Sandinista conciliation and clearly a moment of opportunity for U.S. policy. Real options, both diplomatic and military, were available. Shultz recognized the Nicaraguan statements as "vastly different" from those of six months earlier but indicated that State was marking time. "What we want is reality to be put behind the rhetoric. Also, naturally, we want to probe and find out what is there." But he added that the best forum for the probing was, of all places, in the Contadora talks.

Exactly what could have been achieved in negotiations is uncertain, but those who favored them felt that that December was the time to try. "The most auspicious and best opportunity was around the time of Alfonsín's inauguration [on December 10], with the talks to begin early in 1984," said one Motley aide. He compared it to Jimmy Carter's missed opportunity to break with Somoza in December 1978 or January 1979.

This may also have been the best opportunity to search for terms with Castro. "Grenada caught Castro's attention more than anything since the Bay of Pigs," said a source familiar with Vessey's thinking. "I believe there was a way to cash in. We could have done more than we did." Johnstone disagreed. "I think the Nicaraguans were scared to death. I don't think the Cubans were."*

The failure to seize the opportunity with regard to Nicaragua remains one of the lasting regrets of officials across the government.

Vessey and Gorman, having designed and implemented the pressures of the previous months, felt that Grenada was the peak of success. In El Salvador, the army was implementing major structural reforms, and in Washington, Motley's aides began to express growing confidence that completing this process and holding another round of free elections could turn the war around. At the same time, a combination of military, diplomatic, and economic pressures was forcing Nicaragua to change directions. "We needed to sit down with the comandantes and play hardball with them," said the source close

---

* John Ferch, head of the U.S. interests section in Havana, did approach the Cuban government in mid-1983 after Castro's July 28 offer to withdraw Cuban advisers from Central America and curtail further arms shipments. Ferch proposed that in exchange for normal relations with the United States, Cuba cut its support for the Sandinistas. The idea was a deal that "sells the revolutionary movement down the tubes," according to a high U.S. diplomatic source. Before the talks ever got serious, however, the Cubans broke them off. Ferch made a second attempt early in 1985 with similar results.

to Vessey. "Either through lack of coordination or because the problem was more difficult than people realized, we didn't bring it home."

But Johnstone expressed surprise over the Sandinistas' reaction. "I will confess I was mildly surprised that they were as frightened after Grenada as they were. I mean, the situations are not analogous."[3]

In retrospect, it looks as if Motley and Johnstone may have let the opportunity slip through their fingers. At the time, they and most of their senior staff were preoccupied with the aftermath of Grenada, a matter of top priority to the White House, and apparently did not focus on the broader game. The White House in turn was focusing on the aftermath of the terrorist attack on the U.S. Marine barracks in Beirut.

But it was not merely a question of distractions. The military pressures had not been carefully coordinated to achieve specific aims because the aims were not clearly defined, rather, the concept and pace of the exercises were driven by Gorman and the Joint Chiefs. The build-up had occurred in the months when State was in eclipse as the lead policy-formulating agency. Moreover, if Motley wanted to pursue the diplomatic opening, he had to compete with a presidential envoy who was already circulating through the area and who refused to report to him. The situation in El Salvador meanwhile worsened once again. Human rights atrocities occurred with numbing frequency in the autumn of 1983, and although the Salvadoran army for the first time had taken the offensive, it was caught off-guard and disorganized when rebels attacked army garrisons at San Miguel in September and El Paraíso in December.

Unexpectedly, the power structure in Washington shifted once again. Clark, frustrated by the squabbling within the cabinet and the growing criticism of his role in policy management, asked to be reassigned to the Interior Department, and on October 17, 1983, was replaced as NSC adviser by his deputy, Robert McFarlane. Motley gained suddenly in authority even as Stone lost his patron. This began a three-month struggle to dislodge Stone that ended in a victory for Motley and rancor all around.

Politically, the administration found itself in a straitjacket. The hard right would not tolerate risking the existence of the Nicaraguan insurgents to make an all-out effort for a negotiated settlement. But Congress would not support still more pressures even after the administration's military success in Grenada, so tenuous was the support for Nicaragua policy.

And even as one personnel problem appeared to be getting resolved for Motley and Johnstone, another had just materialized in the person of Constantine Menges, whom Clark had installed as special assistant responsible for Latin America at the NSC before quitting in October. Menges, who earned a Ph.D. at Columbia, had a fertile imagination, passionate convictions, a habit of lecturing his peers, and an "I told you so" attitude that caused his tenure in most jobs to be short. In two years at the CIA he had held the post of national intelligence officer for Latin America until Agency professionals could bear him no longer and was then assigned to a post concerned with paramilitary affairs, which was not filled after he departed. His move to the NSC was a cross between a firing and a promotion.

Menges felt that the United States should vigorously promote democracy everywhere. Thus, he supported agrarian reform in El Salvador, proposed covert U.S. action to deal with right-wing death squads in that country, and opposed the use of the Argentine military to train the contras in Nicaragua. Long before there were contras, Menges had come up with the idea that anti-Soviet "national liberation" movements could be used to unseat newly installed Communist governments. In a 1968 essay published by the Rand Corporation, a think tank with close Pentagon links, Menges proposed a "bizarre alternative" based on the "simple and unproven premise" that "Communist regimes are very vulnerable to a democratic, national revolution that is conducted with skill and determination to succeed." The resistance would not strike until six months or a year after a Communist takeover.

"The tactics used would be precisely the same as those immortalized by the Viet Minh and Viet Cong: systematic assassination of key Communist officials at all levels of government . . . establishment of model governments in areas free of Communist government control; attacks on Communist military units known to be demoralized and the like."

Menges conceded that this might sound "like the daydream of a frontiersman who wants to be the Indian for a while," and added that indeed there was a "pinch of political fantasy in these notions." But he noted it had never been tried. Menges's brief essay did not set out any criteria for backing a movement or analyze why some Communist-led movements succeeded and others failed. And he apparently did not pursue the subject in later writings.[4]

While his positions won him support in many quarters, the

single-minded passion with which he pursued them infuriated friends and foes. His job at the NSC was to prepare option papers for the President in the area of Latin America and review speeches and statements before they were published. But Menges, like North, was an advocate, not a paper shuffler, and he turned his energies to causes in which he believed. With Motley on the rise and his own patron, Clark, out of the White House, Menges could not accomplish much except to block proposals he opposed, but that he did with an intensity that made him public enemy number one at the Bureau of Inter-American Affairs.

By the end of 1983, Menges had become a strong advocate not of sitting down for talks but of applying still more military pressures on the Sandinistas. If Reagan would put a couple of aircraft carriers off the coast, Menges argued, the Nicaraguans would call elections under rules that would put their regime at stake. Otto Reich, the new ambassador in charge of public diplomacy at the State Department, enthusiastically shared that view, as did other neoconservative Democrats.*

According to Harry Shlaudeman, a veteran diplomat and executive secretary to the Kissinger Commission, "that would be the Kissinger approach. Scare the hell out of them." Shlaudeman cautioned that "it is very much a problem how far you can go." But the Reagan administration's national security structure was still a semifeudal system with competing baronies. There was no central authority to determine how far was too far. "That was a wasted opportunity. That would not have been seen as a bluff," Reich later said.[5]

The Menges approach, however daring, sounds tame in comparison with what others were planning in Honduras. All that fall, indeed weeks before Grenada, there was talk at the NSC of a far more risky military project. This was for the contras to seize territory, proclaim a free Nicaragua, and force a series of decisions in Washington and in the region leading to the overthrow of the Sandinistas. The covert war would turn overt.

Like so many ideas concerning the contras, the concept appears to have originated with Álvarez. But it was enthusiastically adopted by

---

* Reich counted Stone as being among them. But Stone said he had grave misgivings about mounting such a bluff. He thought Grenada had presented appropriate political circumstances whereas Nicaragua "would have been much, much tougher. . . . To send in the fleet would have been a lie. We didn't want to invade them."

Dewey Clarridge; and Paul Gorman gave it ambiguous but implicit support.

In advocating a liberated zone, Álvarez had switched strategies. In 1981 he had proposed to Casey, Schweitzer, and Clarridge that the contras spread out across Nicaragua, provoke a civil war, and, he hoped, raise an insurrection. At the least, they would create havoc in the countryside. He never expected that even a 20,000-man guerrilla army could defeat a well-supplied and well-trained Sandinista army. But the contras could cause enough of a crisis to provoke the Sandinistas into a massive attack on contra base camps in Honduras, which would afford Honduras the excuse to request U.S. military assistance under the Rio treaty. Time proved Álvarez wrong on two assumptions. In August 1982, the United States showed it was not willing to back him up in the midst of border tensions but insisted he stand down his red alert. And in mid-1983, Clarridge's on-again, off-again supply tactics and his inability to provide any airlift beyond an old C-47 proved that the CIA could not or would not provide assured logistics to back up this strategy. Álvarez's liberated zone thus was a response to Clarridge's inability to deliver either his government or the goods.

Whether or not Clarridge had authority from Washington—and there is reason to suspect he did not—he seemed to buy into the plan. On October 1, 1983, he sat down with the civilian and military leaders of the FDN in Tegucigalpa and told them it was time to take and hold territory long enough to win outside recognition and support. He also urged them to consider a provisional government and prepare to elect Adolfo Calero president and commander-in-chief once they established themselves. He suggested that this be done by the new year. If all went well, the United States would recognize the government and provide direct supplies. In the meantime, he would travel through Central America to garner support.[6] Clarridge left a similar message with Álvarez.

That same day, on a ranch outside of Guatemala City, Gorman and Álvarez secretly met the defense ministers of El Salvador and Guatemala and the commander of the National Guard in Panama. The project, pushed by Álvarez, was to revive the Central American Defense Council, or CONDECA, an anti-Castro military accord organized in 1963 at the behest of the U.S. Southern Command in Panama under which the United States provided equipment and logistical support to the Central American countries. CONDECA had never been much of an alliance and had been moribund since

1969, when Salvadoran troops invaded Honduras in the so-called "soccer war." Now it briefly came to life again. A joint statement was issued saying the leaders had met to counter "extra-continental Marxist-Leninist aggression." If a liberated zone was created—and Álvarez had elaborate plans for its creation—CONDECA could provide the legal fig leaf for a U.S. intervention.[7]*

Anticipating approval, Álvarez late in 1983 began constructing an all-weather access road with the help of contra labor and CIA funds to cover fuel and the leasing of the equipment. He also offered to break relations with the Sandinistas if the U.S. government recognized the new liberation government, and to provide an air-supply bridge should his ten-mile all-weather road not be ready.

Álvarez's plan for a liberated zone ran up against resistance in Washington. It "would keep on turning up," according to Motley, but was never formally reviewed in the RIG. North supported it and repeatedly brought it up, and Clarridge also backed it. Motley felt it was a valid tactic if it could be pulled off, but the FDN in his estimate was in no shape to do it. Vice-Admiral Moreau, representing the Chiefs, could not support it. But Álvarez read from a different set of signals. He found Clark had clear views "on what was needed to be done in Nicaragua." Fred Iklé at Defense thought it was "a marvelous idea" and favored U.S. recognition of a government in exile, according to U.S. diplomats. Vessey and Gorman never told Álvarez formally that the United States would invade Nicaragua, but he felt their actions, including Gorman's involvement in the attempt to revive CONDECA, indicated "we are going to do something." Álvarez talked over his strategy with Vessey, but with such an aura of haziness and riddles that Vessey felt he never actually tried to sell his grand scheme. Álvarez contended that Sandinista resistance would crumble in the first hour and end in less than three days.†

Vessey, thinking as an Army general, felt he could not support "that thing." He thought the plan needed more work, and had real questions about whether Álvarez could deliver on his promises. Who on the White House staff actively backed the scheme is not clear, but there

---

* The territory Álvarez had in mind was 4,000 square kilometers, or 1,500 square miles, of mountainous terrain in northwest Nicaragua that was sparsely inhabited and easily defensible.

† "U.S. generals, especially Army generals, were concerned about casualties in Nicaragua from a military operation," Álvarez said. "I assured them there would not be too many because the Sandinista army consisted of draftees. In the first hour of combat, you'd have mass desertions. Within seventy-two hours, the real resistance would be finished. You'd see Daniel Ortega addressing the crowds in Havana."

is little doubt it was under consideration. "That was the plan in mid-1983: to set up a rival government," said Norman Bailey, then an NSC senior director. "The idea was to have them liberate territory and declare themselves a government." Kenneth deGraffenreid, the NSC senior director for intelligence programs who oversaw covert operations, reportedly told one disbelieving associate, "It's not necessarily a loony idea." Another NSC official said that Stone and Menges were supportive but "they could never quite get everyone on board." A high State Department official said that one enthusiastic backer was Jackie Tillman, Kirkpatrick's assistant. "She was pushing it," he said.

It may have been the plan at the White House, but the top Central America strategist at the State Department doubted the contras were told to prepare for such a move. "I disbelieve that. I would be particularly skeptical of that allegation," Johnstone said. "I'm not saying that there aren't people who advocated that."

The strategy came to naught for a variety of reasons. Foremost was that the FDN simply could not conquer the territory. Bermúdez said later, "At that time it was easier for us to try to do that. They [the Sandinistas] didn't have the army they have now. At the same time, we didn't have large enough forces to do it." Calero opposed having the FDN leadership become a government in exile. "Politically, it was not advisable," he said. "We couldn't have very well done that without causing more divisions" between the southern and northern fronts, he said. He also feared that Congress would halt all aid.

Clarridge's support for the plan may have been its greatest drawback. Álvarez got the false impression from him that the administration backed it. "Dewey supported the liberated zone. We thought that Dewey had the order. But really he hadn't." Álvarez later speculated that Clarridge had been leading him on in hopes of being able to present a fait accompli to the administration. Clarridge's improvisations generally aroused scorn in the U.S. military establishment unless they had solid State Department backing. And Clarridge's scheme could easily have led to a ground war, which State very much opposed.

A further contributing factor was the failure of the attempt to revive CONDECA. State had opposed the project from the start. "I thought it was a spent force," said Johnstone. "It was born in the Somoza period and was in some respects . . . an instrument of Somoza. It didn't serve a useful purpose to try and resurrect something that was so tied to the Somoza period."

The FDN's military commander, Bermúdez, also was very skeptical. "How will CONDECA work if the governments of Central America are not unified in their policy against the Sandinistas? And the Central American armies were very busy fighting the guerrillas in their own territory."

In pursuing his project, Álvarez seemed oblivious to the major political trend in the region, which was moving from an era of rule by military strongmen into one of government by democratically elected civilians. The reaction in Guatemala, the nominal headquarters of CONDECA, exemplified how badly Álvarez had misread the changing politics of Central America. Foreign Minister Fernando Andrade Díaz-Durán, a banker and confidant of the military and the centrist political sector, had not been told of Álvarez's meeting with the military leaders of Guatemala, El Salvador, and Panama about reviving CONDECA.* When he learned of it the day it occurred, he contacted his Salvadoran colleague Fidel Chávez-Mena and the two of them, both smooth and capable operators, blocked the follow-up planned by Álvarez, a meeting of the presidents of the three countries to establish a political coordinating body. Both felt that Álvarez was pushing far too ambitious a concept. This sealed the fate of CONDECA.

A Latin American expert attached to the Joint Chiefs said he thought Álvarez had "put it over" on Gorman, who had little background in the region. "Gorman had so close relations with Álvarez that he had no choice. But everyone in the region knew that without Guatemala, there was no revival of CONDECA. The only way CONDECA could work is if the political organization is there first."

CONDECA did not actually die until six months later, in April 1984, when it called a joint exercise and almost no one came. Álvarez's vision died that same month, when he himself was ousted by fellow officers.

With war strategies such as these afoot and key people in high places preferring anything but diplomacy, it is understandable that Shultz and Motley did not rush into a diplomatic initiative, however

---

* I was traveling to Miami on October 1 on the same flight as Andrade and asked him about the CONDECA meeting that day, which I had heard about from U.S. sources in Guatemala. "I have no knowledge of any meeting of CONDECA," he said. "However, if there is a meeting which I don't know of . . . it is strictly a military matter . . . it is not my field of jurisdiction." Actually, it was his jurisdiction, for the follow-up meeting would have involved the presidents of the countries; only in Guatemala, with a military chief of state, would that have meant the same individual.

opportune the moment. Before he could attempt anything serious, Motley had to consolidate his authority, which meant outmaneuvering or ousting his rivals. Neither Menges nor Stone was one to keep his head down. In the meantime, Motley signed onto and backed what in the context was a more moderate and less risky military move—the mining of Nicaragua's harbors.

STONE'S OUSTER

On October 17, 1983, the day William Clark left the NSC, Stone and Reich were both in Paris briefing political officers from U.S. embassies around Europe on Central America policy. Reich called his wife in suburban McLean, who told him a small tornado had knocked down trees in their back yard but just missed their house. Reich told Stone: "A tornado hit Washington." Stone, misunderstanding, replied: "Yeah, I know."[8]

Stone's demise, three months after his patron's, left bitterness all around. Stone had thought he still had the presidential mandate. Recognizing that pressures were having an impact in Managua, he had stepped up his diplomatic efforts and was about to make his one big shot at diplomacy with the Sandinistas when Motley launched his counterattack. "We tried as hard as we could to get a deal," said Stone. First he convinced every resistance leader to agree to lay down his weapons and run for office if the Sandinistas would hold elections "on an open playing field." He then prepared to go to Managua to get talks started between the parties with Betancur as mediator. The plan raised eyebrows around the inter-American affairs bureau.

"Stone had developed a view that if the Nicaraguans sign onto elections, it doesn't matter how much Soviet presence there is and whether they were helping the guerrillas in El Salvador," Johnstone said. "He and Betancur started bouncing off of each other. But Stone could never get interagency approval for his approach." Motley was openly contemptuous of Stone and Betancur. "They deserved each other," he would say.

Stone scheduled his visit to Managua for mid-December. But Motley beat him to the punch.

It was Saturday, December 10, in the middle of the Argentine summer, when Motley laid his trap for Stone. The archrivals were in the official U.S. party headed by Vice-President George Bush to attend the inauguration of Raúl Alfonsín as democratically elected president of Argentina. Motley sought a separate meeting with Daniel Ortega but was told that, as head of state, Ortega would receive only Bush. So Motley asked Bush to introduce him to Ortega, and told the latter he wanted to visit Nicaragua soon. Ortega invited him to accompany him on his own airplane; but that was too soon for Motley. Instead, Motley returned to Washington with Bush, stopping in El Salvador on the way. Two days later, Nicaraguan officials phoned the U.S. embassy in Buenos Aires to say that Motley was welcome to visit. Stone, who had not left, was upset; he checked with Washington and found no one who knew what the trip was about. He proceeded to Caracas and checked in again. This time Eagleburger told him that he had not been aware of Motley's trip but that it appeared the vice-president's credibility was on the line because he had introduced Motley to Ortega.

"If Motley goes to Nicaragua, how can I go two days later?" Stone asked. So he broke off his trip and returned to Washington.

Motley then flew to Managua, sat down with the comandantes, and proceeded to slice up his rival. "Let me describe how we work in the United States," he said. "I am the one dealing with policy on Nicaragua. Stone is a propaganda front. I am the man with whom you should talk. That should be clear."

It was a message his listeners had not anticipated. "We found out from that about the conflict" in the Reagan administration, one foreign ministry official said. Another sign of the division was that, unlike Stone, Motley never mentioned the contras in his conversation with the Sandinistas, the official added.

Stone was furious about the snub and persuaded Reagan to state publicly that he retained confidence in his special envoy. He finally got to Managua on January 5, sat down with Ortega, and attempted to pick up where he had left off. But the illusion of power had been shattered.

The second act of the decline and fall of Richard Stone began with another inauguration, this time of the new Venezuelan president, Jaime Lusinchi, on February 2, 1984. Again the two rivals were present, along with Shultz. "You here again? I thought you only attended funerals," Motley gibed at Stone. Lusinchi told the visitors that he wanted to be helpful in the peace process and asked Stone to return to Caracas to talk with him. Motley went back to Washington and began organizing the visit by calling in intelligence experts, whom he asked to prepare a briefing for Lusinchi. Stone was not invited until the second planning session. Learning how Motley had altered his mission, he stormed out and went to Shultz.

"If Motley isn't curbed, I'm going to resign," he said. Shultz replied that that was up to other authorities; meanwhile, the best compromise would be for him to go to Caracas and carry out the mission as Motley envisaged it. While in Venezuela, Stone was told that his resignation had been accepted.

CONFLICTING SIGNALS

The power struggle in Washington, and the conflicting diplomatic signals it generated, had a parallel in the management of the contra program on the ground. In the course of 1983, the contras had been given five different tactical signals by the administration. Early in the year, they had been urged to take the offensive. In late spring, they had been called back, ostensibly because of a shortage of supplies, and supposedly told to shape up or risk losing congressional funding. In mid-summer, they had been told to resume the offense but given no new resources. Meanwhile, Clarridge had launched his own small navy to mount spectacular actions which would be credited to the contras. And in October, they had been encouraged to liberate territory and declare a free Nicaragua.

To end the year, they now got a sixth piece of advice from U.S. sources: Keep your heads down because 1984 would be an election year. This reputedly came from an NSC official involved in congressional liaison, Christopher Lehman, brother of Navy Secretary John Lehman. Lehman was on a familiarization trip to the region and sat down with members of the contra civilian leadership. He told them U.S. experts had studied Central America and had concluded that it was the ideal place for guerrillas because of the difficult terrain. For reasons of proximity and geopolitics, the United States would not allow the Sandinistas to consolidate their political power. The Sandinistas were expansionist by nature and if they were allowed to stay, they would inevitably support guerrillas who would take advantage of the terrain. Thus, it would take a lot of men to get the Communist guerrillas to leave and for this reason the administration had decided the Sandinistas had to be removed from power. However, he told them, they should understand the nature of American politics, that in an election year you do not precipitate a major military action.

The account of Lehman's remarks is from Edgar Chamorro. Lehman confirmed it with the exception of the advice regarding keeping their heads down in 1984. "I didn't counsel them to back off. I would be counseling them to go forward," he said.

Another NSC official said that the advice to the contras to keep their heads down until Reagan's reelection originated with Oliver North in late 1983 and early 1984. "Ollie was putting that message out," said Norman Bailey. It was also a message that originated with members of the Senate Intelligence Committee, who provided the only hope for new funds to sustain the program into 1984 and beyond.[9]

The message should have been driven home by congressional action in mid-November 1983. The administration had sought $50 million for the 1984 fiscal year, which began on October 1. The Democratic House had voted to cut all covert aid twice, in July and in October, whereas the Senate Intelligence Committee had voted 13-2 in September to make almost the full $50 million available. Finally, in conference, both chambers agreed on November 18 to the sum of $24 million for six months, a result that was meant to keep Casey on a shorter leash by requiring him to return for more funds.

This presented Casey with the prospect of an almost year-round dispute with Congress in place of the six-month-long wrangle dictated by the budget cycle. Meanwhile, the program had gotten so big and brought so much grief to the CIA that it was becoming unmanageable. This was the context for Casey's unusual offer late in 1983 to turn the contras over to the Defense Department. Casey brought it up at an NSC meeting, but Weinberger turned him down. For one thing, Defense did not want it. A second reason, raised by NSC staff, was that, by statute, covert programs of this nature must be carried out by the CIA and not Defense. "Pontius Pilate, all over again," said a high military official of Casey. He added: "It just wasn't feasible for us."[10]

MUTUAL VETOES

As 1983 drew to an end, confusion reigned in Central America about the goals of U.S. diplomacy and the process of U.S. decision-making, as well as the goals of the insurgents.

Had Reagan wanted to remove the Sandinistas through direct military action, Honduras had offered him an open invitation.

Álvarez felt a U.S. intervention was the logical next step in the joint venture to support the insurgency that had begun in August 1981. He had developed a plan for the contras to seize territory in order to provoke a clash with the Sandinistas and had begun construction of a road to improve resupply. With the support of his civilian president, Roberto Suazo Córdova, he was prepared to commit the Honduran army and offer the use of Honduran territory as the springboard for an American intervention. Álvarez had even found a fig leaf for a U.S. intervention in the form of the revival of CONDECA. But Reagan had not made up his mind; the Joint Chiefs wanted nothing to do with a military intervention, and while Gorman implicitly endorsed the revival of CONDECA, the State Department did what it could to scuttle it.

On the other hand, had Reagan wanted to use the military pressure to achieve a negotiated settlement on favorable terms with the Sandinistas, there was hardly a better time than in the period following the U.S. intervention in Grenada. The combination of naval maneuvers, ground exercises, and contra strikes deep into Nicaragua had had its impact in Managua; the Sandinistas had even moved up the timetable for national elections. Yet conservatives who were in control at the White House following the ouster of Thomas Enders would not tolerate a negotiated settlement with the Sandinistas.

The two sides exercised blocking vetoes on each other.

As a result, 1983, the year of the big stick, was also the year of missed opportunities.

CHAPTER
9

THE PRICE OF
CONFRONTATION

After three years of frustrating stalemate, U.S. fortunes in El Salvador showed signs of an upturn in the first half of 1984. Vice-President George Bush had paid a dramatic six-hour visit to San Salvador at the beginning of December 1983 and presented a list of demands to the military leadership. Most were met by early January. A new military command was installed; some military officers who had been linked with death squads were transferred, allowing the authorities to get a grip on the free-lance vigilantes; and the army stood back and let the political process unfold. The deal was precooked, for Motley and Johnstone had arranged a visit by Carlos Eugenio Vides Casanova, the defense minister, to Washington three days before Bush's trip. "We told him [Casanova] what was going to happen and, if there was going to be a continuation of assistance, what the Salvadoran response was going to have to be," Johnstone said.

Military setbacks occurred, but the professionalized structure of the Salvadoran high command was better organized to respond. On January 11, the Kissinger Commission issued its bipartisan report endorsing administration policy in El Salvador and asking for a substantial increase in military aid as well as a five-year $8 billion package of economic aid for the region. The recommendations helped assure a stable bipartisan basis of support for U.S. policy in El Salvador. Turning to Nicaragua, the panel assessed that the Sandinistas posed a threat to the security of the region and called for a comprehensive negotiated settlement, but could not agree whether the contras should be supported until that was achieved. On the political front, El Salvador held its first round of presidential elections on March 25, and José Napoleón Duarte, the centrist Christian Democrat with wide support in the U.S. Congress, won a substantial plurality over Roberto d'Aubuisson, his rightist opponent. In May, Duarte won outright. With his victory, obtaining military aid from Congress was no longer a problem. The events in El Salvador left the Sandinistas more isolated than ever.

Fidel Castro took note of the shifting winds when the Cuban state news media dispatched two reporters to San Salvador after Duarte's first-round victory. They obtained press cards like other foreign reporters and asked tough questions at Duarte press conferences, including whether he planned to follow through on pledges to hold peace talks with the leftist guerrilla groups. In this oblique manner, Castro entered into indirect dialogue with the American-backed government. The reporters returned for Duarte's inauguration on June 1.

"The real question is whether Castro is willing to sell out the FMLN to save Nicaragua," noted Harry Shlaudeman. He was referring to the possibility that Castro would cease providing support and transportation facilities for the Farabundo Martí National Liberation Front, the military wing of the Salvadoran guerrillas. Shlaudeman, a veteran U.S. diplomat, had replaced Stone as roving ambassador in February 1984. "I think at one point he may have been close to doing it. That one point was after Grenada."

For pragmatic diplomats, this seemed an ideal time to consolidate gains and test the waters by reopening the negotiating track. Johnstone developed scenarios for the United States and Nicaragua to resolve differences. But it was not to be. From late 1983 well into 1984 "the State Department's schema were serially rejected [by others in the administration]," a Johnstone aide said.

The hard right read the trend line differently than the pragmatists. They saw developments in El Salvador, Nicaragua, and Grenada as vindicating the confrontational approach and called for a ratcheting up of pressures. McFarlane described this as the macho mentality at work, the "we showed them" attitude.

Once again, as in 1983, there was a fundamental divergence in Washington in assessing the political and military situation and remedy. As State searched for a negotiating vehicle, Casey, Weinberger, Kirkpatrick, Meese, and their minions stood ready to block it. To solidify their position the hard right began articulating in public two interrelated theses about Nicaragua that conflicted with any negotiating stance.

The first was to label Sandinista Nicaragua an incorrigible Marxist-Leninist regime with close Soviet and Cuban ties that must not be allowed to consolidate power. Iklé had said it in a controversial speech in Baltimore in September 1983. "We must prevent consolidation of a Sandinista regime in Nicaragua that would become an arsenal for insurgency, a safe haven for the export of violence."[1]

By early 1984, a second notion had taken hold among the hard right. This was that the contras were the instrument to prevent consolidation. Not many thought the contras could topple the comandantes, Iklé least of all, but the Sandinistas' delay in responding to the rebel offensive during 1983 made it an open question. What the right was not prepared to accept was a negotiation with Managua that implied selling out the contras before they reached their potential. Neither idea was new, but articulating them in public helped to establish a self-reinforcing dogma that could be used to fight anyone advocating accommodation with the Sandinistas.

The conservative dogma pointed to confrontation within the administration, with the U.S. Congress, and ultimately with the Sandinistas. But the key question was whether the priority was to neutralize the State Department as a policy-formulating agency, to shore up Reagan's political position at home, or to affect the situation on the ground in Nicaragua, for they were often at odds.

Conservatives argued that confrontation had the twin benefits of polarizing U.S. public opinion while provoking greater repression inside Nicaragua. The end result would be an America awakened to the threat of a repressive Marxist-Leninist state on the American mainland. But the dilemma remained: if democracy in Nicaragua was the goal of U.S. policy, how could this goal be advanced by a plan intended to radicalize the adversary?

"Most conservatives agreed this might drive the Sandinistas faster into the Cubans' arms. They would say it is a marginal setback because they are going into the socialist camp anyway. So it doesn't matter," said a senior U.S. diplomat. Another ranking diplomat commented: "I'm not sure we did anything but speed up the process."[2]

Unwittingly, in creating and publicizing its own dogma, the right also created its own trap. The fruit of confrontation with Congress and the State Department was likely to be a greater reluctance to fund or support the program. Documents released during the Iran-Contra hearings more than three years later revealed that the growing polarization between the White House and Congress over Nicaragua policy was the principal reason Casey in early 1984 launched his secret search for third-country funds, turning first to South Africa, then Israel, and, through Robert McFarlane, Saudi Arabia.

Conflict between pragmatic and ideological viewpoints is common-place in government. What is abnormal is that Reagan refrained from choosing one side or the other but tried to affiliate with both. He favored confrontation with Managua but maintained full diplomatic relations. He called the Sandinistas Marxist-Leninists, implying they could not be trusted in negotiations, but he allowed negotiations to go forth fitfully. While proclaiming Nicaragua a cancer that had to be removed, he ruled out the use of U.S. force. Underlying his ambivalence was the varied advice he was receiving from his aides. The State Department felt the Sandinistas were there to stay, but the hard right insisted the contras had a chance of victory.

Casey played a central role in this endeavor, for he not only oversaw the contra program but also controlled intelligence about contra activities. As Congress became ever more estranged from the program, he became ever more driven to assure its survival. Diplomats who served in Central America believe Casey regularly crafted his intelligence presentations to make the point that the contras were effective and successful in really hurting the Sandinistas. "He carried that garbage straight to the President, who believed him," said one former ambassador.[3]

The fantasy of contras triumphant had no basis in reality; but

Reagan was not one to choose between advisers or discard a dream. The outcome was predictable: confrontation and conciliation were pursued along parallel, competing tracks. Neither could succeed and both could fail.

The problem for the right was that despite the rhetoric calling for confrontation, they had no agreed-upon plan for a military solution. Not surprisingly, it was in the military area that three major problems arose in 1984. Álvarez was ousted as Honduran armed forces commander on March 31. The CIA mined Nicaraguan harbors, which became an international controversy in April; the mining did just enough damage to outrage Congress but not enough to hurt the Nicaraguan economy. The third problem was predictable: starting in mid-1984, the Sandinistas undertook a massive rearmament and military expansion in response to the contra offensive. In the face of these developments, confrontation lost any meaning as a foreign policy and became simply a theme of bureaucratic and domestic politics.

So focused were conservatives on the struggle within the administration and with Congress that many were probably caught unawares when the military option disappeared in the first half of 1984.

It departed in the person of General Gustavo Álvarez.

THE UNRAVELING BEGINS

Álvarez had made many contributions to the resistance. First and foremost, he had offered Honduras as a sanctuary. In 1980, he had supported and supplied the rebels with arms before they were a cohesive force. He had devised the concept of overthrowing the Sandinistas with the help of the insurgents and put it before Casey and the NSC in April 1981. In 1983, realizing that Clarridge and the CIA could not deliver on promises, he had urged the Pentagon to take charge. (The CIA resisted, but later Casey came up with the same idea, whereupon the Pentagon resisted.) When the United States backed away from what he saw as an ideal chance for a direct confrontation with the Sandinistas, Álvarez in late 1983 had proposed creating a liberated zone and set about selling the scheme to U.S. government leaders. In short, to the extent that any one person had provided a guiding vision and strategy for the contras, Álvarez had been it.

But by late 1983, Álvarez's scheme for a liberated zone had been shunned in Washington, and the impact of Reagan's indecision began to be felt in Honduras. Álvarez and Suazo repeatedly put the proposal to Gorman, who kept a prudent distance. Álvarez had put the idea to Vessey, but Vessey felt he could not commit the U.S. government to support that kind of project. "Then the Hondurans got goosey," said a senior U.S. military official. They saw they had 12,000 to 16,000 insurgents on their hands with no clear chance of success, and the thought of so many dissatisfied contras, which Honduras could neither absorb nor control, began to preoccupy different levels in the Honduran armed forces. "That certainly contributed to Álvarez getting the boot," said the official. "The army began to realize early in 1984 that it was being asked to do a lot for the United States but it was not getting much in return. They saw Álvarez as the culprit," said a Honduran officer.[4]*

In the first three months of 1984, Álvarez saw Gorman only once and met Negroponte four or five times, but only when there was a visiting American delegation in town. Meanwhile, he continued working on his plan for capturing Nicaraguan territory. In February, Álvarez consulted other Central American defense ministers on changes in the structure of CONDECA so that it could operate as a combined force. In March, he began moving supplies by Honduran army helicopters to the rear of the proposed liberated zone.

April 1 was a Sunday. Álvarez was planning to travel to Washington for meetings with Vessey, Gorman, McFarlane, Casey, and other top officials; high on his agenda was the topic of contingency plans for a military intervention in Nicaragua. Álvarez never made it. He was ousted that Saturday. There was surprise all around the region, but especially in the U.S. embassy and CIA station in Honduras. Gorman also had had no inkling. Some accounts say Álvarez's foray into politics had provoked a falling-out with Honduran president Suazo. But it appears Suazo learned of the ouster only at the last minute. More likely, this was an internal coup by senior officers who

---

* Another factor was that Álvarez ignored domestic political sensitivities by accepting the U.S. plan for a regional military training center where U.S. Army special forces trained Salvadoran troops. Using Honduran soil to improve an army that had waged war on Honduras a decade earlier was expedient and economic from the U.S. viewpoint but poor political judgment in relation to Honduras, where it aroused nationalist opposition across the political spectrum.

resented Álvarez's leadership style, pressed by Walter López Reyes, the air force commander who succeeded him.*

One day after his ouster, CONDECA's first joint maneuver began. It was called Granadero I (Grenadier I), a transparent wordplay on Grenada, and was to last from April 1 to June 30. Guatemala, El Salvador, and Panama were invited to take part in a ground and sea maneuver, and Costa Rica was invited to observe. The Pentagon handout said the aim was "to reassure Central American nations of our continuing support and cooperation in the improvement of regional defense capabilities."

That was an understatement. "We had a vision of an exercise that would show the Nicaraguans all the players were in our sandbox, while they have only the Russians and Cubans," said a top Gorman aide. But the plan backfired badly. "All the Central Americans said they would play. But they wimped out on us." The result was a U.S. exercise with Honduran participation. There were 800 Army engineers, 250 Air Force personnel, about 800 other U.S. troops, and 1,200 Hondurans. Still, the troops improved two airstrips, one of them at Jamastrán near the Nicaraguan border, adding to the extensive work done in 1983.

Gorman was philosophical about the failure to revive CONDECA. "He described our activities as 'groping in a dark closet,'" said his aide. "We may not be even 50 percent accurate. He did things he would not repeat because they were not productive." But the departure of Álvarez was a real setback. Walter López's first message to Negroponte was "We're anticommunist but we're nationalistic," an embassy official recalled. López began treating Negroponte as an appendage of a previous regime. He refused to confide in him and preferred to let him discover major decisions in the press. Thus,

---

* According to an account told by a top military commander to a U.S. diplomat, Álvarez's Prussian style of command and political ambitions led to his undoing. At a meeting of the high command on March 16, Álvarez apparently berated several unit commanders by name for inadequate performance, among them López and Colonel Riera Lunatti, another powerful commander. On March 30, Álvarez flew to San Pedro Sula by executive jet. Only a duty officer met him; the base commander was at a soccer game. Álvarez phoned López and, using abusive language, either fired him or came close to it. López resented the criticism, for Álvarez's trip was not official business but to attend a meeting of the conservative political grouping called APROH. López met other commanders who had been criticized by Álvarez and threatened personal revenge, but his fellow officers told him: "Don't do that. We'll do it institutionally." López personally arrested Álvarez, forced him to sign a document giving up power, and led him in handcuffs to the plane that flew him to Costa Rica. (Álvarez later claimed he never signed the document.)

Negroponte learned from leaks to the foreign media that Honduras wanted a revision of the 1954 treaty of military assistance. For Gorman, it became a good deal harder to get things done with López. For the FDN, life got more complicated as López, with the concurrence of fellow officers, began to restrict their presence and activities. The contra project began to unravel, and the Hondurans began to reassess their role.

For the true-believers promoting the cause in Washington, meanwhile, the preoccupation was not strategy or facts on the ground, but money. Casey's management of the project and his disdain for the oversight process had made the program all but unsalable in Congress. Skirmishing in the summer and autumn of 1983 had left little doubt in the administration that 1984 would be a lean year for contra aid. Congress had approved $24 million, half the sum sought by Casey, in hopes of keeping him on a tight leash. But the irrepressible Casey had spent funds faster than projected, and in mid-February told Motley that the money would run out within three months.

As he searched for ways to sustain the program, Casey engaged simultaneously in three high-risk ventures. Without telling the State Department, he had begun inquiring into possible support from third countries with whom the CIA maintains close liaison, according to documents released during the Iran-Contra hearings in mid-1987. In January, he had raised the possibility of assistance with a high-level visitor from South Africa. By early March, the South Africans had taken the bait and said they were "optimistic of positive support to past requests" should the CIA send over a high-level visitor. Casey decided to send Clarridge.

His second gamble was in seeking funds from Congress. This time he worked with the State Department, in a move devised by Motley. Circumventing the Senate Select Committee on Intelligence, which supervises CIA programs, he went instead straight to the Appropriations Committee, which writes the checks for supplemental spending, to obtain $21 million in funds. Barry Goldwater, the Arizona Republican who headed the intelligence panel, got wind of the maneuver and called a hearing on March 8 to chew Casey out. The committee was angry and distracted, and when Casey slipped a sentence into his prepared testimony about current contra activities stating that "mines are being placed" in Nicaraguan waters, without saying by whom, neither senators nor staff asked for details.

The bitterness of Casey's clash with the Senate panel, the last haven of support for the program in Congress, alarmed the White House and spurred the search for third-country financial support. In the process, Robert McFarlane set a pattern for intragovernmental deception that later would tear the administration apart. McFarlane's problem lay in Reagan's reluctance to decide a strategy when faced with competing sources of advice. Casey enthusiastically backed the idea of approaching third countries and charged ahead unasked; Shultz was dead set against it. McFarlane resolved the matter by working with Casey and not telling Shultz.

The committee saw Casey again on March 13 and was about to approve more funds when ships in Nicaraguan harbors began to detonate the mines. The mining was Casey's third gamble, and it imperiled funding from all sources.

Casey predicted more "possible difficulties" in Congress and told McFarlane in writing that he was exploring the possibility of obtaining equipment and matériel for the contras from South Africa. Indeed, the white minority regime, according to a CIA cable, agreed to assist. In his "eyes only" secret memo, he also noted that McFarlane had suggested Israel as a possible alternative source. This "should promptly be pursued," Casey said, all but ordering him to initiate the contact. Casey also proposed setting up a foundation to funnel nongovernmental funds to the FDN.

McFarlane thought the program had been run badly, and asked Israel to provide training and direction as well as funds. The Israelis balked. Shultz heard about the request weeks later, in mid-April, from the U.S. ambassador in Tel Aviv and quickly admonished McFarlane against solicitations. "We should not get dependent on others. We must do it ourselves," Shultz said he told McFarlane on April 18. Shultz thought the administration should act to "maximize the chances of persuading Congress to come back on board and give support. I felt if we actively solicited third countries, we would cut against those objectives in our arguments with Congress."

Two days later, McFarlane told Howard Teicher, an NSC staff aide, to try Israel again, this time asking for matériel "of any sort." He was told to say this was "an important matter to us," and if the Israelis "should decide that they can help, it ought to be done bilaterally although we would be pleased to provide a point of contact." McFarlane also passed the word that he had been "a little disappointed in the outcome but we will not raise it further."[5]

Meanwhile, Casey's prediction of "possible difficulties" from the mining had proven to be an understatement. Clarridge visited the white minority regime in South Africa from April 9 to April 13, but in the uproar being raised over the mining received last-minute instructions to seek no assistance. The effort was called off a few weeks later due to what John McMahon, the deputy CIA director, called the "current furor here over the Nicaragua project."[6]

ADMIRAL DEWEY AND THE MOTLEY CREW

The secret mining operation is sometimes described as a scheme hatched by Clarridge and Casey, with the implication that the State and Defense departments were dragged in against their will. In fact, the operation was approved by Motley's Restricted Interagency Group (RIG), and Motley was very much on board. "People who are saying that Dewey did it on his own are casting unfair blame," said a Motley aide. CIA officials and some Motley associates even thought he originated the idea. "Tony was gung-ho on that kind of thing. Tony had all sorts of colorful ideas," said a fellow assistant secretary of state. Motley recalled it as Clarridge's brain child, but admitted that he consciously decided to back it to the hilt. The two men saw the plan through from beginning to end; they explored the idea, won the agreement of the RIG, obtained Reagan's approval, organized the operation, and then in their own fashion briefed the congressional oversight committees.

According to McFarlane, Reagan made the decision over the course of two meetings of his top national security and White House aides. "The President was fully involved and approved the recommendation by most around the table to go ahead. There was some disagreement on it, and then some people kind of waffled." But like the original decision to launch the covert war itself, the discussion was unfocused and notable for its omissions. Absent was a thoroughgoing analysis of options and risks by the Joint Chiefs of Staff. The CIA stressed the advantages without examining the downside.[7]

The mining was an example of the perils of formulating policy in a small, secretive, and homogeneous group. The foursome who comprised the innermost policy circle—Motley, Clarridge, Moreau, and North—were action-oriented men with military or paramilitary backgrounds who had no compunctions about covert operations. But they had little or no background in international politics. Nestor

Sanchez was also present, but stayed in the background. "Nestor would play along, but Moreau was the heavy[weight]," said another member of the inner circle.[8]*

The assumption they made was that the mining, or the news of it, would cause ships to stop calling in Nicaragua for a time. They were wrong, and as a consequence the operation failed. Operational failure was compounded by public exposure, embarrassing Congress. Clarridge and Casey, instead of treading with care, made a bad situation worse by carrying on their feud with the oversight committees.

So Congress terminated the entire contra aid program—or thought it did.

It is not hard to see how the decision-makers went wrong. In order to gain control of a diffuse and unwieldy power structure, Motley had streamlined the policymaking process by confining the key decision-making to the group of five people, each representing one of the central agencies—State, CIA, JCS, NSC, and DOD (Pentagon)—who made up the Restricted Interagency Group. "If you had to make things work as envisioned on paper," said one RIG participant, "it wouldn't work." The four in the innermost circle reached their decisions by consensus; each had a veto. If all agreed that an idea had merit, each made a separate approach to his boss. If Shultz, Casey, Vessey, and McFarlane agreed, the CIA would produce an intelligence finding that would be brought to Reagan for signature. It was the same method Enders had used—winning agreement at the middle level and forcing a decision at the top level.

That ended the consultation process. "We would get agreement at the center and ram it through our buildings," the source said. "At times it was amazing how we could get things done."

The system produced some croppers, but a defender said it also squelched many schemes that were still farther-out. The mining exposed its central flaw: the absence of an expert review, a devil's advocate, or other self-correcting mechanism. The NSC ought to have insisted on such a mechanism so it could present genuine alternative options to the President for decision. But the NSC representative on the RIG was not a disinterested party; North was a zealous advocate. Officials outside the RIG felt uncomfortable about the absence of critiquing but said they were intimidated. From the time of Enders's

---

* Actually, they were not operating in complete isolation from the State Department bureaucracy, because Johnstone was also frequently in attendance.

ouster, the internal debate on Nicaragua had become so suffused with anticommunist ideology that questioning that ideology was tantamount to disloyalty, according to two individuals involved in the outer circle of decision-makers, the interagency groups. Those who doubted the aims or means were quickly removed. "There was a paranoia about questioning the program," said one. Judgments warped. "Everybody's reaction was that this was a logical next step. No one expected there would be a public outcry," said the second official. "*We* thought that the mining was an attempt to convert the program from a brutal war in the countryside to going after government resources."

The process of formulating and implementing policy bore the earmarks of "groupthink." According to Irving Janis, who popularized the term, groupthink is a byproduct of the "concurrence-seeking tendency" of a group. It "fosters overoptimism, lack of vigilance and sloganistic thinking about the weakness and immorality" of the target group.

Nestor Sanchez was probably the most cautious member of the RIG as well as the most experienced, having helped supervise the CIA overthrow of the Arbenz government in Guatemala in 1954. Sanchez summed up the atmosphere in the RIG: "You had to be careful," he said. "To raise a question was to be a negative thinker."[9]*

Reagan approved the plan in December 1983, and the RIG became a targeting committee to decide where the mines would be placed. Intelligence committee staffers later dubbed the enterprise "Admiral Dewey and the Motley crew."†

---

* Janis, drawing from the examples of Pearl Harbor, the Korean War escalation, escalation of the Vietnam War, and the Bay of Pigs, said a similar set of presumptions underlies most foreign policy debacles. There is the illusion of invulnerability and the assumption "luck will be on our side." Group members "become very reluctant to carry out the unpleasant task of critically assessing the limits of their power and the losses that could arise if their luck does not hold." There is the "illusion of unanimity"—when people who respect each other's opinions arrive at a unanimous view, "each member is likely to believe that the belief is true." Some group members suppress personal doubts for fear of being labeled soft or undaring, and their silence is taken for consent.

† The exact date of the decision is not known, but preparations were under way for some months. John Wallach of Hearst Newspapers reported on July 17, 1983, that a team of CIA and Defense officials obtained detailed maps of three major Nicaraguan ports from the Defense Mapping Agency in February and March and the mining originally was planned for May. But Enders apparently blocked it. "It was debated in the Core Group shortly before I left. It was then set aside," he said. In late summer 1983, FDN officials publicly claimed they had mines and were considering using them; this may have been a trial balloon to test public reaction.

Motley viewed the mining as an assault on the Nicaraguan economy that would frighten oil shippers from supplying Nicaragua and place the Nicaraguan economy "in a stranglehold," making them "look inward." In practice, this meant halting all shipments from Mexico, which was the principal oil supplier. It was assumed that no one but the Soviet Union would continue supplying oil under the circumstances. Johnstone saw the aim in slightly different terms, to scare off all world shipping, not just oil transports. Vessey had gotten the impression that the main purpose was to build up the contras' image and other purposes were secondary. North and Clarridge and their principals may have had still other expectations.

The operation was a strange hybrid: a conventional military operation carried out under CIA cover with the overt psychological purpose of making news that would influence decisions by international shipping lines. In function, it was a naval blockade on the cheap. If the official goal had been a conventional sea blockade, it would have had a military back-up plan in case of failure. But U.S. military involvement would have amounted to an act of war, which no one wanted. So there was no back-up. Another flaw was the flimsiness of the cover. Covert operations by definition must be plausibly deniable by the government. For some reason, Motley and Clarridge had failed to plan for the contingency that U.S. involvement would be exposed. "You don't have to assume that it becomes public. There are many things that are never tagged to us," a source close to the planning said. But this was not your average covert operation; this relied on publicity to succeed. Success or failure was likely to embarrass the CIA.

The mines selected for the job were "bottom sitters" containing about 300 pounds of explosives. They were described as "nonlethal," consistent with the objective of deterring and not sinking international shipping. Most navies use mines with deadly intent, and the first problem Motley and Clarridge encountered was that "firecrackers," as nonlethal mines are called, were not being produced for any Western military arsenal. So the CIA had them assembled to its own design specifications at a workshop in Honduras. The choice of location was probably the first operational mistake, for Sandinista intelligence operatives had penetrated the FDN.

Contract employees known as "unilaterally controlled Latino assets," or UCLA in Agency jargon, placed the mines in January and February 1984 in the Pacific ports of Corinto and Puerto Sandino and the Caribbean port of El Bluff. These soldiers of fortune were from Ecuador, Guatemala, El Salvador, and other countries, and had carried out attacks against the same ports the previous autumn. They used speedboats based in a CIA "mother ship" anchored beyond Nicaragua's twelve-mile limit. The ship was believed to be a converted oil rig service ship with helicopter landing pads and ramps to launch the boats.

The planners anticipated that word of the mining would spread quickly and that Lloyds of London, the insurance brokers, would cancel insurance, deterring commercial shipping. Detonations would reinforce the message. But, like so many other things, the notification itself went awry.

The FDN was to claim the credit, thereby distancing the U.S. government from the operation. But Managua radio scooped everyone on January 3. The Sandinista radio account, moreover, accurately asserted that the CIA was directly supervising the mine-laying. The FDN had to play "catch-up," and two days later issued the disinformation that it had done the mining. Edgar Chamorro, then the FDN's head of communications, recalled that "George," the CIA deputy chief of station, woke him up at 2 a.m. on January 5 and "handed me a press release in excellent Spanish. I was surprised to read that we, the FDN, were taking credit for having mined several Nicaraguan harbors. 'George' told me to rush to our clandestine radio station and read this announcement before the Sandinistas broke the news."[10]

Among shipping lines that served Nicaragua, the battle of press releases was more likely to arouse amusement than worry. For not a single mine had detonated. Further, Motley and his planners ought to have been aware how smoothly insurance brokers and shipowners had adjusted to the far more real dangers to shipping of the Iran-Iraq war.

"We assumed a big ripple of news," said a senior State Department official. "The Nicaraguans would sweep them up in due course, but there would be an element of uncertainty. Deliveries would be stopped for thirty days.

"Nothing like that happened," he continued. "No one cared. International shippers ignored it. It didn't affect one shipping line's schedule. Insurance companies were blasé about it."

Two small fishing boats at the Caribbean port of El Bluff were the first to detonate the mines and sank on February 25, demonstrating that the deadliness of the mines was a function of the size of the ship. A Dutch dredger was seriously damaged at Corinto on the Pacific coast on March 1; a week later a Panamanian freighter detonated a mine. On March 20, a Soviet oil tanker reported damage at Puerto Sandino on the Pacific coast, leading to a Soviet protest note. "George" brought an urgent message to Chamorro. "The same agent instructed us to deny that one of 'our' mines had damaged the ship to avoid an international incident," Chamorro recalled. Liberian, Panamanian, and Japanese ships also triggered explosions. On March 22, the State Department denied any U.S. role in the incident and credited the FDN. This was a low point for the State Department's credibility, and within a fortnight the facts came tumbling out.

At first the mining aroused as little interest in the news media as it had in the insurance world. Moreover, despite several weeks of incidents, the Sandinistas withheld comment. "For days before and after I sent the story, officials referred to the mining using a series of euphemisms," said Stephen Kinzer of the *New York Times*, who wrote the first complete account from Corinto on March 15. Only when the Soviet tanker detonated a mine did the Sandinistas make a major flap; it quickly became a focus of attention in Washington. Still it took the Sandinistas time to work out their public relations strategy.

For a short while, the mining had the intended effect. "You could breathe the anxiety of the Sandinistas. This was really the most powerful blow," recalled a former Venezuelan foreign minister who was in Managua at the time. "But this terrible thing was changed in seventy-two hours. It had a boomerang effect when [the administration] had to apologize."[11]

In Congress, the mining became a national issue when Senator Barry Goldwater, the chairman of the Select Intelligence Committee, complained that he had not been briefed. The Arizona Republican, known as "Mr. Conservative," thought he had restored a working relationship with the CIA that had not existed since congressional oversight began; he was dismayed to learn that Reagan, his political soulmate and protégé, had personally approved the operation.

In a scathing letter to Casey, he said he would not have supported the mining had he known about it. "I am pissed off," he wrote on April 9. "Bill, this is no way to run a railroad. . . .

"The President has asked us to back his foreign policy. Bill, how can we back his foreign policy when we don't know what the hell he is doing? Lebanon, yes, we all knew that he sent troops over there. But mine the harbors in Nicaragua? This is an act violating international law. It is an act of war. For the life of me, I don't see how we are going to explain it."*

A few days later, McFarlane stated in reply that "every important detail" of the mining "was shared in full by the proper congressional oversight committees." He said he could not account for Goldwater's claim to have been kept in the dark, for the House committee had been fully briefed on January 31 and the Senate informed on March 8 and March 13. Yet these briefings were well after the mine-laying operation began, the Senate briefings even after the first mines had begun detonating, and Goldwater said it fell short of the 1981 law requiring briefing on "any significant anticipated intelligence activity." The language of the law implied that the briefing had to occur *before* the event. When Casey refused to apologize, Daniel Patrick Moynihan, the Democratic co-chairman, resigned his post in protest.†

The outcome was a rebuke of the CIA in the Senate, which voted 84-12 against the use of U.S. funds to "plan, direct, execute or support the mining of the territorial waters of Nicaragua." It was a nonbinding resolution, but a strong reproof that revealed bipartisan opposition for the first time. The House approved a similar resolution 281-111.

Not until April 26 did Casey apologize to Goldwater for failing to keep the panel better informed. He also said that the mining had been halted. Moynihan then withdrew his resignation. But the damage had been done. As a result of the flap over the mining, supplemental funds were not appropriated and U.S. military support was suspended for more than two years.

Most intelligence professionals view the mining as one of the worst disasters in a covert operation in a decade or more. Its collateral damage was political, ushering in a new era of mistrust in the oversight committees. But Motley felt it was a good plan at the time and years later continued to defend it.

---

* Among CIA officials there is a lingering suspicion that the letter was drafted and disseminated by Goldwater's chief of staff, Robert Simmons. But Simmons said Goldwater dictated the letter himself; however, the staff chief raised no objections to its contents. He suspected the leak of its contents to the press came from a senior Democrat on the committee, but at least one reporter said he got it from the Republican side.
† McFarlane and Casey were technically correct that Goldwater's committee had been informed, since Casey had made his oblique reference to the mining in his March 8 testimony about his appropriations request.

Abroad, the mining caused acute embarrassment. Britain called it a "threat to the principle of freedom of navigation." France called it "a blockade undertaken in peacetime against a small country, which presents serious problems of political ethics." France voted for a UN Security Council resolution condemning the mining. The United States cast a veto; Britain abstained.*

France also offered to send ships to sweep the mines if "one or several friendly European powers" were willing to cooperate, a move that earned an immediate U.S. rebuke. A State Department spokesman said the French offer "might facilitate [Nicaragua's] export of revolution." Diplomatic sources say Richard Burt, assistant secretary for European affairs, called in the French ambassador. "We understand if you send economic assistance. But no military assistance. This is our hemisphere" was how one diplomat paraphrased the message.†

---

* Later that summer, the mining caused deep embarrassment to U.S. diplomacy in the Middle East. Nonlethal mines were sown in the Gulf of Suez, apparently by Libya, which damaged nineteen or twenty ships including vessels from the Soviet Union, Poland, and Saudi Arabia. This time the United States, Britain, France, and the Soviet Union dispatched minesweeping and support ships to help clear the area. But when Egypt sought to bring the issue before the United Nations, U.S. Ambassador Nicholas Veliotis had to urge the government to desist, fearing it would give Nicaragua a new platform for criticizing the United States.[12]

† In fact, what torpedoed the French offer was a diplomatic gaffe in Bogotá. Claude Cheysson, the French foreign minister, sent Colombian president Belisario Betancur a highly sensitive message in which he denounced the CIA mining as "a direct attack against the efforts being made by the Contadora group" and offered French minesweeping vessels if other countries would join in. He also asked Betancur if he would be willing, "alone or with the chiefs of other friendly nations, to solemnly and publicly denounce obstacles to the freedom of navigation and the attack against common law such as the blockade of a nation that is not in a state of extreme belligerence."

Betancur inadvertently published the Cheysson note before he had ever read it. The cause of the blunder according to a Betancur aide was that the French ambassador to Colombia dropped off the note at Betancur's office on the evening of April 2 without alerting anyone to its sensitivity and importance, and it landed in a pile of papers for routine attention by Betancur. Cheysson also had sent a message to Mexico of a far more general nature that was clearly intended for public consumption. The two messages arrived in the respective capitals by coincidence while Mexican president Miguel de la Madrid was visiting Bogotá. The Mexican chancellery forwarded its Cheysson message, and Foreign Minister Sepulveda discussed a joint response with his Colombian counterpart, Lloreda, early the next day. Betancur approved the statement and, assuming he had received the same message as de la Madrid, told his secretary to search it out and hand copies to the press along with the joint statement. The first that Betancur saw of Cheysson's note to him was when he read it in the newspapers.

Attached to the very sensitive letter was their very bland joint statement. It was

On April 9, Nicaragua asked the World Court to find the mining and U.S. support of the contras a violation of international law. State, anticipating the move, had announced the previous day that it would not accept the court's jurisdiction relating to U.S. disputes with any nation in Central America for two years.

As Goldwater's angry letter made clear, the administration had little legal leg to stand on. At least part of the legal research before the mining had been done by Clarridge himself.

"Did you get any legal advice?" Moynihan asked him at a closed-door hearing of the Senate Intelligence Committee after the event.

"We checked on the Geneva conventions," Clarridge replied.

"Who checked?" Moynihan continued.

"I did. I didn't see any problem with it."

Clarridge had not consulted the CIA's legal counsel or the State Department, although he may have spoken with the in-house lawyer in the CIA's operations division.

For the contras, who had resumed their offensive in October and November 1983 after Clarridge had recalled them, the events of spring 1984 were a terrible blow. Not long after the mining flap, the House Intelligence Committee concluded that the Agency had illegally reprogrammed funds to pay for the mining. More than $1 million of the $1.2 million in costs for the mother ship had been charged to "overhead." The House panel already had voted to delete all funding for the covert program for that year. Now the Republican majority in the Senate panel was soured, quashing hopes of further CIA funding for the contras. The final votes to suspend all aid came in October, but the program was dead in the water as early as May.

Reagan was determined to keep the program going and, as the signs of trouble began to multiply, told McFarlane in effect to keep the contras together "body and soul." McFarlane assigned the task of liaison with the contra leadership to North, while the national security adviser himself pursued other foreign donations, this time with more success. The process involved a series of top-level deceptions within the administration. In May, McFarlane sat down

---

high incongruity. "We highly appreciate the interest expressed by Your Excellency for the problems of the region, and your hopes for the success of the Contadora Group efforts in which we are currently engaged together with the presidents of Panama and Colombia," they said.

Had this not happened, Betancur would have explored the possibilities of getting other countries involved, the aide said.

for a routine meeting with Prince Bandar, the Saudi ambassador, and told him the administration was "headed for a substantial setback, a defeat . . . [that] would represent a substantial loss for the President." Days later, the envoy pledged $1 million a month through the end of 1984. He was as good as his word, and the money, deposited directly into a Calero bank account in the Cayman Islands, paid for a stockpile of weapons which the contras drew from into 1987. McFarlane briefed Reagan and Bush as well as deputy NSC adviser John Poindexter on the contribution, but he did not tell Shultz, and in meetings of the National Security Council and the smaller National Security Planning Group pretended to oppose solicitation, according to Shultz. Casey played along, telling Shultz he opposed solicitation when he was secretly egging McFarlane on.*

At the same time that McFarlane was deceiving Shultz, North was deceiving McFarlane.

Without telling his boss, North had already begun talking with Casey in early spring 1984 about creating a private network to supply arms to the contras. At Casey's suggestion, North contacted Richard Secord, a recently retired Air Force major general who had a wealth of experience in logistics from the Vietnam War, where he helped direct the CIA's clandestine support of Laotian mercenaries against North Vietnam. Secord had left the Pentagon under a cloud, due to purported business connections with Edwin Wilson, a renegade ex-CIA agent who became principal arms merchant to Libya's Muammar Gaddafi. With North's help, Secord sold arms to the rebels starting in 1984, delivered them in the course of 1985, and took over the entire resupply operation in 1986. But McFarlane did not learn of this until the Iran-Contra scandal broke at the end of 1986.[13]

EXIT CLARRIDGE, ENTER NORTH

In May, Clarridge brought North to Tegucigalpa, where he introduced him to the FDN leadership as another "top military man." "I bring him to assure you that we will not abandon you even if Congress stops the aid," Clarridge told FDN leaders. "He is going to be very close to this." Calero recalled North's pep talk: "We will

---

* Three years later, McFarlane was full of regrets for this action. "I'm guessing it was probably out of concern for further dissemination and compromise of that relationship, and damage and embarrassment. I don't think there's any justification for it."

keep on pressing, we'll keep on soliciting funds." North also assured him, correctly, that "the President would say it himself."[14]

Clarridge visited again, but this was his way of signaling good-bye. In the wake of the mining, the entire CIA team dealing with the contras was replaced by October.* North traveled to Central America so frequently in the next year that he became known as "Night Rider."

Before closing the chapter on the offshore raids, Clarridge made one last pass at helping his friend Edén Pastora. En route to its home port in a Gulf state after completing the mining and other harassment off the Pacific coast of Nicaragua, the mother ship made a detour. After passing through the Panama Canal it headed, on Clarridge's instructions, for the southeastern coast of Nicaragua, where Pastora was trying to capture San Juan del Norte, a fishing village at the mouth of the San Juan River. Pastora intended to declare a liberated zone and establish a provisional government within ninety days. Clarridge provided gun and rocket support from a helicopter based on the ship on April 9. This incident emerged in testimony before the Senate Intelligence Committee.

"Were you shooting at people or things?" one member asked Clarridge.

"At the weeds," he replied.

"Who's in the weeds?"

"We don't know."

"Why did you do this?" Clarridge was asked.

"Because Pastora asked for it as a favor."[16]

The bottom fell out of CIA funding at a moment when the rebels were at their maximum effectiveness. "We had them under great pressure," said Bermúdez. "They were having problems with the mothers of kids they were recruiting by force. And I felt we couldn't be in a better position."

Pastora held San Juan del Norte for three days. At the same time, the FDN claimed its fighters controlled more than 8,000 square

---

* Even the unflappable Calero seemed piqued at the manner of Clarridge's leave-taking. "I saw a lot of Maroni [Clarridge]. And I have high regard for him. He was very enthusiastic, very deeply and personally involved in the effort of trying to help us out as much as possible. And we were close. You know you deal with these people and then they disappear."[15]

miles of territory. Citing what it called "the biggest military offensive launched by counterrevolutionaries," the Nicaraguan government canceled the traditional Easter vacations for government employees.

But the other side was in even greater disarray. At the time the CIA was trying to unite ARDE and the FDN. Pastora, losing on the ground and under pressure from Costa Rica to lower his profile, turned on the CIA and blamed it for a police raid on ARDE offices in San José. He declared ARDE would "never align" with the "genocidal . . . Somocista guard." The CIA then cut Pastora loose. Actually, that is not the entire story. The CIA all along had been divided over Pastora, with Clarridge his main defender. Now Clarridge was on the way out; the Agency was running out of funds and supplies and Pastora's outburst may have been used as an excuse. Pastora completed the break a month later when, after he was nearly killed by a bomb blast at a press conference, he publicly allowed the possibility that the CIA was responsible.

And there is still another twist. While negotiating, with CIA support, for a union between ARDE and the FDN, Alfonso Robelo, the cooking oil magnate who had headed ARDE's political wing, tried to displace Bermúdez as FDN military leader. "It was a few weeks after Álvarez was changed," Bermúdez said. "Robelo came down to talk with the new armed forces chief and asked them to kick me out. So did Pastora, Carlos Coronel, and all the southern group. They saw an opportunity to destroy me because of our close association with Álvarez." The effort failed, but left Bermúdez with an abiding distrust of Robelo.

For Clarridge, this capped a hectic three-year performance. Many who knew him thought he deserved to be canned for the fiascos ending with the mining, the biggest CIA covert disaster in recent times. Unlike the usual high-risk covert operation which is designed to preserve plausible deniability, this one was so badly conceived that it landed the U.S. government in the dock at the World Court in a case the administration knew it would lose. Clarridge's reward was being named director of covert operations for Western Europe, one of the most prestigious posts in the CIA. This was understandable, said a former CIA official familiar with the events. "If anyone had the ability to kiss and tell, it was Dewey. If he had been badly punished, he would have squawked. You'd have John Dean in the courtroom." The Bureau of Inter-American Affairs did its part by giving Clarridge its "superior honor award," the second highest

award given by the State Department. Motley felt that Clarridge had
been asked to build an army and had done it in magnificent fashion.
In Honduras, Don Winters, the station chief, and his deputy were
removed. They had failed to predict Álvarez's ouster or to put
sufficient time, effort, or money into the new military leadership.
That was a mistake the CIA would not repeat.[17]*

However these events may have embarrassed the CIA, nothing
would prove more damaging to the contras, the long-term security
concerns of the region, or U.S. interests than a process that began
in June 1984—the Soviet Union's decision to supply a new
generation of military hardware to the Sandinistas, including the
Mi-25 helicopter gunship. The mining, which had been linked
openly to the U.S. government, and the contra offensive then
under way handed the Sandinistas two powerful arguments to carry
to the Kremlin in their own quest for military victory. Soviet
approval of the Mi-25s, apparently given in connection with Daniel
Ortega's trip to Moscow in mid-June, in turn not only altered the
tactical situation on the ground and shifted the military balance in
the region to the benefit of the Sandinistas but also quite possibly
stiffened their terms in the Contadora regional peace negotiations
and in direct talks which opened with the United States that same
month. The "flying tanks" began arriving in November 1984 and
were deployed in combat for the first time in August 1985.

Meanwhile, the loss of congressional confidence in the covert
operation constituted a short-term gain of turf for Motley and
Johnstone in Washington. Casey had been cut down in size. At the
same time, Gorman's activities were becoming a political issue. The
General Accounting Office, the congressional watchdog agency,
charged that Gorman had spent funds improperly, and as the fall
presidential election approached, the Pentagon prudently trimmed
the pace of military activities. By the process of elimination, there
was by midyear not much else to try but diplomacy. The idea of a
diplomatic initiative had the added merit—for some the only merit—
of defusing a potentially hot issue in the fall election campaign.

---

* Actually, Winters was also rewarded with a promotion from GS-15 to GS-16 in the
eighteen-grade civil service promotion system. The main reason for his removal was
his close identification with Álvarez. Winters and his wife had adopted a Honduran
child, and Álvarez agreed to be its godfather.

CHAPTER 10

LAST STAB AT DIPLOMACY

THREE YEARS at the center of the policy process had neither broadened Oliver North's vision nor tempered his method of operation. His whole persona remained that of the action-oriented lower-echelon infantry officer who would batter down walls to carry out his mission. After the release of the film about the mythical Vietnam veteran who, in defiance of the bureaucracy, single-handedly liberated a prisoner-of-war camp, he took the nickname "Colonel Rambo."

North wore his patriotism on his sleeve and in the run-up to Reagan's reelection victory, his politics as well. The highest compliment he could give another man was to say "He's a damn fine American."

At one point, he lost his bearings altogether as he mixed up policymaking with the 1984 election campaign. North was in the chair at an interagency meeting to discuss the latest U.S. government publication criticizing the Sandinistas. He opened with a bang.

"I think you ought to understand the purpose of this meeting is to help get the President reelected," North said.

Ambassador Frank McNeil, representing the State Department, said: "We're supposed to be nonpartisan. If the President gets reelected because you've done a good job for him, that's all right."[1]

The working day is not long enough for an NSC staff member to run a personal crusade on top of his other responsibilities; and as his emotional attachment to the FDN deepened, North lengthened his day to sixteen, eighteen, or sometimes twenty hours. As support for the policy fell apart in Congress because of Casey's and Clarridge's mishandling, North readily agreed to take over responsibility from them. North acted as the FDN's champion within the government, encouraged them to keep fighting, advised them on military strategy and weapons purchases, and helped raise funds from third countries and private donors. North was well-placed to help their cause, for the NSC all along was a major actor in the Nicaraguan policy process—often the principal actor.[2]

As his power grew, so did his ardor for getting things done. But North disdained the complexities of international politics. The emotional intensity with which he supported the insurgents brought him into conflict with the State Department after Motley and Johnstone decided in the spring of 1984 that the time had come for diplomacy. As Johnstone tried to prepare the initiative by drafting discussion papers and sample documents that might draw the Sandinistas into talks, North, on behalf of the NSC, systematically gutted them.

If State offered a scheme to get a discussion going with the Sandinistas, "Ollie would come in and want to look at it as the final document," said one U.S. official. "He would say, 'We don't want that.' "

One idea that was floated was that the United States might suspend military maneuvers as part of an overall resolution. "Ollie never devastated anything in one meeting. He'd go back and say the NSC would not tolerate an end or a suspension of maneuvers," this official said.

In the role of nay-sayer, North was not acting entirely on his own but with the knowledge that powerful patrons like Casey and Kirkpatrick were behind him. They, like North, had committed their

name and office to the insurgents' cause. North earned their
gratitude by taking over the account.

Menges on at least three occasions also headed off Shultz's efforts
to open a dialogue with the Sandinistas, according to a former aide to
Casey. "He had a genius for smelling a rat," this aide said. "He'd call
up Bill and Jeane and they'd go to the President." Menges confirmed
this. "There were a number of very dramatic occasions," Menges said.
"These were cases of a unilateral action by the Department of State.
I had a presidential commission, to make sure the President's policy
was carried out. . . . All I did was to take the action needed to get the
issue put in front of the President so he could know what was going on
and then make a decision as to whether he wanted this to be done or
wanted to continue with his current policy." Reagan in each case
decided "by his policy." That is to say, all Shultz's plans were canceled.

The hard-liners had been able to prevent State from exploring the
diplomatic advantages opened by the Grenada invasion in late 1983.
But the constellation of powers had changed by spring 1984. Stone
was gone by March 1. McFarlane had neither Clark's political clout
nor his personal commitment on this issue. Using McFarlane's good
offices, Shultz felt he was beginning to gain the confidence of Reagan
and ascendancy over the foreign policy apparatus. One sign of
Shultz's rise was that political appointees in NSC staff positions
began to be replaced by State Department career officers.

When Shultz decided to take the gamble and reopen talks with the
Sandinistas, he conferred only with McFarlane before seeking
Reagan's approval. The plan, devised by Motley, even circumvented
the members of the RIG. Motley was convinced that more consultation would have stopped the initiative in its tracks. North vehemently opposed talking "with the enemy," and the Pentagon could
never agree on a bargaining position. "You never got more than a
momentary consensus out of that group [RIG]," said a State Department official. "Where they did agree, you got the mining and similar
disasters." Another said the reopening of talks was "designed by
Motley as a coup within the administration."

Shultz used the occasion of a visit to San Salvador for Duarte's
inauguration in June to make a side trip to Managua. Until Shultz
boarded his plane in Washington, few lower-ranking officials knew
the meeting would be held. "We still may not do it," Motley told
another official shortly before take-off. But as they climbed the ramp,
he said: "It looks like it's a 'go.' "

The reason for the uncertainty was fear that Casey and Weinberger would raise objections and scuttle the trip. Casey was the key concern, and Motley briefed him early. It was an oral briefing because Motley believed there was no way to get the scheme going by drafting papers. "Listen, we're going to try a public relations stunt," an aide paraphrased Motley as saying. The aim of the mission was to appease Congress, which was "beating the administration to pieces" by its votes against contra aid. After laying out a scenario, Motley told Casey: "Don't get concerned." Motley had no second thoughts about stressing form almost exclusively over substance. If Casey wanted to believe that domestic U.S. politics was the only element of the plan, it was okay. The private briefing given Weinberger was less selective. Motley later heard that Casey consulted Weinberger before deciding not to demur. Kirkpatrick was traveling in Alaska, and Motley arranged to have her briefed in flight. The major players were thus informed. North, Menges, and Iklé were deliberately kept in the dark.

McFarlane, although the overseer of the decision-making process, did not mind that Shultz had won Reagan's approval for the initiative without first discussing the plan before all of his cabinet colleagues. McFarlane felt that Shultz had been "very frank" about laying out his thoughts and he felt he could support this plan because, unlike Enders's mission three years earlier, it had "teeth"—a "much more demanding standard of performance by the Sandinistas, arrangements that would give some confidence that terms would be adhered to."

Yet there was an obvious drawback to launching a diplomatic initiative as if it was a covert military operation, however delectable the irony that the object was to mislead the CIA director. McFarlane was right that the content had changed from 1981, but the furtive style was vintage Tom Enders, and those kept in the dark reacted predictably.

An added irony was that McFarlane thus became the pivot in two mutually exclusive and simultaneous deceptions. Working with Casey, he kept Shultz in the dark while trying to obtain foreign funds and matériel for the contras. Working with Shultz, he helped keep Casey in the dark as Shultz prepared his trip to Managua. As befit Reagan's style, both approaches proceeded in parallel. The competition spelled problems for both policies.

The Shultz-Ortega meeting took place at the Managua airport, which nine months earlier had been a CIA and contra target. The new U.S. ambassador in Managua, Harry Bergold, had sounded out the Sandinistas about the possibility of the talks about a week before Shultz's arrival. "They said he was coming to discuss with Nicaragua how they could better help the Contadora process," said Victor Hugo Tinoco, Nicaragua's deputy foreign minister. "From the very beginning, they linked [the bilateral talks] with Contadora." Harry Shlaudeman, who had replaced Stone in March as special U.S. envoy, personally delivered the news to Honduras at about the same time.

It was the highest-level contact since December 1981. According to a confidential State Department summary, Shultz told Ortega that Reagan had given his personal blessing to the initiative. Shultz reaffirmed the usual four points of concern about the Sandinistas' foreign military advisers, support for the Salvadoran insurgents, the military build-up, and finally the "failure to fulfill their 1979 promises of pluralism, democracy and elections." All points had to be addressed simultaneously and reciprocally to achieve a comprehensive settlement. Ortega responded that Nicaragua's internal affairs were not subjects for negotiation. But Shultz felt his tone was "businesslike and civil." He described the two-and-a-half-hour meeting as frank, without acrimony or excessive rhetoric, and concluded that "we are proceeding on the premise that a negotiated settlement is possible and that practical reasons exist on all sides to reach agreement."[3] Shultz named Shlaudeman as the U.S. representative in further talks. Ortega named Tinoco.

Hardly had the secretary of state left Managua when he came under sniper fire from White House staff. A senior official accompanying Reagan on an official visit to Galway, Ireland, said that Reagan's aides felt "dissatisfaction" that the Shultz-Ortega encounter would raise public expectations that a solution was in the offing. "There is a feeling of no great enthusiasm about the meeting," the official said.[4]

The Sandinistas were equally wary. Ortega so distrusted U.S. intentions that he asked to have Mexico represented at any subsequent talks. Shultz resisted, but, without specific authorization, said the first meeting could be held wherever the two sides agreed. "We did a trade-off," said Shlaudeman. "The venue would be in Mexico. But we rejected the [Mexican] presence." The compromise was that Mexican officials would stay nearby. Ortega wanted to open the process in a face-to-face meeting with Reagan. Reagan, in Ireland,

dismissed the idea out of hand. "I'm in the wrong country for that."
A day after the Managua talks, D'Escoto told reporters he was "a bit
perplexed" by Shultz's timing and expressed concern that it was "a
publicity stunt," almost the exact words Motley had used with
Casey.[5]

When the Shlaudeman-Tinoco talks began later in June in Manzanillo, Mexico, each side found cause to reinforce its skepticism. In
the succeeding four months, they never did agree on the substance
of the agenda or the form the end result might take. When they
began to exchange proposals, neither wanted to discuss what the
other had submitted. An American official present in Manzanillo said
90 percent of the time was spent discussing what the talks would be
about. In December, after the ninth session, the United States cut
off the talks, blaming the Sandinistas for trying to substitute a
bilateral agreement reached at Manzanillo for a multilateral agreement that could be reached under the Contadora process. That may
have been true at the time the talks broke up, but the real story was
more involved; the Americans enshrouded the Manzanillo talks in
secrecy but paid scant attention to the Contadora forum. As a result,
the United States placed its major proposal on the table at the same
time Contadora did. The two peace plans collided; neither side knew
what hit it.

Johnstone, Shlaudeman, and some other high State Department
officials assert that Manzanillo represented a serious negotiating
effort by the United States to which the Sandinistas failed to
respond. Other high officials say it was doomed from the moment it
began because of the division in Washington. "Manzanillo was a
child born with such deformities that it would have had a brief time
to live anyway," said one. The two views are not mutually exclusive.

The dialogue between Shlaudeman and Tinoco took place in an
atmosphere that, while professional and serious, was wholly artificial.
They were like picnickers in a rowboat on a lake on a sunny
afternoon. A cyclone approaches from the west, a hurricane from the
south, and whirlpools open up to the north and east. The boat
overturns but there are any number of possible causes.

Rarely has a diplomatic negotiation occurred in so difficult a
context. The United States was engaged in a proxy war with
Nicaragua, and both countries were preparing for national elections.
While the U.S. elections gave Motley and Shultz the opening to sell
negotiations to the White House, the timing, as D'Escoto pointed

out, aroused suspicion on the Sandinista side that the move was principally for domestic political consumption. So, without much enthusiasm, the Sandinistas played along in hopes their participation would influence Congress positively and avoid giving Reagan an excuse to move against them should he win a second term. While the U.S. election was not an official agenda item at Manzanillo, Nicaragua's elections, scheduled for two days before the U.S. elections, were on the American agenda. And here the Reagan administration was simultaneously pursuing two courses. State wanted the internal opposition to participate if it could achieve conditions for a fair fight; the White House and Casey opposed participation.

It is unlikely that either side at the time quite understood the other's perspective. The internal politics of both countries were like prisms distorting the critical facts of the U.S.-Sandinista confrontation, namely the facts on the ground. Sandinista officials later told U.S. officials in Managua that the day of Shultz's brief visit to Managua—June 1, 1984—was "the greatest moment of military peril" they had faced. In April and May, there had been almost daily attacks in the south or north on army posts, state farms, and electrical or telephone transmission installations. Contra forces had begun massing in larger groups of up to 500 for some attacks, a sign of increased confidence and freedom of movement. The Sandinista army under the Ortega brothers and the interior police under Borge's command were unable to protect the installations and lacked the manpower or mobility to pursue the guerrillas.

Under the military battering they were taking, the Sandinistas had developed a series of responses. For weaponry, they turned to the Soviet Union, which agreed in the emergency to upgrade Sandinista capabilities. Daniel Ortega's visit to Moscow on June 17 to 20 was reported at the time to be centered on securing military aid. He then stopped in East Germany, Poland, and Bulgaria—all suppliers of military aid to Nicaragua. But it would be autumn before the first Soviet Mi-25 helicopter gunships were delivered to Managua. For strategy, the Sandinistas took advice from Cuba and other sources, but drew also on U.S. counterinsurgency expertise from Vietnam as well as in neighboring El Salvador.

Whether or not they realized it, Shultz and Shlaudeman began talks from a position of relative strength on the field and in Managua, which would erode in the next six months. The Sandinistas also had a number of factors going for them. Congress had halted U.S. aid to

the rebels; the CIA's management of the program was under assault
from both parties; and Walter Mondale, the Democratic presidential
candidate, declared he would cancel all covert funding if elected.
Although Mondale proved to be a weak candidate, for political
reasons alone there was no prospect for a resumption of U.S. funding
until after the election. Merely holding the talks weakened the
contras. But the Sandinistas either failed to perceive the opportunities afforded by the division within the administration or were unable
to agree on how to exploit them.

Thus the stage was set for the real battles of Manzanillo, which
took place within the Reagan administration and in the nine-man
directorate in Managua. In view of the very different nature of the
two societies, a good deal less is known of the Sandinista internal
disputes than of those in the Reagan administration, but the available
evidence indicates that the main controversy in Washington focused
on Manzanillo, while the Sandinista internal dispute related to the
Nicaraguan elections.

GRIDLOCK

Events in Washington that spring had led to the impression in the
press and Congress that the negotiations had been hurriedly arranged by Shultz and Motley following a direct appeal from the
president of Mexico. That was something of a cover story, for the
State Department already had a scheme ready that required only the
political go-ahead.[6]

President de la Madrid had told a joint session of Congress on May
16 that democracy could not be imposed by force and had warned
against "the illusion of the effectiveness of force." De la Madrid had
then gone to see Reagan to urge a dialogue with the Nicaraguans.
Bernardo Sepúlveda Amor, the Mexican foreign minister, took
Shultz the same message.

"Well, we were on the verge of having a dialogue with the
Nicaraguans, anyway," Johnstone said. "We said, 'Fine. Glad to do
so.' Talk about surprised Mexicans! They never would have dreamed
that we'd actually say yes." Sepúlveda laid out a step-by-step
approach that would deal with security issues first and left democratization until last.

"We had already been thinking in terms of a step-by-step approach to the problem, but obviously we weren't going to accept a step in which you do the security things and leave democratization for the end," Johnstone said, "because you give the Nicaraguans everything they want in the first step and you're never going to get the next three steps." Johnstone said the idea sounded very good, but asked, why not do a little in each category instead of one after the other? Sepúlveda stopped.

"He spent three minutes there looking at me. It's a really disarming thing to do to anybody. Finally he replied: 'OK, that sounds very good.' "

This became known in State Department jargon as the "horizontal cuts" approach. "Nobody could ever understand what the hell we were talking about," Johnstone said. The term "came from stacking all the issues on a matrix page and then chopping them off horizontally rather than step-by-step vertically as Sepulveda had proposed."

The matrix proposal (an unofficial translation of which is reproduced in Appendix I) had been in draft form before de la Madrid's visit. But the plan of which it formed one part was far more ambitious. Johnstone's idea was to outline a result that might be achieved on December 31, 1984, and negotiate over the milestones en route. The vision was that U.S. military maneuvers would come to a halt; Nicaragua would have free elections; military advisers would be virtually eliminated in Honduras, El Salvador, and Nicaragua; and the contras would "go away." To avoid criticism at home, Shlaudeman never spoke of the end result as a treaty or an agreement but as an unsigned understanding. In effect, the approach disentangled the four points Enders had announced in August 1982.

Its subtlety was that while putting the focus on democracy, the plan was not to discuss democracy in the negotiations themselves but to work out the issue simultaneously away from the table. To that end, Johnstone devoted considerable effort during the talks to pressing for opposition participation in the Nicaraguan elections under conditions that could arguably be described as fair. Open elections would resolve the democracy issue and remove it from the table. On the other hand, clearly flawed elections would pave the way for a shift in public opinion in the United States possibly for some other remedy.

The main drawback in the State Department scheme was that it was designed as much to cope with opponents of a negotiated settlement in Washington as it was to entice the Sandinistas; and, given its complexity, the underlying intentions probably eluded the Sandinistas. A second flaw was that the rest of the administration never really got on board.

Devising the plan and secretly launching the diplomatic process were simple compared to fighting for the policy through the administration. "Every Manzanillo session tore the cabinet apart," said one U.S. diplomat. "There was a fight about everything," said another. Reagan personally chaired two meetings of his national security advisers to discuss Shlaudeman's instructions. Typically, Shultz, Weinberger, Casey, and Kirkpatrick gave their views, and Reagan made a noncommittal pronouncement at the end. Afterward, Shlaudeman reported to the State Department: "Well, the President agreed, but that doesn't change anything."

The backlash in Washington following Shultz's trip may have been greater than its positive results. Motley's influence peaked with the trip. Those who were not consulted or were not informed of it until the last minute—North, Menges, and Kirkpatrick—were galvanized into opposition and came down hard. Motley was not invited to attend the National Security meetings at which it was discussed. At the subcabinet level, North grew in strength. "I watched Ollie gain power," said one State Department official. "His attitude was that 'we don't want a negotiated end that doesn't give us everything we want. So there can be no negotiated end.' " Throughout Manzanillo, "Ollie's *modus operandi* was to keep the negotiators off balance until something better comes along." This official said he found North's attitude "amoral." "Ollie believed in the great game [against the Soviets]. I think he felt his mission was to undermine everything we did."*

A fellow Marine officer said this attitude fit North's personality. "He likes to avoid complicated solutions to what he sees as simple problems. He is convinced that they are bad and they have to be cut out."

Kirkpatrick fought Manzanillo from the start. "She said Manzanillo undercut Contadora. I think it's baloney," said Shlaudeman. "One thing you can say about Jeane: she's honest," another senior diplomat said. "She did everything she could do to subvert Manzanillo."

---

* I asked North through Otto Reich to comment on this characterization, but he declined.

Kirkpatrick makes no bones about her strong reservations. "The fact is they never sold the matrix, the grid—I call it the gridlock— inside the U.S. government," she said.

The gridlock was partly of her making. "Kirkpatrick knew if the plan had democracy in it, it would fail," said a senior U.S. diplomat. "That was the fundamental cynicism of Manzanillo." "Democracy" was the title of one of the six sections of the U.S. proposal. Kirkpatrick said she fought for it. "I believed in democracy in Central America before I ever supported Ronald Reagan, before the Sandinistas came to power." She also agreed it would be hard to negotiate with democracy on the table.

Not long after Shlaudeman and Tinoco sat down for their first formal meeting, Kirkpatrick exchanged views on the Manzanillo talks with a high Sandinista official. Julio López Campos, head of the party's department of foreign relations, and Kirkpatrick had a mutual fascination. López is a neo-Trotskyite who became an orthodox Sandinista, and Kirkpatrick a neoconservative Democrat who became a conservative Republican. The meeting was in early July at the United Nations and was the fourth in what became an annual series. "We practically became old conversation buddies," Kirkpatrick said. López was "a very smart guy. I sort of liked to talk to him." The content of their conversation is important, for López's report led the Sandinista leadership to conclude that the U.S. intentions at Manzanillo were less than sincere, foreign ministry officials in Managua said.

According to two Nicaraguan foreign ministry sources, Kirkpatrick made it clear to López she was unhappy with the negotiations and the conduct of the policy and felt it was a gesture to Congress in an election year. The administration did not want to go to Manzanillo, and she was convinced that the effort would fail, the sources quoted her as saying. A third source, Deputy Foreign Minister Tinoco, said she did not go quite that far. "She never really said, 'I don't agree with what Shlaudeman is doing.' Of course, it was clear she had a different perspective and she was not very happy with what was going on in Manzanillo."

Kirkpatrick denied the version given by the foreign ministry officials. She said she would not have described Manzanillo as being politically motivated. "Nobody that I knew regarded the administration as under any pressures whatsoever relating to the 1984 elections that would have led them to try to get a quick agreement." She said the only officials concerned with U.S. politics were within the State Department bureaucracy. Her recollection of the talk with López paralleled that of Tinoco. "I think he [López] probably came away with a sense that the United States government was not so eager for an agreement that they would accept a treaty which did not meet minimal U.S. and Contadora hopes for the region," she said.

Menges fought Manzanillo with such tools as were at his disposal. He inserted the toughest possible language in the section of the U.S. proposal on internal democratization, State Department aides said. He was frequently on the telephone to Raymond Burghardt, a former Negroponte aide in Tegucigalpa who became the NSC representative at the talks. Menges also took an active role in influencing the internal opposition in Nicaragua to hold out for election terms that would give them an excuse not to take part. And he fed material to speechwriters preparing Reagan's public statements that signaled repeatedly his disdain for the election process and his disinclination to reach an agreement with the Sandinistas. According to Otto Reich, "He felt that Craig [Johnstone] and Motley had purposely undermined the contras and misunderstood the importance of that leg of policy. Constantine felt they wanted a Paris-type Vietnam agreement and assumed it would suffer the same fate."

This was a formidable set of opponents, and their concerted opposition made give-and-take difficult at best. "The resentment of the other side was so strong that the balance was never restored," said a U.S. diplomat. "They did everything they could to upset the balance. They blocked the instructions and reduced our flexibility." Another U.S. diplomat described Shlaudeman's negotiating latitude as "about one tenth of an inch. . . . His leash was so tight that Victor [Tinoco] could not go to the john without Shlaudeman calling Washington and asking permission. It was ridiculous. It was meant to be unacceptable."

Kirkpatrick thought these constraints were a good thing. "The President was very judicious. . . . While he authorized the conversations, he authorized them within some very broad constraints," she said. There were "constraints on what they could commit and couldn't commit" as well as the obligation to keep Honduras and the other countries informed.

Disagreements over procedure took up the first three sessions at Manzanillo. Tinoco wanted English-Spanish interpretations. But after a trial run, Shlaudeman suggested they speak only in Spanish. Tinoco agreed. Other disagreements centered on who would prepare the transcript and whether to issue a joint statement. Just getting agreement on the Spanish word for stenographer took several hours, said one participant. After talks that ran well into the night, both sides settled for keeping separate notes and producing one-page agreed-upon minutes at the end of each session. About the only event at the third meeting was that Ambassador Bergold broke his arm while changing his shirt. He had rushed back from a tennis game to attend a session and pulled off his tennis shirt, not noticing a metal fan running at full speed. The only thing that saved his arm from being severed, he later said, was his Seiko watch.

Kirkpatrick and some other officials who did not take part in the talks insist that high-level Cuban diplomats were present at most of the Manzanillo meetings. "They were there in the hotel all the time. They were in particular touch with the Mexicans, of course," she said. U.S. officials at the talks dispute this, but Kirkpatrick said, "All of those guys had a vested interest in the Manzanillo talks." Tinoco dismissed the claim about Cubans as flat wrong. "Maybe they are referring to the Mexican army. Because the only people who were around aside from the U.S. delegation and the Nicaraguan delegation were some hundreds of Mexican troops. Nobody was able to get into this place. They even had a destroyer in front of our house."

Not until the fourth meeting, on August 15 and 16, did Shlaudeman present the matrix proposal verbally. Ten weeks had elapsed since Shultz's flying visit to Managua, but Shlaudeman still was unable to get interagency agreement to hand over the piece of paper to Tinoco at this meeting. "He said they considered it not advisable to give the whole thing in writing," Tinoco said. "So what we did was take notes."

Shlaudeman spoke very slowly, dictating in Spanish, word by word. "It took about two hours, maybe more," Tinoco said.

The proposal itself left the Sandinistas fairly baffled. Titled "Timetable of Reciprocal Unilateral Measures," it called for specific Sandinista concessions over a ninety-day period in return for an undefined U.S. response. For example, it proposed that one third of the Cuban and Soviet military advisers be removed from Nicaragua within thirty days, the second third within sixty days, and the remainder within ninety days. After thirty days, "the U.S. military presence in Central America will take Nicaraguan actions into

consideration." After sixty days, "the U.S. continues to take Nicaraguan actions into consideration." And after ninety days, "the U.S.
presence in Central America will have taken Nicaraguan actions into
consideration."

"This taxed our intelligence," said one Sandinista foreign ministry
official. "It was totally unacceptable from the outset. It implied a
unilateral withdrawal."

So it appeared. The reason no incentives were stated was the
internal struggle in Washington. "There was something in every one
of those [matrix] boxes when we started," one State Department
official recalled. "But Ollie, with an almost bizarre smile on his face,
would veto the contents. The plan was emasculated. It became
unbalanced." The Pentagon did not work out the U.S. unilateral
response to the proposed withdrawals. "We were kicking it around.
We never did come up with an answer because they never came back
to us and asked for elaboration," a source on the JCS staff said.

Almost every other area of the six-point proposal contained a hook
that would be hard to swallow. In exchange for closing the centers of
command and control of the Salvadoran FMLN, the United States
pledged that the "anti-Sandinistas agree not to mine or attack the
harbors of Nicaragua or petroleum storage places." The U.S. offer
not to repeat a military and diplomatic failure was taken in Managua
as a less than serious concession. The final goal to be reached after
ninety days was even more interesting: that the FDN and ARDE
would leave Honduras and Costa Rica, and all U.S. aid to them
would be cut off; in return, the two guerrilla groups were to be
incorporated in the Nicaraguan political process.

A section on democracy called for "free and fair democratic
elections" in Nicaragua. In return, the United States committed
itself to similar action by El Salvador in the March 1985 parliamentary elections. Within thirty days, Nicaragua was to invite "all
political tendencies" to compete in elections, restore full political
rights, and grant equal access to news media. Within sixty days, the
election campaign would be under way and amnesty granted to all
who wanted to participate peacefully. Within ninety days, elections
which guaranteed "free and fair democratic" participation by all
political tendencies would be held. The final goal was institutionalized "democratic structures and rights."

Under economic cooperation, Shlaudeman offered restoration of
the sugar import quota, renegotiation of the Nicaraguan debt,

support for international bank loans, and full access to U.S. markets, but said U.S. demands of Nicaragua were under study. The demand relating to arms levels contained a vague offer that "the U.S. presence and exercises [would be] re-adjusted to reflect the advances made." Only the area relating to verification seemed reasonably straightforward.

"This is the only thing we can get from the NSC," a member of the U.S. delegation told his Nicaraguan counterpart. "We are in a double negotiation."

Tinoco told Shlaudeman he had to study the document before responding. Johnstone, hearing of this, interpreted it in the most positive light. That was not how Tinoco had meant it. At first reading, it appeared to be a "proposal for surrender." Tinoco felt he had to return to Managua to study it and decide how to respond. "I was not in a position to say immediately that it was a disaster." Three weeks later, on September 5, Shlaudeman had the authority to hand over the actual document. Yet Tinoco refrained from asking Shlaudeman to fill in the many blanks.

Johnstone was dismayed by the lack of interest. "It was an enormous disappointment to me. We thought we had found a gimmick in which we could get an agreement from them on where it was all going to end up and the fact it would be approached on multiple stages with simultaneous action by both sides across the spectrum of bilateral differences. And then we could quibble, if we wanted to, about how to get there." Had the Sandinistas responded, "you would be cooking. You would have an active, a real negotiation taking place."

Johnstone acknowledged that the U.S. incentives were exceptionally vague. "We had a lot of specific things in mind as to what we'd do. We didn't have exact agreement at that time as to what it would be. But everybody knew that if they signed on to it, we would have to do something that would be regarded by our own public as being an adequate response." Among the possibilities was the "whole question of the U.S. presence in Honduras." With respect to the contras, Johnstone's idea was that "the contras would have to go away." But he added: "We insisted that they had to go away in the context of being absorbed into the political process."

To overcome wariness of the vague U.S. proposal, Johnstone said he sent a message through diplomatic channels in Washington: "Look, this is action-forcing. If you say yes to this, there's no way we cannot do something that is equivalent. Exactly what we will do will be subject to negotiations."

It was a message that the Sandinistas say they never received. Carlos Tünnerman Bernheim, the Nicaraguan ambassador to Washington and a participant in later stages of Manzanillo, said no U.S. official ever called at the embassy from the time of his arrival in August 1984. His deputy, Manuel Cordero, said he could not recall receiving any such message as Johnstone described. Tinoco said he never got it. "Surely not in writing or as a formal message," he said. If he had, "this would be something different," he said. "I don't remember that they even hinted something similar to that concept. Because we could have gotten involved in the whole question of what is equivalent."

The Sandinistas' failure to probe the U.S. proposal puzzled State Department officials long after Manzanillo ended. Tinoco explained that the leadership in Managua had a choice: either to ask for clarifications and thereby accept the American framework, including the reference to Nicaragua's internal system, or to define its view of the concessions and the measures that the United States had to take. They decided to take the latter route in a response tabled at the end of October. There were two reasons for proceeding this way. As the Sandinistas read the matrix proposal, it placed primary emphasis on the political and internal affairs of Nicaragua, and "we were not in a position to accept involvement of the U.S. government in our internal matters." Tinoco said he stated that very clearly to Shlaudeman. Meanwhile, on security aspects, the proposal asked Nicaragua to take a series of steps and did not offer anything clear in return. "So it was not at all a good base."

The Sandinista counteroffer, presented on October 30–31, was remarkably vague in terms of commitments, calling on the United States to halt all maneuvers in exchange for a similar pledge by Nicaragua and demanding that the United States dismantle all military schools, bases, and installations in Honduras, Costa Rica, and El Salvador in exchange for a Sandinista promise not to establish any schools, bases, and foreign installations of their own. (An unofficial translation of this offer is reproduced in Appendix II.) Shlaudeman dismissed the counteroffer as "this half-assed thing" and it was never a subject of serious discussion.

Underlying the Sandinista reserve was their belief that the State Department could not sustain its position with the rest of the administration. "Eighty percent of U.S. policy toward Nicaragua has been formulated outside the State Department. You have to weigh that," said a foreign ministry official. That may well have summed up what had gone before, but with regard to the Manzanillo talks, it could have serious consequences. For in Reagan's cabinet-style government, the course of policy was determined by the constellation of the key players and by who was making day-to-day operational decisions. When Shultz's influence was weak, he could be little more than a brake on Casey and Weinberger, if that; but Shultz's influence was on the rise in the months leading to the Manzanillo talks, which explains how he got away with arranging the meeting with Ortega.

Tinoco said he and his colleagues saw three different tendencies within the Reagan administration. One was interested only in helping reelect the President; the second wanted to test "if Nicaragua is ready for unilateral concessions or a surrender"; the third thought "it was important to make an effort, a real effort for accommodation with Nicaragua."

At the beginning, "we had some doubts about the degree of serious division among the different sectors in the administration." But, Tinoco said, "we were really not in a position to play games with the contradictions inside the administration." At the end, they concluded that it was "more a matter of tactics and that those differences between Shultz, Kirkpatrick, and Weinberger really were not serious."

WHEN PEACE PLANS COLLIDE

The standard explanation for the failure of the matrix proposal among the U.S. diplomats who worked on it in Washington was that the hard-liners in Managua refused to budge. "I can't believe an intelligent person wouldn't have understood where it was going. It was very clear to us and I can't believe it wasn't clear to them, all the possibilities that were there," said one Johnstone aide.

In fact, the shot that crippled Manzanillo came from an entirely different direction: Contadora. The collapse of Manzanillo is the story of rival peace processes in collision.

Until Shultz's trip to Managua in June 1984, the State Department had not engaged in negotiations with the Sandinistas for nearly two years and instead watched warily as the four countries comprising the Contadora group tried to fill the vacuum. Shlaudeman felt it would be improper to send U.S. observers to their monthly meetings in Panama the way the Cubans had; Cuban representatives invited the Contadora participants out for drinks and meals to learn exactly what was going on. "This has been structured to leave us out. I don't think the participants would look with favor," Shlaudeman said. "The Cubans of course could get away with these things." Besides, the Cubans were there "to give the Nicaraguans a hand."[7]

But the arm's-length attitude proved costly when the United States reentered the diplomatic game. Important developments had occurred without American input or, apparently, knowledge since the administration last paid it much attention. That occasion—the unveiling of the Contadora document of objectives in September 1983— showed the division in the administration, with the State Department reluctant to endorse a process consisting largely of rhetoric and improvisation, and the White House enthusiastic about it for that very reason. In the meantime, working groups of the five Central American countries had met from February to April to thrash out the issues, and Costa Rica, the only stable democracy, took the lead role among the little entente of U.S. allies in discussing political issues. It was in this forum that Costa Rica reached the conclusion that democracy in Nicaragua was beyond the reach of its diplomacy. "We just had to give up. We do not have the means to impose our views on Nicaragua," said Jorge Urbina, Costa Rica's deputy foreign minister and chief representative in Contadora. "Nicaragua said it was their internal affair and we had no right to press them."

That concession removed from the table an issue on which Contadora or any peace process might founder, modified the twenty-one points of September 1983, undercut a U.S. policy goal dating back to mid-1982, and reinforced the Sandinista conviction that its internal system was nonnegotiable. When Shlaudeman presented the U.S. proposal at Manzanillo months later, the Sandinistas could ask themselves why they should agree to discuss a demand that the leading democracy in Central America had abandoned months earlier. U.S. officials in Washington and San José said they were not aware of the development.*

---

* Washington *was* aware when Costa Rican officials subsequently met secretly in Paris on three occasions with their Nicaraguan counterparts to discuss a bilateral security deal. U.S. Ambassador Curtin Winsor intervened to block what he called a "pernicious plan" to "sterilize" the border, and the talks were dropped. "We explored [a border agreement], then decided it would be a costly proposition," said Carlos José Gutiérrez, the Costa Rican foreign minister.

Not until June 1984 did the State Department make a serious effort to monitor Contadora activities at the scene. As Shultz arrived in Managua, the political counselor at the U.S. embassy in Panama, Ashley IIewitt, set off on a two-week trip through Central America to meet the delegations assigned to the Contadora process and gain sources for monitoring future meetings.

It was too late. On June 8, the Contadora countries presented a first draft of what they called the Act for Peace and Cooperation in Central America. Prepared in Panama by technical experts, it incorporated areas of consensus reached in the working groups and offered language where there was no agreement. Unfortunately for the State Department and its expert in Panama, the venue of action then moved to Mexico, where the highly secretive Mexican foreign ministry drafted revisions.

Shlaudeman said he had repeatedly stressed all that summer two major U.S. concerns with the draft: the need for a strong mechanism to ensure compliance, and a timetable for simultaneous implementation of the accord's provisions on ceasing aid to irregular forces and reducing military advisers, maneuvers, arms, and armies. Both points were integral in the U.S. "matrix" proposal that was eventually presented.

But the leaders of Contadora were focusing on broader political considerations rather than on technical details.

The single event in 1984 that concentrated the minds of every president and minister engaged in the issue was the prospect of Reagan's reelection in November. This applied especially to Fidel Castro, who had no formal role in the talks but developed a close working relationship with Colombia's Betancur. Encouraged by Castro and working with Mexican foreign minister Bernardo Sepúlveda, Betancur made a concerted push beginning in the spring of 1984 to conclude the Contadora process with a grand finale on the eve of the U.S. elections. Mexico was eager for the same result. "Clearly it had to be done before the elections, or the United States would be much more tough to deal with," said Carlos Rico, a Mexican scholar on U.S. affairs and adviser to the Mexican foreign ministry.

Speeding up the clock for a political deadline is an enormous gamble in any negotiation, more so for a loosely structured mediation run by four countries. From its inception, Contadora was possibly the most complex diplomatic effort of the modern era; taking on the twenty-one points made it the most ambitious as well. All along, the effort was slowed by inexperience, differences among the partners, and their inability to commit national resources.

Sepúlveda and Betancur treated U.S. concerns with disdain.

Mexico's attitude was fed by the perception that the United States was not serious at Manzanillo. "Based on knowledge of what was happening at Manzanillo, not too many people thought the talks would lead anywhere," Rico said. "We had a clear sense that it was done basically to satisfy electoral needs and to buy time. Experience showed that the United States was not willing to compromise."

U.S. insistence on simultaneity was viewed in Mexico "as a delaying maneuver . . . exactly the kind of U.S. position seen as not serious," Rico said.

Although Mexico had the most professionalized foreign ministry of the Contadora countries, it lacked experience in mediating what was in essence a security dispute. Claude Heller, the senior official in charge of the drafting, had no background in security issues, according to Rico. "It was a question of reading books." The military, long relegated to the sidelines of Mexican diplomacy, were consulted, "but not enough."

In addition, the vision that drove the Mexicans was rather more ambitious than resolving the immediate crisis. They wanted a redefinition of the relationship between the United States and the left in Latin America. "In a certain sense a very important aspect in inter-American affairs since World War II has been a search for a new order that accommodates the interests of the Latin American countries with the interests of the United States," Heller said. As examples of the old order, he cited the CIA-sponsored coup in Guatemala in 1954, the U.S. military intervention in the Dominican Republic in 1965, and the American-backed overthrow of Salvador Allende in Chile in 1973. "The question comes down to the ability of the United States to coexist with Latin American experiments that are in contrast with the fundamental interests of the United States." Conceivably, patient, skilled diplomacy by Latin countries over many years might begin to effect so strategic a shift in the U.S. role in the region. A quick fix would not.

Betancur was a newcomer to negotiations but saw in his amateur status a special virtue. In negotiating peace with leftist guerrillas at home, he eschewed verification altogether. The internal process was "very much appearances," according to Fernando Cepeda, dean of the law school at the University of the Andes. The Colombian army and press alleged that the guerrillas were breaking the truce. The guerrillas charged that the army was breaking the truce. "I was on the verification commission. We could not prove anything. There was no staff, no procedure; information arrived very late. So verification was nonexistent."

Betancur theorized that to conclude a binding, comprehensive, verifiable agreement in treaty form was impossible; it was better to produce a document that had the language and use the existence of that to press for results. "It isn't a completely empty theory. It has its validity," said Shlaudeman.

Venezuela and Panama kept a low profile that summer.

As host government in Manzanillo and a key player in Contadora, Mexico theoretically was the link between the two negotiating processes. Shlaudeman visited Manzanillo every third week that summer and frequently saw Sepulveda or his deputies. However, "I never got much out of him," Shlaudeman said. "I never figured out what the hell they were doing."

Sepúlveda claimed equal ignorance of Manzanillo. "The conversations at Manzanillo were private, between the United States and Nicaragua, and the Contadora effort was, I wouldn't say totally independent from the knowledge of the proposals, it was a different forum altogether. So none of the Contadora members knew of the proposals in Manzanillo." As for the U.S. matrix proposal, he said: "I don't remember that particular document."

Actually, both sides briefed the Mexicans after each round. Tinoco confirmed that he gave Sepúlveda a copy of the U.S. proposal.

In short order, the two peace processes collided head-on.

Shlaudeman presented the written matrix proposal at the two-day meeting in Manzanillo that ended on September 6. That night in Panama, the four Contadora partners met and produced a revised Final Act. Suddenly, two peace plans were on the table, and neither the United States nor Contadora understood the content, strategy, or origins of the other's plan.

The new draft took the Americans by surprise. Shultz, in a letter to West European foreign ministers dated September 7, guardedly endorsed Contadora's efforts, calling their draft "an important step forward" that contains "many positive elements."

But he was referring to the June draft, not the one completed that same day.*[8]

The Contadora September 7 act was another example of the dubious procedure of presenting a final product rather than have the Central Americans negotiate it face to face. The substance was also questionable. Security elements that would affect the United States—its military presence and maneuvers—would be subject to removal on a fixed timetable, but those aspects affecting Nicaragua were left largely to subsequent negotiations. Verification procedures had no teeth. Latin America experts on the JCS staff in Washington expressed concern. "For us to have agreed to that revised act would have been the United States getting out of Central America," said a senior analyst. "It would have been seen as a retreat."

Sepúlveda had not only thought up the language but also a public relations plan to promote the document as the answer to Central America's problems. The platform was to be the United Nations, with Mexico playing the lead role. His design was to create momentum for support through international public opinion before anyone could raise serious objections to the draft. He introduced the September 7 act as an official United Nations document almost immediately, before any U.S. official saw it. One of the "friendly countries of the region" made a copy available the next week, but it was September 12 before John Hamilton, a career diplomat in the inter-American affairs bureau who followed Contadora, got to read it cover to cover. Shlaudeman took a copy with him when he left on a tour of Contadora countries and U.S. allies in Central America a few days later to discuss the latest developments. Meanwhile, Sepulveda was pressing to have the act accepted as a Security Council document. Jeane Kirkpatrick heard of the maneuver and helped block it by alerting several Central American countries. "There was an effort here to pull a kind of propaganda coup," she later said. "I'm sure we did [help to block it]."

In the weeks after its release, Sepúlveda, de la Madrid, and Betancur mounted a campaign to induce Central Americans to sign on. Some needed little prodding. Gutiérrez of Costa Rica on

* The letter stated that Costa Rica, El Salvador, Guatemala, and Honduras had welcomed the draft, and that Nicaragua had rejected key elements, a recapitulation of what had occurred since June; Shultz also noted that a meeting on August 25 to resolve differences had made little progress.

September 13 offered to sign the document because it had taken into account all of Costa Rica's objections to the earlier draft.

The first negative signal came from Honduran officials in Tegucigalpa, who on September 19 told Shlaudeman that further revisions were needed. "It was we who told Shlaudeman what kind of observations we had [about] the act," said Jorge Ramón Hernández-Alcerro, the deputy foreign minister. "He didn't have very clear ideas about what the September draft meant." After Shlaudeman left, Honduras issued a statement to this effect. This in retrospect was a "great tactical mistake," Hernández-Alcerro said. "Not only did it appear that the United States was giving orders, but more important, the Nicaraguans with that declaration were sure we would not sign the act."

Two days later, on September 21, Nicaragua announced that it would sign the draft "immediately and without further modifications." The news startled the region, the State Department, and even the Contadora countries. Endorsing the document was a major public relations coup for the Sandinistas, but a shrewdly calculated step with low costs.

A lot of effort had gone into wooing the Sandinistas, but knowledgeable diplomats in the Contadora states believed Managua endorsed the act in the sure knowledge that it was going nowhere. Tinoco backed this up. "Of course, our impression was that it probably would be difficult for the United States to accept that." Or as another foreign ministry official put it: "We perceived realistically that we couldn't expect the Americans to accept the act." If Washington did, Tinoco said, the limits imposed on U.S. military maneuvers and the requirement to withdraw advisers would be "good for Nicaragua."

On September 24, the State Department publicly expressed its objections in phrases lifted from the Honduran statement five days earlier, adding to the acute embarrassment in Tegucigalpa.

All this might have been written off as theater except for the devastating impact it had on American diplomacy. Shlaudeman's talks with Tinoco were arguably the only sustained U.S. negotiating effort since Reagan took office. But in the course of September, the Sandinistas found themselves with a choice—a fairly rigorous U.S. plan and the rather loose Contadora act. Probably no one else was aware what had happened. Tinoco said it was clear that the Americans had lost the initiative. "In a period of about one month, the administration was in a very difficult situation," he said.

The Sandinistas took neither proposal very seriously but under public and private pressure from other Latin countries, including Cuba, agreed to Contadora. When they did, the point of Manzanillo became questionable.

Shlaudeman discovered this at the next meeting on September 25, where Tinoco announced that Nicaragua had adopted the September Contadora draft as its position in the bilateral talks. "Any substantive changes would upset a delicate balance. It is the result of a two-year process," he said.

This was the point of collision. John Hamilton, who took part in the Manzanillo talks, cast it in a more positive light. "The two processes were organically joined."

Shlaudeman concluded that he was dealing not with an organic link but a wall of stones. He returned to Washington and at a session of top national security advisers with Reagan himself in the chair brought the very negative report that the Sandinistas were "just stringing us along."

The State Department became anxious, and conveyed U.S. views about the act to allies in Central America. Costa Rica quickly backed down.

El Salvador's José Napoleón Duarte, after visiting Venezuela, Colombia, and Panama, had promised to send home the fifty-five U.S. military trainers in El Salvador if Nicaragua would remove 8,000 Cuban military advisers. "Let us do something. Let us sign the document," he declared on September 22. He spoke before hearing from his ally. When asked about the U.S. position two days later, he told reporters in San Salvador: "I think that a sovereign country does not have to talk to anyone about the line of conduct to be followed by that country. When we enter into an international treaty, we honor it." This was more than the traffic would bear in Washington. "He had said things he shouldn't have said," a senior U.S. diplomat commented. Shlaudeman met with Duarte and "left him in no doubt as to what the administration wanted."

Early in October, Honduras said that it, together with Costa Rica, and El Salvador, planned "adjustments" to the Contadora document which would delay the signing beyond October 15, the deadline set by the Contadora ministers. Shultz paid a brief visit to Mexico, where he said the United States and its allies wanted the treaty to work better and thought it required improved verification and simultaneous enforcement. Sepúlveda replied: "It might be useful to include those comments in the treaty." With that, the bottom fell out of the September 7 act: Nicaragua had agreed to sign only "without modifications." Honduras called a meeting of the foreign ministers from Costa Rica, El Salvador, and Guatemala on October 19 and they produced a draft of their own. Guatemala, which had withheld any endorsement of the September 7 act, sent only its deputy foreign minister, who did not sign the proposal.[9] The Contadora process went into a stall, from which it did not recover until spring 1985.

Within State, Manzanillo also looked like a lost cause. The matrix scheme had not induced much of a dialogue, and Sandinista acceptance of the September 7 Contadora act put that document at the top of the U.S.-Nicaraguan agenda at Manzanillo. But when other Central American countries and even Mexico agreed that the Contadora act needed further work, the discussion at Manzanillo began to go in circles. Manzanillo had been a costly undertaking for the State Department in terms of internal administration politics, and now there seemed little likelihood it would bring a diplomatic payoff by the end of 1984 as Johnstone had envisioned. The talks proceeded, nevertheless, through the end of the year and might have been extended but for a failure of U.S. policy in a second, related sphere.

Direct U.S.-Sandinista negotiations were only part of the State Department strategy that fall. Johnstone's scheme also had attempted to address in writing a subject that no country except under conditions of military occupation would have been willing to negotiate, namely Nicaragua's internal political system. But, as already noted, Johnstone's plan was not to negotiate directly over democracy but to resolve the issue through the Nicaraguan elections. Indeed, if elections that were seen to be fair could have been held in Nicaragua, democracy would have been swept from the table as an issue. While the talks were going on, Johnstone made an effort to bring this about, but he was up against a formidable array of forces. The wrangling over elections came to a head at precisely the same moment as the collision of the two peace plans.

CHAPTER 11

DIVIDED COUNSEL

NICARAGUA'S 1984 ELECTIONS provide a case study of the impact of loose management on a delicate foreign policy situation that might have been amenable to U.S. influence. The November 4 polling was a turning point not only in the post-Somoza history of Nicaragua but also in U.S. policy. This was the point where low-cost U.S. options ran out. Of the many missed opportunities to achieve at least some of the stated U.S. goals in Nicaragua, perhaps none compared to this. The division in Washington all but assured an inconclusive contest.

"One of the biggest mistakes of all, maybe the biggest mistake, was the handling of the election," said a high U.S. diplomatic source. "The idea of the CIA and White House staff was to avoid participation in the elections. The debate was over whether to go halfway or not."[1]

The State Department's planning for both direct diplomacy and the elections had gone into high gear following Daniel Ortega's announcement on February 21, 1984, of the election date.

About a month later, Johnstone met Arturo Cruz Sr., the former Sandinista ambassador to Washington, to discuss the elections. Over lunch at Germaine's, a French-Vietnamese restaurant in upper Georgetown, he asked Cruz if he would be interested in running for the presidency. "We had to be sure there would be a candidate," Johnstone said. "He was the one leader we thought they might be able to allow into an electoral process."

Johnstone and Motley were preparing a strategy that in theory would offer the Sandinistas an opportunity for reconciliation with the Reagan administration. The two governments would tackle their differences over security in direct talks even as the Sandinistas and their domestic opponents fought out their claims to power through the election process. Conceiving such a scheme in an ideological but loosely managed government may have been unrealistic. Even to test the Sandinistas' intentions convincingly required a unity of purpose that had thus far eluded the administration. There was no assurance that the other side would conclude an acceptable security accord or run a fair election. Yet not to try meant forgoing the unique opportunity offered by the nearly simultaneous elections—Nicaragua on November 4 and the United States on November 6.

A co author of the free election concept was Luigi Einaudi. The grandson of a post–World War II president of Italy, Einaudi was the "institutional memory" of the Bureau who had worked under four administrations. He was no dove. "I always say you do not beat a guerrilla carrying a machine gun by throwing sacks of fertilizer at him unless you happen to be very lucky." Einaudi had drafted Enders's July 1981 speech and held that, even in countries torn by civil war, elections can bring national reconciliation and function as a moment of truth. If rigged, they will be exposed; if fair, they will reconcile. In this particular case, they offered the chance to get the United States off the hook while the time was right.

The State Department scheme drew on professional assessments of the political situation on the ground. In the view of diplomatic observers, the Sandinistas would have won free elections fairly in their first three years in office. But with triple-digit inflation, lowered living standards, the draft, and increasing state control of the economy, an overwhelming victory was no longer assured in 1984. A poll conducted by the Statistic Institute of Spain in

November 1983 showed that the Sandinistas would gain only 35
percent of the vote unless they formed a common front with other
leftist parties and lowered the voting age to sixteen, in which case
they could gain 55 percent.[2]

The Sandinista leadership had its own scarcely hidden rivalries.
Daniel Ortega, the presidential candidate, saw the election as a way
of enhancing his stature abroad and at home; Borge had thought the
honor was his and opposed the election plan. Bayardo Arce, a Borge
ally, later described the contest as a "nuisance" forced on the
Sandinistas by the United States. "If we did not have the war
situation imposed on us by the United States, the electoral problem
would be totally out of place in terms of its usefulness," he said in a
secret speech that spring.

Anthony Quainton, the U.S. ambassador to Nicaragua, anticipated
that Daniel Ortega would win a plurality but thought he would
attempt to govern as head of a broad coalition including centrists, the
same style of leadership he showed in the later stages of the
revolution. In this context, to participate in the elections would
preserve a breathing space for the opposition. Quainton did not press
his views, however.*

The overall assessment was shared by Harry Bergold, who
replaced Quainton in May. Bergold had previously served in
Hungary and had a fascination with Communist systems and the
ways that U.S. influence might be used to encourage them to open
to the West. Bergold knew that discontent was seething beneath
the surface and felt an election contest might "spark something
exciting."

However, the hard right did not agree. For Reagan hard-liners,
the main problem that spring was politics at home. The harbor-
mining calamity coupled with Casey's disdainful attitude toward

---

* The views of the chief U.S. representative in Managua had long since become
relegated to the category of curious communications. Quainton had on several occasions proposed alternatives to military pressures involving contacts with the internal
opposition, but his efforts to influence policy were viewed even at State as quixotic.
Quainton narrowly escaped being fired for refusing to join a White House campaign
portraying the Sandinistas as anti-Semites. In an attempt to win the backing of
American Jews, the administration charged that the Sandinistas had persecuted Nicaragua's tiny Jewish community. But in fact most of them had prospered under
Somoza and left when he did. Quainton reported that he could find no verifiable
evidence of persecution. Shultz saved his foreign service career by insisting that
Quainton be sent to the first open post, Kuwait, even though he was not an Arab expert.

Congress and Mondale's decision to make Nicaragua policy an election issue eroded what little bipartisan support remained for the contra program. With no prospect of funds from Congress, the hard right focused its energies on finding alternate sources. Simultaneously, the CIA had to stop managing the program, and in May Clarridge turned over control to Oliver North. North now had not only had an interest to promote but, with a seat on the RIG, a key role in policymaking. From the time Shultz went to Managua on June 1 and began the Manzanillo talks, he, Motley, and Johnstone were under attack from the hard right: Casey, who had been misled by Motley; Kirkpatrick, who had been briefed on the run; and North, Menges, and others, who had been kept in the dark. For Johnstone, the elections were crucial to the success of his design for a negotiated settlement. "Democracy" was on the table at Manzanillo, but Johnstone wanted to address it through Cruz's candidacy. His scheme assumed that the opposition would register for, if not actually contest, the election. However, where the State Department supported Cruz's candidacy in hopes it would foster a deal in which the contras would "go away," the hard right believed that force was the only way to bring about democracy in Nicaragua and the Sandinistas had to "go away" either through overthrow or removal. They supported Cruz in the expectation he would not participate in the elections, thereby discrediting them. They regarded a negotiated deal with the Sandinistas as a sell-out.

For the hard-liners, the actual political situation in Nicaragua was irrelevant. They argued by syllogism. Communists never allow fair elections; the Sandinistas are Communists; for the opposition to participate in elections will legitimize Communist rule.

Conservatives kept a low public profile but were able to engage their assets without drawing attention. Casey had direct access to Reagan and influence on his thinking and his public statements. He also had a network in Central America which could influence the contras in Honduras and Costa Rica as well as good contacts in the Nicaraguan internal opposition. Even Cruz was receiving CIA funds at the time. "The other guys were able to run it by their complete penetration of the opposition," said a senior diplomat. "None of these people is independent any more."

They worked to convince the internal opposition to insist on election rules so comprehensive that the Sandinistas would never accept them. Menges was convinced that the Sandinistas would stage a sham election. He insisted rigidly that Reagan's demand for democracy not be compromised. To this end, Menges worked closely with the presidential speechwriting staff. Reagan as usual did not choose between competing strategies or impose discipline on his subordinates but allowed the different power centers to pursue policy according to their interpretation of the goals.

Not many people saw anything positive coming out of the election campaign that spring.

Two Americans did, however, and approached Cruz about it independently. John Curry, a foreign service officer who had served in Managua at the time of the revolution, told Cruz not to be too purist. "Of course he couldn't win an election in a Marxist-Leninist state," Curry said. "That wasn't the name of the game. We had a short window of time, the only one in which the opposition politicians could use radio and television, travel around the country, get a semblance of a political organization going, explain their point of view, and show people they were not alone. I said he should take advantage of it." Curry, whose wife is Nicaraguan, was sure the Sandinistas would prevent Cruz from campaigning, but that this fact would be widely shown in the international news media. If he withdrew, it would be seen abroad as justified.

Max Singer, who describes himself as an anti-Communist writer and analyst who at the time was organizing PRODEMCA, a nonprofit group that backed administration policy in Central America, told Cruz to "get your best conditions up front and go all the way." He was convinced the Sandinistas would lose in an honest election. "You put José Gómez on the ballot, you would have gotten a majority. There were two ways we could win. If it forced them to repress the opposition and if we won."

Offsetting these overtures was an invitation to Bergold from John Carbaugh, the former Helms aide who was now a peripatetic lobbyist and still a hyperactive champion of conservative causes. Over drinks at the Metropolitan Club, Carbaugh discussed ways to manage election strategy so as to discredit the Sandinistas. Carbaugh felt the standard for Nicaragua should be the same as in Honduras, El Salvador, Costa Rica, and Argentina, and "we should not give them any special privileges."

Carbaugh's attitude was widely shared among conservatives, who were out of touch with the political situation on the ground.

Their instinctual distrust of Sandinista intentions was reinforced by conservative Nicaraguans who passed through Washington with increasing frequency that summer and spoke of *zancudismo*, or parasitism, in describing the nature of the elections. It was a term drawn from the Somoza era; a *zancudo*, Spanish for mosquito, was a conservative Somoza opponent who collaborated with the regime.

Thus the line was drawn. One group thought the elections could "spark something exciting" and favored taking risks as Enders had in El Salvador to see how things would run; the other felt that the opposition was fated to lose in a Marxist-Leninist election, the Sandinistas should not be legitimized, and the contest should be blocked. Either course was a self-fulfilling prophecy. Johnstone asserted that the entire administration supported the policy formulated at the State Department that Cruz should run if he could get fair conditions. Singer gave this assessment: "It was ARA [the Bureau of Inter-American Affairs] with the support of the secretary of state against the rest of the government."

In addition to the obstacles in his path at home, Johnstone faced a number of challenges in Managua. A major hitch was the divisiveness of the internal opposition, a central feature in Nicaraguan political culture that predated Sandinista rule. In an effort to gain unity, the opposition in 1982 had formed an umbrella group, the Coordinadora Democrática (Democratic Coordinator), which tried to forge unity through decisions by consensus. The group consisted of four political parties, two trade unions, and representatives of six business organizations. Coordinadora generated rhetoric and wish lists, but its cumbersome decision-making method lent itself to the tyranny of the minority of conservative businessmen, and it proved incapable of crafting a workable election strategy. The group found themselves continually outmaneuvered by the Sandinistas and failed to achieve even their most basic goal, to hold a dialogue with the Sandinistas before proceeding.

The only program they had been able to agree on was a nine-point plan in December 1983 which the Sandinistas simply ignored. The first demand was to separate the Sandinista party from the Sandinista army, which meant reorganizing the army. The ninth set talks

between the Sandinistas and the contras as a condition for participating in the elections.*

In their March meeting, Johnstone had cautioned Cruz not to be
caught up with these maximalist terms. Johnstone felt quite a few of
the nine were "killers."

It was early July, and the Coordinadora had yet to choose a candidate. Under prodding by a visiting West German parliamentary delegation, a sort of rump Coordinadora consisting of two political figures
representing both ends of the spectrum got together and made the
decision. They were Enrique Bolaños, a wealthy cotton grower and
head of COSEP (the Superior Council of Private Enterprise), and
Azucena Ferrey, one of the more dynamic women of Nicaraguan
politics, who headed the Social Christian party, a close ally of COPEI,
the Venezuelan Christian Democratic party. The selection process
took place "in the darkness of a tunnel," Bolaños said. They wrote
down five names: Arturo Cruz; Adolfo Calero; Ismael Reyes, head of
the Nicaraguan Red Cross; Alfonso Robelo; and Eduardo Rivas
Gasteazoro, deputy leader of the Coordinadora. "I said, number one
is OK with COSEP. Number two has his finger on the trigger, no good.
Number four is the same as number two. Number five is very ill. So
numbers one and three were okay with us in that order."[4]

Ferrey flew to Washington and asked Cruz. It was July 11, and the
Sandinistas had set a deadline of July 25 for the registration of
candidates. Bolaños and Ferrey agreed that if Cruz was willing, he
should be the candidate of the entire Coordinadora. He agreed.
Ahead of him was a formidable task: it was four months before the
election and nothing had been organized.

Besides diverging from democratic practice, the procedure for
choosing the Coordinadora candidate deprived the anointed candidate of a political base; by virtue of the delays, he had no way of
creating one on returning to Nicaragua. Cruz was everyone's candidate and no one's candidate. Ferrey wanted him to run under any
circumstances. Bolaños's view was close to that of conservatives in

* The nine points amounted to the framework for a constitution: 1. Separation
between the organs of state—the army, police, militias, and news media—and the
FSLN party. 2. Repeal of censorship and laws violating private property rights.
3. Suspension of the state of emergency. 4. Amnesty to allow all Nicaraguans to
participate in the election process. 5. Respect for freedom of religion. 6. Union
freedom, to allow full exercise of rights including to strike. 7. Judicial autonomy.
8. Reinstatement of habeas corpus. 9. A national dialogue with "all the parties and
political movements, including those that have taken up arms" leading to elections.[3]

Washington: he could not foresee circumstances in which Cruz should run.

Cruz's main constituency was in Washington, and Washington was split. Johnstone clearly hoped Cruz could find his way clear to registering. White House officials said they supported the goal, but their sincerity was quickly called into question.

Before leaving Washington, where he was working at the Inter-American Development Bank, Cruz touched several bases. He called on deputy House Majority Whip Bill Alexander (D.-Ark.) and his aide Brent Budowsky, who represented congressional liberals, a group with a lively interest in his candidacy; then met representatives of the AFL-CIO labor federation, and with them he called on Menges at the White House. "Menges thought that we should go. He said that was his first impression." But Cruz said he replied: "Look, we have to see if this is legitimate or not because we cannot afford to legitimize a tyranny."

A better guide to White House thinking was contained in two Reagan speeches. Once again, the President's rhetoric pointed to a different policy than that which the State Department was pursuing. On July 18, the eve of the fifth anniversary of Somoza's demise, Reagan launched a new public relations offensive to gain $21 million in contra aid by labeling Nicaragua a "totalitarian dungeon." Then on July 19, hours before the Sandinistas announced the ground rules for the election contest and four days before Cruz returned to Managua to test the waters, Reagan belittled the scheduled Nicaraguan elections. "No person committed to democracy will be taken in by a Soviet-style sham," he said. "We think that's what it's going to be," White House spokesman Larry Speakes told reporters. The main stress of the President's speech was that the United States had a "moral responsibility" to aid the contras so long as the Sandinistas continued "communist interference" in the region.

The controversial language was drafted by Menges, who felt it should have been even more explicit. "I think my preferred language was 'Soviet-style fraudulent elections,' " Menges said three years later. "Every communist government has these phony Soviet-style fraudulent elections. . . . Obviously I felt it was very important to give the American people, friendly governments and the communist Sandinistas notice that the President was watching them." Menges asserted that Reagan's harsh rhetoric did not prejudge the issue and was "an effort to be constructive." But at the time, according to one of the speechwriters, he argued for the language on the ground that the election would be a Soviet-style sham. This was a different pitch than the one he gave Cruz.

The tenor of the Reagan remarks disturbed some top aides. Robert McFarlane said he had grave doubts about Sandinista intentions but believed that a credible policy required factual evidence, which could be obtained only with Cruz's return. Although Johnstone's effort to encourage Cruz was the agreed-upon strategy, Reagan's speech pointed in the other direction. At the State Department, this was viewed as par for the course. "The watchword around the government is that the White House is entitled to its rhetoric. That goes for any White House," said one knowledgeable official. The problem is that words that easily flow from a speechwriter's pen in Washington and have little impact on U.S. opinion transform into a mighty roar in the village-like context of a small Central American state.

Reagan had sent an important signal, effectively writing off the Nicaraguan elections before anyone in Washington was aware of the political facts on the ground. It was the triumph of Carbaugh's line of thinking. In the context of a drive to renew aid for the contras, the remarks made clear that the White House priority was on external military pressures, not an internal settling of political differences. Either approach was a gamble, but Reagan was placing his chips on the external.

"Reagan's rhetoric produces the triumphalism of the hard-liners. It means you abandon strategy," said Bill Baez, a close associate of Cruz, who as head of the leading organization of Nicaraguan cooperatives was one of the representatives of COSEP on the Coordinadora. Cruz concurred. "As long as the recalcitrant opposition has a reading of things that the United States eventually will invade Nicaragua and kick the Sandinistas out and say, here, now, we will pick a king, we will not be able to articulate our own policy and really address the issues we have to as Nicaraguans." White House rhetoric never did fall into line with State Department efforts.

A second challenge for Johnstone was bringing the FDN on board. That turned out to be easy so long as Cruz was not really going to run. Johnstone laid the groundwork by approaching Calero directly; Cruz also was in direct touch with Calero, as were the congressional liberals. "We were told by this fellow Brent Budowsky and by Bill Alexander that if we were open to the elections, then people would be convinced that the Sandinistas were not to be trusted," Calero said. Calero agreed and went so far as to offer to lay down arms should the Sandinistas accept the conditions of the internal opposition. This was a calculated ploy. "I was sure that the Sandinistas were never going to meet them, so I could be really audacious," Calero said. Calero also had every reason to be confident the opposition would never take part in the elections. "I knew the way the Nicaraguan people think. There was enough history that the fear of legitimation of a fraudulent action would have prevailed. That's why I went out on a limb."

Even before setting foot on Nicaraguan soil, Cruz had reason to be ambivalent. With U.S. counsel divided, he was on his own. On the eve of his departure, Cruz gave a long interview to Fred Francis, an NBC television reporter, in which he assessed his chances. As the crew packed up, Cruz approached Francis. "You know I'm really not going to run. You know that." Francis threw out the interview.

Cruz's ambivalence quickly surfaced in Managua, where he returned on July 23. Without consulting any of his political allies, Cruz raised the ante in a speech on July 24. "Of the Coordinadora's nine points, which are in fact our catechism, we have decided that the ninth will now be first," he said at an opposition rally in Managua, referring to the demand for negotiations with the armed opposition.*

Cruz was worried about being seen as a *zancudo* and was looking for a way out. Ferrey was scornful. "When Somoza gave elections, they were dirty and fraudulent compared to what the Sandinistas were offering. Arturo did not know how to distinguish between the two dictatorships."

Sandinista handling of the rally bore Ferrey out. Cruz's entire speech, including the charge that the "ruling party has a monopoly on television and the other essential communications media," was carried live on Managua radio. So was his statement: "The time has come, compatriots, to choose freely between destruction, hunger, and death caused by the FSLN's stubborn decision to force the country onto a path that is alien to our culture; and bread, peace, and life, as guaranteed by democracy within the community of free

---

* Cruz's impulsive decision was suggested by his son, Arturo Jr. "I advised him that sometimes you have to announce a *fait accompli*. This is the mark of leadership. He did this on my advice."[5]

Western nations—without excluding friendly relations but also without selling out to the Communist countries."[6]

Miguel Obando y Bravo, the Archbishop of Nicaragua, shared Ferrey's sentiment. In a sermon on the eve of Cruz's return, Obando had called on Roman Catholics to vote in the next elections for candidates who "respect dignity and human rights." "If the elections are free," he said, "the people are obliged to vote." Cruz said Obando told him privately that his own informal polling of campesinos revealed a groundswell of support for him. "Why don't you politicians give it a try? I respect what you politicians are trying to do. But why don't you find a way to do it?"

Cruz got the registration deadline extended until Sunday, August 5. In the meantime, he planned three rallies: a closed-door meeting in Jinotepe, his home town, a semipublic meeting in Matagalpa, and a public rally in Chinandega on the Sunday of the deadline.

Chinandega symbolized the election contest that might have been.

The Sandinistas were worried. Ortega had visited the town the night before the rally to try to discourage people from attending, Cruz said.[7] Workers were threatened with the loss of their jobs. Television ads and handbills urged people not to attend. But everything backfired.

Without having any idea of the reception, Cruz decided to drive first through the town. The marketplace was jammed with townspeople and peasants from the surrounding cotton-growing area when the motorcade of station wagons, cars, and vans rolled up. From forty yards, the crowd looked hostile. A fat woman in a red dress was shouting something and shaking her fists in the air threateningly. Others in the throng were also shouting in anger. Cruz sank back in the front passenger's seat of the Subaru station wagon driven by his friend Mario Rappaccioli. "You sons of bitches, go back home," Cruz muttered.

"Look, we're going to get a barrage of insults, so let's lower the window," he told Rappaccioli. "I like insults."

The crowd *was* hostile that Sunday morning, but not toward Cruz. The fat woman had been crying "Down with the Sandinistas." Others shouted: "We don't want communism. We want democracy." And "Food, not arms." The motorcade slowed. More chants. "Viva Arturo. Viva Cruz. Down with the Sandinistas."

It was a political moment. By all accounts, the outburst was spontaneous.

They then drove to a baseball field just outside the town for the rally. Vandals had destroyed the platform and stands at 5 a.m., but opposition backers rebuilt them. About 7,000 supporters had gathered, mostly farmers, cotton pickers, sugar cane cutters, and port workers from nearby Corinto. They had taken a risk in coming, for, as a U.S. embassy staffer noted, state security was present, photographing them. About fifteen minutes into the rally, someone shouted: "The mob is coming on the highway." Supporters began to run. "I thought they were going to break up the rally," said Rappaccioli, a leader of the Conservative party. "Two or three minutes later, I realized what they did. They went out and faced the *turba* [mob] and made them turn back." He said the supporters turned back a *turba* of about 300. "Chinandega was very successful," recalled Bill Baez. "Our mob was bigger than their mob."

Until Chinandega, Cruz had had no idea of the depth of resentment of his countrymen against the Sandinistas. He vividly recalled a peasant woman passing a note to him hand over hand at the rally. The spelling was poor and the handwriting crude but it was "the greatest treasure, because it revealed all." It was brief. "Don Arturo, they're liars. It isn't true what they say to the world. Go and tell the world that they are liars. We are sick and tired of this."

There could have been an insurrection.

One of the most striking facts about the Chinandega rally was that no one in Washington seemed to know about it. No U.S. reporter was present. Sandinista censors chopped so much of the news and photographs from *La Prensa,* the opposition newspaper, that its editorial board decided not to publish the next day, so Nicaraguans never got the full story. For reasons that are not clear, officials at the very top of the Reagan administration right up to McFarlane, the national security adviser, were unaware of the event; yet Bergold said he had cabled a complete report based on the observations of a U.S. diplomat at the scene.

Ferrey tried to convince Cruz that the popular sentiment reflected in Chinandega was more important than the consensus in Coordinadora. "They were not listening to the grass roots," said Ferrey of the politicians. But Cruz, anxious about his lack of a political base in Nicaragua, had already plotted his escape. The day after Chinandega he returned to Washington, and for five weeks suspended his campaign. Most of that time he spent traveling in Latin America in search of advice on what to do next.

Meanwhile, in Washington the struggle had intensified between Johnstone on the one side and Menges, North, and Casey on the other. Johnstone had been working with staff to prepare a new list of demands without the maximalist "killers" while his adversaries worked to thwart him.

North's role by this time extended well into the policy process. At one RIG meeting, Johnstone sought approval for a concept to test Sandinista promises of a pluralistic political system. North was trying to block it.

"At least Constantine believes in democracy," Johnstone snapped. "You don't."[8]

Johnstone won agreement in Washington on a modified set of demands, which Cruz essentially adopted as his own. They were: freedom of the press; freedom of assembly; access to voter registration lists and election returns; international observation of the elections; security of voting places; freedom to campaign on military bases; and postponement of the elections to allow at least ninety days of campaigning. The killer provisions, such as the requirement for a national dialogue between the Sandinistas and the contras, were dropped.

But the scale-back of demands only galvanized the opponents in Washington and Managua. Calero withdrew his commitment to back Cruz. Johnstone responded in a joint approach to the FDN with a high CIA official, which brought the FDN back on board. After other U.S. officials had urged the internal opposition to ignore the stated policy, Johnstone also made an approach to them.

One such message came from the U.S. ambassador in San José, Curtin Winsor Jr., a conservative businessman who was a political appointee and an outspoken proponent of overthrowing the Sandinistas. (Winsor once compared their rule to "an infected piece of meat" that attracts "insects.") He viewed Johnstone and Motley as "the principal villains" in Central America policy, and alleged that Johnstone in particular was "solidly opposed to the freedom fighters."[9] Even among conservatives, Winsor was regarded as having extreme views. "Steam rises from between his ears," said one friend.

Winsor had known Bill Baez through business contacts for many years. At breakfast in San José on August 29, Winsor told Baez he had received word that the White House did not want the opposition to participate. "I think you should be aware of the problems and situation," Baez quoted Winsor as having said. "There is a division in the government. Some people in the State Department are saying you should participate. I represent the views of the White House. My opinion is that it is not appropriate to go." Baez said he did not feel pressured. "But I began to understand that there was a difference of opinion within the administration. When someone tells you the White House says 'don't participate,' you don't have to be stupid to know what to do." Baez responded that the opposition would analyze the situation. He went back to Managua and briefed his associates.*

Johnstone learned of the conversation from embassy reporting and flew to San José for a dinner with Winsor. "I don't know who you're getting your instructions from, but it is no known organ of government," he told Winsor.† Once again, Menges was a source of inspiration. "There was nothing systematic. There was no attempt to communicate a 'White House point of view,' " Menges later said. But he added that if Winsor had asked him, he might have said, "No, I don't think they'll hold a fair election."

A third obstacle on the ground was CIA operatives in Central America. "I know the CIA was all against it. They were transmitting this loudly and clearly," said a source familiar with the thinking of Alfonso Robelo, the opposition leader who at the time was in San José. Cruz's son, Arturo Jr., who was frequently in the Costa Rican capital, concurs. "The State Department behaved in a very civilized way. But the sergeants of 'the Company' were behaving differently in the field. They were talking to their clients and saying Cruz is going to sell you out." And a congressional source stated that Bolaños had at least two meetings with the CIA chief of station in San José at about this time. Johnstone disputed assertions that the CIA was undermining official policy, but said he had detected the erosion in support for Cruz among the internal opposition and acted "with dispatch" to shore it up.[10]

The CIA signals fortified the hard-liners in the Coordinadora in Managua but also led to a profound misunderstanding. Those in Managua agreed with their counterparts in Washington on the intermediate goal of discrediting the elections but not on who should

---

* Winsor's version is that he made a point of being well-informed and tried to give a reading of "what I thought was going on." "There were conflicting views of what the decision should be. Craig Johnstone wanted accommodation . . . on the other hand other elements and common sense, political elements said it makes no sense at all for them to accredit a farcical conclusion."
† Winsor was fired later that year.

be the beneficiaries. The hard-liners in Managua hoped to destroy the legitimacy of the elections but on the assumption that they would benefit. Those in Washington did it in hopes that the contras and the external military solution would benefit.

During a visit to Bogotá in early September, Cruz won from Betancur a promise to work for the Sandinista acceptance of the modified demands. When he returned to Managua, Cruz heard from him every other day. But Betancur had his own agenda: to talk the Sandinistas into accepting the Contadora revised treaty at the same time. On September 19, Betancur notified Cruz of what he thought was a double victory. The call came midway through an indoor rally in León that was marred by government-organized violence.

"Arturo," Cruz recalls his saying, "I have very good, good news. Sergio Ramírez has called me with the full authority from the national directorate of the FSLN to tell me that they are going to extend the campaign period and they are willing to meet most of your demands." He asked Cruz to provide a written presentation of the Coordinadora's demands.

Cruz readily agreed but informed him that circumstances belied an amicable solution. As they spoke, *turbas divinas* were pelting the building with rocks.

"You may observe that I am shouting," Cruz replied.

"Yes, why, Arturo?" Betancur asked.

"I am surrounded by very unfriendly people. And one of the guarantees precisely that we need, Mr. President, is that we can meet freely. We are being obstructed."

Betancur said: "Arturo, by all means that is totalitarian behavior."

Worse violence occurred on September 21, in Boaco, about fifty miles east of Managua, where a crowd of about one hundred broke through police barriers, stoned Cruz's car, and broke the windshield. Cruz was hit by a rock and slightly injured. "They were really mad. Arturo and I were nearly killed," said his friend Bill Baez. The Supreme Electoral Council, headed by Mariano Fiallos, did not investigate the incident on the grounds that Cruz was not a registered candidate.[11]*

---

* One aspect of the violence that puzzled those at whom it was directed was the authorship. At first, the mobs appeared to be at the direction of Borge's interior ministry. The army, under the command of Humberto Ortega, rescued the opposition in León. Then the roles reversed. "In Boaco we were protected by Borge's policemen and the mob were army people," Bill Baez said. Indeed, Daniel Ortega publicly took credit for the violence.

On September 21, the Sandinista directorate agreed to the Contadora draft but did not reach any conclusion regarding Cruz's modified election campaign terms. On September 27, Cruz telexed the new opposition demands to Betancur. Betancur conferred with Bayardo Arce, who was en route to Rio de Janeiro to represent the Sandinistas at the annual leadership conference of the Socialist International, which groups the world's Social Democratic parties.

Betancur then passed the baton to Carlos Andrés Pérez, a senior Socialist International official and former president of Venezuela. Pérez in the meantime had personally invited Cruz and two colleagues to Rio and promised "ample possibilities of having important conversations."

A few days later Arce met with Cruz in Rio. Arce fidgeted in his chair and nervously rolled his shirtsleeves up and down. The bearded, somewhat intellectual-looking former journalist with *La Prensa* was now in charge of political affairs for the Sandinista party. Opposite him was Cruz, who, in an equally nervous state, chain-smoked and moved about uncomfortably in his chair.

The setting was Pérez's suite at the Rio Palace Hotel, overlooking the Copacabana; the date, Sunday, September 30. For three days Pérez cajoled, berated, and pushed the two sides. When the negotiations were over, Arce accused Cruz of blocking the deal and Cruz claimed Arce had welshed.

These were the first real negotiations between the Sandinistas and the opposition since the election was announced. It was the last best chance to resolve the Nicaragua dispute through political means. It was the crunch for U.S. policy. Johnstone said that of all the efforts to reach a peaceful settlement, "that one came the closest, I think."

The importance of the talks is undisputed. Exactly what went wrong in Rio is very much disputed. Nearly two years later, even Pérez, who chaired the talks, said he had not figured it out.[12]

One reason is that both sides were engaged in gamesmanship.

For Cruz to register so late in the election process, it was essential to delay the elections to avoid being accused by his associates of a sell-out. For the hard-liners in the Coordinadora, who wanted to discredit the process, it was essential to block Cruz from reaching a deal.

The Sandinistas wanted to avoid a delay but also to avoid blame for the collapse of the mediation.

The Reagan administration was a major participant at Rio, even if not present. But again it was divided. The State Department hoped for national reconciliation in the form of elections and sought an agreement on terms Cruz could live with. The hard right wanted to delegitimize the election and would distrust any agreement that emerged.

The Sandinistas had been aware of mixed signals all that summer from Reagan's rhetoric, from Kirkpatrick at the UN, and from Manzanillo, showing the gulf between those seeking a domestic political resolution and those favoring an external military policy. However unable they had proved to exploit U.S. divisions for diplomatic gain in the past, they knew how to use them in domestic politics.

Pérez, the Socialist International vice-president for Latin America, also was engaged in chicanery, though of a different sort. He had not told his SI colleagues that he had invited Cruz and his Coordinadora colleagues, paid for their tickets,* and laid all the groundwork for negotiations. Nor did he tell them about the first meeting that Sunday afternoon.

The first disagreement was over what to call the rebel forces. Arce wanted them to be called "contras." After a "very, very long conversation," Pérez said they agreed to call them "groups which have taken up arms against the Sandinista revolutionary government."

Pérez urged Arce to accept conditions within which Cruz could participate. He began with the nine demands that the Coordinadora had presented to the Sandinistas and separated out statements that would be regarded as ultimatums. The meeting lasted three and a half hours.

Arce and Cruz met again the following morning, Monday, October 1, this time in the presence of Hans-Jürgen Wischnewski, a close associate of SI president Willy Brandt, and several West German Social Democrats. Cruz was accompanied by vice-presidential candidate Adán Fletes and Coordinadora president Luis Rivas-Leiva. Hanging over the talks was the latest deadline for registration, running out at midnight that night.

In one hour, the negotiations made remarkable progress. The Coordinadora presented the demands they had sent to Betancur. In return for satisfaction, they promised to participate in the election if the date was postponed to February 24, 1985.

---

* A very wealthy man, Pérez said he picked up the tab for their travel but was reimbursed by the Venezuelan government.

Arce readily agreed to all the guarantees.

Cruz and his two colleagues asked for a break to confer with Managua. At the other end, opposition leaders gathered around a speakerphone in the offices of the Social Christian party. Bolaños kept a low profile; the spokesman was Daniel Bonilla, an industrialist associate of Bolaños and perhaps the hardest of the hard-liners. And he was deeply skeptical.*

After lunch the three negotiators denounced Arce's concessions as demagoguery, demanded additional access to the official news media as a condition, and required that the Sandinistas immediately agree to February 24 or some other postponement of election day. Then Arce dropped a bombshell. If Coordinadora registered before midnight, the contest would be delayed until January 13, 1985, provided there was an effective cease-fire with the contras. Arce insisted that Coordinadora declare a cease-fire by October 10 and that Calero's and Pastora's groups withdraw from Nicaragua by October 25. On the other hand, if the Sandinistas did not live up to their part of the bargain, the opposition could withdraw its registration any time up to October 25.

The atmosphere in the room was suddenly electrified.

Cruz called Managua again. "My advice to you is you go and register," Cruz told his associates. "Do it, register, because we have all the necessary safeguards not to be trapped. Do something really meaningful and we will really grow in stature."

"Arturo," Bonilla intoned, "whatever is going to be done is going to be done here. That is what the Coordinadora wants." Bonilla objected that the Coordinadora could not represent both the armed and the civic resistance. "I cannot have one single man representing the whole, because that would get the civic in bed with the military."

In Washington, Johnstone closely monitored the progress. He was in frequent touch with Baez, who was in Washington. Johnstone asked to be kept informed but felt Cruz should proceed. He also was in touch with SI officials. "The United States government asked the SI to do its utmost to help the Coordinadora reach a deal," said a close associate of Brandt.[13]

---

* Bonilla was an ideologue. "Communists don't convene an election unless they have all the means to win it," he said in an interview more than a year later. "We don't believe in the elections. We would have lost. And there is nothing worse in politics than losing. That is not the worst thing. . . . It is that we would have made the Sandinistas win with our presence. My God, do you know what that means?"

Working along with Johnstone was a senior CIA official. Johnstone
said each called his contacts in the opposition and the FDN to keep
them from backing away in the midst of the negotiations. The FDN
"were extremely concerned about not being undercut by third force
representation in elections that would legitimize the Sandinista
regime," Johnstone said. He asserted that the CIA supported his
plan. "I was working out of the same room as the CIA guy and unless
some other part of the Agency was trying to undermine him, we
were giving the same advice: take part if you can get fair terms."*

Despite the cold reception, Cruz thought he saw a way to bridge
the differences. "This is the most exhilarating day in my whole life,"
he told Brent Budowsky on the telephone that night. "We actually
have a chance to have an election and stop the war." Cruz asked for
advice: "I probably need forty-eight hours to go back to tell my own
people. Is that unreasonable?" Budowsky said he replied: "My
judgment is no, you're talking about stopping a war. I don't think it
is that big a deal."

The deadline passed without action.

A dejected-looking Pérez received Wischnewski the next morning
and pronounced the negotiation a failure. Actually, he had another
card up his sleeve. Without telling his SI colleagues, Pérez had asked
Arce to prepare a typed summary of the points of agreement,
including the election postponement on condition of a cease-fire.
Unannounced, an aide to Arce appeared with the document. (A
translation is reproduced in Appendix III.)

Pérez gave a copy to Cruz, who promised to return with a
response at 4 p.m. Cruz checked with Managua, where he received
more discouragement.

Bonilla reiterated that the decision must be made in Managua. To
drive the point home, he had the Coordinadora reaffirm its stand in
a terse telegram. "Ratifying our conversation that you come back.
Anything that is going to be done is going to be done in Nicaragua,"
it said. Cruz said he never received it.

Now Cruz dropped his own bombshell. Appearing at the appointed time, he went through Arce's paper point by point, wrote in

---

* Other U.S. diplomats familiar with the negotiations say Clarridge's replacement as
the senior CIA officer in charge of operations in Central America, Alan Fiers, saw the
value of encouraging the opposition to take part in the elections, but that this view
had not taken hold down the line. A total turnover in CIA personnel took place
between June and October. As a result, these sources said, CIA officials in Central
America told their opposition contacts to hold out for the toughest terms possible.

changes of wording, then agreed to it. He conditioned his signature upon a "vote of confidence" by the Coordinadora in Managua. If they did not back him, he would withdraw as their candidate. Arce reacted angrily. "In the beginning, they said a big fat 'no,'" Pérez said. "They [the Sandinistas] said it was a joke to discredit the electoral process by doing this."

"I represent the Sandinista Front, and although only five comandantes are now in Nicaragua, I have committed myself here and now," Arce said. "But I have received no comparable pledge from Arturo Cruz, otherwise the Coordinadora could have registered before the deadline. Either you sign now," he insisted, "or I don't sign."

Pérez became visibly peeved with Arce and in what appeared to be a slip of the tongue, addressed him as "Comandante Bastardo." "I was watching his expression," Rivas-Leiva said of Arce. "The first time, no reaction. The third or fourth time, I noticed it bothered him."

Pérez stressed the significance of Cruz's personal commitment to return to Managua and put his name on the ballot, and for a brief moment Arce seemed to relent.

It was about 5 p.m. "For twenty minutes we had an agreement," said Thorwald Stoltenberg, a former Norwegian defense minister who had joined the talks for the SI. The two sides shook hands. "They were very, very pleased. We were starting to drink cognac." Stoltenberg suggested they type out the contents of the accord. Cruz dictated the final wording to Pérez. "Luis Rivas-Leiva, as president of the Coordinadora, accompanied by Adán Fletes and Arturo Cruz, also agrees, both parties *ad referendum* to their respective organizations." Stoltenberg took a call from *Dagbladet*, a Norwegian newspaper, and broke the news to the press. An hour later, he had to phone the newspaper back and say the negotiations had fallen through.

Arce suddenly stood up, shook hands with the West German SI participants, and bolted.

Cruz thought the signal had been given in New York by Daniel Ortega. In an interview published that morning in the *Washington Post*, Ortega had declared that the election would take place on schedule. "We were flexible on the date until a few days ago," he said. "The elections are going to take place on November 4. At this point we cannot continue to play with the date."*

---

* Johnstone concurred with Cruz. "It was unbelievable. A moderate [Ortega] undercutting a hard-liner [Arce]."

Later, in a UN General Assembly speech, Ortega predicted that the United States would invade Nicaragua on or before October 15 in order to sabotage the elections.

But Arce had been bluffing all along.

"Extending the campaign was never a position for us," said Ramírez, the campaign manager and candidate for vice-president of the ruling party. "We always considered that it would be damaging for us because people would not be confident about our own elections if we did." Arce had made the offer in the knowledge it was unacceptable. Moreover, according to Ramírez, "Cruz never had authority over Bermúdez and Calero . . . and the Coordinadora didn't have that authority."

Cruz said he had known that the Sandinistas were bluffing. "We had to be forthcoming and call their bluff or to reach a real agreement if it was possible."

Arce went before a press conference. "Yesterday at midnight they lost their last chance to register. There is no longer any question. The elections will be held in Nicaragua on November 4."

Pérez said that information he received subsequent to Rio gave the impression that "the CIA had given instructions, had put pressures [on representatives of the Coordinadora] against Cruz's candidacy and therefore it wasn't accepted. They just didn't want someone with the prestige of Cruz to enter the elections, because it would validate them. They wanted to demonstrate there was no freedom of elections in Nicaragua." Pérez felt the "game" of the Coordinadora had been "simply to take away legitimacy."

Neither Ortega, after he became president, nor Ramírez, after he became vice-president, could cite specific evidence that the CIA was responsible.*

On returning to Managua, Cruz found that the Coordinadora was anything but supportive. Bolaños felt that Cruz had agreed to "a bunch of foolish things. I don't know how he could promise that. He was saying yes to everything." Bonilla's view was: "I don't think any

---

* Ortega said, "The best evidence was that Mr. Cruz was receiving funds from the CIA," a reference to a stipend which Cruz confirmed receiving that summer. "Cruz is part of the whole works. All these gears were oiled by CIA money. It is possible that Cruz was really excited about the possibility of running, but CIA money oiled the works, and the machinery wouldn't let him participate." The only evidence Ramírez could cite was a *New York Times* account quoting administration officials who said that Bolaños and other COSEP leaders had met CIA officials in Washington and San José that summer. (The *Times* account said Bolaños denied any CIA links.)[14]

plan proposed by [Arce] would have been any good except for them."
Cruz said he told them: "There are some elements among you who
might think that I am risking your interests. Accordingly, I am going
to go away."

On October 11, a full week after the break-up in Rio, the
Coordinadora changed its mind and backed the election accord.
Stoltenberg of the SI flew to Managua, followed by Brandt, to ask for
a postponement in the elections. But the Sandinistas refused. "The
case was lost in Rio," Stoltenberg said.

Johnstone blamed the collapse of Rio on the Sandinistas. Had they
given Cruz the forty-eight hours he desired and had he decided to
run despite the criticism of the Coordinadora, it would have caused
an uproar among the armed resistance and their backers in the
Reagan administration. "Too bad the Sandinistas didn't stick it out.
They might have forced the FDN to back out," Johnstone said.

The crisis then would have come home to roost in Washington.

REGRETS

After the mediation collapsed, the Reagan administration quickly
agreed that no democratic opposition party should take part in the
elections. "In an election that the opposition could not win, it was
better to have them out," said one Johnstone aide. The State
Department also took it upon itself to urge other countries not to
send official teams of observers. "We felt the elections were fatally
flawed and were hoping to expose their lack of credibility," said
another.[15]

There were two problem cases. One was Virgilio Godoy of the
Independent Liberals, who already had registered as a presidential
candidate, and the second was Fletes of the Social Christians, who
U.S. officials feared might run anyway. Motley, under pressure from
Casey, instructed the embassy in Managua to "firm up Fletes." A
diplomat in the embassy's political section was dispatched with the
message. "We were told to make sure that Fletes knew we wanted
him to stay with the Coordinadora," said a U.S. source.

To deal with Godoy, the ambassador himself was dispatched along
with his political office director, Michael Joyce. His instructions
were to lay out U.S. objections and conclude: "Accordingly, we hope
you do not run." Bergold felt his instructions were "fuzzy" and

ignored the last part of the message. It proved superfluous. Godoy told him the party was evenly divided and he would follow the party's will. The next day, the party voted overwhelmingly against his participation.

Godoy thereupon went to the Supreme Electoral Council and gave written notice that the Independent Liberals were withdrawing from the race and wanted their candidates' names removed from the ballot.

The collapse of the Rio talks had unexpected repercussions in Congress, which at the time was still grappling with the contra aid question. The Democratic House had voted a total cut-off, but the Republican Senate defeated a similar measure, and the conference was unable to bridge the difference. The compromise, to delay a vote on $14 million until February 1985, was suggested by liberal Democrats who had supported Cruz's candidacy and felt the Sandinistas were to blame for the breakdown. Bruce Cameron, then the lobbyist for Americans for Democratic Action, and Robert Leiken, a senior associate with the Carnegie Endowment for International Peace, drafted a *Washington Post* opinion article which they and the State Department distributed prior to publication on October 9. "The fate of a country—even a region—may be in the balance," the article, which appeared under Leiken's byline, said. "Our best hope to avoid regional war and national bloodbath would be to suspend a decision on aid to the contras until after the Nicaraguan elections."[16] On October 10, a few days later, the conference did that, keeping the issue open until another day. The compromise allowed the administration to return for another vote on $14 million in military aid in March 1985.

The elections themselves produced an intriguing result. The Sandinistas captured 67 percent of the vote, a remarkably low figure for a "Communist dictatorship." Although Godoy had quit the race, his name remained on the ballot; he received 9.6 percent and his party got nine seats of the elected ninety seats. The Sandinistas took sixty-one.

On the day of the election, Reagan told reporters: "I have just one thing to say. It's a phony." And Shultz, through his spokesman, commented: "The Sandinista electoral farce, without any meaningful political opposition, leaves the situation essentially unchanged."

Many observers thought that Cruz would have received at least 40 percent of the vote had he run. The most consistent and supportive backers of his participation, the leaders of Venezuela's two parties, derived two conclusions from the elections.

One was that Cruz should have run. "I hold the conviction that if Cruz had gone to the elections, the democratic opposition would have gotten not less than 45 percent of the vote," said Luis Herrera Campíns, the former Venezuelan president and a leading figure in the COPEI, or Christian Democratic party.*

The other was that the Reagan administration tried to block him. Venezuela's parties were well plugged into the internal opposition parties in Nicaragua. "They kept on telling us that the United States was telling the internal opposition not to participate in order to sabotage the elections," said a senior U.S. diplomat in Caracas.

Pérez, a leader of Acción Democrática, the Social Democratic party in Venezuela, who had organized the mediation, said he had had no expectation that the Sandinistas, as a group of guerrillas who had fought their way to the top, would let power go because of elections, but thought elections might have put Nicaragua on a course similar to that of Mexico: left-of-center, semidemocratic, broadly based one-party rule. He viewed the Nicaraguan election as "not a solution to the problem, but it certainly was an opening."

Cruz agreed, and his will be the judgment that lasts.

"In hindsight," said Cruz, "we should have gone, with or without conditions. In hindsight, I feel you must go to elections to prove there has been a fraud. From a purely political standpoint, against a totalitarian system, you might as well go and bloody your nose."

Four weeks later, Harry Shlaudeman sat down with Victor Tinoco in Manzanillo for their seventh session. "I think you just missed the great opportunity," Shlaudeman said.

"From now on," Bergold told Saul Arana, head of the North America desk at the Nicaraguan foreign ministry, "you have to understand that everything will center on the contras. That is our main instrument. Security issues will be secondary."[17]

---

* Herrera Campíns's prediction coincides with the assessment in November 1983 of the Statistic Institute of Spain.

CHAPTER 12

RHETORIC AND REALITY

THE NOVEMBER 4 ELECTIONS marked a watershed in Nicaragua's internal politics and relations with the United States. Daniel Ortega had been elected president, but his title did not confer the power it implied, and he adopted a militant stance at home and abroad as he worked to consolidate his authority. The internal opposition claimed that their boycott had denied legitimacy to Ortega's election. But whatever it did, they now found themselves without a role, a leader, or a future. Skillful and magnanimous treatment of them would have gained Ortega political credit abroad and support at home. Instead, he now presided over a crackdown.

The comandantes' minds were elsewhere. Having gotten through the moment of greatest danger in June 1984, the nine began to overcome their fear of a U.S. invasion and turned their attention to surviving a certain second Reagan term. They defined the threat in military terms and, to deal with it, acquired advanced Soviet weapons, restructured their army, and developed a new counter-insurgency strategy.

Two days after the Nicaraguan elections, Reagan won his second term with 58.4 percent of the vote, a forty-nine-state landslide. For Casey, who had fought to save his contra program with little help from the White House during the campaign, the result was a shot of adrenaline. Mondale had sought to make Nicaragua a campaign issue by pledging upon election to halt the contra program for good. The public had shown little interest, but Congress, perhaps more in reaction to Casey's mismanagement than to Mondale's campaign, had nevertheless suspended all contra aid just three weeks before the election. Casey and other conservatives read Reagan's tremendous victory as a mandate to restore military aid to the contras. Saudi funding secretly arranged by the White House would sustain them for the moment.

The political windfall and secret funding were two factors in the new foreign policy equation. The third was a policy vacuum. Shultz, Motley, and Johnstone had bet the house on the combination of Manzanillo and the Nicaraguan election. But their strategy, relying on the acquiescence of opponents in both capitals, had proved overly ambitious. U.S. officials said the Sandinistas conducted their election fairly on voting day, and probably won the two-thirds majority they claimed. But the absence of a contest in Managua left State empty-handed; and officials had few ideas on what to do next. Ortega's margin of victory became Shultz's margin of defeat.

The combination of political windfall, secret funding, and policy vacuum allowed conservatives to turn Nicaragua policy into the political fight of the year. Their strategy succeeded. In June 1985, Congress voted $27 million in nonmilitary aid; one year later, Congress narrowly approved $100 million, including $70 million in military aid. In so doing, they transformed Nicaragua from a foreign policy concern into pure domestic politics.

But as the issue became politicized, the concepts underlying U.S. policy increasingly fell out of touch with the real world; the facts on the ground became props in the domestic debate.

In place of a strategy, those advocating politicization offered public relations. Otto Reich's public diplomacy office mounted a vigorous and effective propaganda campaign to alter the image of the Sandinistas from Robin Hood to Stalinist thug. Casey had lobbied behind the scenes for a public relations campaign and supported the project by releasing intelligence on the Sandinistas. North, from his perch in the NSC, pressed the bureaucracy to release data quickly. With such heavyweight support as this, Reich hired an outside public relations firm, then proceeded to build a staff with more than a dozen full-time foreign service or other government professionals. The administration capitalized on the Sandinista military build-up and Managua's growing dependency on Moscow by treating them as PR pluses in the struggle with Congress. Yet in terms of policy goals, these were setbacks to U.S. interests that rendered the insurgency or any other course of action by the United States more difficult and costly to pursue. The emphasis placed on the contras as cure-all also made no sense in strategy terms. Historically, domestic political oppositions always play the decisive role in an uprising, and the external armed forces are the adjunct. In the administration's PR terms, however, the opposite was the case. The polarization within Nicaragua that caused more and more of the internal opposition to leave the country became a plus in efforts to sway Congress to back the contras.

A lack of coordination had plagued U.S. policy in the period from 1981 to 1984, when the CIA had managed the contra program and State had intermittently had control of the policy. But that period was smooth compared with what followed. Reagan's hands-off style of management, his readiness to turn foreign policy into domestic politics, and his preference for can-do subordinates operating under his inspiration rather than on carefully formulated guidelines encouraged a kind of free-enterprise competition.

A stunning example of the confusion occurred on the night of the U.S. election. News reports quoted U.S. intelligence to the effect that the Soviet freighter *Bakuriani*, heading for Corinto, might be carrying Soviet MiG-21 combat aircraft. More than a year later, military intelligence and the CIA were not sure if the MiGs had been on board. If so, they were sent back. But the story, fed by administration threats of retaliation, took on a life of its own. The White House compared arms shipments to Nicaragua to the build-up in Cuba shortly before the Soviets installed offensive missiles in 1962. The Pentagon, asserting that Nicaragua had "designs" on its neighbors, announced a series of previously scheduled naval exercises in the Caribbean and ground exercises in Honduras. The Sandinistas renewed their state of emergency, sent tanks and armored vehicles rolling through cities, and put troops and militia on a nationwide alert against the threat of a U.S. invasion. Meanwhile, the Pentagon spokesman said government officials and the news media had jointly contributed to the "hysteria" over the MiGs.*

The false scare set back U.S. policy. If MiGs had in fact been on board, administration goals would have been better served by keeping quiet until they were unloaded. These would have been the first fighter planes possessed by a Soviet ally within range of the Panama Canal. U.S. public opinion would have supported retaliation. More significant militarily was that the nonarrival of the MiGs obscured the actual arrival of a fast, valuable armored aircraft—the Mi-25 Hind helicopter gunship, the export model of the Mi-24 used by the Soviets in Afghanistan. Shortly before the elections, at least five Hinds were delivered to El Bluff on the Atlantic coast of Nicaragua by Bulgarian freighter. These could be used in the counterinsurgency but also in an offensive cross-border operation. Because the public focus was on the higher-threshold response of the MiGs, the Hinds became a secondary issue—in public, that is.

Behind the scenes, the arrival of the Hinds provoked panic, leading North into a step fraught with legal peril, as was revealed during the Iran-Contra hearings nearly three years later. Calero apparently provoked it by complaining that the FDN had not been warned of the Hinds' arrival and adding that the FDN could still destroy the choppers on the ground if it had timely intelligence. Nothing the FDN had done pointed to such a capability, but North swung into action. CIA task force chief Alan Fiers insisted he did not supply the intelligence data, but North obtained it somehow, possibly from the Pentagon. And despite the explicit congressional ban, North turned over maps and other intelligence material to Robert Owen, a volunteer courier, who hand-delivered them to the FDN. Poindexter, then deputy NSC adviser, said he was aware of the handover, but McFarlane, his boss, could not recall giving North any such authority.[2]

Official U.S. threats of retaliation proved to be bluster, thus

---

* David Martin of CBS, who has excellent military intelligence sources, broke the story, but it took off for other reasons. One news account blamed an "overzealous Reagan campaign official" for hyping the story. An administration official "familiar with the process of intelligence dissemination" was quoted as saying: "Originally I got a signal from the White House to go ahead and tip selected reporters about the ship early this week. But then we got a countersignal to hold off until after the election." However, when Martin broke the story, the White House reverted to the earlier plan and confirmed the report.[1]

squandering administration credibility in the region and political support at home. Moreover, radicals in Managua used the bluster to enforce a crackdown on the internal opposition. Most significantly, Nicaragua acquired its most advanced and valuable weapons system to date without any U.S. reaction.

The supercharged atmosphere in the weeks after the election reflected the White House's ambivalence to further direct talks with the Sandinistas.

But the Sandinistas misread the American political signals and, without weighing the impact on U.S. policy of their own uncontested elections and the collision between Contadora and the Manzanillo endeavors, indicated they thought an agreement was in sight. With the encouragement of Fidel Castro, they had convinced themselves that Reagan, reelected, would act like a traditional Republican president and come to terms with an elected Sandinista government as well as with the Castro regime.

At the eighth session at Manzanillo on November 19-20, "we engaged in serious negotiations" on possible Nicaraguan agreement to modify the September 7 Contadora accord, which the Sandinistas had already agreed to sign, according to Raymond Burghardt, who represented the White House at Manzanillo.[3]*

Tinoco made concessions on a key technical question. "It was clear to all of us that they were ready to go a good distance," another U.S. participant said. "They agreed to on-site verification [of arms levels] and were amenable to a fairly complex scheme." But they still had to work out a formal plan as well as agreements regarding arms limitation and a timetable for implementation.

What Bergold termed "the Cuban fantasy period" lasted through February 1985. In December, Daniel Ortega received the ambassador for a rare audience and tested out a theory about the Reagan administration. According to this theory, which presumably originated with Castro, there were two factions. Weinberger, Casey, and Kirkpatrick were implacable enemies of the Sandinistas. The other faction, led by Shultz and McFarlane, had gained great political power and would dominate the second administration; on their advice, Reagan would be amenable to a deal or deals that contained

---

* For example, Shlaudeman proposed that if Nicaragua agreed bilaterally to the continuation of U.S. military exercises, the United States would limit such exercises to agreed levels.

something for everyone. Bergold tried to disabuse Ortega. "You are characterizing it in an inaccurate way," he said. "Perhaps Shultz and McFarlane have a higher tolerance for a negotiated outcome. But the others do not trust the State Department. That is where the differences are. If you knew what Shultz thought of you, you wouldn't be any happier."

At the ninth and final meeting on December 10–11, the Sandinistas apparently drew back from earlier signs of a willingness to modify their stance on Contadora. Instead, the two sides explored the outlines of a security accord that would have committed the Sandinistas to limit their military build-up, halt support for foreign insurgencies, and send home their Cuban and Soviet military advisers in return for a U.S. commitment to halt its support for the contras. These were the last three of Enders's four points of August 1982. The proposal included on-site verification: in short, everything but democratization.* That was an important omission.

According to the Sandinistas, the meeting broke up in disagreement over the question of democratization. According to Shlaudeman, it was over the form the accord might take. To an outside observer, democratization appears to have been the real stumbling block.

Shlaudeman had sought changes in the Contadora act of September 7 along lines demanded by Washington's Central American allies in October. Tinoco parried that the act "as it now stands is unacceptable for you without modifications just as it is for us with modifications." Instead, he suggested "bilateral agreements that could help overcome the problems that emerge at a regional level." His aim was an understanding leading to normal diplomatic relations. Yet that sort of accord had long since ceased to satisfy leading figures in the administration, whose sole object was to regain aid to the contras.

---

* Daniel Ortega, in response to questions in an interview with Peruvian author Mario Vargas Llosa at about this time, spelled out their bottom line. "We're willing to send home the Cubans, the Russians, the rest of the advisers. We're willing to stop the movement of military aid, or any other kind of aid, through Nicaragua to El Salvador, and we're willing to accept international verification. In return, we're asking for only one thing: that they don't attack us, that the United States stop arming and financing the gangs that kill our people, burn our crops and force us to divert enormous human and economic resources into war when we desperately need them for development." Vargas Llosa had put his questions on behalf of the Venezuelan president Jaime Lusinchi, who viewed Ortega's response as a satisfactory answer.[4]

An official Sandinista account of the final session states that Shlaudeman rejected the offer on the grounds that the Sandinistas refused to negotiate with the contras. "We have emphasized the importance of the process of national reconciliation, which implies the incorporation of all opposition sectors into the political process," Shlaudeman was quoted as saying. "You have rejected the possibility of a dialogue with a sector of the opposition, the sector under arms, and this is why we feel it is difficult to reach bilateral agreements."

However, according to Shlaudeman and Burghardt, the meeting foundered on something else, the Sandinistas' effort to supplant the Contadora act, with its vague references to democracy, with a bilateral U.S.-Nicaraguan security accord which would contain no references to democracy. "I don't get it," Shlaudeman said. "This would contradict Contadora. How do you match up the bilateral agreement and Contadora?"

Shlaudeman's statement on its face may appear illogical, for the Manzanillo talks were a bilateral forum with no integral connection with Contadora. But it should be recalled that the context in which Shlaudeman was operating was not the traditional diplomatic pursuit of safeguarding defined national security interests but an internal negotiation with those in the Reagan cabinet who adamantly opposed direct talks and absolutely opposed a security accord with the Sandinistas. To go to Manzanillo, the State Department had had to devise the convoluted explanation that the talks would supplement, not supplant, Contadora. This proved to be a cover story, for State had given little attention or support to the Contadora process. Subsequent events revealed that as late as December 1984 the United States was not coordinating its actions with those of the Contadora mediators but operating unilaterally. Thus, Shlaudeman's reaction to Tinoco should be understood in the domestic context in which he was operating: to negotiate exclusively security issues was politically untenable.

"Perhaps you could have a secret agreement," he quoted Tinoco as replying. Shlaudeman said the United States was not interested.

Tinoco insisted that the problems were between Nicaragua and the United States; Shlaudeman replied that they were between Nicaragua and its neighbors. He added that the only logical way to interpret Tinoco's statements was that Nicaragua did not want a comprehensive Contadora accord but a bilateral treaty, dealing exclusively with Nicaragua's security concerns. Tinoco, according to

an aide-mémoire distributed to other governments by the Nicaraguan foreign ministry, promised that once agreements were reached
guaranteeing the security interests of both the United States and
Nicaragua, "increased efforts must be made to achieve a regional
agreement, which, under these new conditions, would have more
possibilities of success." Up to this point only Nicaragua had said it
would sign the September 7 act and not retracted its statement.

According to Tinoco, the meeting broke up with Shlaudeman's
summing up of the Nicaraguan position: "That is interesting. It is a
new approach, something different. We will review your position,
and at the next meeting we will answer this proposal."

According to the version of Shlaudeman and Burghardt, Tinoco
distanced himself from his own proposal by saying he had been
floating some personal ideas.

Burghardt passed a note to Shlaudeman saying if the U.S.
delegation head were his friend Henry Kissinger, he would get up
from the table, telling Tinoco he was not there to listen to his
personal ideas.

Shlaudeman concluded by reiterating that Nicaragua's internal
political arrangements were the primary issue, not security matters.
His parting words to the Nicaraguan delegation were: "If you don't
talk to the contras, there will be no peace in Central America."

Without setting an exact date, the two sides agreed to hold
another meeting in the second half of January. Ortega was sworn in
as president on January 10. On January 17, Tinoco called the U.S.
embassy to propose January 24–25 as dates. Two days later, Bergold
called on him. "For various reasons it is not prudent to set a date for
another meeting," he said. In terms of the U.S. position, the
Manzanillo talks were not making progress. Now it was time for the
multilateral talks to move forward. The following day, Notimex, the
Mexican news agency, reported that the Manzanillo talks had been
suspended. The State Department never announced the suspension
and waited hours to confirm the report. In doing so, an artful "spin"
was put on the event, downplaying its real significance. Denying that
the U.S. side had "broken off" the talks, the department said: "We
have not scheduled any further meetings at the present time,
however, pending an evaluation of the talks to date and further
evolution of the Contadora process."

The news was obscured by another announcement earlier that
day—that the United States would boycott the World Court pro-

ceedings brought by the Sandinistas the previous April. A State
Department spokesman said the Court had "ventured into a political
question that is beyond its competence" and the "haste with which
the Court proceeded" to a 16-0 ruling on November 26 to hear the
case "only adds to the impression that the Court is determined to
find in favor of Nicaragua in this case."

Shlaudeman later complained that the Sandinistas had begun
saying publicly that Manzanillo would supplant Contadora as the
major forum to resolve Central American disputes. "We have to see
what happens in Contadora," he said in an interview. "If it goes
ahead, we probably would resume direct talks. I hope this will help
rather than hinder Contadora." Contadora eventually went ahead,
but the direct talks did not.

Contadora was at best a pretext for breaking off Manzanillo. Ten
days before Washington suspended the talks, the four Contadora
foreign ministers urged the United States and Nicaragua to "intensify
the dialogue that they are holding in Manzanillo in order to conclude
agreements furthering a normalization of their relations and regional
detente." Clearly, a suspension was not their idea of help. At the end
of January, Simon Alberto Consalvi, the Venezuelan foreign minister, declared that Contadora was "at a dead point. Unless we obtain
a clear definition of support from the Reagan administration for a
realistic agreement in the region, our good offices are not going to
prosper."[5]*

The real reason for breaking off the talks was somewhat different.
The administration could no longer achieve its goal of democracy
through negotiations and as a result the political basis for the process
had collapsed.

"We could have done a security negotiation if Washington was
interested. But Washington never was," said one member of the
U.S. delegation. "If it were just security issues such as the question
of assistance to insurgents, as difficult as these security issues are,
you have obvious trade-offs, the stuff of which agreements are made.
The problem is that the other thing on the table is democracy.
Nobody can figure a way to negotiate that one."

Or, as Shlaudeman put it, "The fact is, the basic issue is their

---

* This was the first time the Venezuelan government had publicly blamed Washington for impeding efforts toward a negotiated settlement. One reason Consalvi
spoke out was that Venezuelan president Lusinchi had just received Ortega's answers
to his questions put through Vargas Llosa (see p. 261n).

internal political arrangements. The rest is not all that important."

Tinoco saw things the other way around. "We can't accept the United States meddling in our internal affairs in the way they have been used to doing. But it doesn't mean that it is not possible to fulfill some of the concerns of the United States regarding internal matters," he said in January 1986. If the United States accepted the Nicaraguan revolution and stopped financing the insurgency, the rebels under an amnesty could return to Nicaragua and engage in political activity. "There is no ideological contradiction in terms that Washington wishes a pluralistic election and we don't. Really, it is possible to do it. But in the context of an aggression, it is not possible." He suggested as a trade-off ending the war in exchange for holding elections with "the participation of everybody."

Tinoco's trade-off would have involved risk but also the possible payoff of ending the dispute peacefully. Yet there is no indication the administration ever explored the possibility, if indeed it knew of it.*

The formal U.S. explanation for breaking off Manzanillo did not even hint at the motive forces at work. Power had shifted in Washington after Reagan's election landslide, and the opponents of negotiations—chiefly Casey and North—had gained the upper hand. Casey had a visceral dislike of negotiating with Communists and wanted his contra program restored. North pressed the point. As the diplomacy was winding down, financial aid for the contras, albeit from a "third country," Saudi Arabia, was going full speed ahead.

Two days before Tinoco asked Bergold to schedule more talks, North summed up the position of the newly revived hard right. In a lengthy memo to McFarlane, North contended that a negotiated settlement would run counter to U.S. interests. There were only three options, he said: a negotiated solution leaving the Sandinistas in power in return for assurances that they will not "export revolution"; a resumption of aid to the contras "to prevent the consolidation of a Marxist-Leninist state" and to establish in its place a "truly democratic and pluralistic" government; or the use of U.S. military

---

* If the Sandinistas had any doubts about the meaning of the suspension, they were set straight ten days later when Shultz wrote the Inter-American Development Bank asking for deferral of a $58 million loan that Nicaragua sought for food production and funding small and medium-size farms. Stating that the money could be used to support Nicaraguan aggression against its neighbors, Shultz all but threatened to cut off bank support if the loan went through. (The United States controls the major part of bank resources.)

force to remove the Sandinistas to achieve the same goal. North concluded that letting the Sandinistas remain in power was unacceptable to U.S. strategic interests. "The most prudent course of action, given the threat we face from the Soviets and their surrogates in Central America, is to seek congressional approval for resuming our support to the Nicaraguan resistance." This in hand, McFarlane left on a quick tour of the region to assure allies of administration "steadfastness" despite its inability to convince Congress to back its policy.

Within a few weeks, North and Casey acquired the financial resources to sustain the drive for a military solution. Unbeknown to Shultz, Motley, or the Congress, the Saudis had been subsidizing the contras at the rate of $1 million a month since July 1984. During a February 1985 White House visit, King Fahd told Reagan he would step up the pace, and within a month he deposited another $24 million for a grand total of $32 million.[6]

Casey in the meantime launched his own campaign in support of the contra program by offering a new foreign policy vision based on the sweeping aim of backing anti-Communist resistance worldwide.

CASEY AT BAT

It is hard to imagine a less likely candidate to shape political strategy than William Casey. But according to congressional leaders, no other senior cabinet officer would identify with the program. Casey had practiced confrontation with Congress for most of Reagan's first years and was not about to shrink from a fight. His loose management and cavalier disdain for the oversight process had finally so soured Congress that, on October 11, it had suspended the use of funds for the insurgency by any government agency until March 1985. Four days after the ban, known as the second Boland amendment, took effect, Casey found himself in yet another imbroglio with Congress, this time over a CIA "terrorist training manual." Once again he charged into the fray.

On October 15, the Associated Press reported that the CIA had produced a manual advising the rebels on intimidation tactics, kidnappings, and assassinations. The aim behind the manual was to help discipline a force that one adviser to the Joint Chiefs of Staff called "the strangest national liberation organization in the world

. . . just a bunch of killers." Casey himself had proposed the project on a visit to Tegucigalpa in June 1983. But something had gone badly awry. Instead of discouraging wanton violence, the manual had seemed to glorify it. Based on the 1968 lesson plans of the Army Special Warfare School at Fort Bragg, North Carolina, the contents drew largely from the practices of the Vietcong during the Vietnam War. Its cover featured a drawing of fifteen heads with holes in them; the author used the pseudonym "Tayacán," Nicaraguan slang for a macho man. A chapter on the "selective use of violence for effects of propaganda" advised the rebels to "neutralize" prominent Sandinista figures and hire professional criminals to carry out specific "jobs," such as creating "martyrs" or provoking mob violence.

When the manual became a political issue in Congress on the eve of the election, Casey thumbed his nose at lawmakers by defending it as an attempt "to make every guerrilla persuasive in face-to-face communication."[7] Not until early December did Casey admit to negligence in managing the operation. After an internal investigation, the CIA disciplined five midlevel employees and fired "John Kirkpatrick," a former employee who wrote the manual under contract. Investigators acknowledged that the manual had violated the law barring funds to aid in the overthrow of the Sandinista government. But they asserted the violation had been unintentional on grounds that senior officials in the field and at headquarters had never read it. Clarridge, who should have supervised the project, got off without a reprimand.

For the congressional oversight committees, this was the last straw. No one wanted responsibility for a project that the Senate committee estimated had taken up 25 percent of its time and repeatedly ended in embarrassment. Goldwater and Boland gave up the chairmanships of the Senate and House committees and their successors, Republican Dave Durenberger of Minnesota and Democrat Lee Hamilton of Indiana, became outspoken opponents of resuming covert aid to the contras as a covert program.

Casey had ushered in a new era of mistrust.

But his star was on the rise. On January 7 the Senate committee criticized the CIA for its "inadequate supervision and management" of covert operations in Nicaragua in connection with the manual. On January 9, Casey took the offensive with a vast and different concept.

In its first four years, the Reagan administration had accomplished much of its domestic agenda through higher defense spending, lower taxes, and trimmed domestic programs. But it had achieved nothing that resembled a foreign policy legacy. The Grenada intervention was hardly a policy accomplishment, and its significance paled in comparison with Beirut, where a terrorist bombing had led to Reagan's withdrawal of the U.S. military presence. Now Casey would offer his version of the Reagan legacy.

In his six years as CIA director, Casey never held a press conference and, until early 1985, his public speeches attracted little attention. When he spoke, it was often before an exclusive men's club to which he belonged.

He chose the Union League Club in New York City, of which he was a member, to kick off what would later become known as the "Reagan Doctrine."* The untitled speech said little about practical responses to complex problems, but its sweeping assertions and inconsistencies said a good deal about Casey's mind. The probable origin of the speech is a story in itself.

Reagan, Casey, and their ideological soulmates fervidly desired the rollback of Soviet influence in the third world, and the Soviet invasion of Afghanistan in 1979 gave the theme an aura of political respectability in Congress. But it was difficult to find a link between the Afghan resistance and other rightist-led anticommunist struggles that could provide a basis for a new U.S. policy and for politically sustainable programs of support. Enter Jack Wheeler, a self-styled adventurer whose most noted previous feat was a parachute jump at the North Pole that had earned mention in the *Guinness Book of World Records*. Wheeler had been a friend of Dana Rohrabacher, a member of the White House speechwriting staff, and prodded by him, decided in 1983 to explore the phenomenon of anticommunist insurgencies. With funds provided by the libertarian Reason Foundation, Wheeler set off on a six-month tour of Nicaragua, Angola, Afghanistan, Cambodia, Mozambique, and Ethiopia. On his return, Rohrabacher invited Wheeler to give an illustrated lecture to about twenty-five White House aides. Wheeler's concept—that anti-Soviet rebellions were occurring worldwide and "we ought to take advantage of it"—caught on and "excited everybody," Rohrabacher said. Wheeler briefed Kirkpatrick and North, and got to know Casey "very well" and briefed him "extensively" on his concept, Rohrabacher

---

* The phrase "Reagan Doctrine" was coined by writer Charles Krauthammer in a *Time* essay by that title, April 1, 1985.

said. Wheeler confirmed that he had presented a memo to Casey arguing that anticommunist struggles worldwide were a single movement at a one-and-a-half-hour meeting in November 1984.

Casey gave his speech on January 9. Wheeler believed his argument influenced Casey's language; but in setting the main theme of the speech Casey also drew from his personal experience fighting the Nazis.[8]

His topic was the global struggle against communism. For Casey, the third world was divided into two groups: "occupied countries," in which Marxist regimes have been "either imposed or maintained by external forces," and "unoccupied countries," that is, all the rest. He identified five countries as "occupied"—Afghanistan, Cambodia, Ethiopia, Angola, and Nicaragua—without differentiating the unique circumstances in which leftist governments had come to power in each. Interestingly, Nicaragua, whose regime was neither installed nor maintained by external forces, did not fit his own definition of "occupied."

Casey put the behavior of the Marxists in these countries on a par with that of Adolf Hitler. "In the aggregate there has occurred a holocaust comparable to that which Nazi Germany inflicted in Europe some forty years ago," he said of the five countries. But the "aggregate" evil did not apply equally in each case. The Marxist Khmer Rouge had undertaken a systematic slaughter in Cambodia, but no such bloodbath had occurred in Nicaragua.

His logic suggested that America's goal should be the destruction of the regimes in the "occupied" countries, but Casey ducked altogether the question of policy goals. Instead, he announced "the good news is that the tide has changed . . . the 1980s have emerged as the decade of freedom fighters resisting Communist regimes." Even better news was that joining this tide against communism was cheap as well as vital for U.S. interests.

Although "the Communists . . . are spending close to $8 billion a year to snuff out freedom in these countries, it is not necessary to match this in money, manpower, or military weapons. Oppressed people want freedom and are fighting for it. They need only modest support and strength of purpose from nations which want to see freedom prevail and which will find their own security impaired if it doesn't."

Casey's proposal for "modest support" was self-serving in more ways than one. On the most obvious level, funding insurgencies was by charter a CIA responsibility, and adding covert programs translated into an expansion of his empire. Less obvious was the fact that Casey's aggrandizement would be at State Department expense. The context in which he proposed support implied not only more programs but also a bigger hand in policy. Casey omitted mention of any rational process under which support for insurgencies would be decided case by case, in a local context, and to achieve specified policy aims and, instead, substituted global anticommunism as the criterion. In making an ideological aim the test of merit, he removed any concrete measurement of success. Indeed, the modest levels of expenditure he advocated assuredly would accomplish little beyond making the Soviets and their client states bleed. That would reinforce the need for his programs. Moscow would step up aid; Washington would follow suit; and the insurgencies and the support programs would become ends in themselves. If insurgencies became ends in themselves, the State Department role would be further reduced, for according to hard-line doctrine there was no place to negotiate settlements with leftist governments since they were not to be trusted. Casey happened to oppose such negotiations anyway. By rendering negotiated solutions impossible, Casey would in time justify conservative ideology, which posits inevitable, unending conflict with the Soviets.

In short, the inconclusive bloodletting under way in Nicaragua would become the model for combatting Marxist regimes throughout the third world.*

---

* Casey modified and embellished his vision in the course of speeches that year and in 1986. To cope with the anomaly that the Sandinistas had not perpetrated a bloodbath, he invented one. "In Nicaragua, the Communist government killed outright a minimum of 1,000 former Somoza national guardsmen during the summer of 1979," he told New York's Metropolitan Club in May 1985. No such event had been reported at the time or since, and the CIA press office was unable to point to a source for this fact. Casey subsequently dropped the reference. In a backhanded way, he eventually acknowledged that Marxism in Nicaragua had not been "imposed or maintained by external forces." In a June 1986 speech he substituted the less sweeping phrase "installed or co-opted." Casey also added Mozambique and Yemen to his "occupied" list. Still, inconsistencies continued to abound from speech to speech. Reminiscing on his World War II OSS background, Casey said in that same speech: "In my opinion, Nicaragua can and should be a perfect example of how some of our experiences of World War II can be applied with great effect in support of a resistance movement." But he switched examples to suit convenience. Three months later, he spoke admiringly of the Communist model as applied by the Sandinistas. "Two can play the same game. Just as there is a classic formula for Communist subversion and takeover, there also is a proven method of overthrowing repressive government that can be applied successfully in Nicaragua."[9]

Casey was only one very important voice in the internal debate, and his speech did not constitute official policy. But he laid down a concept (rollback by proxy), rhetoric ("freedom fighters"), and a shrill tone that became the inspiration for Reagan. Although the specifics of Casey's conversations with Reagan are not known, he was a friend and ideological soulmate of the President with cabinet rank, direct access, and ample opportunities to discuss an issue on which he felt strongly. And he brought "good news," which is what the President liked to hear. When White House speechwriters later in January came up with similar language and proposed it for the State of the Union address, Reagan quickly endorsed it.

The role of the speechwriting shop had grown since Enders's ouster. Speechwriters all along had been the guardians of Reagan's conservative conscience, and with some reason they felt that they made a difference. In a reversal of the practice under Jimmy Carter, they, not the policy formulators, were the last to sign off on presidential foreign policy statements, according to high State Department aides. Speechwriting in the Reagan White House was a rhetorician's dream come true. Here was a president who visualized policy through speeches, who tried to achieve goals through aggressive advocacy rather than aggressive management. "Speechwriters are part of the policymaking process along with the secretary of state, the National Security Council, and the Department of Defense. The only difference is we're anonymous," boasted one. They subscribed to the view on the right that the State Department was "the other side." "We always said we needed an American desk at the State Department," joked Bently Elliott, then speechwriting director.

Reagan's State of the Union address on February 6 picked up Casey's concept of aiding freedom fighters without reference to any specific policy goals. Rohrabacher and Wheeler had helped pave the way for what essentially was an update of Menges's 1968 "daydream." The actual words at the core of the "Reagan Doctrine" came from Elliott and Menges. "That was Constantine and me on the word processor," Elliott said.[10] "We must not break faith with those who are risking their lives—on every continent—to defy Soviet-supported aggression and secure rights which have been ours from birth," Reagan stated. "The Sandinista dictatorship of Nicaragua, with full Cuban and Soviet-bloc support, not only persecutes its people, the church, and denies a free press, but arms and provides bases for Communist terrorists attacking neighboring states. Support for

freedom fighters is self-defense and totally consistent with the OAS
and UN charters. It is essential that the Congress continue all facets
of our assistance to Central America. I want to work with you to
support the democratic forces whose struggle is tied to our own
security."

Reagan's attachment to the notion of anti-Communist "freedom
fighters" was largely romantic, in the judgment of many foreign
policy experts, and he may have had little in mind beyond sending
money. But Casey, as the head of an action agency, seemed to fall in
a different category. He had managed the program essentially as a
supply relationship. But he had never insisted on developing a
workable military strategy, a task well within the capabilities of the
CIA. The omission of so obvious a step raised basic questions. Was
Casey also a romantic, or did his motivation lie more in gaining
programs and power than in making the programs work? Diplomats
who struggled against the consequences of Casey's thinking in
Central America saw the Reagan Doctrine as a pipedream whose
major impact would be to block the normal functions of diplomacy.
"What they are doing is building a model of how the United States
can take a socialist revolution which we regard as inimical and
reverse it without the use of military force," said a high U.S.
diplomat. "Democracy would emerge as the alternative and take
over. The Sandinistas would either participate as a minority or go
away. This would be a first in American international politics, a
casebook study of how to shrink the Soviet empire at its extremities."
It was as attractive as any dream could be. "It would raise morale. It
would make people think we are on the right side of history."

The problem with confrontation by proxy was the absence of a
politico-military theory to underpin it and a program to apply
resources to concrete ends. Only a handful of American military
theorists actively work on developing counterinsurgency doctrine,
and fewer on insurgency. Moreover, rightist insurgency against a
leftist police state presents a different set of problems from leftist
insurgency against an unpopular rightist regime. Words and money
are not sufficient to the task. Leftist insurgencies usually have a
unified military structure, a political command that presents a united
front to the world, intelligence and support infrastructures within
the target country, and an external source of financial and moral
support, military and political advice. But the administration failed
to think through the problem in Nicaragua or anywhere else, and not

until late in 1986 did it create a support structure for the anti-Sandinista military or political front. The manner in which Reagan pursued his goals in Nicaragua alone suggests that the so-called "doctrine" was a rationalization for ad hoc actions undertaken in large part for reasons of the internal administration power struggle.

Two weeks after Reagan spoke, Shultz struck back with a considered statement that offered support to "democratic revolutionaries" worldwide—not just in Casey's five "occupied" countries, but also in South Africa, Chile, South Korea, the Philippines, and Poland. Unlike Casey or Reagan, Shultz differentiated among struggles. "The nature and extent of our support—whether moral support or something more—necessarily varies from case to case," he told the Commonwealth Club in San Francisco on February 22. Wherever possible, the path to freedom, human rights, and the rule of law should be "through peaceful and political means." In Nicaragua the U.S. policy aim was to change Sandinista behavior along the lines of Enders's four goals: removal of Soviet-bloc personnel, a reduction in Nicaraguan armed forces, a halt to Sandinista support for foreign insurgencies, and "a political opening" that would allow for the participation of Nicaraguan opposition, armed and unarmed. Shultz went out of his way to leave open the possibility for a negotiated solution. "Whether it is achieved through the multilateral Contadora negotiations, through unilateral actions taken by the Sandinistas alone or in concert with their domestic opponents, or through the collapse of the Sandinista regime is immaterial to us," he said.*

Shultz's policy statement, which might have attracted bipartisan support for administration programs, had only a brief life, for other developments, helped along by rightists at the NSC and the speechwriters, all but foreclosed a peaceful resolution in Nicaragua. Reagan's rhetoric became increasingly strident, thanks in part to the

---

* Shultz was unequivocal in advocating "material assistance" for those resisting "aggression of the kind committed by the Soviets in Afghanistan, by Nicaragua in Central America, and by Vietnam in Cambodia"—in other words, cross-border intervention or subversion. But he stressed the importance of negotiated outcomes with respect to civil wars in Nicaragua and Angola. In Nicaragua, the armed opposition was "the only incentive that has proved effective" in leading the Sandinistas to negotiating compromises. As for Angola, "foreign forces, whether Cuban or South African, must leave. At some point there will be an internal political settlement in Angola that reflects Angolan political reality, not external intervention." And he spoke vaguely of "armed insurgencies" in Ethiopia, referring to the separatists who sought to break up the Ethiopian empire before the leftist Mengistu regime took power.

talents of Patrick Buchanan, a conservative's conservative who had joined the staff as director of communications. It was also a heady time for North. "I helped write some" of the "innumerable" speeches Reagan made about Nicaragua, North later recalled. Elliott confirmed this was the case. "We were in constant contact with Ollie and Constantine Menges. We relied on them constantly for our information." Under Reagan's loose structure the Marine lieutenant colonel in effect could draft the guidelines for the policy he would so vigorously implement.[11]

In February, Reagan stated as his goal to "remove" the Sandinista government "in the sense of its present structure, in which it is a Communist, totalitarian state and . . . not a government chosen by the people." If the Sandinistas would "say uncle" and invite the contras into the government, their removal would not be necessary. In March, the President said the contras were the "moral equivalent of our Founding Fathers and the brave men and women of the French Resistance." And in April, he announced as U.S. policy the demand of opposition figures that the Sandinistas dissolve their constituent assembly, call new elections, and hold a dialogue with the armed internal opposition.

The toughened terms trace in part to backstage maneuvers by North and associates and in part to the Sandinistas' own ineptitude. The Sandinistas had treated Cruz and others in the internal opposition with disdain since November, and North skillfully exploited this for domestic political purposes.

Ten days after the election, Cruz had publicly criticized U.S. military pressures during the "MiGs" crisis, called Daniel Ortega's faction the most moderate in the Sandinista leadership, and urged Washington to "give Ortega a period of grace" so he could work for national reconciliation. But the Sandinistas were not into politics. Heavy censorship of La Prensa resumed, opposition leaders could not obtain exit visas to travel abroad, and the Sandinistas scuttled a national dialogue in late November by demanding that the opposition first sign a statement condemning U.S. "aggression." Cruz began to shift.

On January 3, Cruz joined Pedro Joaquín Chamorro, editor of La Prensa, and did an about-face, endorsing U.S. aid to the contras.

This was a welcome development in Washington, where North and others were "in a panic" over the abysmal legislative prospects for contra aid, according to FDN sources. Building on Cruz's change of heart, North began working with Arturo Jr. on a project to broaden the political leadership. Although formerly married to a Cuban and known for his ties with the Cuban embassy in Washington, Arturito said he was a frequent visitor to North's office, "charmed him [North] as he charmed me," and began dating his comely secretary, Fawn Hall.*

Late that month, North brought Cruz Sr. and Calero together to produce a combination peace initiative and unity statement. The final drafting was done in North's Miami hotel room on January 29 and 30, and the Marine lieutenant colonel took credit as coauthor; Alan Fiers, who had succeeded Clarridge at the CIA, also claimed a major role. Cruz Jr., who was not present, asserted *he* was the principal drafter. Cruz Sr., who was, said North's claim to coauthorship was "a lot of bullshit." Whoever was responsible, North portrayed the resulting document as an elaborate deception. "The only reason Calero agreed to sign [the peace initiative] was because the criteria established for the Sandinistas were, he knew, impossible for them to meet. He personally wrote several of the democratization provisions," North later confided to McFarlane.

As for demonstrating the unity of the external opposition, North told his boss that all participants saw the goal as "to convince the U.S. Congress that the opposition was led by reasonable men." He noted that Calero had felt uncomfortable working with Cruz and Robelo, who had been on the Sandinista junta when his property was expropriated, and "has only cooperated in the unity effort because he trusts . . . North and McFarlane." The agreement became but another prop in North's efforts to renew contra funding.

Despite its disputed origins and disingenuous goals, McFarlane thought the document had been an "extremely solid platform and peace proposal" for which he credited the "enormous diplomacy of Col. North."[13]

On March 1 in San José, Costa Rica, Cruz, Calero, and Robelo signed the "document on national dialogue of the Nicaraguan resistance."

It described the November 4, 1984, election as a "farce," referred to Ortega's new government as an imposed interim regime, and

---

* Although North's calendar showed him visiting between thirty and thirty-seven times between September 1984 and December 1985, Arturito said often he scheduled a meeting as an excuse to see Hall.[12]

demanded the dissolution of the national constituent assembly and
the calling of new national elections—all positions sure to be
rejected. It also revived the Coordinadora's demands of December
1983, in effect calling for a new constitution, and called for a
Church-mediated dialogue with the armed opposition and a cease-
fire in place.* Two days later, the State Department distributed the
statement in Washington. One month later, Reagan publicly embraced this position as U.S. policy.

As powerful individuals worked to block reconciliation with the
Sandinistas, some major agencies of government endeavored to
preserve an alternative option, a policy of containment. The uniformed military leadership agreed with the State Department that
walking away from Central America was irresponsible, that overthrow of the Sandinistas by the contras was unlikely, and that
intervention by the United States was undesirable. Following the
suspension of Manzanillo, State and the staff of the Joint Chiefs put
a good deal of energy and thought into Contadora. They drafted
language and urged verification procedures which if incorporated in
a revised act would address U.S. security concerns and those of allies
but leave the Sandinista government in place. It was a long shot, but
there was a glimmer of hope that a deal would come off.

Paul Gorman summed up the Joint Chiefs' attitude toward
Nicaragua. "I don't see any immediate prospect that these guys in
blue suits in the hills are going to march into Managua. . . . I think
that therefore the answer lies in some kind of pressures and
diplomacy. I believe the formulae we have been reaching for in
Contadora are an adequate basis of proceeding. They're the only
kind of basis that I think realistically people in the region would live
with."[14]

Underlying this analysis was also a desire to avoid the other
option, direct intervention, which according to most experts would

---

* The only major external opposition figures not to sign on were Edén Pastora and
Alfredo César, former head of the Central Bank under the Sandinistas and a close
associate of Pastora. They were convinced that the document had been drafted within
the White House. Pastora by this time had been adopted by the office of Senator
Jesse Helms, and on his advice, Helms denounced the document as "a blueprint for
fuzzy-minded socialism" that would cripple the insurgents. Helms assumed the
Sandinistas were so cunning that they would take the bait of a cease-fire in place.
They did not.

be an enormously costly enterprise. A study by the Rand Corporation, a California think tank with close Pentagon ties, estimated that 100,000 or more U.S. combat troops would be required and nearly all the available U.S. strategic reserve forces, and asserted the task could "bog the United States down in a prolonged military occupation and counterinsurgency campaign."*

Military logic drove the armed services' leadership to view Contadora as the best available option. Ideology drove those on the hard right to avert a negotiated solution. Many conservatives also opposed intervention, but they discounted the Chiefs' thinking as reflections of the Vietnam syndrome. Casey, in a May 1985 speech, dismissed the Contadora talks on the grounds that Communists cannot be trusted. He declared the only solution in Nicaragua to be a change of regime, but he did not specify the means.

"There are some who will be content with an agreement that the Nicaraguans will now forgo further aggression. Our experience in Korea and Indochina provides some lessons on the value of agreements with Communist governments. . . . We believe the Sandinistas' main objectives in regional negotiations are to buy time to further consolidate the regime," he said.

"History and the record and purposes of Marxist-Leninist regimes in general and the Sandinistas in particular lead us to believe that unless Nicaragua has implemented a genuine democracy as required by the Organization of American States, such assurances could not be adequately verified and would not be complied with."[16]

Winning government-wide acceptance of positions in support of Contadora was difficult, and North and Casey were not the only ones to present problems. Motley had tried to recreate the centralized decision-making method that he had used with mixed results in the harbor-mining in 1983, although with a slightly different cast of characters. On one occasion early in 1985 he had convinced Shultz to

---

* Georgetown University professor Theodore Moran estimated that 50,000 to 60,000 combat troops would be needed, while a U.S. military source in Managua estimated 150,000 to 200,000 troops would have to be deployed for one and a half to two years to pacify Nicaragua. The Rand study extrapolated from the U.S. intervention in the Dominican Republic in 1965, in which 23,000 combat troops required a year to restore order in a single city with no organized opposition. In Grenada, 7,000 combat troops required three days to overcome the resistance of 300 lightly armed Cubans. But there the population was friendly. The assumption could not be made in Nicaragua, which in addition has the biggest trained army in Central America and a vast stockpile of Soviet-bloc arms.[15]

approach Weinberger, Casey, and Vessey and ask each to appoint a representative to thrash out a deal in their name. Motley, Iklé, Moreau, and the CIA representative spent two and a half hours in a conference room and emerged with agreement on the guidelines for a Contadora treaty. A few hours later, Weinberger vetoed the deal. Apparently Iklé had changed his mind. "Shultz threw up his hands," said a source close to Motley.

The other major obstacle to progress in the Contadora forum was the Sandinistas. They had allowed Contadora to grind to a halt at the end of 1984 over an incident almost unrelated to the larger issues of war and peace in Central America—the case of José Manuel Urbina Lara, a twenty-three-year-old Nicaraguan draft-dodger who sought political asylum in the Costa Rican embassy and was later arrested. Although President Daniel Ortega indicated he wanted Urbina released, Interior Minister Tomás Borge refused. Costa Rica, Honduras, and El Salvador boycotted all sessions of Contadora until the Sandinistas finally released him in March 1985.*

Instead, for months after the U.S. negotiators left Manzanillo in January 1985 Sandinista diplomacy focused on reviving the bilateral

---

* The case of Urbina Lara provided a vivid example of the infighting among the Sandinista directorate that in some ways mirrored the turf battles within the Reagan administration. Over the course of three months, their position changed a half dozen times as the Ortega and Borge factions fought over the outcome. Urbina Lara first entered the Costa Rican embassy in August 1984. The Sandinistas refused him permission to leave the country. Months passed. Over Christmas, the Costa Rican ambassador and his staff went home and shut down the embassy except for their visitor. By coincidence, presumably courtesy of Borge's interior ministry, Urbina Lara's girlfriend came by on Christmas Eve and invited him out for companionship; on leaving the embassy grounds he was captured and jailed. In Costa Rica, a traditional land of asylum, the rightist press, with the encouragement of Ambassador Curtin Winsor, treated it as a sensation. In the course of trying to resolve it, the divisions between the Ortega brothers and Borge became obvious. Each side exercised a veto. Shortly after Urbina Lara's arrest, the Sandinistas sent word that they had no intention of backing down. They then dispatched a high official to Carlos José Gutiérrez, then foreign minister in Costa Rica, to reinforce the message. "Forget about it. He will stay in jail," Gutiérrez recalled him as saying. Later, a second official approached Jorge Urbina, Gutiérrez's deputy, with a different message. "Ortega was perfectly willing to make a deal with you but Borge is against it," he said. The Costa Ricans subsequently learned to their surprise that the second official, who seemed to be critical of Borge, was not an Ortega ally but a representative of Borge. With the situation in deadlock, the Costa Rican ambassador in Managua approached Borge, who said he would take the matter under consideration. A short time later, Urbina Lara was released to go to Colombia. "That gave me the idea that they work by consensus," commented Gutiérrez. "Because of the situation they are in, that is the only way they can harmonize differences."[17]

forum—until it became clear that the Reagan administration was adamantly against it. Finally, and most fundamentally, the Sandinistas had thrown their energies into achieving a military solution to what they saw first and foremost as a military challenge. Joaquín Cuadra Lacayo, the Sandinista army chief of staff, summed it up in January 1985. The strategic defeat of the contras would be possible by the end of the year, he said. He defined "defeat" as forcing them out of the area around Jinotega and back to the border. Militarily, it was a sound approach that could be accomplished with the help of training, reorganization, and new equipment. Politically, it left much to be desired. The Sandinistas were ignoring the most important lesson of Vietnam, which was that the war would be won or lost not on the battlefield but in the halls of Congress in Washington.

Other tendencies within the Sandinista government supported a Contadora accord, with the encouragement of Fidel Castro. "Castro really was pushing the Nicaraguans quite strongly to reach a Contadora agreement," according to Shlaudeman. At Ortega's inauguration in January, "he did a real number on the Contadora foreign ministers. He convinced them he was being helpful. In a way he was. His principal interest was to prevent another Grenada, to assure above all else the survival of the Nicaraguan revolution." According to one minister, Castro said Cuba "is absolutely ready to help the process and to take any action in this direction, including withdrawing every adviser in Nicaragua, no matter what the designation."[18]

Contadora was also changing. Having yielded to the pressure of Mexico and Colombia for a quick solution in September 1984, it now began to bend to demands from a different quarter. Responding to criticisms by the United States and its allies, the ministers began revising their document. Canada, which had had extensive experience in sending out peace-keeping forces, offered to advise on verification and monitoring.

Contadora resumed its sessions on April 11–12, 1985, and briefly made genuine progress when Tinoco agreed that verification could be overseen by an international inspection corps. This resolved a major issue, leaving only the question of who would comprise the corps. The document was moving in a direction that U.S. military and diplomatic professionals viewed as solid.

Two sets of developments intervened. One was that Castro stopped playing a supportive role. The reason was that in mid-May, the Reagan administration started up Radio Martí, beaming news about Cuba to Cuba, and Castro was infuriated. The other was a string of actions in Washington, including Reagan's April 4 endorsement of opposition demands that the Sandinistas hold new elections, the imposition of a trade embargo on Nicaragua on May 1, and the forceful and eventually successful drive to restore funding to the insurgency on June 12.

In May, Tinoco backed away from the verification agreement of the previous month. And after the House approved the $27 million contra aid in June, Tinoco walked out of the talks, insisting that Contadora deal before anything else with the growing war on Nicaragua's doorstep. In the meantime, the Sandinistas launched a major attack against the last strongholds of the southern front on the Costa Rican border. Two Costa Rican civil guardsmen were killed and nine wounded in the offensive, in which Sandinista troops may have crossed into Costa Rica. The OAS sent out a fact-finding delegation consisting of officials from the Contadora countries, but Contadora as a diplomatic process had become irrelevant. The result of these events in the first part of 1985 was that Contadora lost the initiative it had briefly regained. Although Contadora lingered around a good deal longer, 1985 was the year it ran out of steam. With it went the alternative of a negotiated containment arrangement at current arms levels.

THE PAYOFF OF CONFRONTATION

As we have seen, the aim of those who had Reagan's ear that year was not to devise a workable scheme for containing Nicaragua, but to resume aid to the contras through an all-out battle with Congress. State Department professionals had resisted the idea of a battle over contra aid altogether. As a result, they were hardly involved in the planning phases. Indeed, Motley and Johnstone tried to get a discussion going in the State Department about the possibility of life in Central America policy after the contras, but conservatives recoiled even at contingency planning and took aim at both of them. Motley also got in trouble for not being vigorous enough in congressional testimony about the paramount importance of restoring contra aid.

Behind the scenes, meanwhile, Casey, North, and Buchanan, emboldened by the influx of Saudi funds for the contras, were busy orchestrating a campaign to propel Reagan into a confrontation with Congress. In a letter to Chief of Staff Donald Regan, Casey said it was "crucial that we move quickly and strongly." North the same day asked McFarlane to request Regan to seek a presidential decision within forty-eight hours. Attached to his March 20 memo was the outline of a ten-week public relations extravaganza he had worked up with Buchanan.*

North's PR plan laid out more than ninety events, many of them already under way, "including military operations and political action . . . timed to influence the vote." There were sabotage attacks against Sandinista targets by British mercenaries, a $2 million advertising program by unnamed conservative groups, TV interviews by Cruz, Calero, and Robelo, op-ed pieces by friendly Democrats such as Zbigniew Brzezinski, congressional appearances by Sandinista atrocity victims, a news conference with "articulate freedom fighters with proven combat records," and a presidential speech in Miami's Orange Bowl that North promised to help draft.

The next day, March 21, Casey tried to force the issue by telling McFarlane the administration should not be "content" to seek nonlethal aid. McFarlane knew from his preliminary soundings that Congress would vote down lethal aid and referred the question to Reagan.

In the face of conflicting advice, Reagan put off his decision. But he agreed, according to North, to base his judgment on "the effects of a major P.R. campaign waged by outside entities"—an apparent reference to the campaign being waged by North himself. Reporters

---

* Casey's and North's memos, with their cross-references to each other and to Buchanan, added up to a classic "snow job." "The battle for contra funding is viewed in Central and Latin America as a litmus test of U.S. resolve and intentions . . . any delay in this endeavor, for whatever reasons, will be interpreted by all observers, friendly and unfriendly, as a weakening of US resolve," Casey told Regan. He said the March 1 statement that North had engineered had been "widely acclaimed by all observers as a positive development." Reagan's rhetoric, which Casey, North, and Buchanan had helped craft, had given new confidence and unity to opposition leaders, "steeled the resolve" of regional allies, and prompted in the Sandinistas "an atypical hesitancy and lack of surefootedness," Casey added. The long, rambling letter was another case of tailoring facts to suit policy goals. "It is our assessment that without renewed aid, advice and guidance, the Sandinista effort to destroy the effectiveness of the armed opposition will be successful, probably within a 12 month period," Casey told Regan. In addition, the unity and effectiveness of the internal opposition will "quickly disintegrate." The director of Central Intelligence concluded with a fervid "God save America!"

that spring found themselves covering a series of bizarre events.* It was only with the release of White House memos two years later during the Iran-Contra hearings that the aim of the campaign became clear. The target never had been the general public, the news media, or Congress. The audience that mattered to North and Casey was Ronald Reagan himself, and *he* was impressed.[19]

Under terms of the October 1984 postponement of the aid vote, Reagan could request $14 million in military aid in an expedited procedure that, circumventing committee hearings, had to be approved by both Houses. Senator Dave Durenberger had said his committee, the Select Committee on Intelligence, wanted no part of it.†

Dante Fascell, the Florida Democrat who headed the House Foreign Affairs Committee, wrote Reagan suggesting a sixty-day delay. On April 3, House Minority leader Robert Michel of Illinois told Reagan the plan was "dead in the water." That night, on the eve of the congressional Easter recess, Reagan formally asked Congress to renew the paramilitary aid. The plan justifying the aid, drafted in the White House, was still undergoing revisions as State sent out the cables to inform foreign leaders of its contents.

The White House chose a visit by Colombian president Betancur, a key figure in the Contadora process, to unveil what was billed as Reagan's "peace initiative." It was built on the "last and definitive summons" contained in the "document on national dialogue" which Cruz, Calero, and Robelo had signed on March 1. Under their ultimatum, if the Sandinistas did not begin a dialogue with the contras by March 20, and make progress toward agreement on a cease-fire and the holding of new national elections by April 20, the dialogue "will be definitely suspended by the Nicaraguan Resistance, thereby terminating the possibilities for a peaceful resolution of the national crisis."

Reagan embraced this plan as U.S. policy but extended the first deadline until June 1. If the Sandinistas began the dialogue by that

---

* For example, Bermúdez, appearing at his first Washington press conference, said the FDN was prepared to seize territory inside Nicaragua, even though the Sandinistas would quickly destroy his forces, if this sacrifice would lead to the renewal of lethal aid. The offer was baffling because lethal aid was politically out of the question.

† "The previous formula for covert assistance is simply at a dead end. Congress won't be party to the illogical and illegal absurdity of pretending that we are not providing military assistance when it is widely and publicly known that we are," he said.[20]

day, he would use the $14 million only for food, clothing, and medicine. If no agreement was reached, the funds would be released for arms and ammunition. The State Department was unsure about whether Reagan's final time limit was 60 or 120 days after he made the offer, the basis on which he would judge whether to resume military aid, and the exact goals in the talks. Shultz briefed Betancur on it for about ten minutes, stressing the positive aspects; Betancur asked no questions.

Appearing on the White House south lawn with Reagan a few hours later, Betancur treated the plan as a positive development. But ten days later he said that he had not realized Reagan's plan implied resumption of military aid, and that this made it "no longer a peace proposal but a preparation for war." Durenberger denounced the "peace plan" as a "box of candy with a razor blade inside." House Speaker Thomas P. O'Neill called it a "dirty trick" that Congress would reject. The Sandinistas dismissed it as a public relations maneuver. "You drop dead, or I will kill you," was how D'Escoto paraphrased its real meaning.

The reaction in the democratic governments of Latin America was astonishment. A top Venezuelan official commented that the administration had encouraged Cruz and other opposition leaders to boycott the electoral process, but the opposition had nevertheless won a good share of the seats. "Then the United States asked for new elections, which has no precedent in any country. You cannot ask a country to do what you want it to any day."[21]

Tony Motley had long been looking forward to a vacation, and shortly after Betancur left he drove his family to Lorton, Virginia, boarded the Auto-Train, and departed Washington for Florida for ten days. He was away during the final planning phase of the public relations campaign for contra aid. At the end of April, he resigned.

By the time Reagan kicked off the public campaign, his peace initiative for all intents had been laid to rest. Speaking at a fund-raising dinner on April 15, the President made only a passing reference to it.*

The emotional speech was largely composed at the White House by Buchanan with little input from State. One State Department

---

* The $500-a-plate dinner was organized with White House help by the newly created "Nicaraguan Refugee Fund." According to an investigative account, only $3,000 of the $220,000 raised that night went to aid refugees; most went for "consulting fees."[22]

official described the scene at the final drafting. "At the White House 'war room,' they have a Wang that projects onto a screen. People sit around and shout out corrections." In the speech, Reagan accused the Sandinistas of "institutionalized cruelty that is the natural expression of a Communist government, a cruelty that flows naturally from the heart of totalitarianism." He accused them of atrocities, massacres, and setting up concentration camps.*

The next day Reagan claimed a new celebrity endorsement. Pope John Paul II had been supportive of "all our activities in Central America," he said. When questioned by reporters if this included promoting the contras, he said: "I'm not going into detail, but *all* our activities." The Vatican replied that its policy excluded "the possibility of [the Pope's] support or endorsement of any concrete plan dealing, in particular, with military aspects."

Confrontation is a two-way street. O'Neill moved up the date of the House vote to coincide with the Senate's. This forced the White House to divide its lobbying efforts. Reagan denounced the move as "immoral."

Meanwhile the speechwriters were running out of rhetoric. What Reagan had called "one of the greatest moral challenges in postwar history" was headed for defeat. So on April 18, the President formally discarded the "peace initiative" and asked for funds for food, medicine, and clothing only. But he kept up the attack on House Democrats, who had in the meantime unveiled an alternative plan to provide $14 million in aid to the region, to refugees, and to wind down the contra war. Reagan denounced this as a "shameful surrender."

This was the context in which Senator Robert Byrd (D.-W.V.), the Minority leader, initiated bipartisan talks at the White House on April 22, the day before the vote, to try to draft a new bill that Democrats could support. Byrd, a skilled legislator, brought together northern liberals like Christopher Dodd of Connecticut, who openly opposed any form of contra aid, and southern conservatives like Bennett Johnston of Louisiana, who was

---

* The venue of the speech was the topic of a bitter struggle within the White House. Menges and Buchanan wanted Reagan to go over the heads of Congress and deliver a major televised public address. North opposed the idea and prevailed, annoying those in the speechwriters' shop. "He's just a bull-headed Marine," Dana Rohrabacher said. "He didn't have the expertise to make political judgments but felt he could."[23]

committed to backing almost any form. The talks were held around the long oval table in the White House cabinet room with McFarlane representing the administration and seven senators from each party representing the Senate. The Democrats had agreed among themselves that the price for supporting an aid package was to reopen direct U.S.-Nicaragua negotiations and close down the CIA as the aid conduit.

On the other side, though not physically present, was William Casey. "Casey was involved the whole way through," said a senior aide to Robert Dole of Kansas, the Senate Majority Leader. McFarlane, who acted as mediator, summed up Casey's attitude. Casey felt Congress had "thrown down the gauntlet" and that any hostility to his program was motivated by partisan politics. Others might have viewed the analysis as self-serving, but Casey was "a person of enormous conviction and confidence in what he believed in." For him, "there simply wasn't going to be any possibility of bipartisanship" and "promoting it was a waste of time," McFarlane said.[24] The CIA chief insisted that there be only one meeting with the Sandinistas to encourage and discuss modalities of a cease-fire and direct contacts between the Sandinistas and the contras. Shultz and Richard Lugar of Indiana, chairman of the Senate Foreign Relations Committee, were both out of town that day, so there was no effective counterweight to Casey. The talks failed, and with them the chances for forging a long-term bipartisan policy on Nicaragua. The administration now had to scramble to get a majority in the Republican-controlled chamber.

In a last-ditch move, McFarlane brought over the draft of a policy letter that Reagan would sign and send to Dole.[25] Prepared by Casey, it contained neither concession sought by the Democrats. Shultz and McFarlane set up shop in Dole's office just off the Senate floor, and all afternoon conservative Democrats and swing-vote Republicans trooped in and out, adding language to the letter that would ensure their support. Foreign policy was being formulated one vote at a time. Lloyd Bentsen, a Texas Democrat, felt that the administration should exhaust nonmilitary means before exerting military pressure and asked for strong language about economic sanctions against Nicaragua. It was added. Sam Nunn, a Georgia Democrat, was concerned about human rights abuses. Reagan promised to urge the contras "to take steps to investigate allegations of such acts and take appropriate actions against those found to be guilty." When the page was illegible, staff would produce a new printed version.

"Manzanillo was the toughest thing to negotiate into the letter. Having terminated those talks, they didn't want to resume them," Dole's aide said. It came down to Casey. "Casey didn't want to go the negotiating route. He has very strong feelings about the whole thing, partly because it's his program," said a high-ranking U.S. diplomat. Had there been twenty or thirty Democratic votes, a pledge to undertake direct negotiations might have been possible, but once it became clear the administration could get fifty-one or fifty-two votes without Manzanillo, weak language was used instead. About an hour before the vote, Reagan signed the letter agreeing to resume talks, but only for the purposes stipulated by Casey.

Thus, the possibility of gaining broad bipartisan support for the policy was discarded largely because Casey, as the cabinet's leading contra supporter, did not want the Manzanillo talks to resume. It was an example of consensus decision-making, American-style. Casey played the role that Borge had exercised within the Sandinista directorate: he cast the veto.

"I intend to resume bilateral talks with the Government of Nicaragua and will instruct our representatives in those talks to press for a cease-fire as well as a church-mediated dialogue between the contending Nicaraguan factions," the letter said.

This was not the same as direct talks to resolve the differences. Byrd told Dole that Democrats were being asked to endorse a Gulf of Tonkin resolution with assurances contained in a nonbinding letter. He voted against the bill.

But, for wavering Republicans, the letter came just in time, and the Senate voted 53–46 in favor, the closest margin for this issue in the Senate. An hour later, the House defeated the plan 248–180, the widest margin on the issue to that date. On April 24, it narrowly adopted a Democratic move to give $14 million in aid to the region, and narrowly rejected a Republican plan to provide $14 million in nonlethal aid; then House liberals and administration loyalists combined forces to scuttle the entire bill.

On April 25, Reagan decided informally that the letter was no longer operative.

Angered by the rebuff in Congress, Reagan called an urgent policy review, then ordered a trade embargo and abrogation of the

U.S.-Nicaraguan treaty of friendship. Under terms of the International Emergency Economic Powers Act, Reagan declared a national emergency and stated that Nicaragua posed "an unusual and extraordinary threat" to the United States. Clearly, that language had lost all meaning. "It came so fast that all we had was a paper trail," said one State Department official of the decision. Every good reason for not imposing a trade embargo was well known. U.S. officials had warned that the impact on the economy would be limited and could be made up through aid from other Western countries. As a punitive measure, they added, the embargo would become an issue in itself instead of focusing attention on Sandinista political behavior. Finally, it would give the Sandinistas an alibi for their economic mismanagement. All these prophecies came true but were irrelevant, for the decision was purely political in nature.*

Reagan's announcement of the embargo on May 1, 1985, as he landed in Bonn for an economic summit, combined abysmal timing with inadequate preparation. No advance effort had been made to win support of other countries. Only Salvadoran president José Napoleón Duarte later endorsed the decision. The European allies and Canada bought much of the $53 million worth of bananas, coffee, beef, and shellfish that would have been exported to the United States, and countries throughout the region scrambled to make up the $115 million in lost U.S. exports.

This was yet another signal to the internal opposition that their economic survival was not a priority for the United States. "The embargo did not do anything to Nicaragua. It was an internal political maneuver by Reagan," said Enrique Bolaños, head of COSEP. "Politically it is a blessing for the Sandinistas. They have a scapegoat and can holler to the world 'foul.' And the world listens. I don't think the United States had to do it. It was a mistake."[27]

In the context, it may seem remarkable that seven weeks later the House did an about-face and voted $27 million in nonlethal aid for

* These arguments were also articulated in an internal State Department dissent memorandum submitted in April 1984, when the idea first came up, by Stephen McFarland, the Nicaragua desk officer at the State Department. A group of opposition leaders led by Cruz met Shultz in late November 1984 and also warned him against the consequences. "The effect won't be what you think it will be," Mario Rappaccioli recalled saying. "It will be used by the Sandinistas as an alibi. The people who are going to suffer are the Nicaraguans."[26]

the contras. The shift resulted from a combination of factors. The Democrats quickly found themselves in a triple embarrassment. The House leadership, after agreeing on the need for a positive alternative, had lost control when the House unexpectedly voted down every option on April 24. Second, as the House was voting down the alternatives, Daniel Ortega announced that he was about to travel to Moscow, giving no specific reason. That would not have mattered so much had he made some conciliatory gesture along the lines he had discussed with visiting members of Congress in mid-April. Ortega had promised that if Congress defeated the aid bill he would feel "morally obligated" to make political concessions such as easing press censorship and resuming a national dialogue with government critics. In the event, he did little beyond expelling one hundred Cuban advisers.*

After sustaining its worst foreign policy setback in more than four years in office, the administration could not have been happier with this turn of events. Reagan had portrayed the Sandinistas as pawns of Moscow, and by traveling at this moment without making any conciliatory gesture, Ortega made the vision seem true. Indeed, according to Otto Reich, the administration knew of Ortega's trip to Moscow a full week before the vote in Congress.[29]

The trip was hurriedly arranged, the timing unfortunate, and the cause so embarrassing politically to the Sandinistas that they were reluctant to acknowledge it: their closest noncommunist ally and

---

* Ortega's offer to lift press censorship and the state of emergency was carefully drafted, and he took a legalistic view of his obligations. "I spoke with many congressmen, and we did not make any commitment of that nature . . . the only aide-mémoire that was worked out was with those members of the Senate," he said, referring to Senators John Kerry (D.-Mass.) and Tom Harkin (R.-Iowa). That stated if the Reagan administration and Congress discontinued direct and indirect, overt and covert support to the contras, and immediately reinitiated the Manzanillo dialogue, to include delegations of observers from both houses and with the aim of normalizing relations, Nicaragua would call for a cease-fire, grant an amnesty, "*as well as immediately guarantee full freedom of the press and reaffirm political pluralism and fundamental freedoms*" (italics added). Ortega commented that this was agreed with Kerry and Harkin. "It wasn't with anyone in the House." And he added: "We were talking about the response of the Congress, not the position of the House. The vote in the House was not a vote against aid to the Contra but a result of the internal mechanisms of the House." In other words, short of renunciation of the policy by Reagan, the Sandinistas had no obligations. That was Ortega's explanation. Other Nicaraguan officials have said that Ortega wanted to make the gestures called for but was overruled by other members of the directorate.[28]

principal oil supplier, Mexico, had informed them that their credit had run out and they would have to obtain oil elsewhere.*

"It was a strategic matter. We simply didn't have oil," a Nicaraguan diplomat in Mexico City said. Ortega "had to conclude an agreement very formally and at the highest levels to avoid the risk of a U.S. naval blockade that would block the supply of oil. We knew there was a price to it."[30]

The price was the U.S. Congress.

State Department officials observed that almost no one had spoken up for the Sandinistas during the April debate and felt victory was possible if the administration produced the right package. In early May, as the Ortega trip continued to command headlines, Lee Hamilton, chairman of the House Select Committee on Intelligence, predicted the House would reverse itself on whether the CIA could provide intelligence support to the contras. This had been the hidden agenda in the votes on April 23 and 24. The Senate agreed to lift the restrictions, but the House explicitly supported the ban. The defeated Republican alternative would have omitted this provision.

What helped end the confusion at both ends of Pennsylvania Avenue was the beginnings of a dialogue. Casey and others favoring confrontation had shot their bolt in April, and McFarlane, with the help of North, now took charge. The House Democratic leadership, undercut by the combination of liberal Democrats and pro-Reagan conservatives, had failed to achieve the compromise it sought. Representative Dave McCurdy, a third-term Oklahoma Democrat who served on both the Intelligence and Armed Services committees, was moderately conservative and also Spanish-speaking. McCurdy had made Central America his specialty and his views carried weight among a bloc of thirty to forty centrists. He regularly voted for aid to the government of El Salvador and against aid to the contras. For advice, he turned to three Democrats who had abandoned the liberal viewpoint—Bruce Cameron, Robert Leiken, and Bernard Aronson, a speechwriter in the Carter White House.

---

* Mexican president Miguel de la Madrid formally notified Henry Ruiz Hernández, the comandante charged with maintaining relations with Mexico, on April 16. Ironically, Ortega need not have traveled to Moscow. Mexico's action preceded Reagan's trade embargo, but the embargo provoked an outcry among the Mexican left, which asserted that the only country effectively supporting it was Mexico. Thereupon, de la Madrid reversed himself and sent a tanker-load in July. A far more effective embargo would have been in place if Reagan had not declared one.

Cameron suggested the figure of $28 million in nonlethal aid in exchange for a letter from Reagan committing himself not to overthrow the Sandinistas. Cameron drafted the letter; McCurdy agreed to it; North got it approved and signed. McCurdy stopped short of demanding a return to Manzanillo because his advisers and members of his coalition were divided on the merits of requiring negotiations of an administration that was dead set against them. But he won from Reagan what he thought was a commitment to a peaceful resolution of the conflict.[31]

Reagan wrote on June 11 that he was "determined to pursue political, not military solutions in Central America" and that he did not seek the overthrow of the Nicaraguan government, nor did he desire "to put in its place a government based on the supporters of the old Somoza regime." He did not directly promise a return to Manzanillo, but said it was possible "that in the proper circumstances, such discussions could help promote the internal reconciliation called for by Contadora and endorsed by many Latin American leaders. Therefore, I intend to instruct our special ambassador to consult with the governments of Central America, the Contadora countries, other democratic governments and the unified Nicaraguan opposition as to how and when the U.S. could resume useful direct talks with Nicaragua." He added that the talks could resume "only when I determine that such a meeting would be helpful in promoting . . . a church-mediated dialogue between the contending factions and the achievement of a workable Contadora agreement." McCurdy thought he had a sufficient commitment by Reagan to back the aid package. He brought his bloc with him.

On June 6 the Senate approved $38 million in nonmilitary aid, 55–42. And on June 12 the House voted by a wide margin, 248–184, $27 million in so-called humanitarian aid. In conference, both houses agreed on $27 million.

Then, at the end of August, Reagan backed away from Manzanillo once again. In a letter to McCurdy he said that Shlaudeman had found that "while the Contadora countries generally favor a resumption of the U.S.-Nicaraguan talks, a different view is held by Nicaragua's neighbors."* This was true but it was also a convenient

---

* The August 31 letter said Nicaragua's three neighbors felt that resuming the Manzanillo talks "in the absence of a clear demonstration of Sandinista intention to negotiate seriously in the Contadora process would undermine the process. . . . A return to the Manzanillo talks now would likely be viewed by the Sandinistas as a reward for their disruptive behavior in June, when the multilateral talks were

excuse. Clearly, the United States alone was the country that could end this Catch-22 if it wanted a negotiated solution.

With the approval of nonlethal aid, Reagan had won the short-term legislative contest while failing to resolve any of the fundamental questions. The margins of victory were sizable but as volatile as the political atmosphere. In the meantime, an opportunity had been lost to craft a bipartisan policy that could be sustained and avert continued battles on Capitol Hill. The level of discourse descended as the administration succeeded in framing the debate in ad hominem terms of good guys and bad guys and demanded that Congress choose sides. Such an approach is part and parcel of domestic politics, but is fraught with dangers when applied to foreign policy. Writ large, the United States would be at war with half the world; for there are not that many "good guys" out there and many places where it is hard to tell the good and bad apart.*

The means approved by Congress corresponded to the fundamental contradiction in Reagan's Nicaragua policy. Humanitarian or, more accurately, nonlethal supplies could keep the contras alive but not fighting. ("How can we win a war with humanitarian aid?" was Bermúdez's reaction to the congressional vote. "You think you are going to win a war with enough medicine for the wounded?") In fact, most of the $32 million from Saudi Arabia went toward arms purchases, and the stockpile served the FDN well into 1987. But U.S. involvement remained at arm's length.[33]

The final legislation permitted the CIA to share intelligence with the contras but not to be involved in dispensing aid; the Pentagon was excluded altogether. Yet it was widely agreed that the contras needed U.S. training and advice to improve their tactics and strategy if they were to become a threat to the Sandinistas. A new organization—the Nicaraguan Humanitarian Assistance Office (NHAO)—was

---

aborted because of Sandinista refusal to discuss agenda items previously agreed to by all the parties. These serious concerns have been heightened by a new wave of aggressive Nicaraguan actions," a reference to four Sandinista army attacks against Costa Rica and repeated "aggression" against Honduras.

* An exception to the descent into name-calling was the State Department publication "Revolution Beyond Our Borders," which contained a wealth of declassified details about U.S. diplomacy toward the Sandinistas since Reagan took office. The title was misleading, however. Tomás Borge indeed said in a July 19, 1981, speech: "This revolution goes beyond our borders," but quickly qualified his remark: "This does not mean that we export our revolution. It is sufficient—and we cannot avoid this—that [the people of Latin America] take our example, the example of gallantry, courage and determination of our people."[32]

created at the State Department to dispense the aid, and by late 1985 funds began to flow.

But even as they acquired their new resources, McFarlane and North took a grave risk by misleading Congress about North's role during the time U.S. government aid was barred. The *New York Times* reported on August 8 that North was running the contra program and guiding FDN military and fund-raising activities. The House Foreign Affairs subcommittee on Latin America led by Michael Barnes and the House Select Committee on Intelligence headed by Lee Hamilton asked for explanations. McFarlane cleverly deflected Barnes by offering to show him documents without staff present, which Barnes turned down. He deliberately misled Hamilton. "None of us has solicited funds, facilitated contacts for prospective potential donors or otherwise organized or coordinated the military or paramilitary efforts of the resistance," McFarlane wrote Hamilton.*

Nicaragua was not the only policy area where the White House, working closely with Casey, spun a web of deceit to exclude the State Department, Congress, and the public at large from a major policy decision. That same month, August 1985, Reagan shipped arms to Iran in hopes of securing freedom for U.S. hostages in Beirut. Like the Nicaragua policy, the decision was based on a highly controversial analysis pushed by Casey. Shultz and Weinberger strongly opposed the move, and Reagan refused to decide in their presence. So McFarlane went to him privately and secured authority to tell Israel to send TOW antitank missiles which the United States later would replenish.

This had been a busy summer in the White House, and at the end of the battle over contra aid, it was unclear which group could claim

---

* McFarlane said in his letter it was "patently untrue" that North had offered the FDN tactical advice and direction, used his influence to facilitate the movement of supplies, been the focal point for private fund-raising. Yet internal White House memos released two years later show that the allegations were accurate. For example, North, in February 1985, had urged that FDN forces in northern Nicaragua disperse to survive an anticipated Sandinista offensive. He had urged that a retired British expert in special operations be hired using Saudi funds to mount sabotage raids against the Sandinistas. And in May, he had told McFarlane that the FDN had cut the Rama road for the first time "in response to guidance that the resistance must cut Sandinista supply lines and reduce the effectiveness of the Sandinista forces on the northern frontier." As for facilitating the flow of logistics, North in a March 5 memo had urged McFarlane to reward the Guatemalan military for providing phony end user certificates the previous month to obtain arms for the FDN.[34]

credit for turning the House around—the confrontationists, who helped create a volatile atmosphere conducive to reversal, or the accommodationists, who brought about the actual deal. As a result, there was no serious effort to preserve the coalition in the year ahead, and 1986 saw a replay of the contest, although for higher stakes: $100 million *and* military aid. This time, McCurdy was on the other side.

SPRINGTIME FOR ZEALOTS

In the meantime, there had been a wholesale turnover in the administration team dealing with Central America. General Paul Gorman had departed from the U.S. Southern Command in March 1985 for reasons that were not made clear at the time or since. Jeane Kirkpatrick left the United Nations in April to be replaced by Vernon Walters. Constantine Menges remained at the NSC but his involvement in the 1984 elections, and in particular his reported encouragement of Curtin Winsor, had given Motley a lever which he readily used to "marginalize" him by excluding him from interagency meetings. Menges stayed on at the NSC handling public diplomacy until mid-1986, when he resigned under pressure. John Negroponte left Honduras at the end of May 1985, and was replaced by John Ferch, a career officer who had headed the U.S. interests section in Havana.

At the State Department, Tony Motley resigned effective July 3 to pursue business interests. Motley's problems had begun with his appointment in 1983, when he attempted to consolidate his authority. This meant getting rid of rival power centers. Some thought he was on the skids from the time he went to Managua in December 1983 and told the Sandinistas that Richard Stone was a front man and not the U.S. negotiator. "That was unique in the annals of bureaucratic back-stabbing," commented Otto Reich. At a hearing in late winter 1985 before the House Foreign Affairs Committee, Motley, according to his critics, was "not supporting the President" on the contras. (Craig Johnstone, too, when it looked like Congress would stop the contra program, said "the contras are dead," according to Reich.) Motley's efforts to replace Curtin Winsor and other conservative political appointees in Central America late in 1984 weakened his base of support in the White House, as did the departure of

Richard Darman, a presidential assistant and Motley ally, who went with Chief of Staff James Baker to the Treasury Department in January 1985. Officially, Motley resigned; but there are indications he was pushed. One such indication is that Nestor Sanchez, the Pentagon's chief civilian point man on Central American issues, began criticizing Motley to other State Department officials. "Nestor said that Motley had been taken over by the career types and was totally under their control," said one diplomat. "I knew it was the end to Motley." By "career types," Sanchez was referring to Johnstone, this diplomat said.

Motley was replaced in July 1985 by Elliott Abrams, a young neoconservative Democrat who already had held two top State Department posts, assistant secretary for international organizations and then human rights and humanitarian affairs. Abrams, a veteran Hill staffer with little background in Central America, took up the public relations challenge with the intensity of a zealot. A very ambitious man who knew what the White House wanted to hear, Abrams ruled out negotiations on anything short of changing the Nicaraguan system. Instead, he became a supporting player in schemes to provide aid to the rebels first as directed by law, and then, when Congress balked in mid-1986, soliciting third countries for funds through a loophole in the law.

Craig Johnstone that same month was named ambassador to Algeria and was replaced by William Walker, a career officer who had been deputy chief of mission in Honduras and Bolivia. Shultz had asked Johnstone to take over the embassy in El Salvador, but Johnstone declined. McFarlane then suggested that Johnstone replace Negroponte in Honduras, but when the idea surfaced in the Evans and Novak column, conservatives quickly wrestled it to the ground. Finally Shultz, who had developed some sizable business deals with Algeria in his previous position as head of Bechtel Corporation, proposed to send him there. No one objected.[35]

Last but not least, Robert McFarlane quit the White House in early December, overwhelmed by the job, the pressures, and the back-stabbing. McFarlane had been the broker among the various independent power centers who deeply distrusted and did their best to thwart each other. As ideologues and zealots threw their weight around, McFarlane presided. In the circumstances, the straight-arrow ex-Marine had amassed a remarkable record of double-dealing. He had misled Shultz about contra fund-raising and Iran policy, Casey about Shultz's negotiations, and Congress about North's war efforts. He had been steamrollered by Casey, who wanted a confrontation with Congress, only to save the program through old-fashioned give-and-take. None of this was known at the time to the public, the Congress, or, apparently, to the principals.

The wave of personnel shifts raised questions among Central American governments about the direction and sustainability of U.S. policy in Nicaragua, but the implications did not become clear until early 1986. The State Department team that had sought to test whether a settlement was possible with the Sandinistas was gone, and no one who remained behind would try that again. Meanwhile, there were plenty more within the administration to replace Kirkpatrick and Negroponte, who had fought for the contra program in Washington and facilitated it on the ground respectively. The upshot of the changes, in other words, was that U.S. policy would become monodimensional.

In October 1985, Harry Shlaudeman briefly resumed the Nicaragua contacts in Washington, but only to demand that the Sandinistas negotiate with the contras. The talks led nowhere.* The Contadora four had proposed a new treaty draft that September and Nicaragua formally rejected it in November. Contadora went into a tailspin

---

* The Shlaudeman sequel is a tale of protocolary one-upmanship. Shultz informed one of the Contadora foreign ministers about the plan for a meeting before anyone told the Nicaraguans. After getting a tip, I asked for a comment from D'Escoto, who was in New York for the UN General Assembly. This was the first he had heard of it. Some days later, shortly before Daniel Ortega's arrival in New York to address the UN General Assembly, the State Department proposed that Abrams, accompanied by Shlaudeman and Bergold, call on Ortega in New York. Nicaragua replied that Ortega was willing to call on Reagan or receive Shultz, but if Abrams wanted to be received by Ortega, he would have to travel to Managua. On the other hand, D'Escoto was willing to receive Abrams in New York. If they wanted to meet in Washington, D'Escoto would send his deputy, Nora Astorga. Astorga had been denied agrément when proposed as the Nicaraguan ambassador to Washington because of charges that at the time of the Sandinista revolution, she had lured a Nicaraguan military official who also was a CIA asset into her house where he was murdered. The State Department declined all these options, but offered to have Shlaudeman call on D'Escoto. The Sandinistas rejected the gambit and said Astorga could meet Shlaudeman in New York. This the Americans rejected. Finally, they agreed that Shlaudeman would meet with Nicaraguan ambassador to the United States Carlos Tünnerman. When they finally met, both reiterated their already stated positions, according to both diplomats.

until mid-1986 when, on the eve of another vote, the four produced a new draft which all sides rejected.

For the leaders of Contadora, who still hoped for a peaceful settlement, these were grim times indeed. "What has happened is that you are introducing either from one side or the other elements which are foreign to the whole process and which disrupt the process in itself," said President Betancur of Colombia. "It would seem that every single morning either those on one side or those on another look at a list of what mistakes haven't still been made. And they decide to choose one of them."

"Contadora is breathing its last breaths," said a foreign ministry official in Managua late in June 1985. "Contadora really said nothing about the embargo or the further funding of the contras. There is no protection for Nicaragua in Contadora."

Indeed, for a grouping that produced endless statements, Contadora's silence was remarkable. If ever there had been a time for an even-handed joint statement condemning U.S. aid to the contras, the embargo, and the Ortega trip, this was it. Yet Contadora had said nothing. The reason is that they made decisions by consensus, and Mexico refused to go along. Embarrassment was a factor. "It was Mexico's fault that Ortega had to go. So it would have been exaggerated for the Mexicans to criticize Ortega," noted a leading Mexican diplomatic reporter.[36]

"Sometimes I feel Central America is a Greek tragedy," said a Costa Rican official. "Everyone knows the end, but everyone is playing his role to fulfill the prophecy. A very important part of the ideology of those in power in Nicaragua is a willingness to die to promote the revolution." Rationally, Nicaragua should have stayed in Contadora, he said, because it was "the only security umbrella they can get. The only way they can stop the U.S. administration from funding the contras is signing an agreement." The revised treaty would impose very hard decisions on Nicaragua. "Are they willing to pay the price and stay in power? Or will they fulfill the prophecy and die promoting revolution in Central America?"[37]

In September 1985, the Contadora group presented a revised treaty representing a compromise between its own draft of September 7, 1984, and the objections raised by Costa Rica, Honduras, and El Salvador. In November, Daniel Ortega rejected the treaty and said Nicaragua would not begin talks on arms reductions until the United States ceased support for the contras.

The stagnation of peace efforts was of no concern in the administration, where Casey and North in the course of 1985 had effectively taken control of formulating policy for Nicaragua. But much had changed in Washington as a result. In place of the traditional policy process in which the State Department seeks to accommodate presidential goals to domestic political reality and the real world, the two activists had opted for ever more strident presidential rhetoric and a stance of confrontation with Congress to back their program in order to avoid a negotiated solution. It was a high-risk method of governance for Reagan to allow them to ignore the views of experts and to hide their schemes from the rest of the executive branch and Congress. If they achieved the goal they set for him of overthrowing the Sandinistas, they could get away with it; but no one except possibly Reagan himself thought that likely. Reagan took an even greater risk by allowing their power grab of Nicaragua policy to become the model for the secret arms-for-hostage sales to Iran. McFarlane, who had facilitated both policy takeovers, saw the sidelining of the State Department on these and other foreign policy issues as a cause of lasting regret. It may have been a factor as well in his resignation. "The organization of the administration for the conduct of foreign policy is, I believe, intrinsically unworkable," he said eighteen months after he quit. "There must be one person who is advocate, conceptual creator, implementer of foreign policy. That is the Secretary of State."[38]

The policy implication of these shifts was that Washington no longer would pursue a diplomatic track. In Managua, meanwhile, a combination of new arms and military reorganization and the strong rhetoric from Washington gave hard-liners the excuse to reject the Contadora mediation. Thus, at the end of 1985, both the Sandinistas and Reagan were headed in the direction of a military solution. The difference was that Reagan's approach was largely rhetorical, whereas the Sandinistas were well on their way to changing the facts on the ground.

CHAPTER 13

"POINT OF NO RETURN"

AFTER TWO YEARS OF A RELATIVELY FREE RUN, the contras were nearly routed in 1985. The shift in the military balance that led to this reversal reflected differences in strategy, military structure, and sources of external support of the two sides. The setback should have raised alarm bells in Washington, but the administration, focusing on its precarious majority in Congress, pretended in public that nothing had happened. North addressed the crisis by wresting control of finances and logistics from the contras and turning them over to his associate Richard Secord.[1] The fix was inadequate, and by the time Congress restored military aid in late 1986, the difficulties facing the contras looked almost insurmountable.

The emergence of Ejército Popular Sandinista (EPS), or Sandinista Popular Army, as an instrument capable of containing the contras was the central event on the ground in 1985. It could not have been achieved without flexibility and imagination by the Sandinista leaders, who revamped their military structure and strategy, improved their training, command, and communications, and introduced powerful new weapons.

They drew on their experience as guerrillas and their somewhat less successful counterinsurgency efforts in 1983 and 1984, but they also had to revise earlier plans built around the assumption that the United States intended to use the rebels as the trigger to an invasion. From intelligence reports, presumably from infiltrators, they had learned that Argentine officers had told the commandos that if they did certain things and took certain objectives, the United States would intervene. "We know the North American government is arrogant, but they're not fools," Bayardo Arce, one of the nine comandantes, had said. "We thought this [the FDN] was a complementary force leading to an invasion. It was going to play the role of destroying our forces in the northern zone, where an invasion of regular forces is less likely."[2] The Sandinistas had planned to allow the rebels to advance into the interior; meanwhile they had structured their forces and organized their strategy on the assumption of an American invasion of the main population centers on the Pacific coast. (American military experts throughout 1983 had expressed surprise that the Sandinistas were using mostly semitrained militia forces, often from outside their area of origin, and holding back the regular army.)

"We didn't have anything like a trained army," commented Luis Carrión, another of the comandantes. "We fought the contras in 1982 and 1983 on sheer numbers. Thousands of people were mobilized from all over the country to fight but without any training. The commanding officers were not really officers. They were people from the cities without adequate training trying to fight in the bush. And that was really a mess." The chain of command was weak, as was discipline. Militias made up of semitrained local people had to go out of their operational area "and that didn't have good results."

The troops had been volunteers from all backgrounds. During one major mobilization in 1983, authorities had noted a fall in the crime rate in Managua. "Criminals were among those who mobilized themselves," Carrión said, adding that this had led to human rights abuses in the field. "These people would many times [cut off] the hands of the peasants, treat them badly."

By 1983 the leadership had concluded that owing to internal U.S. politics, an intervention was "not easy." "Meanwhile," Carrión said, "the contras had begun making serious inroads. They were on the rise. They had reasons to be optimistic . . . from the military view."

This, then, led to a restructuring of the Sandinista forces and the creation of irregular warfare battalions, known as BLIs—Batallón de Lucha Irregular. "We decided that the type of training our people received didn't make any sense," Carrión continued. "We had to change that and recall some of our own experience as guerrilla fighters." The comandantes decided that the government forces should have more physical training, intensive target practice, and training in irregular tactics such as ambushes, silent marches through the woods, reconnaissance, and camouflage. The troops were trained to operate in dispersed companies, each with a great deal of autonomy coordinated by the battalion commander. The seventeen BLIs, with 700 to 800 men each, came to constitute nearly half the EPS regular force.

By the start of 1984, the Sandinistas had introduced the draft, organized the BLIs, and also weighed an agrarian reform. Through that summer, the contras had them very much on the defensive.

"In 1984, we were in our best moment," Bermúdez noted. "We were a large force with good experience. We had relatively good support. We were causing many casualties." The high point came around June and July. Even though aid was cut, they continued on the basis of supplies on hand. "And I felt we couldn't be in a better position than at the end of 1984."

Carrión disagreed, calling 1984 a military draw. "But a draw is a bad thing for them [the contras] because the only way an irregular force can have any hope to achieve its goals is if it is always advancing. They were no longer on the rise." Yet he conceded that on the psychological front Bermúdez had made important inroads among the rural population. "Things were not clear for the population. They were not sure who was winning the war. I'll tell you that for a peasant that's the most important thing to determine: who's winning the war. That's how I'm going to lean." This was the context in which the Sandinista leadership convinced the Soviet Union to step up military deliveries. The first Mi-25 helicopters arrived in October 1984.

What is interesting to note is that even after a run of two years of relative success, the contras' military achievements were limited.

They were highly successful in disrupting the 1984 coffee harvest in mountainous northern Nicaragua, depriving the Sandinistas of needed foreign exchange. North of Matagalpa, government vehicles had to move in convoy because of the threat of ambush. The contras had a support infrastructure in the border region and in other rural areas that allowed them to remain in the country. Yet the movement failed to obtain a firm toehold or to ignite the least sign of popular support in Nicaragua's cities.

Leaders of both sides agreed that the military balance shifted significantly in 1985, although they cite different reasons. According to Carrión, the improvement came in the Sandinista military training, strategy, and structure and their political motivation. According to Bermúdez, the FDN did not have a reliable source for supplies. Both are probably correct.

According to Joaquín Cuadra Lacayo, the EPS chief of staff, there were at the beginning of 1985 10,000 contras total, 6,000 on the northern front, of whom about 5,000 were inside Nicaragua at any time and some of whom had penetrated as far as 150 kilometers (90 miles) inside the border. Cuadra said the "strategic defeat" of the contras would be possible by the end of the year. He defined "defeat" as getting them out of the Jinotega area and back to the border region. In this sense, by the end of 1985 the contras were indeed "defeated." Throughout 1985, the Sandinistas kept up pressure on the contras in the north. They used their Mi-8 and Mi-17 helicopters to transport the BLIs to contest the contras, laid extensive mines in the border region, intensified bombardment with long-range artillery, and relocated civilian supporters from areas where the contras operated. The effect was to isolate those fighters remaining in the country.*

In mid-May, the Sandinistas had mounted a major offensive against the remnants of Pastora's ARDE forces in the south by bombing airstrips and wiping out contra camps. "Operation Sovereignty" led to an international incident when one Costa Rican civil

---

* Bermúdez's Washington representative later recounted that "the effect of this strategy, as Unit Commander Segovia informed me, was that in one ten-month period, during which his troops faced numerous engagements, they spent fifteen days without sighting a single peasant. They were totally dependent upon what they obtained in the mountains or captured from the enemy or the meager supplies received by air in order to survive."[3]

guard was killed and eleven others wounded. But it achieved its desired effect as the southern front completely collapsed.*

Another innovation of Sandinista strategy which helped improve their fortunes in 1985 was in the nonmilitary sphere—the effort to win over the peasantry. In its earlier form as a volunteer army, the EPS had found it "very difficult to keep the population on our side," Carrión said. "With better preparation and training we needed less troops because we had a greater operational capacity and more effective troops. We sent some people out with a lot of money to go to the field to find out whatever damage had occurred to the property of the peasants, explain it to them, and pay them." The attitude of troops toward peasants improved, abuse problems diminished very dramatically, and "we started to defeat the contras."

A second element in this effort was the agrarian reform program, under which the Sandinistas distributed land to almost 5,000 families in 1985. "That has something to do with the war also," Carrión said. The government also sent civilians or, in areas of risk, small armed groups to the countryside to talk to as many people as possible to "find what they were thinking, how they were feeling, give them confidence to talk in order that we could better identify their fears, their needs and try to organize in response to that."

A third element was improved methods of repressing sympathizers and supporters of the resistance. "When you are trying to win the population for your side, you have to be firm and fair," Carrión said. "If people think you are weak, they won't support you. They will support the one who is stronger. This is not an ideological decision. It is a survival decision."

It was important in arresting anyone "to make sure before you arrest him that he's clearly involved and that that involvement is known or can be made easily known for all the people." Carrión said the interior ministry, which he runs day to day, knew "of a lot of people" who collaborated with the contras but did not arrest them. Instead, "we go to them and make them know that we know." For some, collaboration is unavoidable. "A group of armed men come

---

* The Sandinistas later offered to create a demilitarized zone, an offer about which Costa Rican president Luis Alberto Monge expressed serious interest. The United States moved quickly to discourage any such arrangement. Congressman George Brown, a member of the House Intelligence Committee, said he called on Monge with George Jones, the chargé d'affaires of the U.S. embassy. "He said it diplomatically: 'We would prefer you not to do it.' " Monge subsequently backed off.[4]

and what are you going to do? You give them food or whatever. We understand that. We do not consider that a crime. The only thing we ask them is, let us know." The ones the interior ministry arrests, according to Carrión, are the activists: "the one who moves around collecting information, who recruits other people, who collects money for them—militant contras." They are put on trial before "people's tribunals," a system of courts set up by Interior Minister Tomás Borge which has been very sharply criticized by U.S. human rights groups.

Carrión said that the repression "was not very well directed" in 1983 and 1984. "We did not hit who we should hit." But starting in 1985, methods had improved and the Sandinistas were operating "with very good results."*

On the other hand, 1985 was Bermúdez's worst year. "In 1985, we didn't grow," he said. "It was a bad year for us. On the contrary, many people who saw we were getting no support abandoned the movement. We diminished a bit."

Yet the administration repeatedly claimed that the FDN continued to grow in size despite the lack of U.S. aid. U.S. military intelligence experts at the Southern Command in Panama said the FDN was growing by 1,000 fighters a month through mid-1985; Bermúdez estimated the growth at 500. "Each time a unit goes deep into Nicaragua, despite their losses, they come back with more," said one expert. A glossy U.S. document issued in June 1986 depicted a steady rise in numbers to 20,000 resistance fighters in 1985, up from

---

* "Very good results" for the Sandinistas translated into something very different for those arrested. Human rights sources in Managua knew of 600 cases in 1985 of disappearances, physical and psychological torture, and holding prisoners without charge for extended periods. These sources said 4,000 political detainees were in prison by the end of 1985, most of them rural campesinos or peasants. Another 3,000 people were arrested in the first six months of 1986, of whom only 700 had been released by July. Typically, an individual was arrested and placed incommunicado for two to three months, when a confession was sought. It might take up to two years to be sentenced. Amnesty International, the human rights watchdog group, criticized the Nicaraguan government for "prolonged pretrial incommunicado detention of political prisoners" and for restricting their right to a fair trial. But in a report in early 1986, it credited the Sandinistas with establishing a "pattern of investigation and prosecution of government personnel alleged to be guilty" of human rights abuses. As for the contras, Amnesty concluded that the "targeted assassinations of government officials and real or supposed supporters, the abduction of civilians, and the abuse or ill-treatment of captives, far from being isolated and questionable incidents, have become a constant feature of military operations by the irregular anti-government forces." It asserted that the contras had killed several hundred.[5]

14,000 in 1984 and 7,500 in 1983. Elliott Abrams claimed that in the year without U.S. assistance, the resistance doubled in size to 18,000. The FDN, which constituted the bulk of these forces, asserted that its numbers never exceeded 15,000.[6]

Appearances were deceiving. Bermúdez's forces did grow and then again they didn't. They grew in the sense that growth was required by political strategy. "Our policy was grow, grow, grow so we can play" in the policy game, Bermúdez said. "That was a basic strategy for the movement." Yet he also conceded the growth was only in numbers. "We haven't improved our forces. We have grown. But we haven't improved. We are fighting only with rifles."

North was among those who lobbied for higher numbers. In May, he asked McFarlane to approach Saudi Arabia for another $15 to $20 million, arguing that with it the FDN could more than double its troops to 35,000 or 40,000 inside six months. McFarlane turned him down, but North predicted that the force would grow to 30,000 anyway. (In fact, it never did.)[7]

According to CIA and Honduran army sources, the FDN's numbers inflation concealed a serious military weakness. From 1983, growth came largely by sending out recruiters into the villages of northern Nicaragua. Early in 1985, the Sandinistas cleared a swath along the border zones where the resistance were getting support and resettled some 180,000 peasants inland, according to the Sandinista minister of social security.[8] The FDN's reaction was to haul in its support structure. Thus the numbers stayed more or less steady and ostensibly even grew while in fact the FDN's strength diminished. This helps account for the situation noted by one observer of guerrilla warfare that unlike most guerrilla movements, the FDN had virtually no urban or rural auxiliary support within Nicaragua.*

---

* According to the rule of thumb that counterinsurgency forces need a 10:1 ratio to prevail, the Sandinistas easily had the military advantage. While 20,000 contras seemed formidable on paper, equal to one third of the Sandinista regular army, only 4,000 to 5,000 rebels were in the country on active operations at any time. Thus the real ratio was about 16:1. By comparison, Angola's army with Cuban combat troops had a 7:1 advantage over Jonas Savimbi's UNITA forces; the Mozambique government had only a 4:1 advantage over South African-backed Renamo insurgents; Ethiopian forces augmented by Cuban combat troops had a 12:1 advantage over insurgent forces in Eritrea and Tigre; the Afghan government supplemented by Soviet troops had a 10:1 advantage over the Mujahadeen. "The prospect for the Nicaraguan insurgents to win on the force of their own arms is not a bright one," concludes one expert.[9]

In building up his numbers, Bermúdez had a single aim in mind. He never had conceived of the FDN as able to conquer Nicaragua and doubted its ability to capture territory at any stage. Bermúdez's real aim may not have fit classic guerrilla doctrine, but it did fit a classic aim of Nicaraguan politics: to get the United States to solve the problem.

Bermúdez, in short, hoped to bring about a situation by mid-1986 that would constitute "a point of no return, where the United States would have such a big investment politically and financially that it would be more expensive to stop it than to let it go ahead."

Bermúdez, however, had a problem of timing. He was convinced that Republicans would lose control of the U.S. Senate in the November 1986 elections, an astute prediction. "Therefore, we are in a hurry to act," he said one year earlier. But in order to carry out actions that would bring the United States to the "point of no return," funding had to be approved by April 1986.

The stress on numbers played well in Washington, but it was a poor answer to the sort of reorganization, restructuring, and retraining that had been undertaken by the Sandinistas. McFarlane had tried to provoke the FDN into such a shake-up, but found himself stymied. In January, he had told Calero the FDN had failed to develop a political leadership and program with authentic appeal to the general population or to demonstrate "sufficient competence" on the battlefield to constitute a threat to the Sandinistas. He had believed that 1985 would be a critical year of testing for the contras and that if their deficiencies were not corrected, "we owed it to them and to ourselves to cut both our losses and theirs by changing our strategy to a more overt combination of U.S. force and U.S. diplomacy."

But McFarlane had been working at cross-purposes with Reagan, who offered uncritical support. "The President repeatedly made clear in public and in private that he did not intend to break faith with the contras," McFarlane noted. The rhetoric was not accidental. Although North had agreed to carry out McFarlane's agenda, he and Casey also had their own agenda, which was not to close down his program under any circumstances. They used their influence with White House speechwriters to ensure this remained a feature of Reagan's rhetoric.

A further complication in reaching the goals sketched by McFarlane was North's penchant for focusing on image over substance. His initial concern had been that the EPS would deliver a humiliating blow to the FDN in an offensive that U.S. intelligence predicted would occur in March or April. North had sent a CIA map to Calero to be passed to Bermúdez, his second such deliberate circumvention of the October 1984 Boland amendment ban. In a note North had urged the FDN to disperse its forces in northern Nicaragua to avoid the Sandinista "firestorm." He had added: "While I know it hurts to hide, now is the time to do it."

His other worry had been short-term congressional politics, and in the absence of tactical gains, North had tried to dream up military spectaculars. In February, he had proposed seizing the Nicaraguan merchant ship *Monimbo* on the high seas to prevent it from carrying a cargo of arms back to Corinto from the Far East. John Poindexter, the deputy NSC adviser, had concurred that "we need to take action to make sure [the] ship does not arrive in Nicaragua." Nothing happened. On March 6, a hired British special operations team had attacked a major military complex, touching off explosions with a force that rocked Managua. But the operation went awry. The main damage had been done to the country's principal military hospital, where casualties included women and infants in a maternity ward. The FDN wisely avoided claiming credit.

Although his spectaculars had all fizzled, North claimed to have reorganized the contra force. In mid-April, he had boasted to McFarlane that based on his guidance, the FDN in less than a year had become "an effective guerrilla army." He cited introduction of a traditional staff structure and the reorienting of officer training and recruit schooling "from conventional to guerrilla warfare tactics." By late May, North had begun crowing about tactical military gains. "For the first time in the war, the FDN [succeeded] in interdicting the Rama-Managua road, launched simultaneous operations in the Boaco area less than 60 km from Managua and inflicted heavy losses on Sandinista troops in the vicinity of Siuna-Bonanza." The operations had been conducted "in response to guidance" that the FDN must cut Sandinista supply lines and reduce their effectiveness on the northern frontier, he told McFarlane. The "guide," of course, was North.

North had also been active on the political front, but here as well the changes had been superficial and aimed mainly at impressing Congress. After helping orchestrate the March 1 "peace initiative" by Calero, Cruz, and Robelo in San José, North had set to work creating a civilian leadership structure. On May 31, North had reported to McFarlane that "two weeks of intense dialogue with the resistance leadership" had resulted in a document of objectives. This, in theory, was just what the boss had ordered. It established civilian primacy over a unified military organization and committed its leadership to a democratic process to elect a new government once the Sandinistas were toppled. The new organization was to be called UNO, Unidad Nicaraguense Opositor, an umbrella organization.

"In short, the political and military situation for the resistance now appears better than at any point in the last 12 months," he had boasted in the same memo. Even by North's standards, however, this was a gross overstatement.[10]

UNO served as the vehicle to distribute $27 million in nonlethal U.S. aid approved by Congress in late June. But UNO really existed only on paper. Calero played along, but Bermúdez was openly contemptuous, and that rendered UNO powerless. Bermúdez saw it as a power grab. Cruz and Robelo, he said, tried to "take over the FDN. They have nothing. They want to impose themselves. That is not fair. We worked harder to bring this organization to what it is now. They were on the rival side. They kept attacking us." UNO "is somebody's invention . . . artificial without any support of the basis," created to please Congress.*

In a narrow sense, he was right. UNO most assuredly was an artificial creation. Yet the FDN also lacked a base of popular support. Instead of expanding the base, Calero and Bermúdez had in fact narrowed it between mid-1984 and mid-1985. Both eased out opponents and consolidated their position within the movement. Calero appointed his brother, Mario, to handle all the procurement and deliveries to the forces. As a result of this narrowing of the base, the large exile community in Miami shunned them. Yet only new political leadership could devise clear goals and an ideology that

---

* They apparently never actually agreed on the name in English. Reagan's policy letter to McCurdy in August 1985 called it the "Unified Nicaraguan Opposition." Robert Leiken, a supporter and adviser to Arturo Cruz, called it the "Nicaraguan Opposition Unity" in an op-ed piece in the *Washington Post* in July 1986. UNO's own literature named it the "United Nicaraguan Opposition." Months after opening a duplex office suite over a Chinese restaurant near the Washington Zoo, UNO did not have a listing in the Washington telephone directory. Then again, the FDN, which previously had operated out of cramped quarters adjacent to the Cuban-American National Foundation in Georgetown, did not either.

could be sold to Nicaraguans who had stayed behind, to Nicaraguan émigrés, and to Americans who had to pick up the tab. What Bermúdez really wanted was a boost for his own leadership.

"Why do you insist on failure? Why don't you take the successful people and make one group? Think about it. How can a guy belonging to a rival group who hasn't had any success come to me and say: 'Listen: you are doing things wrong. You have to behave. You have to change.' I could ask: 'Do you have any moral position to say this? What have you done? What is your success?' " This attitude, grounded on what Bermúdez felt were his achievements, was also the bottom line for Calero in UNO.[11]

The impotence of UNO and the "civilian primacy" it represented became clearer when the military situation worsened in June. As the impact of the Sandinista offensive in the south sank in, North became agitated and around June 1, called a "program review."

Disregarding his own political creation, UNO, North summoned Bermúdez and Calero, the real powers, to an all-night session at the Miami airport hotel with Secord and two associates in attendance. There he harshly criticized the contras' resupply arrangements. He cited rumors that Mario Calero had botched deliveries and that certain individuals were lining their pockets. When the meeting ended at 5 a.m., there was agreement on three points: the FDN required better air resupply; a southern front must be revived; and the contras had to begin operating in urban areas. Apparently, North had something quite different in mind: Secord would take over logistics, resupply, and financing, and North would play a far more active role in diplomacy and fund-raising. But he did not reveal this at the time to Calero; nor did he tell McFarlane, who said he could not recall authorizing North to organize the meeting, much less assign a role to Secord.

After the meeting, North quickly took four steps. First, he asked Secord to put together the resupply operation. Next, he called in Lewis Tambs, the ambassador-designate to Costa Rica. Tambs, who in 1981 had been Jesse Helms's candidate for the job of assistant secretary of state in the Bureau of Inter-American Affairs, had most recently served an ambassador to Colombia. North "asked me to go down and open up the southern front," Tambs recalled. "If that's what they want, that's what we'll try and do," was his reply. Tambs said he assumed North was "speaking for the RIG," the Restricted Interagency Group, but North apparently had no authorization for the instruction. Third, he had the NSC staff aide responsible for Asian affairs, Gaston Sigur, introduce him to the head of the Taiwan trade office, from whom he solicited $1 million. (Sigur had been Helms's candidate in 1981 for assistant secretary for East Asian and Pacific affairs.) The funds were sent to an account Secord had established in Geneva under the name of a dummy firm, "Lake Resources." Finally, he directed Robert Owen to travel to Costa Rica to help locate the site for an airstrip in northwestern Costa Rica for emergency landings of aircraft supplying what was hoped would be the southern front. Tambs arranged the necessary clearances with the Costa Rican government, arguing that the strip would be required if Nicaragua provoked Costa Rica into invoking U.S. assistance under the Rio treaty. Later that autumn, North obtained another $1 million from Taiwan. This was apparently the seed money for the airstrip. Once again, Shultz and Abrams were not informed.[12]

Meanwhile, the FDN on August 1 implemented point three of the Miami accord by capturing La Trinidad, a town of about 8,000 on the Pan-American Highway about fifty miles north of Managua, and holding it for five hours. This was the opportunity the Sandinistas had been waiting for; they deployed their Mi-25 helicopter gunships and recaptured the town. It was the first and last contra offensive of the year and was marred by reports that FDN troops "marched people outside and hacked off their heads," according to congressional sources.

Things were not going according to North's plan. Instead, a series of calamities, some of their own making, gravely weakened the contra fighting force.

Congressional approval of the $27 million in June 1985 should have been a shot in the arm for the FDN, but it was nearly the beginning of 1986 before the nonlethal aid began to arrive in quantity, more than eighteen months after the aid cut-off. The slow-down was due to a combination of political uncertainties in Honduras and the FDN's own ineptitude. On the second flight in, on October 10, 1985, Mario Calero, who was running the supply operation for his brother, Adolfo, brought along an NBC camera crew. The Honduran military ordered the crew off the plane, seized the contents, and suspended all further shipments.

Honduras was in the middle of an election campaign, and the new U.S. ambassador, John Ferch, focused on ensuring an orderly hand-over of power, had held up aid funds for fear that Suazo would misappropriate them, and then was unable to get the ban lifted. The impasse caused concern in Washington. At the suggestion of North, Vice-Admiral John Poindexter, who had succeeded McFarlane as national security adviser on December 4, visited Tegucigalpa in mid-December and asked the Honduran military commander, Walter López Reyes, to lift the ban. López indicated he might. Poindexter called on only military officials during his one-day five-nation swing, and did not see Suazo Córdova, who was about to leave office. Suazo refused to lift the ban, and the deliveries were not resumed until his successor, José Azcona Hoyo, took office in late January 1986.

For the contras, the picture could not have been bleaker at the end of 1985. The main FDN fighting force was sitting in its camps in Honduras, without boots, ponchos, hammocks, and—for many— hope. The returning columns "looked like prisoners returning from Buchenwald," Bermúdez's representative in Washington said. Shortly after Christmas, Secord briefed Casey at the latter's request. He expressed "grave reservations" about the contras' abilities to achieve significant military victories, and ticked off the problems: no viable southern front, inadequate logistics and intelligence capabilities, and poor leadership. Secord got the impression that Casey agreed. Retired Army General John Singlaub, a volunteer adviser and fund-raiser for the contras, summed up the situation: "very desperate." Alan Fiers, the director of the CIA Central America task force, described concern about the situation as being "high, almost on the edge of panic."

In short, according to EPS chief of staff Cuadra's definition, the contras were close to being "defeated." They had been forced out of north-central Nicaragua and reduced once again to be a border-raiding force.

Only Elliott Abrams, heeding the political aspects of the issue rather than the military facts, whistled a happier tune. "There is a lot of fighting going on in Nicaragua today, probably never been more," he said in an interview at the end of 1985. "The performance of the FDN in the last month or so is . . . better than they've done before." But he declined to supply details on the grounds that they were classified.[13]

But military professionals viewed the contras disparagingly. General Paul Gorman called them a "cross-border raiding force" capable only of "clumsy attacks on fixed points" and "crude ambushing."

Lacking an intelligence network or a political infrastructure, they were unable to tap the prevailing discontent in Nicaragua's cities and were forced to operate in "the uninhabited fringes" of the country.[14]

In January 1986, Representative Dave McCurdy tried to prepare for the forthcoming funding battle in Congress by consulting some of the leading experts on insurgency and Latin America at an off-the-record two-day seminar. He concluded that the contras had failed on almost every count of what constitutes a successful insurgency. They needed leadership training at every level from squad leader to task force commander. They lacked a political-military strategy—that is, a way to transmit a positive political message to the population of Nicaragua about their goals. They were organized more as a conventional force than as guerrillas, "which makes it easier for a counterinsurgency plan to interdict them." The Sandinistas had appropriated the nationalist message. The contras lacked "charismatic, confident leaders" and had limited indigenous support. On the positive side, they had a secure sanctuary, which was essential in the initial organizational phase, and external support.

One counterinsurgency expert at the McCurdy seminar said afterward that the administration had established "self-defeating" criteria for measuring the success of the fighters. "For the past three years, the United States has relied on quantifying personnel, quantifying the fighting, and quantifying attacks. It may be a false measurement." Far more effective guerrilla forces operated with far smaller numbers. The Sandinistas up until a year before their triumph had less than 500 fighters. In El Salvador, 6,000 to 8,000 guerrillas threatened to bring down the government in 1980-81. Fidel Castro had had no more than 3,000 armed supporters at the very end.[15]*

In the politically charged atmosphere generated by the White House when Reagan threatened to campaign against contra aid opponents in the 1986 elections, few besides McCurdy devoted much attention to the basics. The administration propaganda machine had effectively shifted the debate away from the facts on the

---

* Addiction to the numbers game continued at the State Department, however. As late as July 1986, James Michel, the principal deputy assistant secretary of state in the Bureau of Inter-American Affairs, told a meeting of congressional staffers that the administration goal was for the contras to grow in size to 30,000 and to bring the situation in Nicaragua "to a head within the next two years" through "internal opposition or insurrection against the Sandinistas."

ground to the ad hominem question of good guys and bad guys. Liberals took the bait and devoted great energies to proving that, for example, 46 of the 48 contra leaders were, as the Sandinistas alleged, Somocistas. The administration countered that of the 153 "senior military personnel," only 41 had prior National Guard service, leaving aside the fact that these 41 occupied most of the senior positions.[16]

Much less notice was given to the question of who the foot soldiers were. According to Dave Durenberger, the chairman of the Senate Select Committee on Intelligence, nearly all of the FDN rank and file were illiterate peasants who lived in primitive conditions and had never been outside their home region just south of the Honduran border. "To them, the coastal plain is France and Managua is Paris." Bermúdez, who often boasted about his peasant army, had turned away middle-class volunteers, Durenberger said.[17] The implication was that the FDN commander preferred unlettered soldiers because their loyalty would be unquestioning.

Thus, at the end of 1985, even as a fragile political consensus began to build in Congress behind limited financial support for the contras, the situation on the ground had become militarily untenable. The gap between U.S. political support and the military reality was nothing new; they had never been synchronized, because Reagan had at no point required that his chief diplomatic, defense, and intelligence aides pursue an agreed-upon strategy that could be sustained in Congress. As a result, at the very time Bermúdez seemed to be on the verge of his goal to bring the United States to the political point of no return in backing his forces, the Sandinistas were on the verge of ensuring a military "point of no return" for Bermúdez's forces in Nicaragua.

CHAPTER
14

MANIPULATING THE
PRESIDENT

UNLIKE THE REBELS, who found themselves in difficulties at the start of 1986, Casey and North, their benefactors in Washington, were in their heyday. As Reagan entered his sixth year in office, the two activists had taken control of perhaps the riskiest initiative in recent American diplomatic history: the secret arms sales to Iran.

The broader role that Casey and North came to play in U.S. foreign policy was built around the zealous implementation of Reagan's instructions in mid-1984 to keep the contras alive "body and soul" when Congress refused to renew CIA funding. The two worked as a team. Casey, by appealing to Reagan's romantic attachment to the concept of "freedom fighters" and feeding him distorted intelligence, was able to dominate the policy process. North, by directing fund-raising and arms drops and advising the rebels on military and political strategy, kept day-to-day control of

313

the program. But Nicaragua was only a springboard. In the summer of 1985, Reagan overruled the objections of Shultz and Weinberger and followed Casey's advice in approving the secret arms transfers to Iran. Policy implementation followed the Nicaragua model. Casey fed Reagan distorted intelligence assessments centering on the Soviet threat to Iran, and North took charge of sales and negotiations. In late 1985, Casey also helped force a shift in Southern Africa policy by defeating Shultz in a hard-fought battle that resulted in renewal of CIA arms deliveries to anti-Communist rebels in Angola. Casey tried to expand his covert aid empire to the South African-backed insurgents in Mozambique, but here Shultz managed to block him.[1]

For his accomplishments and his ambitions, Casey gained a nickname among U.S. diplomats: "Secretary of State for the Third World." (A variant was "Secretary of State for the Reagan Doctrine countries.")

That same winter, Casey mounted an indirect challenge to Shultz after he and other hard-liners persuaded Reagan to introduce lie detector tests for government employees from the cabinet on down. Shultz had threatened to quit two years earlier over a similar scheme, and in mid-December 1985, after learning that Reagan had signed a secret executive order six weeks earlier, he repeated his threat. "The minute in this government I am told that I'm not trusted is the day I leave," he said. Casey publicly rebutted Shultz with a statement that there was an "acute need" for "selective" polygraphing. Weinberger concurred. His cabinet divided and squabbling in public, Reagan rescinded the order. Shultz stayed but was weakened by the dispute.[2]

The Casey-North style suited Reagan's preference for action over deliberation, but their rapid accretion of influence in 1985 and 1986 should be seen in the context of the more permissive environment in which they operated. This environment was due largely to four factors. For one, in January 1985, as Reagan passively looked on, Treasury Secretary Donald Regan had taken over as chief of staff in a job switch with James Baker. A Casey protégé had replaced a Casey rival. The former head of a Wall Street investment firm whom Casey had brought into the administration, Regan had a limited background in foreign policy. Unlike Baker, he made no effort to save Reagan from the consequences of his unstudied impulses. Regan's watchword was to "let Reagan be Reagan."

A second factor was the replacement of Tony Motley by Elliott

Abrams at the State Department in July 1985, which removed the only real challenge to their foreign policy power base, Central America.

Unlike his predecessors for more than a decade, Abrams had no experience in a diplomatic post abroad, no regional expertise, and no background as a foreign policy professional. "He didn't know much about Latin America, but he knew his way around Washington," said Nestor Sanchez.[3] Abrams had a quick mind, a combative manner, and boundless ambition. He had served on the staff of two conservative Democratic senators, Daniel Patrick Moynihan of New York and Henry Jackson of Washington, and had married into the "royal family" of neoconservatism—his wife, Rachel Podhoretz, was the daughter of neoconservative Midge Decter and stepdaughter of Norman Podhoretz, editor of *Commentary,* the leading journal of the neoconservatives. He had impressed Shultz with his handling of another political hot potato, human rights, as assistant secretary for human rights and humanitarian affairs from 1981 to 1985.

When Shultz asked him to take over Latin affairs, Abrams consulted Podhoretz. "One of two things has happened. Either they're looking for you as a cover for a surrender because you've got good hard-line credentials, or the policy is changing," his father-in-law said. Abrams replied that he knew Shultz well enough to think "the former is probably not a good idea, so the latter is more likely." It was the first of many such surmises by Abrams. He later said his appointment was "probably a sign of how far right [the administration has] gone . . . a sign that the battle's over."

According to Abrams, Shultz did nothing to alter this impression. Instead, he complimented Abrams on the harmony he had achieved at the subcabinet level, which removed Central America as a cabinet-level dispute. Abrams had agreed with North's position that U.S.-Nicaragua talks should not resume until the Sandinistas began negotiating with the armed resistance. "At my level there was unanimity," Abrams said. "We all thought that was what the policy should be and sold it upstairs." Abrams took Shultz's reaction as a green light to pursue the hard line in Nicaragua.[4]

Abrams never asked Shultz for his views on negotiating with the Sandinistas, and Shultz never volunteered them. Abrams, unlike his predecessors, chose to interpret this as lack of interest. Motley also had never asked Shultz to define his position, but saw the veteran labor negotiator as a pragmatist who wanted to test the possibilities abroad within the political constraints at home. "See if we can get anything done, if there's any give on that side. And make sure we don't get nuked here at home," was how he had read Shultz's mind.[5] While Shultz's public utterances were hard-line and his private statements Delphic, his actions suggested a genuine desire to keep the diplomatic option open.*

On September 4, 1985, Shultz sat down with Abrams. News accounts the previous month had alleged that North was raising money for the contras, giving them military advice, and running the program. Shultz asked Abrams to watch North closely. Abrams tersely noted down his instructions. "1. Monitor Ollie. 2. Report to the Secretary on the effectiveness of the contras. 3. Diplomatic track very important; keep alive. 4. Economic aid, boom everywhere, but Nicaragua, look at our economic resources. Get more mileage out of them. . . ."

Coming from a bureaucratic survivor like Shultz, the instructions seemed to suggest that Abrams should collect a file on North for possible future use; that Shultz wanted reliable facts about the situation on the ground in order to calculate his timing; and that it was essential to stay on top of the diplomatic process to preserve options for another initiative.

Abrams ignored the instructions.

Abrams occasionally asked North "whether he was doing anything violative of the law." North said he was not, and Abrams did not press the matter. "I was careful not to ask Colonel North what questions I thought I did not need to know the answers to." The reason Abrams gave was that "it was not my practice . . . to try to reach out and supervise these coordinate agencies, least of all the White House."[6]

Nor did Abrams "keep alive" the diplomatic track. Abrams argued that Shultz in his presence deliberately avoided committing himself for or against negotiations, presumably because of the high political cost attached to either position. The smart thing was not to ask him, and Abrams thought of himself as very smart. Besides, U.S. terms had hardened in mid-1985, when the administration demanded that the Sandinistas first begin a dialogue with the contras before negotiations could begin between the two governments. So there was no need to address the issue.

Late in 1985, Abrams preempted the discussion by renouncing the

---

* Shultz's efforts to take control of the policy process in 1983, discussed in Chapter 6, pp. 133–34, and his decision to go to Manzanillo are examples.

diplomatic track. "I want to be the first guy to reverse a Communist revolution," he told an ambassador under his direction that fall. "Anyone who believes that this president will go out of office with the Sandinistas in power doesn't know Ronald Reagan," he told a group of Democratic contra backers early in December. "There is a unanimity behind the policy," he said later that month, referring to the demand for "democracy" in Nicaragua, the code word meaning replacement of the Sandinista regime. Abrams also asserted that Shultz now saw his June 1984 trip to Managua as "an error" and said "that error . . . had a lot to do with undermining his relationship with Motley." Shultz, commenting some time later, said only that the Manzanillo effort had been "not productive."[7]*

Poindexter's appointment to succeed McFarlane, on December 4, 1985, was a third factor adding to the clout of Casey and North. A Navy rear admiral with a Ph.D. in nuclear physics, Poindexter had been with the NSC since 1981, starting as military aide to then-adviser Richard Allen. Poindexter survived the rapid turnover of NSC advisers by being the perfect staff man, with a photographic memory, a no-nonsense "can-do" style, an obsession with secrecy, and the ability to project himself into the mind-set of his boss. Other than a posture of hard-line anticommunism, Poindexter had no world view and he showed little aptitude in the give-and-take of politics or public affairs. As NSC adviser, Poindexter made his agenda the implementation of what he felt was in the mind of Ronald Reagan.[8]

Poindexter saw negotiations principally as a way to distract public attention. In November 1984, when the Manzanillo talks were stalled, Poindexter had summarized his views to McFarlane: "Continue active negotiations, but agree on no treaty, and agree to work out some way to support the contras, either directly or indirectly. Withhold true objectives from staffs." Poindexter later said he thought a treaty would be "very dangerous" because "I did not personally believe that even if the Sandinistas agreed to a treaty that they would ever live up to it."[9]

On the other hand, after taking over as NSC adviser, Poindexter gave an enthusiastic "full speed ahead" to North for contra fund-raising. "My instruction to Colonel North was to continue on course.

---

* Asked to explain what he *really* had in mind, Shultz said through a spokesman that he could not remember giving Abrams the instruction, "Diplomatic track very important; keep alive," and therefore would not comment.

And that certainly would have included the coordination and discussion between the private parties, the private support network, and the contra leadership to get them the right kind of arms they need." He did not want to know details of North's activities, which meshed with North's preferred operating style. North put it succinctly: "Unless otherwise directed I will proceed as follows. . . ." Or as Poindexter put it, "Colonel North was given a very broad charter to carry out a mission, and I did not micromanage him."[10]

The final factor in the rise of Casey and North was George Shultz. Having done battle over Iran, Angola, Mozambique, and polygraphing, he had little room to maneuver and effectively withdrew from the highly politicized low-gain Nicaragua dispute. The start of 1986 was not ripe for a Nicaragua initiative, and after McFarlane's departure, Shultz had few allies in the administration. He turned his focus to U.S.-Soviet affairs, which promised real progress after the November 1985 Geneva summit.

The State Department's passivity coupled with lax White House supervision gave Casey and North carte blanche. For the State Department, there were short-term benefits and long-term costs.

Abrams found his position strengthened with conservatives in the White House and Congress, but in making the measure of his success the harmony he reached with the "can-do" military men who favored a military solution, he added new tension to the policy trap that the administration had set for itself. By acting as cheerleader for a flawed policy and not trying to reshape it, he gave a gloss of validity to the illusion that there was a cheap and effective military solution. Any military expert knew that the contras could not finish off the Sandinistas or even threaten their hold on power in the near term. About the only thing that Casey and North were sure to achieve by vigorously promoting the program was to enhance their own influence at the expense of State. By supporting them, Abrams ensured the eclipse of State as the lead policy-formulating agency and ultimately the humiliation of George Shultz.

RIDING HIGH

At an earlier point, North may have viewed the contras as the magic bullet to rid Central America of the Sandinistas, but his actions after July 1985 suggest that the romanticism had palled, and the program turned into a crude key to other goals. That month he had taken a big step away from the contra leadership by asking Richard Secord, the retired Air Force major general, to set up an offshore financial enterprise to bankroll the contras, buy and deliver arms, and reestablish a southern front.

There was no way the rebels could derive immediate benefit from the new scheme and it quickly merged into a bigger project. Known as "the Enterprise," it grew out of Casey's desire, according to North, to develop a capability for mounting covert operations outside congressional oversight. The immediate problem was cash; Taiwan and other foreign conservative sources could provide only so much.

At this very moment, thanks largely to the prodding of Casey and North, an opportunity came along in the form of secret arms transfers to Iran.

As foreign policy, it was an incredibly amateurish initiative. To jettison the policy of neutrality in the Iran-Iraq war would unsettle U.S. allies occupying some of earth's most valuable real estate. To provide arms as an inducement to free U.S. hostages held by a pro-Iranian faction in Beirut violated the principle of not rewarding terrorism. Short-sighted as these goals appeared, they were only secondary or tertiary objectives for North. He wanted to sell arms at inflated prices to pay for other things: Secord's resupply of the contras, profits for Secord and his partner, Albert Hakim, and finally the contingency fund for Casey's off-the-books covert operations. But by selling arms for such purposes, cash flow, not hostages, became the U.S. goal.

North, as NSC counterterrorism director, was involved in the planning from early summer 1985. The first diversion of profits from the Iran arms sales occurred in November after he arranged for Secord to deliver eighty Hawk missiles to Iran. At North's request, Israeli arms merchant Adolph Schwimmer on November 20 deposited $1 million in the Swiss bank account that Secord had set up for activities related to support of the contras. The stated reason had been to cover the cost of transport, warehouse space, and expenses. Only about $200,000 was required to meet expenses for the shipment, and the rest was available for other purposes.

"At some point in this period of time, I told [Secord] he ought to go ahead and use some of that money to support the Nicaraguan resistance," North said.[11] The pattern was thus set.

McFarlane, about to end his government career, had abandoned hope that arms transfers would result in release of the hostages or any other achievement. Not so North, who on the day McFarlane departed the White House sent a memo to Poindexter urging a vast expansion in arms sales, to 3,300 TOW missiles and another fifty Hawk missiles. "If we do not make at least one more try at this point, we stand a good chance of condemning some or all [the hostages] to death and a renewed wave of Islamic Jihad terrorism," he wrote. "While the risks of proceeding are significant, the risks of not trying one last time are even greater."

North was planning for more than "one last time." Two days later, he reportedly told an Israeli official in New York that the United States hoped to finance contra activities in Nicaragua from future sales. North then flew to London and met Secord, arms dealer Manucher Ghorbanifar, the Iranian-born middleman who helped inspire the deals, and Israeli officials to discuss the additional sales.

In January, North drafted the covert action finding that provided the basis for him to take operational control over the initiative with Secord's support. No mention was made of the diversion. Early in February, he informed Poindexter.[12]*

"Using the Ayatollah's money to support the Nicaraguan resistance," North said, is "a neat idea."

Poindexter was enthusiastic. "He clearly was looking for a signal from me whether or not to proceed ahead along this line . . . and I gave it to him," Poindexter said. "Frankly I thought it was a neat idea, too." Poindexter's only concern was that "this had better never come out." Under oath, Poindexter said he told no one, including Reagan, believing "the buck stops here with me."[14]

North was at his peak of power. One close associate observed a "real transformation" between 1985 and 1986. "Ollie thought he was God," this associate said.[15]

He had a patron at the highest reaches of government whose star was still rising, an immediate boss who would protect him and his secrets, and no serious challengers at his level. North had drafted the

---

* North later claimed that the diversion had been suggested at the end of January by Ghorbanifar in a conversation in the bathroom of a London hotel suite. Ghorbanifar denied it, and a secret tape recording of the meeting showed that the diversion was discussed in the open, implying it had already been agreed to some time earlier. In fact, Ghorbanifar during a lengthy interview on January 13 with Charles Allen, the CIA's senior expert on counterterrorism, commented that funds from the project could be used for "Ollie's boys in Central America."[13]

ultrasecret presidential finding on arms sales to Iran, taken over the implementation, and then, with Poindexter, changed U.S. policy priorities. He had day-to-day charge of contra and Iran arms sales. A soldier with no background in special operations, he was in control of a miniature CIA. He even set up a private communications network, using fifteen encryption devices provided by the National Security Agency. CIA, military, and State diplomatic operatives on the ground in El Salvador, Honduras, and Costa Rica reported to him directly, as did at least one ambassador, Lewis Tambs in Costa Rica, and one CIA station chief, Joe Fernandez, also in San José.[16]

CONFRONTATION AND PAYOFF

With its newfound consensus on means and ends, the administration did not spend much time debating legislative strategy in 1986. Casey, North, Poindexter, and Abrams worked in harmony. Poindexter made sure that no one even considered searching for a bipartisan middle ground. "When I took over, I got everybody to agree we wouldn't compromise," Poindexter recalled. "I wish we had done that earlier."[17] (Actually, Casey and North had sought a confrontation with Congress to obtain military aid in 1985, but lost that vote and had to settle for nonlethal aid.)

Casey provided intelligence to Reagan to support a confrontational stance. An internal CIA assessment indicated that the contras' acute supply shortages had eased by early January 1986. But Casey chose to ignore this and at a preparatory session for an NSC meeting, said he wanted "to make the insurgency choice stark—either we go all out to support them, or they'll go down the drain."[18]

This was the motif of the first month of the 1986 contra aid battle, one of the longest and least conclusive foreign policy struggles of that or any other year. The political energies consumed were staggering.

On February 25, 1986, Reagan formally requested $100 million— nearly four times the $27 million approved the previous year and equal to the total amount Congress had provided in the five preceding years. Some $70 million was to be spent on lethal arms and $30 million on nonlethal equipment.

The origin of the figure is not certain, but North, who had been running the program, may well have been the author. North had suggested $100 million in writing a full year earlier, arguing that the very act of requesting a large amount conveyed greater seriousness to the endeavor. "It was to some extent pulled out of thin air," Abrams later said. "We knew we wanted to put someting like 15,000 men in the field and we knew roughly the level of weaponry we wanted them to have and we knew how many people were to be trained. So if you're at that general level, make it a good round number."[19]*

The drive opened in a rush of rhetoric. Shultz told the Senate Foreign Relations Committee that the Sandinista regime was a "cancer, right here on our land mass." Reagan, addressing conservative backers, said defeat of the contras could jeopardize the survival of Central America's new democracies, lead to Soviet missile bases on "America's doorstep," threaten the Panama Canal, and cause a migration of hundreds of thousands of refugees. "And those who would invite this strategic disaster by abandoning yet another fighting ally of this country in the field will be held fully responsible," he said.[20] Patrick Buchanan portrayed the vote as a test of loyalty. "With the vote on contra aid, the Democratic Party will reveal whether it stands with Ronald Reagan and the resistance—or Daniel Ortega and the communists," he wrote. Finally, Reagan, in a nationally televised speech, called the Sandinistas "the malignancy in Managua" and warned they could become "a mortal threat to the entire New World." If the United States failed to curb the Sandinistas, "there will be no evading responsibility—history will hold us accountable." The overstatement was a boon to the Sandinistas, who broadcast the speech live with simultaneous translation over radio and television.

The strident tone alienated centrist Democrats and moderate Republicans and made rhetoric the issue. But Poindexter was not interested in a middle ground, and no effort was made to build a bipartisan coalition.

Instead, North sought to reach over the heads of Congress to the public through a domestic television advertising drive. A conservative Republican fund-raiser named Carl Russell ("Spitz") Channell, working closely with North, arranged for $1 million in television ads in the districts of swing Democrats; the crude advertising campaign proved counterproductive.

---

* In a January 1985 memo to McFarlane, North complained that the "low" request of $14 million that year was based on the "thinking that this amount would be more palatable to the Congress. . . . A figure closer to $100 million would indicate to the Congress the urgency of the situation."

This was the caricature of a legislative strategy. And as it began to backfire, Shultz proposed an appointment that would appeal to the center by reviving the diplomatic track. For over a year, Harry Shlaudeman had been plotting his escape from his dead-end job as special envoy for Central America, and he readily accepted appointment as ambassador to Brazil. Shultz proposed as his replacement Philip Habib, a retired foreign service officer and one of the most experienced U.S. negotiators. Habib had served as special envoy in Beirut and had just returned from the Philippines, where he had represented Reagan during the political upheaval that saw the ouster of Ferdinand Marcos. Habib saw his role in Manila as helping create conditions that would force the pro-Marcos lobby in the administration and Congress to abandon the Filipino strongman, which some said they would never do when Habib first undertook the mission. When those conditions came about, Senator Paul Laxalt of Nevada, a longtime conservative associate of Reagan's, telephoned Marcos, and Marcos left. Habib thought he could bring about a similar situation in Central America that would permit the hard right to detach from the contras. Reagan liked Habib for his bluntness and his willingness to plunge into any job. Habib had many admirers in Congress. But his appointment so close to the vote looked like a gimmick to potential "swing" votes and did not affect the outcome.[21]

On March 20, the House defeated the $100 million by a close 222–210. Dave McCurdy, the central figure in the administration's 1985 victory, voted against. He had been burned among his colleagues by Reagan's failure to carry out his commitments to broaden the contra leadership and to seek a nonmilitary outcome; besides, no one had sought his support until a day or so before the vote.

Eventually, Reagan got the $100 million, but it took two more votes in the House, defeat of a filibuster by the Senate Democratic leadership, and months of parliamentary wrangling before a cent was released. As in 1985, Reagan's continued political strength and his readiness to make this issue the test of party loyalty were elements in his ultimate victory; so was his marginally less flawed performance in the "competition of blunders" with the Sandinista directorate. Contadora was moribund, and no diplomatic alternative was on the horizon. Finally, North had gotten control of a source of cash for a congressional lobbying campaign—Spitz Channell—who in turn raised funds from wealthy conservatives for whom he organized White House pep talks by Reagan, North, and Abrams. Channell set up multiple tax-exempt nonprofit foundations which functioned as an above-board domestic financial counterpart to North's "off-the-books" covert "Enterprise" managed by Secord.

The blunders began after the defeat in the House. Abrams rushed off to Honduras the next day. The mission was apparently thought up by North, who drafted a memo to Reagan predicting negative reaction in Honduras and El Salvador. Without taking advance soundings, he asserted that the civilian and military leaders of both countries needed reassurance "of our determination to succeed in aiding the resistance and in ensuring their security." In fact, the entire Honduran government was about to leave Tegucigalpa for the traditional Holy Week break and had not had time to react.[22]

Two days later, in the early hours of Sunday, March 23, two Sandinista army battalions moved into El Paraiso province, east of Tegucigalpa, in an attack apparently intended to destroy the main rebel bases. Between 800 and 1,500 Sandinista troops were involved in the fighting, which lasted two to three hours. CIA analysts called it a routine incursion and Defense Intelligence Agency experts said it was "a target of opportunity." But Casey insisted that the incursion be portrayed as a strategy to try and "knock the contras out while we debated in the U.S."[23] Abrams joined in, telling White House reporters on March 24 of "a very large Sandinista incursion into Honduras." The White House wanted maximum publicity and to this end decided to make available $20 million in emergency military aid to Honduras. But the law required a formal request from the recipient. Honduras refused to admit there was an incursion because that would confirm the presence of contra camps. The Honduran army refused even to call a state of alert. So a few days after visiting Tegucigalpa on an unnecessary errand, Abrams had to cajole the Honduran government into formally requesting the aid.

"You have got to tell them to declare there was an incursion," Abrams's deputy, William Walker, shouted on the telephone at the embassy chargé, Shepard Lowman. (Ambassador John Ferch was incapacitated by influenza at the time.) Honduran president José Azcona Hoyo's press secretary responded in public that the announcements of the incursion in Washington were "part of the publicity campaign by the Reagan administration to secure approval of the $100 million for the counterrevolution."

Ferch got up from his sickbed, donned three sweaters and a bathrobe, and called on Azcona at the latter's modest bungalow.

"Mr. President, I'm living death," Ferch said. "Let me give you a personal opinion. You don't have a choice now." Azcona replied: "Okay, let's draft something." Azcona met his military commanders and the request was sent forward. On March 26, U.S. Army helicopters ferried some 600 troops to a point well away from the front but close enough to dramatize the "stark" alternatives viewed by Casey. That day, Azcona left for the beach. [24]

On March 27, the Senate approved Reagan's $100 million request with some modifications by a tight 53-47 vote, the exact ratio of the Republican majority. Reagan called the Sandinista offensive "a slap in the face to everyone who voted against aid to the freedom fighters thinking it to be a vote for reconciliation." Meanwhile, the State Department indulged in casuistry of its own. Judge Abraham Sofaer, Shultz's legal adviser, branded Nicaragua an "aggressor state" that did not have the right to claim self-defense against contra incursions. "Our position with respect to Nicaragua is that Nicaragua is an aggressor state, that it has acted in an aggressive way with respect to Honduras, Costa Rica and El Salvador," he said. [25]

The timing of the incursion was a Sandinista blunder embarrassing to those in Congress who had voted against contra aid. But the administration tripped itself up badly. Had it waited instead of rushing Abrams into an unnecessary mission, it could have taken advantage of the Sandinista mistiming. Instead, by exaggerating the incursion and gratuitously blaming it on Democrats, the administration lost credibility. The upshot was a draw for the administration and the Sandinistas.

Next to blunder was the House Democratic leadership, which promised another vote on contra aid to McCurdy and other centrists looking for political shelter, but attached it to a supplemental spending bill that Reagan had promised to veto. McCurdy's plan would have imposed strict conditions and required a second vote on contra military aid; it also would have provided $325 million in aid to the four countries with elected civilian governments surrounding Nicaragua. Through a parliamentary maneuver, Republicans torpedoed the plan and demanded a simple up or down vote. In the process, the McCurdy compromise was swept aside.

Official U.S. funding was now in some doubt. Meanwhile, cash was flowing from the secret sale of arms to Iran into Secord's Geneva account. In mid-February, Secord had delivered one thousand TOW antitank missiles to Iran for North, and the difference between what Iran was charged and what the Pentagon was paid left up to $6,300,000 available for Secord's contra project.

On April 1, Secord began an arms airlift to contra forces in Nicaragua.

North visited the contra camps on April 18 and reported it was "the most depressing venture in my four years of working" on the issue. In an internal memo, he quoted Bermúdez as saying that the remaining troops in Nicaragua would have to withdraw completely within three weeks unless there was an immediate resupply. Their rations were down to one meal a day and they were out of radio batteries, boots, uniforms, ponchos, and weapons.[26]

He of course made no mention of Secord's newly revved-up supply operation.

In mid to late April, Casey telephoned Reagan to "impress upon him my concerns about the loss of Central America and the loss of our intelligence capabilities." Casey recapitulated the conversation in an April 23 note to Regan. "We need an all out effort, laying out the stark alternatives," he said. "We are at a critical juncture. Either we get funding for the contras to implement the policy or scrap our present policy and move ahead with final alternatives." The alternatives were "embargo, blockade or direct military action."

Although Casey told Regan that the President "agreed on the urgency of taking strong measures to improve our position on both of these matters," Reagan was more likely preoccupied with his thirteen-day trip to the Far East, which began on April 25.

But a week later, on May 2, Reagan signaled his alarm to Poindexter en route from Jakarta to Tokyo on board Air Force One. " 'Look, I don't want to pull out our support for the contras for any reason,' " Poindexter quoted him saying. " 'This would be an unacceptable option. . . . I am really serious. If we can't move the contra package before June 9, I want to figure out a way to take action unilaterally to provide assistance,' " he said. By this, Reagan meant an executive action that did not require the approval of Congress. He cited the precedent of sending emergency aid to Honduras in March. "I told him that I didn't think it would apply here, since we are not dealing with a government," Poindexter said in a memo to his deputy. "But the fact remains that the President is ready to confront the Congress on the constitutional question of who controls foreign policy." Poindexter added that Sofaer "and other stalwart lawyers" should be asked to think "in these terms to see if there is some way we could do this, if all else fails."[27]

As the administration struggled to find a way to get funds from Congress or other sources, countries in the region struggled to find a way to head off the administration. The Contadora mediation had been halted in November 1985 by Daniel Ortega's rejection of the latest draft act. To induce the Sandinistas to return to the table, the four mediators—Colombia, Mexico, Panama, and Venezuela—augmented by four other South American countries with newly elected civilian governments—Argentina, Brazil, Peru, and Uruguay—met in Caraballeda, Venezuela, on January 11 and 12, 1986, and reaffirmed the Revised Contadora Act of September 1984, which Nicaragua had accepted. When the eight ministers came to Washington a month later to deliver the message of Caraballeda—an end to contra aid and a reopening of U.S.-Nicaraguan talks—Shultz gave them the cold shoulder. But every delay in Congress encouraged them to press on.[28]

So did the newly elected presidents of Guatemala—Vinicio Cerezo—and Costa Rica—Oscar Arias—who announced that they would not take sides in the Nicaragua conflict. At his inauguration on January 16, Cerezo convinced the other Central American leaders to endorse the latest Contadora statement. Within a month after his election, Arias urged the United States to halt contra aid. "I do not think with that aid he [Reagan] is going to obtain what he wants. On the contrary, the result of the aid to the contras has been a more dictatorial, more totalitarian government in the north," he said in a U.S. television interview. "You won't get a negotiation with the Sandinistas, giving more money to the contras." Newly elected Honduran president Azcona had campaigned on a platform that the contra presence was unwanted and unconstitutional; but the complex election rules under which he was elected yielded him a minority mandate and left him vulnerable to pressures from the United States and his own military forces. His message was mixed, calling for Contadora to resume its involvement but, during a Washington visit in late May, supporting the renewal of contra aid.[29]

Contadora meanwhile was faltering. On April 5–6, the mediators had brought the Central Americans together once again in Panama and sought their commitment to sign a new draft treaty by June 6. Nicaragua alone had refused.

Although Contadora was in disarray, the White House saw it as a real threat to its strategy in Congress and felt the matter would come to a head in late May, when Cerezo had scheduled the first summit of Central American leaders since the Sandinista revolution. North's concerns surfaced on the eve of a meeting of the National Security Planning Group, an informal grouping of the key NSC members, called on May 16 to discuss "bridge funding" for the contras. A May 15 memorandum for Reagan coauthored by North and Raymond Burghardt, a foreign service officer nominally in charge of Latin American affairs at the NSC, was a model of manipulation, steering the President to a course of action based on distortions of the diplomatic and military situation. Congress's delay and the Contadora talks "are creating expectations and anxieties in the U.S. and in Central America," the memo said. In fact, the principal anxiety specified was on the part of the contras, who were "increasingly desperate as available supplies are depleted." It added that "no further significant support appears readily available."

This was untrue. As North noted in a later memo, "Money truly is not the thing which is most needed at this point." The contras had "several million rounds of most types of ammo now on hand" and another three million dollars' worth on the way by ship. Boots, ponchos, and uniforms were being bought locally and Calero had received $500,000 to buy food.

To deal with the hypothetical shortfall, Reagan's top aides agreed that Shultz should draw up a list of countries that might be solicited for aid. North was about to speak up, but Poindexter, suspecting he would reveal the secret source of outside funding, "cautioned him not to say anything."

Later North reminded him in a memo "that the resistance support organization now has more than $6 million available for immediate disbursement. This reduces the need to go to third countries for help."[30]

But Poindexter decided that Shultz's effort should go forward. It was not until North learned that Shultz planned to approach Saudi Arabia for funds that anyone remembered the secretary of state had been kept in the dark for two years. Poindexter asked McFarlane to inform Shultz. Yet Shultz, for reasons that remain unclear, did not tell Abrams or his assistant for Near Eastern affairs, Richard Murphy.

Shultz then decided to solicit Brunei, where he was to travel in June. Abrams had obtained account numbers from North and Fiers but decided to use North's account because "we were having a bit of a tug of war" with the CIA "and we weren't really keen on . . . enhancing the role of the CIA in what was supposed to be a State Department initiative." At the last minute, Shultz decided not to ask for money directly, but sent Abrams to London in mid-August to speak with a Brunei official. They met in a London park. Abrams began with a fifteen-minute discourse on the need for help. "How much money?" the official asked. "Ten million dollars," Abrams replied. "What will Brunei get out of it?" Abrams said Reagan would know of it "and you will have the gratitude of the Secretary and of the President for helping us out in this jam." The official persisted in asking if Brunei would receive anything concrete in exchange. "You don't get anything concrete out of it," Abrams replied. Abrams handed him a slip of paper with an account number at the Crédit Suisse bank, 368-430-22-1. In copying the number out of North's files, however, North's secretary, Fawn Hall, had inadvertently transposed the second and third digits, and the funds wound up in the account of a Swiss citizen.[31]

On Contadora, North's May 15 memo to Reagan predicted, inaccurately, that the Sandinistas would proclaim readiness to sign "another version of the treaty, containing proposals which our friends have rejected. We will then find ourselves engaged in a propaganda contest in which each side will claim the other is intransigent." The U.S. object, it said, was "to support our friends' position as a positive and constructive Central American effort to deal with the region's problems, while denouncing the Sandinistas for refusing to negotiate."

At State, this was viewed as another White House "panic" over a nonevent. "We called it the 'peace is breaking out syndrome,'" one official said. U.S. diplomats believed there was no need to worry because the Sandinistas "will never accept something really significant" at Contadora.[32] In point of fact, when the Central American presidents assembled on May 24-25 in Guatemala at Esquipulas, a religious shrine built around an ancient statue of a black Christ venerated by Central Americans, the group quickly came to loggerheads over the issue of democratization. Instead of discussing substance, they found themselves fighting over the joint communiqué. Arias objected to Ortega's being described with the others as "freely elected by the majority wills of their respective countries"; Ortega resisted committing himself to sign the Contadora treaty, and the five failed to agree on the June 6 deadline.

In retrospect, the Sandinistas were probably not ready to negotiate. Ortega agreed to restrictions on offensive arms but not on what he called defensive arms. He also balked at cutting the size of the Sandinista army. The underlying reason seems to have been that the Sandinistas, seeing the contras in retreat and disarray, felt that a military solution was within reach.

In Washington, meanwhile, Philip Habib had run into a buzz saw of right-wing criticism. After a few get-acquainted trips to the region, he began conferring with members of Congress, and in response to questions from liberal and centrist Democrats, asked the Bureau of Inter-American Affairs to draft a letter for his signature summing up the U.S. position on Contadora. Dated April 11, it said that U.S. aid to the contras would end "on signature" of a verifiable Contadora agreement by all the Central American states. The letter drew little notice until a month later, when Constantine Menges brought it to the attention of Representative Jack Kemp, the conservative New York Republican. Kemp, contending that Habib was ready to sign an accord that would "sell out" the contras, publicly demanded that Reagan fire Habib. Reagan refused. Instead, Poindexter fired Menges. Then Abrams backed the administration away from the letter, telling reporters it had been imprecise and that if he could rewrite it, "I'd just change the word *signature* to *implementation*." Habib said Abrams and North had cleared the draft, and he was angry that Abrams seemed to have blamed him. "He played a nasty, dirty game," Habib later said of Abrams. "I didn't speak to him for a while." Once again, the State Department's own inattention to the Contadora forum was partly to blame. For in the meantime, the Contadora draft under discussion had loosened the terms of what would occur on signature and delayed most key actions until after the ratification of the accord.[33]

The right-wing outcry in Washington over the Habib letter surprised the Sandinistas and raised the question whether signing the accord would force a decision on cutting aid to the contras. On May 27, Daniel Ortega said he would be willing to sign the agreement on June 6. But the deadline passed without signature. And although the Sandinistas on June 20 announced they would accept the treaty, it was a step short of signing. Honduras, followed by El Salvador and Costa Rica, said the draft was inadequate.[34]*

LAST HURRAH

However inept its diplomacy and its politicking, the administration's relentless drive on Capitol Hill slowly made headway. Centrist Democrats joined Republicans seeking yet another vote on the $100 million aid request, and the Democratic leadership gave in. For the administration to win, it needed a shift of only seven votes, and every conceivable pressure was brought to bear.

One unlikely but effective source was a group of Democratic liberals whom critics dubbed "the four meddlers": Bruce Cameron, Robert Leiken, Penn Kemble, and Bernard Aronson. Abrams and North worked closely with them, and Abrams gave them "a considerable amount of credit" for the victory. The grease that made the effort work was money provided by Spitz Channell. Bruce Cameron had worked as a human rights lobbyist for the liberal Americans for Democratic Action for nine years but threw himself behind the cause of Arturo Cruz Sr. after his election negotiations with the Sandinistas foundered in September 1984. Cameron was fired by the ADA in June 1985 for helping win passage of nonlethal aid to the contras; he offered his services to McCurdy, who put him on his payroll briefly for $1,000 a month, but was out of work until January 1986. That month Penn Kemble arranged for him to meet Spitz Channell. In February, Cameron went on Spitz Channell's payroll as an administration lobbyist and earned $40,000 in three months.

Robert Leiken was a writer on Soviet and Central American affairs with the Carnegie Endowment for International Peace, a center-left

* Like previous drafts, it spoke in general terms about national reconciliation and democratization. On security issues, it was noticeably looser than the September 1985 draft in terms of commitments by the Central American states, putting off until ratification by all five countries a freeze on importing new arms, a ninety-day period to negotiate limits on arms, troops, and military installations, and a ninety-day halt to joint international maneuvers. The September 1985 draft had called for these actions upon signature. The prohibition of outside support of irregular forces was to take effect immediately upon signing, however; and the closing of foreign military bases or installations within 180 days of signature. The United States had pressed for simultaneous implementation of all main security provisions as well as a looser regime on maneuvers.

think tank. At the time of El Salvador's constituent assembly elections in 1982, Leiken had testified against U.S. policy and advocated a power-sharing arrangement dividing control of the country between the army and the leftist guerrillas. These views made him unpopular in official circles, and many observers think Leiken was looking for a new vehicle when the Nicaraguan elections came along in 1984. Leiken attracted wide attention and, with official help, wide distribution as well, for his article titled "Sins of the Sandinistas" in the New Republic on October 8, 1984. In it he confessed that he had been a sympathizer with the Sandinistas but now the situation was "far worse than I had thought." When Cruz became a resistance leader, Cameron and Leiken became his principal advisers. Leiken wrote a steady stream of articles attacking the Sandinistas in the New Republic and an extended two-part panegyric of Cruz in the New York Review of Books. He received a travel grant from Channell. Leiken and Cameron worked with Penn Kemble, who headed PRODEMCA (Friends of the Democratic Center in Central America), a foundation formed to encourage popular support for Reagan's Central America policies. PRODEM-CA's funds came from conservative sources, including Channell, who provided $88,000. Its board was largely neoconservative Democrats; Kemble also chaired the Coalition for a Democratic Majority, a neoconservative group. The National Endowment for the Humanities used PRODEMCA to funnel grants to favored administration recipients such as La Prensa, the Managua opposition paper. Bernard Aronson was a speechwriter during Mondale's vice-presidency. Aronson had close ties to the organized labor movement; he supported U.S. El Salvador policy. There is no indication he received any financial benefit from Channell.

The foursome went after the key Democratic swing votes. In April, Leiken and Aronson took Les Aspin, a Wisconsin Democrat and the influential chairman of the House Armed Services Committee, on a guided tour of Nicaragua, concluding with a meeting in Chinandega at which all those assembled criticized the Sandinistas. Aspin switched his vote. A ranking U.S. diplomat in Managua described the arrangements, set up by an anti-Sandinista lawyer, as a "Potemkin village." Cameron organized a tour for thirteen House members led by McCurdy. It featured a meeting with Ortega, who "horrified" all, according to Cameron. Four who took the trip switched their votes.

Kemble took out newspaper ads in the name of PRODEMCA supporting aid to the contras. This turned PRODEMCA into a political lobby, and he had to give up administering the *La Prensa* account. The Endowment's congressional charter prohibits the distribution of funds through political lobbies.

One critical service rendered the administration by Leiken and Cameron was convincing Cruz to remain in the contra civilian leadership of the United Nicaraguan Opposition (UNO) while they and Abrams pressed for "reform." Reform was a euphemism for eliminating Calero's role or at least curtailing his influence over the military force controlled by his close ally, chief of staff Enrique Bermúdez. Cruz had wanted to resign since August 1985, when he realized that Calero would never allow him and Robelo to take control. But "reform" of this situation had been demanded by moderates in Congress such as Senators Sam Nunn (D.-Ga.) and Nancy Kassebaum (R.-Kan.) as the price for their support of the program. There was no meaningful reform, however, of UNO, as the three civilians called their umbrella group. Instead, Cruz was put on Spitz Channell's payroll. At the time of his troubles with Calero, Cruz was also having financial problems. Cameron approached North. North sent word to Spitz Channell, and Cruz, without knowing the source of his income, went on his payroll from January until November 1986 at $7,000 a month. Channell also provided funds to Robelo. Abrams later denied knowledge of the North-Channell financial operation but had acted as if he knew. According to Cameron, Abrams practically ordered him, along with Cruz and Robelo, all of whom were on Channell's payroll, to lobby members of Congress before every vote.[35]

The contra "reform" talks took place in Miami in the first week in May and June, and were completed in time for the final aid vote on June 25. The outcome of the talks was highly ambiguous, but Cruz claimed victory. Henceforth, he said, he and Robelo could overrule Calero and make key decisions such as appointing and dismissing field commanders. Cameron recalled that Alan Fiers lauded him as the "hero of Miami." Within a month, the thirty FDN field commanders formed a Regional Commanders' Council with powers to help choose military leadership and influence major political decisions, thereby negating the "reform" of Miami.[36]

Aronson provided a different sort of service by drafting a speech for Reagan to be delivered before a joint session of Congress. The speech was carried only on the Cable News Network and probably swayed no votes, but Aronson's repackaging of the issues changed the tone of the debate.*

Twelve votes shifted on June 25, five more than needed to approve the $100 million. Cameron later claimed in a memo to Channell that their "success" in Miami on the eve of the vote helped sway three members. He also cited Reagan's telephone calls to every one of the twenty potential swing votes, Habib's appointment, and the decision to add an economic aid package for other Central American countries devised by McCurdy to the contra program. Channell concurred and paid Cameron a bonus of $26,000 on top of the $40,000 he had already earned. He also provided $3,600 to Leiken for a trip to Central America.[37]†

McCurdy had a different analysis of Cameron's success: "Because he worked with me, he knew the inner workings" and "how to slice away the guys" from the McCurdy coalition. "He was the only one who could do it." Cameron's device was to include in the administration bill $300 million in economic aid for the Central American republics surrounding Nicaragua, a sum just below the $325 million which had been a central selling point of the McCurdy alternative.

Reagan hailed the House victory as "a step forward in bipartisan consensus in American foreign policy," but in truth, it was a shaky base for sustaining the policy.[38]

The Republican Senate, after overcoming a filibuster by the Democratic leadership, voted 53-47 in favor of the aid in August. House leaders were unable to do much but slow the progress of the bill, which did not reach Reagan's desk until October 25.

For the Contadora process, the House's approval of aid was the last blow. At home, the Sandinistas launched a crackdown, closing down *La Prensa,* expelling several dissident Roman Catholic priests, and strengthening the emergency law. On July 28, Nicaragua filed suits at the International Court of Justice against Costa Rica and

---

* Stressing the importance of building a bipartisan consensus, Reagan for the first time acknowledged that the contras had engaged in "intolerable" human rights abuses. He also paid special tribute to Democrat Leiken, quoting him as saying the Sandinistas were "detested" by the population, and Aspin, who he said had heard in Chinandega from tradesmen and farmers who wanted the United States "to aid the armed resistance."

† Leiken said he returned the money to Channell after news accounts broke in late 1986 indicating that Channell, through a supposed nonprofit organization, had funded ads supporting a political cause directed at Congress.

Honduras, charging them with "cooperating with rebel groups attacking the Nicaraguan Government." This injected new strains into relations with the two countries and closed down the Contadora forum. "We thought they were abandoning the negotiations," a senior Honduran official said. "[They knew] we could not undertake adjudication and negotiation at the same time."[39] Honduras removed itself from the talks.

But the Sandinistas felt that they were on the high ground, morally as well as militarily. On June 27, the World Court had ruled favorably on fourteen of the sixteen counts of their suit against the United States. It rejected the U.S. argument of collective self-defense. There was insufficient evidence that the Nicaraguan government was responsible for the arms flow since early 1981; even if that could be proven, under international law the Court did not feel that "provision of arms to the opposition constituted an armed attack on that State." However, it said the mining of Nicaragua's harbors in 1984 and economic sabotage by CIA commandos did constitute a use of "force against another State." Supporting the contras was an attempt to coerce the government of Nicaragua "in respect of matters to which each State is permitted, by the principle of State sovereignty, to decide freely." If one state supports armed bands to overthrow the government, that "amounts to an intervention of one state in the internal affairs of the other."[40] The administration ignored the ruling, arguing that the World Court had no jurisdiction in what it maintained was a political dispute.

With the key legislative victory behind him and even a World Court ruling causing hardly a ripple in Washington, Abrams was riding high and decided to flex his muscle. A few days after the vote, he telephoned John Ferch, the ambassador to Honduras, and fired him. Ferch had helped save civilian rule in Honduras by heading off Suazo Córdova's design for a second term. He had developed an excellent rapport with the new president, Azcona, overseen the restoration of contra aid, even talked Azcona into asking for emergency aid in March. But Abrams believed that Ferch was unenthusiastic about the administration's contra policy and built a case against him based on management problems in the embassy. Shultz backed Abrams.

Azcona was surprised at the abruptness of Ferch's removal. "I thought this happened only in Honduras," he told him.

Ferch saw his dismissal as linked to policy differences. "I thought we meant what we said. We wanted pressure so we could negotiate. I'm beginning to think I accepted something that wasn't true." From the manner of his dismissal, he said, "I gather our goal is something different. It's a military goal."[41]

As Abrams celebrated his triumph, Shultz again found himself under pressure from Casey and North and once again decided to resign. This time, Jonathan Miller, the White House director of administration and a close associate of North, had begun to reject routine Shultz requests for presidential aircraft for overseas trips. Reagan restored Shultz's perquisites, and once again he withdrew his resignation.[42]

Outwardly the victory in Congress brought an appearance of harmony in the administration on Nicaragua policy. But beneath the surface, intense rivalries over power stirred among the key players. The State Department, to which the new legislation gave responsibility for directing the program, and the CIA, which had to carry out all operations, vied with each other for control. This was the context in which Abrams devised a strategy that said little about the realities on the ground but would serve him well in the internal power struggle. Late in the summer of 1986, in conversations with foreign diplomats he set out three policy goals for the year that followed. First was to isolate Nicaragua politically and diplomatically from all sources of support except for Cuba and the Soviet Union, so as to convince the world that Managua was allied with Havana and Moscow. Second was to gain credibility for the contras as a capable military force. Third was to rally the support of Central American countries for the strategy, which translated into closing down the Contadora forum. These goals were hardly in keeping with the stated foreign policy goals of the United States in this century, but were fully consistent with implementation of Nicaragua policy under Reagan.[43] Habib and Abrams were barely talking to each other at this time, and Habib said he was not even aware of these policy goals and certainly did not try to implement them.

A second rivalry pitted the CIA task force headed by Alan Fiers against North. They vied over their respective influence over the contras and ability to exchange intelligence with them. North, about to be removed from his advisory role to the contras, was bitter because the overt aid program was starting up and the CIA, U.S. military, and State Department were to take charge. In October, he called up an old friend, Nat Hamrick. Since 1981, when he and John

Carbaugh had helped smooth the way for Argentina and Casey to support the movement, Hamrick had had little involvement in the movement other than to stay in touch with Bermúdez and North. Hamrick piloted his own light plane up to Washington. North was aroused. The movement into which he had invested so much energy appeared to be going nowhere. North had made a proposal in the RIG that spring to bring matters to a head but it had been shot down by the CIA and JCS representatives. Now he would try an end run to get his proposal to Bermúdez via Hamrick. The idea was for the FDN to capture territory, declare a government there, appeal for U.S. aid, and force the United States to break diplomatic relations with Managua and intervene militarily. "Tell them to go bite off some territory," North told Hamrick. "This would be the first cheap victory for the West since 1917. It would be a powerful psychological message to the entire world. It would inspire people."

"Ollie, I don't think it's a smart idea, because there won't be the follow-up," Hamrick said.

"Don't you worry about the follow-up," North replied.

Hamrick returned to his home in Rutherfordton, North Carolina, and thought it over. He decided to do nothing. "I have a big moral problem. It's wishful thinking," he said a few days later. "I'm almost sorry we started the whole project."[44]

TURNING POINT

Four events in swift succession in late 1986 destroyed the administration's cheerful facade and undermined its political base in Congress.

The unraveling began at about noon on Sunday, October 5. Thirty miles north of the Costa Rican border, a patrol of twenty-six young Sandinista soldiers, part of the Gaspar García Laviana Light Hunter Battalion of the 55th Infantry Brigade, Fifth Military Region, were resting in their hammocks in the jungle. They had lost contact with their commanding officers, run out of food, and were living on monkey meat as they awaited supplies. There was a noise overhead, and José Fernando Canales, a nineteen-year-old pharmacist's assistant, looked up. Through a break in the clouds, an old C-123 plane could be seen lumbering across the sky at close range and about 800 feet altitude. He set up the SAM-7 ground-to-air missile he usually carried on his shoulder and fired, hitting the right wing. It was a very easy shot. The plane caught fire and lost altitude. Eugene Hasenfus, a strapping forty-five-year-old ex-Marine employed as a "cargo kicker," stepped through the hatch, pulled the rip cord of his borrowed parachute, and jumped into history. His interrogators found a stash of logbooks and papers on the plane and he cooperated by telling them what he knew. Hasenfus thought he had been employed by the CIA to deliver arms over Nicaragua, a point the Sandinistas were quick to publicize.[45]

"I'm glad you asked. Absolutely not," Reagan replied when asked if there was any U.S. involvement whatsoever in the flight. There was "no connection with the U.S. government at all," said Shultz. "No government agencies, none" were involved, said Abrams. Actually, the project had been directed by North from its inception, but in preparing the guidance for Reagan, Shultz, and himself, Abrams had never questioned North directly. Hasenfus was found guilty and sentenced to thirty years by a Sandinista people's tribunal in November, but was pardoned and released the following month. But the shoot-down had immediate and broad repercussions. Secord halted his supply operation; the FBI, Federal Aviation Administration, U.S. Customs Service, congressional committees, and the news media began investigating; and two weeks after the shoot-down, the House Judiciary Committee asked the attorney general to appoint an independent counsel to investigate North, Casey, Poindexter, and others. North's entire program in support of the contras began to unravel.

Two days after Hasenfus was shot down, a Canadian businessman named Roy Furmark called on Casey and told him a scandal was about to break. Two Canadian investors and Saudi financier Adnan Khashoggi had provided bridge loans for the Iran arms sales, but had not been repaid because North had dumped Manucher Ghorbanifar, the Iranian middleman, without paying him off, and chosen another intermediary. Furmark knew of the diversion to the contras and may have hinted at it on this occasion. He warned that unless there was another arms sale to Iran that would ensure repayment of the $10 million the investors claimed, Ghorbanifar was going to tell the Senate Select Committee on Intelligence about the arms sales. The Canadians, too, were threatening to go public.[46]

On November 3, *Al-Shiraa*, a Beirut magazine known for its sympathies with Syria, published an extraordinary article reporting that McFarlane had traveled to Iran in late May with gifts, including a Bible inscribed by Reagan. The publication led to a string of press revelations about how Reagan had sold arms to Iran. The speaker of the Iranian parliament, Ali Akbar Rafsanjani, confirmed the main elements of the account the next day, but Reagan said the reports had "no foundation," and his spokesman claimed that the U.S. arms embargo remained in effect. Shultz, in the dark as much as the general public, urged Poindexter to tell the whole story. Poindexter fobbed him off. More revelations followed in the press about the sale of arms for hostages.

On November 4, in mid-term elections, Democrats swept the south and regained control of the Senate 54-45. Reagan lost his effective working majority in Congress.

The ultimate revelation came on November 25, when Edwin Meese, by now attorney general, announced the discovery that North had diverted millions of dollars in profits from the Iran arms sales to the contras.

The self-exposé coming on top of the serious political setback unnerved the administration. Poindexter and North lost their jobs. Casey, disabled by a brain tumor, went into the hospital on December 15. Reagan, at the zenith of legislative success, saw his ratings nosedive.

Arming the country that had held American diplomats hostage shattered Reagan's credibility as a tough-guy president.* Turning over custody of the nation's foreign policy interests to unsupervised amateurs cast a harsh light on his carefree style of governance. Allowing his staff to implement secret policies through a parallel government suggested violations of law, beginning with the restrictions on contra aid authored by Representative Edward Boland.

In a parliamentary democracy, the government would have fallen. But under the U.S. Constitution the only remedy was impeachment, a course which found little favor in Congress so soon after the Watergate scandal and the resignation of Richard Nixon.

The government did not collapse, but Reagan's ability to govern in many areas did. Nicaragua policy, integrally linked with his political

---

* Reagan said in public statements that the aim of the initiative was to assist moderate forces inside and outside the Iranian government. But at least three shipments of arms went directly to the radical Revolutionary Guards, and at all times during North's talks with them, the Iranian delegation was headed by or included a member of the Guards.[47]

strength, was one such area, but the $100 million cushion voted in 1986 allowed him to postpone any test for some months. The evidence of weakness was in his repeated delays in seeking new aid. The administration had hoped to obtain $105 million in 1987, but amid press disclosures, experts' reports, and four months of congressional hearings, it put off the day of reckoning. On December 1, 1986, Reagan appointed John Tower, formerly a Republican senator from Texas, to head a board of inquiry along with Edmund Muskie, secretary of state in the Carter administration, and Brent Scowcroft, national security adviser under Gerald Ford. That same day, the Senate Select Committee on Intelligence began its investigation. On December 19, Lawrence Walsh, an Oklahoma lawyer, was appointed independent counsel to investigate possible criminal charges in connection with the arms sales and diversion of profits. The House and Senate, on January 5 and 6, 1987, respectively, set up separate investigating panels, which they later combined into one.

On the eve of the hearings, conservative fund-raiser Spitz Channell pleaded guilty to conspiracy to defraud the government by illegally using the tax-exempt status of his foundations to provide funds for the contras and to place television advertising to support candidates favoring the policy. He named as co-conspirators Oliver North and Richard Miller, a former administration aide and head of a public relations firm that had received contracts from the Office of Public Diplomacy at the State Department. On May 6, Miller pleaded guilty to felony charges and also named North as co-conspirator.

Some of the most damning testimony at the joint congressional Iran-Contra hearings, which ran from May 5 to August 3, came from current and former aides who criticized the policy and the decision-making process that spawned it.

McFarlane suggested that calamity was inevitable. "There is something wrong about the way this country makes foreign policy . . . [people] don't know how wrong," he said. The covert war had been launched in 1981 "in a policy vacuum" and without any assessment of U.S. interests, analysis of options, or calculation of costs. To "engage in conflict with a Soviet client, you must have the American people and the U.S. Congress behind you. Yet it is virtually impossible, almost as a matter of definition, to rally public support behind a policy that you can't even talk about." He came down hardest on those Reagan aides who, to overcome the inherent weakness of their approach, had advised confrontation with Congress. "When the President and the Congress cannot agree, to charge ahead is to invite disaster," he said. "Policymakers who create conditions like this must bear some of the moral responsibility for the failures that follow." Such "shortsighted behavior can well take the country to the brink of disaster" and "threaten to destroy our position of leadership among allies and put at risk even our ability to provide for our own security," he said.

As for the contras, McFarlane called them "well-meaning, patriotic but inept Coca-Cola bottlers," a reference to Adolfo Calero, who had managed the soft drink franchise in Managua, and judged that "they just cannot hack it on the battlefield."[48]

McFarlane also admitted that he had misled Congress over North's role and had kept it and Shultz in the dark about soliciting funds from Saudi Arabia and other countries. The son of a congressman who had spent years working with Congress, McFarlane had violated his own principles and now was trying to redeem himself.

Abrams admitted on the stand that in a closed-door appearance before the Senate Intelligence Committee on November 25, 1986, he had concealed the solicitation of funds from Brunei. He asserted that he had promptly gone back to the committee to correct the record after mulling over his testimony; but they read about it first in the morning newspaper, for the *Los Angeles Times* had broken the story in the meantime. His only note of contrition was to admit that "there is such a thing as being too clever."

North impressed many at the hearings with his straight-arrow appearance and his boy scout's sincerity, but he jolted official Washington when he casually revealed Casey's plan for a stand-alone, self-financing offshore enterprise capable of mounting covert operations on behalf of the U.S. government "off the shelf." North seemed almost boastful about the fact that he had repeatedly lied to Congress and had shredded vast quantities of memos in his office at the time he was fired.

Reagan had claimed to the Tower board not to have known of the funds diversion, and in its report issued February 26, 1987, the board found no evidence to the contrary. Poindexter backed him up. But Poindexter's defense before Congress that "the buck stops here, with me" was an astonishingly arrogant statement for an unelected official, particularly a high-ranking military officer.

Only Shultz and Weinberger emerged unscathed after telling of the good fight they had waged against the Iran initiative. But Shultz puzzled many by defending Abrams against the clamor for his resignation from Democrats and some leading Republicans.

Documents released at the hearings undercut the credibility of the White House and the Office of Public Diplomacy in selling the program. Since 1984, officials had credited the contras with raising the funds needed to survive the congressional cut-off; in truth, the White House had solicited other governments on their behalf. Contra "reforms" had been mainly public relations exercises engineered by North to impress Congress. The growth in numbers, portrayed as proof of the contras' popular appeal, was shown to have been a PR tactic. Military strategy had been crafted largely to impress Congress on the eve of a vote.

The administration's innermost secrets had been exposed. Top officials routinely had lied to each other and to Congress. Only one or two cabinet members, whose advice Reagan ignored, had given any thought to the consequences of foreign policy actions. Casey had doctored intelligence and used it to argue policy choices before Reagan. This most damaging assertion came from Shultz and was borne out in subsequent research by the Joint Committee.*

The revelations, like an acid, dissolved the nonstick coating that had shielded Reagan and his administration from criticism.

This was the opportunity for which the opponents had been waiting. But it took a new group of players in Washington and Central America to seize on it.

Centrists who had been excluded from a role in the polarized debate instigated the change. In the House of Representatives, Jim Wright, a Texas Democrat with a long-standing interest in Central America, had replaced Tip O'Neill as Speaker in January 1987. In Costa Rica, President Oscar Arias had launched his own Central American peace initiative that same month. At the White House, Howard Baker, a moderate Republican and former Senate Majority leader, had replaced Donald Regan as chief of staff in February. A further change was the appointment of Frank Carlucci to replace

---

* For example, in November 1986, following his final swing through Central America, Casey told Reagan in a letter that "the leaders" of Central America were "scared to death that we would not stay the course. . . ." In fact, one leader, Arias of Costa Rica, refused to meet with Casey, a second was critical of U.S. policies, and the ambassador in one country told him that most Latin American countries opposed U.S. policy in Central America.[49]

Poindexter as national security adviser. Carlucci was a veteran Washington insider and foreign policy professional with a wide following on Capitol Hill. He was also a Weinberger protégé, and in reorganizing the NSC bowed to the wishes of the hard right in naming aides to manage Central American policy. He picked Kirkpatrick's deputy at the United Nations, José Sorzano, a conservative Cuban-American known as an ideologue, to be director of NSC affairs for Latin America. Jackie Tillman, Kirkpatrick's former secretary-researcher, took over Central American affairs. But Carlucci compensated for these appointments by supporting Baker when he decided to take the lead in reshaping Nicaragua policy.[50]

For months, House Speaker Jim Wright had been warning Baker of the erosion of Reagan's strength in Congress. Baker told Wright he thought that there was a window of opportunity for an alternative policy leading to a negotiated settlement and in mid-July proposed that Wright undertake a bipartisan peace initiative.

The timing coincided with the assessment made by Philip Habib in early spring of 1987 that the contras, newly equipped and retrained, would begin putting military pressure on the Sandinistas by the summer or fall of 1987, and that this would be the time to launch a peace initiative, including his first talks in Managua. Habib had been preparing the Central Americans from early 1987 for such an initiative and had developed a good rapport particularly with Arias.

Arias was a driven man. Well before his election, he had argued that a peaceful solution was possible "if the comandantes are willing to accept the original commitments of the principles of the revolution: pluralistic society, mixed economy, and nonalignment." Costa Ricans, having supported the overthrow of Somoza, "feel they have been betrayed. We feel they lied to us." By the time he launched his initiative, not only had the Sandinistas lied, but the United States had as well. Arias had reason to be angry. When Arias took office in May 1986, U.S. Ambassador Lewis Tambs told him about the secret airstrip that Secord had built in the winter of 1985–1986 in northwest Costa Rica. Arias demanded that it be shut down permanently, and Tambs agreed. But the Tower board hinted that the airstrip was used even after it was supposed to have been shut down.

Arias demanded an explanation after the Tower report was published on February 26, 1987, but Abrams brushed off the protest, saying that a response had to await congressional hearings. Indeed, the airstrip had been used on June 9, 1986, when a C-123 loaded with 10,000 pounds of munitions, uniforms, and medicines made an emergency landing there and got stuck in the mud. The Tower report also revealed that in September 1986, when Arias was about to announce the closing of the airfield, Tambs at North's request and with Abrams's endorsement called Arias to demand that he cancel the press conference and threatened to call off a forthcoming visit to Washington. Arias gave way, but several weeks later announced that the airstrip had been closed.[51]

The initial spur to action came in mid-January 1987, when the foreign ministers of the eight Contadora and support group countries toured Central America along with the secretaries-general of the United Nations and the Organization of American States. They reported on January 21 that the Central American leaders lacked the "will" to reach an agreement.

On February 15, Arias brought together fellow elected civilian presidents from El Salvador, Guatemala, and Honduras to discuss his plan, calling for a cease-fire, amnesty, a dialogue between government and opposition, free elections according to the constitution of each country, and a halt in aid to irregular forces.* But the presidents decided not to agree on the proposal's contents right away and instead presented it to Ortega along with an invitation to a five-nation summit within ninety days.

The summit, to be held in Guatemala, was postponed from the scheduled date of May 15 until August 6 because Honduras and El Salvador insisted on preparatory meetings among the foreign ministers, which the Sandinistas initially rejected. Ultimately, the summit succeeded due to parallel events in Washington.

Independent of Arias's effort, Howard Baker on July 7 had Reagan appoint former Republican congressman Tom Loeffler as special lobbyist for contra aid. Loeffler, a conservative Texan, was a consistent backer of the contra program, making him acceptable to the hard right, but he also had good relations with Jim Wright, a fellow Texan. After briefings by Baker, Carlucci, Shultz, and Abrams,

---

* The Arias proposal did not stress simultaneity, which opened it up to U.S. criticism. It called for an end to outside support for insurgent forces; an immediate region-wide cease-fire and opening of talks with unarmed opposition groups; amnesty decrees within sixty days and full implementation within six months; a calendar of "democratization" including restoration of freedom of the press within sixty days; and arms reduction talks within sixty days.

Loeffler tested the waters on Capitol Hill. "There was an absolute stalemate," he reported back. "Nothing would give. The votes were not there." On July 22, Loeffler went to see Wright. The new House Speaker, a centrist who had opposed U.S. policy in Nicaragua but backed it in El Salvador, was an obvious partner for a deal. He was a powerful figure, all the more so due to the administration's weakness.

"I have been hired to lobby for contra aid," Loeffler told Wright. "I want you to know that I think and the White House agrees that we have a shot at working out a peace agreement." Baker was well aware that the White House "does not have the credibility with Congress or in the region to do this. The only way they can is if Jim Wright is involved," he added. "Well, Tom," Wright replied, "if you can prove the President is sincere about the diplomatic track, maybe we can work together." The courtesy call turned into a forty-five-minute meeting. Wright invited Loeffler to his home in McLean, Virginia, for dinner and further talks. Loeffler said he had support from the President on down. "Let's find out what is possible if there is anything possible," he quoted Reagan as saying. According to Loeffler, Shultz "played a hell of an active role" and "gave everything he could to this process." Shultz may have had no choice but to become deeply involved, for both his principal advisers were taboo to different groups on Capitol Hill. The center and left wanted Abrams's head, and the hard right wanted Habib's. The right more or less had their way on Habib, who at about this time told Shultz that he was quitting. But Shultz held off accepting his resignation. During the negotiations, Loeffler never conferred with Habib, even though he was the government's resident expert on diplomacy in Central America.

The Wright initiative also had critics within the administration, chiefly Abrams and Sorzano. The political furor over his misleading testimony the previous December had cost Abrams his political base in Congress, and he became totally dependent on two disparate sources of support: the hard right, including the Heritage Foundation, a conservative think tank, and his boss, George Shultz, who was at odds with Heritage on nearly everything else in foreign affairs.

With his job at stake and his loyalties in conflict, Abrams later asserted that he was highly critical of the initiative. But according to Loeffler, this was posturing aimed at Abrams's right-wing constituency. "I don't think Elliott was quite that stout on it, on trying to block it, but if he wants to say he did, that's fine. He needs to be saying what he's saying."

The negotiations between Loeffler and Wright began on Tuesday, July 28, and were over in less than a week. Wright invited Nicaraguan ambassador Carlos Tünnerman to his office along with Republican Minority leader Robert Michel of Illinois. Wright asked the ambassador what it would take for Nicaragua to loosen restrictions on its internal opposition. "If you shut down the contras, we will restore civil liberties," he replied.

At a July 30 meeting with Shultz, Wright insisted that if Nicaragua showed interest in the plan, the administration must put off any request for contra aid because "if not, my colleagues will say I've led them into a trap." Shultz's concern was that cease-fire talks must "include those who fought for freedom. They have to have genuine representation." But he added that this could be worked out by Habib. "Habib is good at that." This was the first hint from Shultz that he intended to involve Habib in the process.

On Friday, July 31, Wright dictated a first draft and showed it to Senate Majority leader Robert Byrd and Minority leader Robert Dole. Ambassador Guido Fernández of Costa Rica stopped by and urged him to remove references to national elections, because the Sandinistas were sure to reject them. Wright concurred. Tünnerman was out of town, and before even showing the draft to the administration, Wright gave a copy that afternoon to Sofia Clark, who maintained congressional liaison for the Nicaraguan embassy. On Monday, Wright passed the draft to Shultz in a large meeting with more than a dozen congressional leaders. Shultz said he would study the contents. After conferring with Habib, whom he had summoned from his home in California, the secretary of state returned it with four or five penned-in corrections.*

Abrams said he and Sorzano found the plan "barely acceptable." They bitterly opposed the accompanying "gag rule," under which Reagan and Wright agreed not to criticize each other and the administration agreed to abstain from requesting contra aid until

---

* The plan called for three simultaneous actions: immediate cease-fire in place, an immediate halt in U.S. military aid to the contras, and an immediate halt in Soviet-bloc military aid to Nicaragua. It also called for the lifting of emergency laws and amnesty. If the Sandinistas did not comply, the United States would be free to resume contra aid. The final wording called for an election timetable but omitted the demand for a new general election which Reagan had insisted on since early 1985.

October 1. "We fought and fought and fought and fought and we lost to Howard Baker, I think wrongly," Abrams recalled. "It was a big mistake." Loeffler had a different recollection. "It wasn't quite that vicious," he said of Abrams's opposition.

Shultz backed the plan. "I think he went along because he thought it was a good idea," Abrams said.

The proposal was announced on Wednesday, August 5, the eve of the Central American summit in Guatemala, in a manner that indicated the administration's underlying ambivalence. The White House issued the document on blank paper without any indication that it was an official document. The State Department had copies delivered to the attendees at the summit but neglected to send a top official to explain its implications.

Fernández was already in Guatemala and called Wright for guidance. He felt the agreement was "too good to be true," but his government had many questions. Wright agreed to Fernández's suggestion to send a representative to answer them and dispatched Richard Peña, a Latin affairs expert formerly with the House Foreign Affairs Committee. He arrived the next day, as the Central American presidents began their meetings.

With Peña as their intermediary, Fernández and Wright transformed the Wright-Reagan plan into a blank check for Arias to use as he saw fit. Their dialogue thereby changed the course of American foreign policy and very possibly the history of Central America. Or, as Loeffler saw it, "once Wright-Reagan came into place, it broke the stalemate in the Congress and the stalemate in the Western hemisphere."

Costa Rica's most critical question concerned the timetable. Arias envisioned ninety days for compliance, whereas Wright-Reagan spoke of sixty days. Was this rigid? Back came the answer from Wright: "No, you can modify it. The plan is meant to complement, not substitute [for the Arias plan]."

Would the White House agree to such changes? Back came the answer: "Wright offers himself as interlocutor with the White House for all things we want to amend."

What was the Sandinista reaction? Foreign Minister Miguel D'Escoto "was consulted" and had replied in a letter to the Speaker that the plan was interesting.

Could Wright guarantee there would be no contra aid for the first ninety days? Peña delivered the answer: "Wright believes he has

enough swing votes behind him." Wright also advised that he
believed there could be no negotiations through third parties
between the Sandinistas and the contras.

It was not the first time that an individual without line responsibility would set U.S. policy in Nicaragua; Wright's distinction from
Carbaugh, North, and Casey was that he had been formally placed
into his coequal role by the White House itself and with Shultz's
support.

When the talks began on Thursday, August 6, Arias was in an
enviable position. Four of the five participants were more or less
supportive and the fifth was operating in the dark. Moreover, Arias
was the only participant with an official interpretation of the U.S.
plan. He used the opportunity to the fullest.

El Salvador was reluctant. (Wright was in touch with Duarte, but
it is not clear whether he ever needed to use his leverage or to
remind him how much support he had provided in obtaining
economic and military aid over the objections of liberal Democrats.)
Guatemala clearly wanted the peace process to succeed. The challenge for Arias was the Hondurans, who were as usual the main
holdouts. Wright had dealt with this by not informing them of the
plan. The administration also made the fatal error of not keeping its
vital ally posted.

The Iran-contra scandal, combined with the political shift in
Congress, had had its impact on Honduras, the use of whose
territory was critical to the continuation of Reagan's policy. "The
scandal debilitated the standing of the U.S. government before the
eyes of the Central American governments," said a senior Honduran
diplomat. "State secrets were on page one of newspapers. Many [top
officials] got worried about what the contra program means for future
relations with a Democratic Congress and for a possible Democratic
administration." According to other diplomats, Honduran military
leaders began to suspect that the contras' military struggle had
assumed greater importance for the administration than the security
of states such as Honduras. The Sandinistas were astonished at the
process unfolding in Guatemala. "We didn't expect an agreement,"
said one senior official. "We thought the best we could get was a
communiqué." But the shift of power in Washington quickly became
apparent to Ortega and his aides. "Something had changed in the
way the Central American presidents perceived the level of strength
[of Reagan]. The Wright-Reagan proposal confirmed it."[52]

To build up the pressure, at about 4:30 a.m. Friday Fernández telephoned Wright at his home and said an outline agreement had been reached; according to observers, this was not actually the case, for the Hondurans were holding out. But once Wright announced the news in Washington and warmly welcomed the agreement, Honduras, not wanting to be the spoiler, backed it. And the deal was made.

The plan, announced Friday, August 7, followed Arias's earlier draft but relegated all security-related matters to the Contadora forum. These could not be negotiated among the five, for the United States first had to define its position on retaining its military trainers in El Salvador, its sizable military presence in Honduras, and its plans for maneuvers in the region. The plan put strong emphasis on enlarging democratic institutions and national reconciliation, but within the framework of existing constitutions.*

Habib saw his chance. He and Abrams read the document in Shultz's office as it arrived page by page from the U.S. embassy in Guatemala.

"We're home free," Habib exclaimed. He said the Guatemala accord was a great achievement for U.S. policy and interests, and recommended going to Central America immediately, but added: "It's time to go to Managua."

Shultz concurred. "He agreed with me 150 percent," Habib recalled.

Abrams said he "violently" opposed that view both orally and in writing. For Habib to travel at that moment "would have been extremely unfortunate and would have given very much the wrong signal" to the four U.S. allies—Costa Rica, El Salvador, Guatemala, and Honduras—and also provoked a firestorm from the right at home, Abrams said. He thought that Habib should not be traveling at all, but that the United States had to give a very tough message to its four allies and that Habib was not the man to deliver it.

The message that Abrams wanted to have delivered was an ultimatum. "Either you work closely with us to protect your national

---

* The plan was a model of simultaneity, setting a ninety-day initial deadline. All five countries committed themselves to take all necessary steps to achieve a cease-fire, enact an amnesty for all armed groups, release political prisoners, and provide full freedom of the press, speech, and assembly by November 5. That same day, the five countries were to request a halt in all outside assistance to armed opposition forces in the region.

security or your national security isn't going to be protected. You people have gone off here and done something which may well result in a disaster for your national security and ours. . . . And you're going to have to live with the results in a much more direct sense than we are. Think it through carefully because we would like to restore the closest possible level of cooperation."

Shultz disagreed, Abrams said. He viewed discussions with the Sandinistas as a "boil that had to be lanced. Sooner or later we are going to have to do it. There is no good moment. Let's just do it and get it over with using the treaty as a justification."

Abrams was prescient in predicting a firestorm from the right. Just in case it did not catch, he worked closely with Sorzano at the NSC to see that Secretary of Defense Weinberger, who had been completely excluded from the deliberations, was made fully aware of the negative consequences. Weinberger had influence with National Security Adviser Carlucci, and Abrams made his view known that there were two distinct viewpoints in the administration, his and Habib's; a choice had to be made. Abrams felt that both Weinberger, "the hardest line guy at the top," and Carlucci had lost confidence in Habib. "Phil symbolized a weaker policy; he symbolized an alternative to the hard-nosed pro-contra policy of Ronald Reagan," Abrams said.

Habib drafted a memo for Shultz and began to select his staff the following Monday. "My idea was to go down immediately, improving, filling the gaps, strengthening the security aspects which were non-existent, and making sure the Central American democracies got it together. I considered it an opportunity to end the war on terms acceptable to us."

But Abrams drafted a countermemo arguing against a Habib trip on the merits. He also told Shultz that politically it was an unwise move.

Shultz replied that he was making a policy choice which he thought was correct. When Shultz went in to see Reagan later that day, he endorsed Habib's recommendation.

"Phil should leave now and go down there and meet not the four but the five." But he quickly added: "I have to tell you, Mr. President, that Elliott Abrams does not agree." Weinberger was present, along with Baker and Carlucci. Having been out of the loop and heard the views of Abrams, Sorzano, and his own hard-liners such as Fred Iklé, Weinberger now gave his view. He was "very much opposed to Phil's traveling," a high State Department aide said.

This was one of the most important decisions in the history of the Nicaragua policy. For the first time, the entire region, the White House, and the Congress were briefly united; but Reagan's aides, as usual, were sharply divided. Weinberger and Carlucci apparently got to Reagan first and carried the day. According to Loeffler, the NSC framed the issue rather differently than Shultz and Habib. The line given Reagan was that the United States had suffered the conse-quences of its long reputation as the "colossus of the North." "Do we send someone now and get accused of trying to tell them what to do, or do we wait and let them try to work it out and try to assist them?" That, said Loeffler, "is the decision that was put to the President."

Reagan had no difficulty in making up his mind. Faced with the conflict among his aides, he hoped to put off the decision.

"I don't want Phil traveling," Reagan said.

"If he can't travel, Mr. President, you've lost confidence in him," Shultz replied. "And if you have lost confidence in him, I should tell him to leave. He should quit."

Reagan responded: "No, I don't want him to quit. I just don't want him to travel right now."

According to several sources, Shultz made a second attempt to convince Reagan a day or two later but failed to change his mind.

Shultz called in Habib. "They don't buy it," he said.

"Fine. I won't stay," Habib replied. He went back to his office and typed out his resignation.

The first to learn of it was an ad hoc group of conservative leaders who had demanded to see Reagan after the Reagan-Wright agree-ment and attacked him for it. They were told that Friday, August 14, of Habib's departure more than three hours before the general public.

"I thought a real opportunity was there and should be taken," Habib said later. "I wanted to take advantage of it, really make it work." He added, "I would have taken what they did in Guatemala City, and gotten agreements that would meet our objectives." His first move would have been to meet the contra leadership, "make them under-stand what I would be doing." If the mediation was successful, they would have to "fold their tent." But they "could be protected while you test [the agreement]. That is what I was going to do."

Instead, the administration withdrew from playing an active role in the process.

DIPLOMATIC VACUUM

In the weeks after the Guatemala meeting, the administration acted as if it had lost its compass. Under attack from his core constituency for signing the joint statement with Wright, Reagan clumsily groped for a way to discredit the Guatemala accord. At first, he officially welcomed it, but within a month declared "yes, yes" when asked whether the accord was "fatally flawed." Shultz, on the other hand, said the United States should take full credit for the outcome, which he said was due to military pressure by the contras, then proceeded to request a quarter of a billion dollars in aid for the following eighteen months. The conflicting signals, according to Abrams, reflected the division among Reagan's top advisers, some of whom urged him to reject the proposal and others to embrace it. Reagan settled for a "compromise in which we said we'll accept it but we don't like it." Amid these strange goings-on in Washington, the Central American leaders worked with a rare adroitness and common purpose to discredit administration policy.[53]

Because Reagan, Shultz, and Abrams spent most of August on vacation and Habib's ouster meant there was no special envoy to send around the region, it took weeks to assess the impact of the Guatemala accord. Abrams's deputy, William Walker, visited the area in late August and returned, a colleague said, "in the pit of despair." No one wanted to hear U.S. views. Most discouraging was the cold shoulder he received from Duarte in El Salvador. By challenging the leftist guerrillas to lay down their arms and enter the political process, Duarte had gained needed political capital. He refused to distance himself from the process.

"What we didn't realize is that you have five incumbent presidents who wanted to delegitimize any threat to their incumbencies," Walker said upon his return. "There is a commonality of interests between Duarte and Ortega."[54]

Early in September a replacement was named for Habib—Morris Busby, a foreign service officer who since early 1987 had run the contra program at State. Busby was junior compared with Habib or Harry Shlaudeman and had no background as a diplomatic troubleshooter.

From Abrams's viewpoint, the problem with Habib was that he had failed to "realize that he was just a symbol" and instead saw himself "as a negotiator." Habib "wanted to get something negotiated. That is what his supporters liked, and that is what his opponents feared." Busby, whose highest previous post had been deputy chief of mission in Mexico, fit what Abrams saw as the Shlaudeman model—"an honest and able envoy who was not exceptionally vigorous" and who enabled "all elements of the administration to maintain their ambiguity."

This was important, because "ambiguity allowed all views in the administration to coexist" whereas "a really vigorous envoy who seemed to be pushing for a treaty elicited opposition. And then you had crunches and arguments and so on."

To ensure that the special envoy did not stray from the path laid out by Abrams and Sorzano, Jackie Tillman accompanied Busby on every trip. "I request the aircraft. He doesn't get a plane unless I'm on board," she boasted to an associate.

The restoration of ambiguity allowed Abrams to resume his drive for policies favored by the hard right, now his sole source of political support. But it did nothing to help the administration regain the confidence of Congress or its influence over diplomacy in Central America. Instead, Central Americans saw this development as a cue to work closely with Jim Wright in order to thwart the administration.

Sooner or later, the ambiguity would have to give way to clarity; meanwhile, Shultz found himself twice embarrassed as he charged up Capitol Hill for more contra aid only to beat a retreat days later.

Abrams pushed hard for another battle over contra aid. He favored "an absolute confrontation with the Hill not because of principle but because it maximizes our chances, such as they are, of winning and forc[ing] the Democrats to pull the plug." This coincided with the preference of spokesmen for the hard right in Congress and conservative groups, most of whom had wanted a showdown over Central America since Reagan came to office. The thesis was that if Democrats could not be bludgeoned into supporting the program, defeat could be transformed into political capital by charging them with being soft on communism. "I know where he's coming from," said Loeffler. "That means that we have a bloodbath. And I don't want to see that."

Another flaw in the thesis was that it overlooked the views of the Central American leaders, who worked together to block the request.

On September 10, Shultz went before the Senate Foreign Affairs Committee and announced that Reagan planned to request $270 million after October 1. But ten days after he spoke, Arias, visiting Washington at Wright's invitation, urged the administration to "give peace a chance" and postpone any request for contra aid until November 7, when democratization, amnesty, and region-wide cease-fires were to take effect. The administration backed down. On October 13, Arias was awarded the Nobel Peace Prize. A few hours later, Shultz appeared before the House Foreign Affairs Committee and stated that Reagan would seek a vote on the $270 million before Thanksgiving.

The new aid proposal had a life of ten days. To Abrams's surprise, presidents Duarte of El Salvador and Azcona of Honduras also spoke out against an early vote on contra aid. Both had come to Washington on White House invitations. On October 15, Duarte urged that the vote be deferred until January 7, when the presidents of the five countries planned to meet and evaluate the results to date. A week later, Azcona said after seeing Reagan that contra aid should be suspended at least until January. Once again, the administration backed down. Shultz formally announced on November 10 that "to give peace every chance," the $270 million would not be requested before 1988.

Abrams also found himself outmaneuvered on the peace plan itself. In August, he assessed the Guatemala plan as a "disaster" for Central American and U.S. security and dismissed each Sandinista concession as it arose. In the naming of a national reconciliation commission to be headed by the Sandinistas' leading critic, Cardinal Miguel Obando y Bravo, Ortega had failed to include enough government opponents, the State Department said. The reopening of *La Prensa* and the Roman Catholic radio station were derided as "cosmetic gestures of compliance." But by mid-October, Abrams, in a bid to regain the public relations initiative, changed tack. "We came in the course of time to think that the Sandinistas had agreed to things that were very remarkable and that by demanding compliance and in a sense getting behind the treaty, we could actually get pretty far." Or, as he told a British television interviewer, "the more I look at it, the more I like it." Indeed, Abrams found he could focus public debate in the United States and in Central America by pressing the Sandinistas to hold cease-fire talks with the contras and then implement a full amnesty. "The refusal of the Sandinistas to meet their insurgents is becoming a major issue. That's not an accident," a source close to Abrams said.

But Ortega outfoxed Abrams on November 5 by announcing that he would hold indirect cease-fire talks with the contras. He also declared a wide-ranging amnesty and the lifting of emergency laws, but turned the decision on the timing over to an international verification commission, which he said could trigger implementation when it determined that Honduras and other countries were also carrying out the agreement. Ortega followed up by asking Obando to be the mediator in the talks and flew to Washington the following week and presented Obando with a cease-fire proposal.

The administration refused to have any contact with Ortega during his visit to Washington, but he called on Wright twice to discuss his cease-fire proposal. He then delivered it to Obando in Wright's presence at the Vatican embassy in Washington. For weeks Abrams had been trying to get Shultz to "be tougher on exposing" and "denouncing" Wright's forays into diplomacy. Shultz had resisted. He was "too busy, probably; other priorities," Abrams surmised. Now Abrams had his chance. Speaking as an anonymous senior official, he told the *Washington Post* that Wright's involvement in the Ortega visit had been an "exercise in guerrilla theater" that had dealt a "serious setback" to the regional peace process. This led to a major blow-up between the White House and Wright, which Shultz allayed with a personal visit to the speaker's office.[55]

Abrams went a step further and had his military adviser, an army colonel, brief reporters. "The war continues to move forward in spite of all the politics that go on. The troops are fighting. They are widening the war," he said. If funded for another year, the guerrillas could overthrow the Sandinistas. Actually, the war was being widened by the administration, for, as the official noted, the CIA had stepped up its arms deliveries into Nicaragua, with the amount in October double that of the previous month.

Yet he also acknowledged that the contras as a force had been "built on its head," beginning with a military operation before there was an economic infrastructure or political support inside the country. So it could not find food to support itself and could not survive a total cut-off of U.S. aid.

Seldom had the contrast been so clear between U.S. rhetoric calling for democracy and the reality of its hands-off approach to diplomatic efforts to that end. Seldom had a U.S. policymaker been as isolated politically in Washington as Abrams or in pursuit of a policy so contrary to the stated wishes of the elected leaders of a region. The five presidents seemed united behind a locally initiated peace process, which week by week had advanced toward agreed-upon goals. But an important portion of the U.S. administration was suggesting that a military solution lay just around the corner and was doing what it could to help that come about.

The approach might have made sense if the object of the expanded fighting was to arrive at a cease-fire, but the U.S. goal was veiled in the ambiguity that Abrams valued so highly as he promoted the hard right's vision of the policy. No doubt, the Abrams approach made sense in terms of the short-term interests of those whose careers were identified with the program, including himself. Less clear at the start of December 1987 was where it fit into long-term U.S. national interests. For the risk in betting on war when the region was betting on peace was that U.S. influence over events would be reduced and the influence of the Sandinistas heightened, and that U.S. interests as a result would be adversely affected. Dating back to 1981, U.S. security interests had been defined as requiring the Sandinistas to undertake arms reductions and expel their Cuban and Soviet-bloc military advisers, matters that would be easy to pin down in verifiable international agreements. But these issues had taken a back seat to "democratization," a process that was internally con-trolled and therefore ultimately reversible.

Indeed, ironically, in the absence of Habib, as the Central Americans moved toward fulfilling the Arias plan, the Sandinistas distanced themselves from the security requirements of the Conta-dora accord. A top aide to Defense Minister Humberto Ortega defected to the United States in October and claimed that the Soviet Union had agreed that same month to support a dramatic expansion of Sandinista military forces by the mid-1990s. The resulting political furor helped the administration win an extension for contra military aid through February 1988. The Soviet Foreign Ministry later denied categorically that Moscow had made any such commitment. Yet a senior Sandinista official who accompanied Daniel Ortega to Washington in November affirmed that Nicaragua wanted to retain its army of 70,000 and have 200,000 reserves that could be mobilized in forty-eight hours. "If Nicaragua invades any of the surrounding countries, the United States will quickly come to their rescue. But if the United States invades Nicaragua, neither Cuba nor the Soviet

Union will come to its aid," Victor Hugo Tinoco noted. He compared the Contadora plan to the 1976 Helsinki Final Act, an East-West accord containing commitments on human rights that have proven unenforceable. Guatemala, this official said, "offered much more than Contadora." In other words, the Sandinista response to the ambiguity of the U.S. position was to remain armed to the teeth.

As the year drew to a close, U.S. policymakers were locked in stalemate with each other, with Congress, with the Sandinistas, and with the other leaders of Central America. Without active participation by the United States, the Arias plan could never achieve its ambitious goals; but a top State Department official said he could not foresee a U.S. negotiating role without the restoration of contra aid, for it would be a vital bargaining chip in any final settlement. Yet the restoration of contra aid seemed certain to doom the Arias plan, for the Sandinistas had repeatedly said they would then abandon the negotiating process. And Congress seemed unlikely to restore the aid unless the Central Americans pronounced the Arias plan dead. This was the impossible set of choices before Congress, the country, and Central America. It was the fruit of seven years of a policy-making process that was as inept as it was politicized, as corrupt as it was chaotic, a process that had given rise to the biggest scandal of Reagan's administration. It had more in common with the foreign policy of the banana republics of the past than of a superpower in the late twentieth century. Indeed, the Central Americans and the United States seemed to have reversed roles.[56]

With policy in worse disarray than hitherto had seemed possible, many of the country's most respected diplomats abandoned their patience with the administration. Habib, speaking in mid-November, was exasperated. "I saw an opportunity to get what we wanted. I would have been down there working. I would have had a cease-fire agreement by now."

His only hope was that the matter might be taken out of U.S. hands.

"The Central Americans," he said, "might save us from our own folly."

EPILOGUE

ON FEBRUARY 3, 1988, the House of Representatives rejected Ronald Reagan's request for another six months of contra funding by an eight-vote margin. Since the White House and Congress had previously agreed that defeat in either house killed the request, this vote effectively ended the funding program. Many observers, including some members of the Reagan team, believed that the administration would be unable to revive military aid funding.

The Sandinistas had acted shrewdly during the run-up to the vote, using conciliatory rhetoric and timing their concessions for maximum effect. On January 16, Daniel Ortega seized the initiative and bowed to the administration's demand for direct talks with the contras and a suspension of the nation's state of emergency. On the defensive, the administration responded with reluctance to Democratic appeals for a new round of U.S. negotiations with the Sandinistas. Elliott Abrams said negotiation with a communist nation was a chip to be played only once. And this, he said, was not the time.

On the eve of the showdown, Reagan gave his twentieth major speech on contra aid in five years. Claiming that Daniel Ortega's concessions were the result of military pressure, Reagan pleaded for his package as an "insurance policy" to support the Arias peace initiative.

But Democrats said the package amounted to a "death warrant" for the Arias initiative. They asserted that the funding package which Reagan described as $36.25 million (including only $3.6 million for lethal aid) was actually closer to $60 million, with five-sixths to be used for military aid or transport. House Speaker Jim Wright, summing up the argument against aid, said the Arias initiative had wrung more concessions from the Sandinistas in six months of peace efforts than the contras had in six years of fighting. He disparaged the U.S. refusal to engage in direct talks as "childish and ridiculous."

The 219–211 outcome was a watershed for U.S. policy in Central America. Defeat, Abrams had said before the vote, would amount to a "Sandinista triumph over us" and a "tremendous undercutting of U.S. influence in the entire region, instantly." He predicted it would lead to military coups in Honduras, El Salvador and Guatemala before the end of 1988. "The dissolution of Central America," he said, "will be fast and it will come on Ronald Reagan's watch."

Guido Fernández, Arias's ambassador in Washington, agreed that the vote would have "overwhelming repercussions" in the region, among them "a complete reversal" of the U.S. policy of trying to solve Latin American problems with force. He welcomed the change and predicted that the United States would begin using diplomatic means to achieve its foreign policy goals, although not until Reagan left office.

After the vote, the administration found itself, as a result of its previous actions, at the margins of the region's diplomacy. On February 5, the third-ranking Soviet diplomat in Washington, Yevgeniy Kutovoy, called on Fernández and informed him that Moscow was prepared to begin talks leading to military disengagement in Central America. Kutovoy complained that he had tried to see Abrams three times in the previous two weeks to discuss this but Abrams would not receive him. Fernández informed Arias of the conversation, and the next day the Costa Rican leader publicly called on the Soviets and Cubans to halt their shipments of military hardware to the Sandinistas and to the guerrillas in El Salvador and Guatemala. The State Department learned of this development from news reports; Abrams had frozen Fernández out of official contacts months earlier.

U.S. aid deliveries ended February 29, causing an acute crisis for contras inside Nicaragua. Speaker Wright proposed a $30.8 million package of food and nonlethal necessities, but Reagan insisted on the restoration of military aid and refused to negotiate with him. On March 3, House Republicans, backed by the White House, joined liberal Democrats to scuttle Wright's plan by an eight-vote margin.

This was the final blow for the rebels, who reacted bitterly and announced their first withdrawals from Nicaragua. In the meantime, the Sandinistas began an offensive in the remote Bocay valley on the Honduran border, which choked off the principal contra supply and escape route. On March 15, the administration claimed that up to 2,000 Sandinista troops had crossed into Honduras and were advancing on the contras' strategic headquarters and main supply depot. On March 16, a few hours after four key figures in the Iran-Contra scandal—Poindexter, North, Secord, and Hakim—were indicted on criminal charges, Reagan dispatched 3,200 soldiers to Honduras on a "training exercise." Even supporters felt he had overreacted. So low were Reagan's credibility and strength that Wright was able to hold off pressures for a new military aid vote as he worked behind the scenes to spur on cease-fire negotiations.[1]

On March 21, Sandinista and contra leaders met face-to-face in Sapoá, a dusty outpost near the Costa Rican border. Both sides agreed to major concessions, and shortly before midnight on March 23 they announced a preliminary 60-day cease-fire. The administration was stunned and, as usual, divided. Shultz welcomed the truce and hinted that he might soon open direct talks with Managua. Reagan expressed serious doubts about the accord, and Abrams let it be known that he opposed direct negotiations.

The accord did not formally terminate the war, but it opened the way. Once again, Central Americans themselves, defying the administration, had taken an enormous step toward ending what Habib called "our folly."

NOTES*

In researching the making of U.S. policy in Nicaragua during the Reagan administration, I tried to interview those on both sides of the issue in the government, in Congress, in the region, and among the parties in and out of Nicaragua. The Iran-Contra hearings in mid-1987 provided many useful documents relating to the policymaking process after 1984. I sought documents for the prior period through the Freedom of Information Act, but most of my requests were denied. As a result, this book is based largely on interviews. Sources are named except where an official insisted on confidentiality as a condition for speaking.

The following abbreviations are used:

FBIS: Foreign Broadcast Information Service, a daily U.S. government publication which monitors foreign publications and radio stations

FOIA: material obtained through the Freedom of Information Act

Tower: report of the Tower board (President's Special Review Board), Washington, D.C., 1987

ICR: *Report of the Congressional Committees Investigating the Iran-Contra Affair*, Washington, D.C., 1987

ICH: Iran-Contra hearings, May 5 to August 3, 1987; ICH page references are based on the unofficial transcripts provided by Federal News Service.

1. The Pattern Is Set

1. Interviews with Carbaugh, Washington, D.C., November 1985, April 1986, October 1987. Platform hearings of the 1980 Republican National Convention, Detroit, July 8, pp. 13–16, 243, and July 10, pp. 530–534, National Archives. Interview with Schamis, Miami, March 1986; the Committee of Santa Fe report, "A New Inter-American Policy for the Eighties," published by the Council for Inter-American Security; interviews with Sumner, telephone, April 1985, and Santa Fe, N.M., October 1985.
2. Testimony of Robert McFarlane, ICH, May 13, 1987, a.m., p. 7/2.
3. Allen recounted his remarks in an interview with Susan Page of *Newsday*, May 1983. They appeared in "Central America. The Making of U.S. Policy," a three-part series by Roy Gutman and Susan Page, July 31–August 2, 1983. Reagan interview, *Time*, January 5, 1981, pp. 30–32.
4. *Barricada* published the Allen letter on March 25, 1981, on page one. Cardenal described the contents of his letter to Reagan in an interview in Miami, May 1986.
5. Interview with Nestor Sanchez, former CIA director of operations for Latin America, later deputy assistant secretary of defense, Washington, D.C., September 1987. Telephone interview with Haig, April 1987. Senate Select Committee on Intelligence report on Casey, 97-285, December 1, 1981.
6. Interviews with Carbaugh, Washington, D.C., October 1985; Enders, Madrid, December 1985; Haig, Washington, D.C., March 1986.

---

* Unless otherwise stated, interviews are by the author.

7. Interviews with Sumner, Santa Fe, N.M., October 1985; Haig, Washington, D.C., March 1986.
8. Interviews with Enders, Madrid, December 1985, and New York, December 1986; Pezzullo, New York, March 1986. State Department statement as handed to reporters April 1, 1981.
9. Letter from Allen to author, March 26, 1986; Haig interview, Washington, D.C., March 1986.
10. The quoted statements are from FBIS monitoring of Nicaraguan radio and newspapers, April 2–6, 1981; also unclassified cable April 13, 1981, U.S. Embassy Managua, detailing the *La Prensa* letter, released under FOIA request.

2. The Slide into Confrontation

1. Shirley Christian, *Nicaragua, Revolution in the Family* (New York: Random House, 1985), p. 176, and Robert Leiken, "Battle for Nicaragua," *New York Review of Books*, March 13, 1986, p. 5. Telephone interview with Bermúdez, Miami, March 1986. Interview with Pallais, Miami, April 1986.
2. Telephone interview with Bermúdez, Miami, March 1985.
3. Interviews with Pallais, Miami, April 1986; Bermúdez, Washington, D.C., May 1986.
4. Interviews with Carrión, Managua, January 1986; García, Miami, March 1986; Bermúdez, Washington, D.C., January 1986.
5. Interviews with Álvarez, Miami, March and April 1986.
6. Interviews with Bermúdez, Washington, D.C., January 1986, and Miami, October 1985; Cardenal, Miami, October 1985; Sumner, Santa Fe, N.M., October 1985.
7. This account is pieced together from U.S. military and diplomatic sources as well as interviews with Álvarez, *op. cit.*
8. Interview with Binns, Washington, D.C., March 1986.
9. Interview with Haig, Washington, D.C., March 1986.
10. Interviews with Pezzullo, New York, March 1986; Enders, New York, December 1986.
11. Interviews with Colonel Richard Lawrence (USAF, ret.), Washington, D.C., April 1986; Angelo Codevilla, former aide to Senator Malcolm Wallop (R.-Wy.), telephone, March 1986.
12. "Foreign Aid to Central America, 1981–1987," Senate Democratic Policy Committee, February 18, 1987.
13. This and the account that follows are based on interviews with Bermúdez, Washington, D.C., May 1986; Hamrick, Rutherfordton, N.C., December 1985; Carbaugh, Washington, D.C., November 1985; Aguirre, Washington, D.C., November 1986.
14. Letter from Allen, March 26, 1986.
15. Interview with Shlaudeman, Washington, D.C., March 1986.
16. Interview with Aguirre, *op. cit.*
17. Interviews with Bermúdez, Washington, D.C., March 1986; Aguirre, *op. cit.*
18. Interviews with Hamrick, Carbaugh, Shlaudeman, Aguirre, and Binns, *op. cit.*
19. Letter from Allen, March 26, 1986. Interviews with Enders, *op. cit.*; Álvarez, *op. cit.*; Haig, *op. cit.*
20. Quote of Clarridge's statement is from interviews with Álvarez, *op. cit.*; other material based on interviews with Bermúdez, *op. cit.*; Enders, *op. cit.*

3. Enders Takes Charge

1. Interview with Muskie, Washington, D.C., April 1986.
2. Interviews with Carbaugh, Washington, D.C., April 1986 and November 1985.
3. Interviews with Enders, Madrid, December 1985; Sumner, Santa Fe, N.M., October 1985; Einaudi, Washington, D.C., December 1985.
4. Interview with Nutting, Boston, April 1986. José Napoleón Duarte, *My Story*, with Diana Page (New York: G. P. Putnam's Sons, 1986), pp. 170–171.
5. Interview with Woerner, Panama, June 1985.
6. Interviews with Pezzullo, New York, March 1986; Hamrick, telephone, April 1986.
7. Interview with Haig, Washington, D.C., March 1986.
8. Reported in *Newsweek*, November 8, 1982, and the *Los Angeles Times*, March 3, 1985.
9. Interview with Otto Reich, Washington, D.C., April 1986.
10. Interviews with confidential CIA source; Nutting, *op. cit.*
11. Interview with Colonel Lawrence Tracy, former aide to Nestor Sanchez, Washington, D.C., November 1985.
12. Interview with Carbaugh, Washington, D.C., November 1985; confirmed by Enders, N.Y., December 1986. Interview with Enders, Madrid, December 1985.
13. The account of the Managua talks that follows is based on a partial transcript of the Enders-Ortega talks submitted to the World Court by Nicaragua in 1984, and interviews with a confidential U.S. source at the talks, March 1986; Enders, Madrid, December 1985; Pezzullo, *op. cit.*; D'Escoto, N.Y., October 1985; Daniel Ortega, Managua, August 1986; Frank McNeil, Washington, D.C., March 1986.
14. Interview with McNeil, Washington, D.C., March 1986.
15. Good biographical sketches of Ortega and other leading Sandinista personalities are contained in Merle Linda Wolin, "Nicaragua Under the Sandinistas: Portrait of an Enemy," *Los Angeles Herald*, May 5–10, 1985.
16. Interviews with Johnstone, Algiers, December 1985; Pezzullo, *op. cit.*
17. Interviews with McFarlane, Washington, D.C., June 1986; Enders, telephone, New York, October 1987.
18. Interviews with Arce, Managua, July 1985; Sandinista official, Managua, January 1986; Ortega, *op. cit.*; Enders, New York, December 1986.
19. This excerpt is taken from the original copy of the message, shown this writer by the foreign ministry in Managua. Portions of this chapter first appeared in my article, "America's Diplomatic Charade," in the Fall 1984 *Foreign Policy*.
20. Interview with López, Managua, September 1983.
21. Texts of the written exchange following the Nicaragua talks are contained in Bruce Bagley et al., eds., *Contadora and the Central American Peace Process* (Boulder: Westview Press, 1985).
22. Interviews with Colonel Richard Lawrence (USAF, ret.), Santa Fe, N.M., October 1985, Washington, D.C., April 1986.
23. Interview with Enders, Madrid, December 1985.
24. Interviews with Johnstone, *op. cit.*; Cruz, Washington, D.C., June 1984.
25. Interview with Enders, Madrid, December 1985.
26. Interviews with Sanchez, Washington, D.C., November 1985; Stoessel, Washington, D.C., July 1983; Johnstone, *op. cit.*; Haig, Washington, D.C., June 1984.
27. Background briefing to reporters accompanying Defense Secretary Caspar Weinberger on a Central America tour, Panama, September 1983. Interview with Pezzullo, *op. cit.*

NOTES

28. Texts of letters quoted are contained in Bagley, *op. cit.* Interviews with López, *op. cit.*; Arce, *op. cit.*; Enders, Madrid, December 1985; confidential U.S. source at the talks, March 1986; Pezzullo, *op. cit.*

4. The Game Shifts

1. These and other factors cited by U.S. officials were mentioned in the first detailed account of the negotiations by Don Oberdorfer in the *Washington Post*, December 10, 1981, p. 1.
2. Interview with Enders, Madrid, December 1985.
3. Interviews with Pezzullo, New York, March 1986; Johnstone, Algiers, December 1985.
4. Interviews with Haig, Washington, D.C., June 1984, April 1986; Enders, *op. cit.*
5. *Role of the U.S. Military—Caribbean Basin*, Army War College, October 16, 1981. An unclassified and updated version based in part on the report was published in 1984 as an Atlantic Council Book titled *Western Interests and U.S. Policy Options in the Caribbean Basin* (Boston: Oelgeschlager, Gunn & Hain).
6. Interviews with Carbaugh, Washington, D.C., April 1986; Woerner, then commander of the 193rd Brigade, Panama, June 1985; Johnstone, *op. cit.*
7. McFarlane testimony, ICH, May 11, 1987, a.m., p. 3/1. Interview with former senior NSC official, Washington, D.C., July 1986.
8. Interviews with Kirkpatrick and McFarlane, Washington, D.C., June 1986.
9. Interview with Arce, Managua, June 1985.
10. *New York Times*, November 5, 1981.
11. Interview with Colonel Lawrence Tracy, then a staff officer working for Nestor Sanchez at the Pentagon, Washington, D.C., November 1985.
12. The contents of the documents were reported in detail in the *Washington Post*, May 8, 1983, by Don Oberdorfer and Patrick Tyler, "Rebel Army Swells to 7,000 Men."
13. *Washington Post*, May 8, 1983.
14. Source is a staff member on the Senate Select Intelligence Committee.
15. Interview with Johnstone, *op. cit.*; House Permanent Select Committee on Intelligence, Report 98–122, May 13, 1983, Part I, p. 8.
16. Interview with D'Escoto, New York, October 1985.

5. A Formula for Stalemate

1. Interview with Michael Smith, reported in the Fort Worth *Star-Telegram*, July 11, 1987. Conversation with Richard Pipes, former NSC staff member, June 1987; conversation with outside NSC consultant on terrorism, March 1987.
2. McFarlane testimony, ICH, May 14, 1987, a.m., pp. 20–21.
3. The mission is recounted in Frank Snepp, *Decent Interval* (New York: Random House, 1977), pp. 295–297 and 405–509; and in David Butler, *The Fall of Saigon* (New York: Simon & Schuster, 1985), pp. 269–273 and 358–361.
4. Christopher Dickey, *Washington Post*, November 28, 1982.
5. Text of the document, called "U.S. Policy in Central America and Cuba Through Fiscal Year 1984, Summary Paper," was published in the *New York Times*, April 7, 1983.
6. Information is from an April 4, 1982, Enders memo to Haig and an April 6, 1982, Haig letter to Castañeda obtained through a FOIA request. Telephone interview with Enders, October 1987.

7. Interview with Johnstone, Algiers, December 1985. The original U.S. proposal was made available by the Nicaraguan embassy in Washington, D.C. The State Department's rendition to reporters is contained in an April 13, 1982, State Department cable to Enders in London, obtained as a FOIA request.
8. Interviews with Haig, Washington, D.C., June 1984; Einaudi, Washington, D.C., December 1985; Quainton, Washington, D.C., August 1986. The letter from D'Escoto is contained in Bruce Bagley et al., eds., *Contadora and the Central American Peace Process* (Boulder: Westview Press, 1985), pp. 34–39.
9. The U.S. reply is contained in Bagley, *op. cit.*, pp. 40–42.
10. Source is an undated Nicaraguan fact sheet prepared by the foreign ministry in Managua.
11. Interviews with Johnstone, Washington, D.C., July 1984; Algiers, December 1985; with other officials (confidential), July 1984.
12. Norman Bailey, former director of strategy and plans, also senior director for economic affairs, NSC, 1981–83, in an interview in Washington, D.C., April 1986.
13. Interviews with Pezzullo, New York, March 1986; Eagleburger, New York, November 1985; see Roy Gutman, "Battle Over Lebanon," *Foreign Service Journal*, June 1984.
14. Interview with Phillips, Bethesda, Md., April 1986.
15. Interview with Victor Meza, director of the Centro de Documentación de Honduras (CEDOH), Tegucigalpa, January 1986.
16. Interview with confidential source, June 1986.
17. Interview with Johnstone, Algiers, December 1985.
18. Interview with Mariano Mendoza, Miami, October 1985; interview with Senate staff source, Washington, D.C., April 1986.
19. Interviews with Álvarez, Miami, March and April 1986.
20. Interviews with Enders, Madrid, December 1985; Johnstone, Algiers, December 1985; Cardenal, Miami, October 1985.
21. Interview with Haig, Washington, D.C., April 1986.
22. Interview with Bermúdez, Miami, October 1985.
23. ICR, p. 32.
24. The Pastora story is based on interviews with Johnstone, telephone, January 1986; Álvarez, Miami, *op. cit.*; Pastora, Washington, D.C., December 1985, March 1986; Pallais, Miami, April 1986.
25. Interview with Eagleburger, *op. cit.*
26. Interview with Jorge Ramón Hernández-Alcerro, Tegucigalpa, January 1986. Others in the Honduran brain trust included Carlos López Contreras, who went on to become foreign minister in 1986, Policarpo Paz Callejas, Leo Valledares, and Robert Galvez.
27. Interviews with confidential U.S. military source, June 1986; Johnstone, Algiers, December 1985.
28. House Permanent Select Committee on Intelligence, Report 98–122, May 13, 1983, Part I, p. 8; McFarlane testimony, ICH, May 13, a.m., p. 18/2.
29. Interviews with Cardenal, *op. cit.*; senior U.S. military official (retired), Washington, D.C., May 1986; Meyer, telephone, April 1986.

6. Turf Wars

1. Telephone interview with Nutting, Boston, May 1986.
2. Interviews with Kirkpatrick, Washington, D.C., July 1983, June 1986.

3. Cole's article, blandly titled "Air Power in the Western Hemisphere: A New Perspective," appeared in the *Air University Review*, an Air Force scholarly journal, in July 1983. Connally, head of JCS Western Hemisphere division, spoke at a conference sponsored by the Keck Center, Claremont College, California, in December 1984.

4. Interview with Eagleburger, New York, October 1985.

5. Telephone interview with Theberge, Washington, D.C., May 1985.

6. Talk with Goshko, Washington, D.C., April 1986; interview with senior State Department official, Washington, D.C., May 1986.

7. Don Oberdorfer and John Goshko, "El Salvador Ascends the U.S. Agenda," *Washington Post*, March 6, 1986.

8. Interview with Enders, Madrid, December 1985.

9. Confidential interview with two members of the task force, Washington, D.C., May 1986.

10. Telephone interview with Feldstein, Washington, D.C., May 1986.

11. Interview with Eagleburger, New York, November 1985.

12. Oberdorfer and Goshko, *op. cit.*

13. Confidential interview, Washington, D.C., April 1986.

14. Remarks regarding the Reagan speech are by Luigi Einaudi, State Department interview, May 1986.

15. Telephone interview with Enders, New York, October 1987.

16. The account of the North meeting is based on interviews with the Pentagon representative at the meeting, Colonel Richard Lawrence, USAF (ret.), Santa Fe, N.M., October 1985; the State Department representative, Stephen McFarland, Washington, D.C., June 1986; and the CIA representative, Constantine Menges, telephone, January 1988. The account of the Shultz-Reagan meeting is from a knowledgeable source; telephone interview with Enders, October 1987. Documents relating the exchange were released as ICH Exhibit GPS-1. Shultz's memo to Reagan had Shultz's initials while Reagan's reply was neither dated nor signed, suggesting the material had been obtained from NSC files.

17. Bob Woodward, *Veil* (New York: Simon & Schuster, 1987), pp. 255–256.

18. Drawn from two information memoranda released as ICH Exhibit OLN-220. The memos are dated August 9 and August 29, 1983, and are from Walter Raymond, a former CIA staff member in charge of public diplomacy at the NSC, to William P. Clark and John M. Poindexter.

19. Interview with RIG member, Washington, D.C., December 1986.

20. Conversation with Colonel Lawrence Tracy of the State Department Office of Public Diplomacy, April 1986.

21. Telephone interview with Elliott, May 1987; interview with Herbert Meyer, former Casey assistant, Washington, D.C., September 1987; Woodward, *Veil*, pp. 235–236.

22. Interview with Bailey, Washington, D.C., May 1986.

23. Interview with former NSC official, Washington, D.C., area, May 1986.

24. Document obtained by author from government sources.

25. The polls were cited in Ronald Brownstein, "Reagan Reaches Out for Public Support for CIA Aid to Nicaraguan Insurgents," *National Journal*, April 13, 1985.

26. Documents obtained by author from government sources.

27. Robert McCartney, "U.S. Will Oppose Loans to Nicaragua," *Washington Post*, July 1, 1983, p. 1.

28. Report of the Congressional Committees Investigating the Iran-Contra Affair, Washington, D.C., November 1987, pp. 34–35.

29. Quoted in Roy Gutman and Susan Page, "Central America: The Making of U.S. Policy," *Newsday*, July 31, 1983. Additional telephone interviews with Sanchez, October 1987.
30. Interview with former Gorman aide, Palmerola AFB, Honduras, January 1986; interview with second Gorman aide, U.S. Southern Command HQ, Panama, June 1985.
31. The account of the fleet movements is based on Roy Gutman, "Quick Gunboat Move Leaves Lasting Work," *Newsday*, August 14, 1983, p. 4; interview with Johnstone, Algiers, December 1985; House Permanent Select Committee on Intelligence, Report 98–122, May 13, 1983, Part I, p. 11; North referred briefly to Casey's interest in 1983 in testimony on July 8, 1987, p.m., p. 30/1.
32. Shultz testimony, ICH, July 23, 1987, p.m., p. 16/1.

7. Force Without Diplomacy

1. Interview with Fagoth, Miami, March 1986.
2. Bermúdez material in this chapter based on interviews in Miami, October 1985, and Washington, D.C., January, March, and May 1986.
3. Telephone interview with Kepner, October 1987; see also Peter Kornbluh, *Nicaragua: The Price of Intervention* (Washington, D.C.: Institute for Policy Studies, 1987), pp. 34–38.
4. Report of the Select Committee on Intelligence, U.S. Senate, January 1, 1983, to December 31, 1984 (printed 1985), p. 5.
5. Interview with former Chafee staff aide, Washington, D.C., April 1986.
6. Interviews with Edgar Chamorro, Miami, September 1985; former congressional staff aide, telephone, October 1987; Álvarez, *op. cit.*; source close to Vessey, *op. cit.*; for more on Suicida see Christopher Dickey, *With the Contras* (New York: Simon & Schuster, 1985).
7. Interviews with Álvarez, Miami, March and April 1986; source close to Vessey, Washington, D.C., May 1986.
8. Telephone interview with Johnstone, Algiers, January 1986.
9. Don Oberdorfer, "CIA Planning to Back More Nicaraguan Rebels," *Washington Post*, July 14, 1983, p. 1.
10. Interview with former White House aide, Washington, D.C., May 1986.
11. Interview with Chamorro, Miami, November 1985.
12. Shultz's secret four-page memorandum and the new finding were released in heavily redacted form as ICH Exhibit GPS-1B.
13. Interview with Pérez-Chiriboga, Caracas, May 1985; texts of the letters are contained in Bruce Bagley et al., eds., *Contadora and the Central American Peace Process, Selected Documents* (Boulder: Westview Press, 1985), pp. 153–155, 6–7.
14. Interview with Jorge Ramón Hernández-Alcerro, Honduran deputy foreign minister, Washington, D.C., May 1985.
15. Interviews with Amado, Panama, June 1985; Herrera Campíns, Caracas, May 1985; aide to Enders, Washington, D.C., May 1986; State Department official, Washington, D.C., January 1988.
16. Interview with Hernández-Alcerro, *op. cit.*
17. Interview with State Department official, Washington, D.C., April 1987.
18. Interview with Johnstone, Washington, D.C., June 1984.
19. Interview with Bolaños, St. Louis, October 1985.
20. Documents discussed are contained in Bagley, *op. cit.*

21. Interview with Lloreda, Washington, D.C., September 1987; confidential interview with a Latin American diplomat, Washington, D.C., September 1985.
22. Interviews with Johnstone, Algiers, telephone, January 1986; Hernández-Alcerro, *op. cit.*
23. Interviews with Shlaudeman, Washington, D.C., Sept. 1985; former Contadora foreign minister, Washington, D.C., Sept. 1985; State Department official, Jan. 1986; source close to Motley, Washington, D.C., Dec.1986; Calero, Washington, D.C., March 1986; Chamorro, Miami, Oct. 1985.
24. Interviews with Saúl Arana, head of North American desk, Nicaraguan foreign ministry, Managua, June 1985; Stone, Washington, D.C., August 1985.
25. Interview with Dr. Fernando Cepeda, dean of the Law Faculty at University of the Andes of Bogotá, Washington, D.C., February 1986.
26. Interviews with Norman Bailey, former NSC official, Washington, D.C., April 1986; former NSC official, Alexandria, Va., May 1986; Eagleburger, New York, November 1985.

8. Opportunities Missed

1. Interview with Julio López Campos, director of the Sandinista party's department of international relations, Managua, September 1983 (quoted in *Newsday*, October 3, 1983).
2. The letters were contained in a hoard of guerrilla literature captured by the Salvadoran army. The State Department has made available a two-foot-high stack of the captured documents.
3. Interviews with former Motley aide, Washington, D.C., April 1986; source close to Vessey, Washington, D.C., May 1986; Johnstone, telephone, Algiers, January 1986; high U.S. diplomatic source, Central America, January 1986.
4. Constantine Menges, "Democratic Revolutionary Insurgency as an Alternative Strategy" (Santa Monica: Rand Corporation, 1968).
5. Interviews with Stone, Washington, D.C., August 1985; Reich, Washington, D.C., April 1985; Shlaudeman, Washington, D.C., May 1985.
6. Interview with Edgar Chamorro, Miami, November 1985.
7. The following account of Álvarez's liberated zone strategy is based on interviews with Álvarez, Miami, March and April 1986; source close to Motley, Washington, D.C., December 1986; source close to Vessey, Washington, D.C., May 1986; Norman Bailey, former NSC official, Washington, D.C., April 1986; unnamed former NSC official, May 1986; unnamed senior State Department official, Washington, D.C., May 1986; Johnstone, Algiers, December 1985, and by telephone, Algiers, January 1986; Bermúdez, Washington, D.C., May 1986; Calero, Washington, D.C., March 1986; JCS expert, Washington, D.C., January 1986.
8. Interview with Reich, Washington, D.C., April 1986. The account of Stone's final months is based on interviews with Stone, *op. cit.*; Johnstone, Algiers, December 1985; source close to Motley, Washington, D.C., December 1986; a State Department official, Washington, D.C., May 1986; Saúl Arana, head of the North American desk in the Nicaraguan foreign ministry, Managua, June 1985.
9. Interviews with Lehman, Alexandria, Va., May 1986; Chamorro, Miami, November 1985; Bailey, *op. cit.*
10. Interview with source close to Vessey, Washington, D.C., May 1986.

9. The Price of Confrontation

1. Interview with Johnstone, Algiers, December 1985; talk with Michael Drudge, former UPI correspondent and head of the Salvadoran Press Corps Association, San José, Costa Rica, June 1985; interviews with Shlaudeman, Washington, D.C., August 1985; former Johnstone aide, Washington, D.C., April 1986; McFarlane, Washington, D.C., June 1986; and Iklé, prepared remarks before the Baltimore Council on Foreign Affairs, September 1983, made available by the Department of Defense.
2. Confidential interviews with U.S. diplomats in Central America, July and August 1985.
3. Confidential interview, Washington, D.C., July 1987.
4. This account of Álvarez's ouster is based mostly on sources who refused to be quoted by name. They included interviews with a source close to Vessey, Washington, D.C., May 1986; senior State Department official recently posted in Central America, Washington, D.C., May 1986; Honduran officer, March 1986; U.S. military officer recently posted in Central America, Washington, D.C., June 1986; former deputy to Gorman in Honduras, January 1986.
5. Casey's memo dated March 27 was released as Exhibit 29 and McFarlane's memo to Teicher of April 20 as exhibit 30 during McFarlane's appearance at the Iran-Contra hearings. Shultz's testimony, July 23, 1987, a.m., pp. 17/2–18/1; also Shultz's "Chronology of non-USG Support for Nicaraguan Opposition Forces," released as Exhibit GPS-Chronology 4A, p. 1. McFarlane testimony, ICH, May 11, 1987, a.m., pp. 11/1–13/1.
6. Clarridge testimony, ICH, August 4, 1987, pp. 64–89, 98–105, 189–193, official transcript. Also, series of nineteen cables released as Clarridge Exhibit 19, ICH.
7. McFarlane testimony, ICH, May 13, 1987, p.m., pp. 22/1–23/1.
8. The account of the mining and the policymaking process that led to it is based on interviews with a member of the RIG, Washington, D.C., December 1986; two members of the interagency group on Central America, Washington, D.C., May 1986; former senior staff aide on the Senate Intelligence Committee, Washington, D.C., April 1986; senior U.S. official, overseas location, December 1985; Enders, telephone, New York, October 1987; Sanchez, Washington, D.C., October 1987; Colombian diplomat, Washington, D.C., September 1985.
9. Irving Janis, *Victims of Groupthink* (Boston: Houghton Mifflin, 1972), pp. 13, 37–39.
10. Affidavit of Edgar Chamorro for submission to the World Court, September 5, 1985, p. 19.
11. Talks with Kinzer, Managua, June 1985; Aristides Calvani, Caracas, May 1985.
12. Interview with a senior U.S. diplomat, Cairo, November 1984.
13. McFarlane testimony, ICH, May 11, 1987, a.m., pp. 13/1–16/1; May 12, a.m., p. 22/1; Shultz's "Chronology of non-USG Support for Nicaraguan Opposition Forces," released as ICH Exhibit GPS-Chronology 4A. North testimony, ICH, July 9, 1987, p.m., pp. 13/2, 15/1; July 8, a.m., p. 43/1; p.m., p. 3/2.
14. Interview with Edgar Chamorro, Miami, September 1985.
15. Interview with Calero, Washington, D.C., March 1986.
16. Contents of a CIA internal report detailing the activities of the "mother ship" were reported by David Rogers and David Ignatius, *The Wall Street Journal*, March 6, 1985, p. 1. Account of Clarridge testimony at closed-door hearing based on interview with Senate source, Washington, D.C., May 1986.

17. Telephone interview with Bermúdez, May 1986; interview with a source close to Motley, Washington, D.C., December 1986; confidential interview, former CIA official.

10. Last Stab at Diplomacy

1. Telephone interview with McNeil, December 1986.
2. The account of events leading to Shultz's Managua trip that follows is based on the following interviews: aide to Motley, Washington, D.C., April 1986; Herbert Meyer, former assistant to Casey, Washington, D.C., September 1987; Menges, telephone, September 1987, January 1988; source close to Motley, Washington, D.C., December 1986; Robert McFarlane, Washington, D.C., June 1986; Tinoco, Managua, January 1986.
3. This summary is drawn from talking points used by Johnstone to brief Western diplomats in Washington and later distributed in a confidential cable to foreign posts, June 12, 1984; obtained by the author under the FOIA.
4. Francis Clines, "Nicaragua Policy Is Affirmed by U.S. After Shultz's Trip," *New York Times*, June 3, 1984, p. 1.
5. The account that follows of events leading to the Manzanillo talks is based on interviews with Johnstone, Algiers, December 1985, and follow-up by telephone, January 1986; Shlaudeman, Washington, D.C., March 1986; senior U.S. official, Washington, D.C., April, July 1985, October 1986.
6. The account that follows of the presentation of the matrix plan is based on interviews with Johnstone, *op. cit.*; Shlaudeman, January, August, November 1985, March 1986; another senior U.S. official at the talks, Washington, D.C., April, July 1985, October 1986; former high U.S. diplomat in South America, New York, February 1986; officials of the Nicaraguan foreign ministry, Managua, June 1985, January, August 1986; Tinoco, Managua, January 1985, January 1986; Reich, Washington, D.C., September 1985; Tünnerman, Washington, D.C., May 1985, January 1986; Cordero, Washington, D.C., January 1986; source on the JCS joint staff, Washington, D.C., August 1985; State Department official, Washington, D.C., January 1988.
7. The account that follows of the Contadora talks is based on interviews with Shlaudeman, Washington, D.C., May, August, November 1985, March 1986; Jorge Urbina, San José, Costa Rica, June 1985; Winsor, Washington, D.C., June 1986; Gutiérrez, San José, June 1985; Hewitt, Panama, June 1985; Rico, Washington, D.C., February 1986; Heller, Mexico City, August 1985; Cepeda, Washington, D.C., February 1986; Tinoco, Managua, January 1986; Colonel James A. Connelly (USAF), JCS, Washington, D.C., January 1986; Hamilton, telephone, Washington, D.C., September 1985; Kirkpatrick, Washington, D.C., June 1986; Hernández-Alcerro, Tegucigalpa, January 1986; Sepúlveda and Colombian Foreign Ministry Ramírez Ocampo, New York, September 1985; Betancur, Bogotá, June 1985.
8. Shultz letter obtained from Center for International Policy, Washington, D.C.
9. Duarte press conference September 22, Panama, reported by Panama radio, quoted in FBIS, September 25, 1984; Duarte press conference in San Salvador, El Salvador radio, September 24, quoted in FBIS, September 25, 1986. Interview with source close to Motley, Washington, D.C., December 1986. Sepúlveda reported by Mexico City News, October 13, 1984, and quoted in FBIS, October 16, 1984; Central American positions reported by ACAN-EFE news agency on October 5 and reproduced by FBIS on October 9, 1984, p. A1.

11. Divided Counsel

1. The account of the debate within the U.S. government that follows is based on confidential interviews with a senior U.S. official in Central America, January 1986; and interviews with Johnstone, Algiers, December 1985, and by telephone, Algiers, January 1986; Arturo Cruz, Washington, D.C., November 1985, Miami, April 1986; Einaudi, Washington, D.C., December 1985; Quainton, Washington, D.C., August 1986; Singer, telephone, Washington, D.C., June 1986; Curry, telephone, San Salvador, June 1986; Carbaugh, Washington, D.C., April 1986; Menges, telephone, January 1988.
2. The poll was cited by Dennis Volman, "Free Elections in Nicaragua?", *Christian Science Monitor*, March 2, 1984, p. 8.
3. Contained in Douglas Payne, *The Democratic Mask* (New York: Freedom House, 1985), pp. 43–45.
4. The account of developments in Managua is based on interviews with Bolaños, St. Louis, October 1985; Cruz Sr., Washington, D.C., November 1985; Ferrey, Managua, June 1985; Bently Elliot, former chief Reagan speechwriter, telephone, January 1987; Calero, Washington, D.C., March 1986; Francis, Washington, D.C., April 1986; Bacz, Washington, D.C., October 1985, Miami, October 1985 and April 1986, Managua, January 1986.
5. Interview with Arturo Cruz Jr., Washington, D.C., February 1986.
6. Translations of Cruz's speeches of July 24 and 25 are carried in the FBIS of July 25 (p. P12–13) and July 26 (p. P22–23), respectively.
7. The account of events at Chinandega that follows is based on interviews with Cruz Sr., Washington, D.C., November 1985; Rappaccioli, telephone, Miami, December 1985; Baez, Washington, D.C., Miami, and Managua, October 1985, January and April 1986; Jaime Chamorro, editor of *La Prensa*, Azucena Ferrey of the Social Christian party, and Luis Rivas-Leiva of the Social Democrats, all Managua, January 1986; senior U.S. official in Central America, January 1986; McFarlane, Washington, D.C., June 1986; Bergold, Managua, August 1986.
8. Interview with former Johnstone aide, Washington, D.C., April 1986.
9. Sources for the Winsor clash were interviews with Winsor, Washington, D.C., September 1985; Baez, Washington, D.C., October 1985; Johnstone, Algiers, December 1985; Menges, telephone, January 1988.
10. Interviews with source close to Robelo, Washington, D.C., March 1986; Cruz Jr., *op. cit.*; unnamed congressional source, Washington, D.C., July 1986.
11. Interview with Fiallos, Managua, June 1985; Cruz Sr., Washington, D.C., November 1985; Baez, Washington, D.C., October 1985.
12. This account of the Rio talks, and that which follows, is based on interviews with participants in the discussions and minutes kept by the Socialist International. Those interviewed included Pérez, New York, June 1986; Arce, Managua, June 1985; Cruz Sr., Washington, D.C., October 1985; Hans-Jürgen Wischnewski, Washington, D.C., January 1986; Thorwald Stoltenberg, San José, June 1985, and by telephone, Oslo, July 1986; Rivas-Leiva, Managua, June 1985; Daniel Ortega, Managua, August 1986; Sergio Ramírez, telephone, November 1986; Johnstone, Algiers, December 1985; Bonilla, San José, January 1986; Budowsky, Washington, D.C., July 1986.
13. Dr. Klaus Lindenberg, personal secretary to Brandt and a spokesman for the West German Social Democratic party, speaking at a conference on the Contadora process at Johns Hopkins University School for Advanced International Studies in Washington, D.C., February 4, 1986.

14. Philip Taubman, "Key Aides Dispute U.S. Role in Nicaraguan Vote," *New York Times*, October 21, 1984.
15. This account of U.S. intervention in the election campaign is based on confidential interviews with U.S. officials in Washington, D.C., and Managua.
16. Interview with Cameron, Washington, D.C., September 1987.
17. Interviews with Herrera Campíns, Caracas, May 1985; Arana, Managua, June 1985.

12. Rhetoric and Reality

1. Alfonso Chardy, "Missing MiGs Caper: U.S. Leaks Led to Flap," *Miami Herald*, November 9, 1984.
2. Top-secret North memorandum to McFarlane, "Clarifying Who Said What to Whom," November 7, 1984, released as Exhibit 31, ICH. Also Poindexter appearance, July 20, 1987, p.m., p. 1; McFarlane appearance, July 14, 1987, p. 60/1. North memo to McFarlane, "The Nicaraguan Resistance: Near-Term Outlook," May 31, 1985, released as exhibit OLN-152.
3. This account of the Manzanillo talks is based on a speech by Burghardt delivered before the Royal Institute for International Affairs in London, April 30, 1986; an aide-mémoire by the Government of Nicaragua dated February 1985; interviews with Shlaudeman, Washington, D.C., January, August, September, and November 1985, and March 1986; interviews with Victor Hugo Tinoco in Managua, January 1985, Washington, D.C., February 1985, and Managua, January 1986; an official Nicaraguan account of the final three meetings obtained by the author; interviews with other U.S. and Nicaraguan participants in Washington, D.C., and Managua.
4. Quote is from Vargas Llosa's article "In Nicaragua," *New York Times Magazine*, April 28, 1985; interpretation from a senior aide to Lusinchi, interviewed in Caracas, May 1985.
5. Consalvi quote is from Juan de Onis's article in the *Los Angeles Times*, January 29, 1985. Consalvi was quoted as a "cabinet-ranked adviser" to Lusinchi in the article; another Venezuelan cabinet member told me that Consalvi was the source.
6. North memo to McFarlane, "Nicaragua Options," January 15, 1985, Exhibit 24, Poindexter deposition, ICH. For description of McFarlane visit to Honduras, see Roy Gutman, "U.S. Policy Squeezes Honduras," *Newsday*, February 3, 1985; Fahd contribution discussed in ICR, p. 45.
7. Letter from Casey to the oversight committees, October 25, 1984.
8. Telephone interviews with Wheeler, January 1987; Rohrabacher, June 1987.
9. June 25, 1986, speech to the Society for Historians of American Foreign Policy, reproduced in the *Congressional Record*, August 13, 1986. September 18 speech before the University Club, Washington, D.C.
10. Telephone interview with Elliott, January 1987.
11. Confidential interview with high U.S. diplomat, July 1985; North testimony, ICH, July 9, 1987, p.m., p. 41/2; telephone interview with Elliott, *op. cit.*
12. The frequency of Cruz's visits was determined by investigators for the Iran-Contra special prosecutor. Telephone interview, Cruz Jr., September 1987.
13. McFarlane testimony, ICH, May 11, 1987, a.m., p. 8/1; July 14, 1987, pp. 50/1–59/1. North memo to McFarlane, "Using the March 1 San José Declaration to Support the Vote on the Funding for the Nicaraguan Resistance," April 1, 1985, Exhibit OLN-260, ICH. Fiers's claim was reported by an American

associate of Cruz in a September 1987 interview in Washington, D.C. Cruz Sr.'s reaction was given in an October 1987 telephone interview from Miami.

14. Gorman testifying before the Senate Armed Services Committee, Feb. 27, 1985.
15. The study, by four of Rand's top experts on Central America—Edward Gonzales, Brian Jenkins, David Ronfeldt, and Caesar Sereseres—was submitted to the Kissinger Commission in October 1983 and published separately in 1984. Moran's assessment was contained in "The Costs of Alternative U.S. Policies Toward El Salvador, 1984-1989," in Robert Leiken, ed., *Anatomy of a Conflict* (New York: Pergamon, 1984).
16. Metropolitan Club of New York, May 1985; first published in the *Washington Times*.
17. Interview with Gutiérrez, San José, June 1985.
18. Interview with Shlaudeman, Washington, D.C., August 1985; Colombian Foreign Minister Augusto Ramírez Ocampo, United Nations, September 1985.
19. Casey letter, March 20, 1985, released as Exhibit DTR-1, ICH; North March 20 memo to McFarlane, released as OLN-218; CIA memo for the record by Deputy CIA Director John McMahon, March 22, Exhibit 36A; McFarlane testimony, ICH, July 9, 1987, p.m., p. 37/2.
20. Speech before the National Press Club on March 26, 1985.
21. Interview with Simon Alberto Consalvi, Caracas, May 1985.
22. Robert Parry, Associated Press, "Nicaraguans Net $3,000 from $220,000 Dinner," as quoted in the *Washington Post*, January 25, 1986, p. 2.
23. Telephone interview with Rohrabacher, January 1987.
24. McFarlane testimony, ICH, May 12, 1987, a.m., pp. 24/4-25/1.
25. The account of the negotiations over the Reagan letter that follows is based on an interview with a senior aide to Dole, Washington, D.C., April 1985; confidential interview with U.S. diplomat, Washington, D.C., April 1985.
26. Telephone interview with Rappaccioli, Miami, December 1985.
27. Interview with Bolaños, St. Louis, October 1985.
28. Interview with Ortega, Managua, August 1986.
29. Interview with Otto Reich, Washington, D.C., July 1985.
30. A fuller account of this episode is contained in Roy Gutman, "Mexico's Oil Is Leverage on Nicaragua," *Newsday*, September 2, 1985.
31. Interview with Cameron, Washington, D.C., September 1987. Also see Michael Massing, "Contra Aides," *Mother Jones*, October 1987, pp. 23–26, 40–42.
32. State Department Special Report 132, published in September 1985, was drawn up as the countermemorial within the inter-American affairs bureau for use in the World Court deliberation over Nicaragua's suit. A complete transcript of Borge's quotes is contained in the FBIS, July 21, 1981, p. 10.
33. Interview with Bermúdez, Miami, October 1985.
34. McFarlane letter to Hamilton, October 7, 1985, with specific questions and answers attached, OLN-109, ICH; undated letter from North to Calero, RWO-3, ICH; North memo to McFarlane, "Assistance for the Nicaraguan Resistance," December 4, 1985, OLN-256; North memo to McFarlane, "The Nicaraguan Resistance: Near-Term Outlook," May 31, 1985, OLN-152; North memo to McFarlane, "FDN Military Operations," May 1, 1985, OLN-261; North memo to McFarlane, "Guatemalan Aid to the Nicaraguan Resistance," March 5, 1985, OLN-145; McFarlane memo to Shultz, Weinberger, Casey, and Vessey, March 11, 1985, OLN-146.
35. Interviews with Reich, Washington, D.C., August 1985, April 1986; confidential interviews with former high U.S. diplomat in South America, February 1981; high U.S. diplomat, overseas location, December 1985.

36. Interviews with Betancur, Bogotá, June 1985; D'Escoto, New York, October 1985; Mexican journalist Jorge Castañeda, Mexico, July 1985; foreign ministry official, Managua, June 1985.
37. Interview with Jorge Urbina, deputy foreign minister of Costa Rica, San José, June 1985.
38. McFarlane statement, ICH, May 13, 1987, a.m., p. 11/1.

13. "Point of No Return"

1. Testimony by Major General Richard Secord (USAF, ret.), ICH, May 5, 1987, a.m., pp. 12/2-13/3.
2. The account of the military situation that follows is based in part on interviews with Bermúdez, Miami, October 1985; Arce, Managua, June 1985; Cuadra, Jinotega, Nicaragua, January 1985; Carrión, Managua, January 1986.
3. Bosco Matamoros, "Our Struggle," unpublished paper made available by Matamoros in Washington, D.C., January 1987, p. 6.
4. Telephone interview with Brown, Washington, D.C., August 1986.
5. Figures are from Lino Hernández, head of the independent Committee for the Protection of Human Rights, interviewed by Nancy Nasser, Managua, August 1986; "Nicaragua, the Human Rights Record," Amnesty International, London, March 1986; Amnesty International press release July 28, 1987; Ian Martin, secretary general of Amnesty International, letter to Assistant Secretary of State Elliott Abrams, July 1, 1987.
6. Reference is to "The Challenge to Democracy in Central America," issued by the Departments of State and Defense.
7. North memo to McFarlane, "FDN Military Operations," April 11, 1985, OLN-149, ICH, later resubmitted May 1, 1985, with slightly higher numerical predictions, OLN-261; North memo to McFarlane, "The Nicaraguan Resistance: Near-Term Outlook," May 31, 1985, OLN-152.
8. Quoted in "Sandinistas Press Attacks on Rebels," New York Times, June 4, 1985.
9. Colonel Rod Paschall, former commander of Delta Force, writing in Parameters, the journal of the U.S. Army War College, Summer 1986.
10. Casey's influence with speechwriters discussed in interview with Herbert Meyer, Washington, D.C., November 1987; North testimony, ICH, July 19, 1987, p.m., p. 41/2. McFarlane prepared statement, ICH, May 11, 1987, a.m., p. 6/1. North memo to McFarlane, "Nicaraguan Arms Shipments," February 6, 1985, OLN-143, ICH. Letter from North to Calero, February 1985, RWO-3. Calero testimony, ICH, May 20, 1987, pp. 18/1–18/2, p. 48. Roy Gutman, "Blast an Accident or Sabotage?", Newsday, July 15, 1987. North memo to McFarlane, "Timing and the Nicaraguan Resistance Vote," March 20, 1985, OLN-217, ICH. North memo to McFarlane, "FDN Military Operations," op. cit. North memo to McFarlane, "The Nicaraguan Resistance: Near-Term Outlook," op. cit.
11. Interview with Bermúdez, op. cit.
12. Secord testimony, op. cit. Robert McFarlane, ICH, July 14, 1987, p.m., p. 50/1. Lewis Tambs, ICH, May 28, 1987, a.m., pp. 2/1-2/2. Gaston Sigur, ICH, May 14, 1987, p.m., pp. 2/3-5/3. Robert W. Owen, ICH, May 19, 1987, a.m., pp. 2/2-4/3.
13. Interview with Bosco Matamoros, FDN Washington spokesman, Washington, D.C., January 1987. Secord testimony, ICH, May 5, 1987, p.m., p. 2/2. Fiers deposition, ICH, August 5, 1987, p. 10. Singlaub and Abrams quoted in Roy Gutman, " 'Year of Decision' Seen for Contra Aid," Newsday, January 5, 1986, p. 4.

14. Testimony of retired General Paul Gorman before the Senate Armed Services Committee, January 28, 1987.
15. Interviews with McCurdy, Washington, D.C., January, 1986; Caesar Sereseres of Rand Corporation, Washington, D.C., January 1986; aide to Senator Robert Byrd (D.-W.Va.), Washington, D.C., August 1987.
16. References are from the two central documents in this exchange: "Who Are the Contras?" by the liberal Arms Control and Foreign Policy Caucus, April 18, 1985, and "Documents on the Nicaraguan Resistance: Leaders, Military Personnel and Program," Department of State, Special Report 142, April 1986.
17. Speech before the Senate, August 11, 1986, during the debate on providing $100 million in aid to the contras.

14. Manipulating the President

1. Source on the infighting over the Mozambique and Angola policies was an interview with former senior State Department official, January 1988. Casey indicated publicly on at least one occasion that he viewed Mozambique as a "Reagan Doctrine" country. In a speech on November 8, 1986, at the Center for the Study of the Presidency in Atlanta, he said there were "half a million resistance fighters" in Afghanistan, Angola, Ethiopia, Mozambique, Yemen, and Nicaragua who had "taken up arms against some 400,000 Soviet, Vietnamese, and Cuban troops occupying these countries."
2. Tower, pp. B19–B23, B6–B10; Bernard Gwertzman, "Forcing Officials to Take Lie Tests," New York Times, December 20, 1985, p. 1.
3. Telephone interview with Sanchez, October 1987.
4. Interviews with Abrams, Washington, D.C., December 1985, December 1987.
5. Telephone interview with a former administration official, November 1987.
6. Abrams testimony, ICH, June 2, 1987, a.m., pp. 18/2, 7/3; p.m., p. 10/2; June 3, 1987, a.m., p. 9/2.
7. Interviews with a former ambassador, Washington, D.C., September 1987; a member of the Democratic party group, Washington, D.C., September 1987; Abrams, Washington, D.C., December 1985; senior State Department official, Washington, D.C., December 1987; Shultz interview by the Newsday editorial board, New York, October 1, 1987; conversation with Shultz spokesman, Charles Redman, Washington, D.C., November 9, 1987.
8. Gutman, "Poindexter Too Perfect a Staff Man?" Newsday, July 12, 1987, p. 5.
9. Poindexter memo to McFarlane, November 23, 1984, released as ICH document JMP-4. Also Poindexter testimony, ICH, July 15, 1987, p.m., p. 43/1.
10. Poindexter testimony, ICH, July 17, 1987, p.m., p. 12/1; North testimony, ICH, July 13, 1987, p.m., p. 3/2. Poindexter testimony, ICH, July 20, 1987, a.m., p. 5/1.
11. North testimony, ICH, July 7, 1987, p.m., p. 12/1.
12. ICR, pp. 194, 197. The unnamed Israeli official was cited in the historical chronology provided by the Israeli government to the joint congressional committee investigating the scandal; Tower, pp. B57–B67; ICR, p. 216.
13. ICR, p. 205.
14. North testimony, ICH, July 8, 1987, a.m., p. 15/1. Poindexter testimony, ICH, July 15, 1987, a.m., pp. 42/1, 48/1; July 15, 1987, a.m., p. 45/1.
15. Quoted by Bruce Cameron, former contra lobbyist, in interview, Washington, D.C., September 1987.

16. ICR, pp. 65–68.
17. Poindexter testimony, ICH, July 15, 1987, p.m., p. 26/2.
18. ICR, p. 382.
19. Interview with Abrams, Washington, D.C., October 1987. North memo to McFarlane, "Nicaragua Options," January 15, 1985, Exhibit 24, Poindexter deposition, ICH.
20. Shultz remarks reported by the *New York Times,* March 3, 1987, p. 4; Reagan speech, March 3, 1987, Presidential Documents.
21. Buchanan's opinion column appeared in the *Washington Post,* March 5, 1986; Reagan's speech, March 16, 1986, contained in Presidential Documents; ICR, pp. 91–98; account of Habib's intentions based on information from a senior U.S. official, Washington, D.C., January 1988.
22. Interview with McCurdy, Washington, D.C., June 1986; North memo to Poindexter, March 20, 1986, ICH Exhibit OLN-274.
23. Address to the nation by José Azcona Hoyo, April 4, 1987, carried by Honduras radio, April 5, and quoted in FBIS, April 7, 1986, p. P9; ICR, pp. 382–383.
24. Interview with an aide to Abrams, Washington, D.C., September 1986. Azcona spokesman Lisandro Quezada was quoted by AFP, March 24, 1986, reported by FBIS, March 25, 1986, p. P4; account of Ferch-Azcona conversation based on an interview with a U.S. official, Washington, D.C., October 1987.
25. Philip Shenon, "U.S. Aide Terms Nicaragua 'Aggressor State' in Region," *New York Times,* March 29, 1986.
26. Tower, pp. 180–181; ICR, p. 79; North memo to Donald Fortier, April 21, 1986, Exhibit OLN-277, ICH.
27. Casey memo to Regan, April 23, 1986, released as ICH Exhibit DTR-26; Poindexter testimony, ICH, July 15, 1987, p.m., p. 14/1; Poindexter memo to Donald R. Fortier, May 2, 1986, Exhibit JMP-45, ICH.
28. See William Goodfellow, "The Diplomatic Front," in Thomas W. Walker, ed., *Reagan vs. the Sandinistas* (Boulder: Westview Press, 1987), p. 152.
29. Arias interview on "One-on-One" with John McLaughlin, February 23, 1986.
30. Memo by North and Raymond Burghardt to the President, May 15, 1986, released as ICH Exhibit JMP-50; North memos to Poindexter, June 10, 1986, Exhibit JMP-53, ICH; May 16, 1986, Exhibit JMP-51, ICH.
31. Abrams testimony, ICH, June 2, 1987, a.m., pp. 26/1–29/1; ICR, p. 352.
32. Telephone interview with William Walker, deputy assistant secretary of state, December 1987.
33. Evans and Novak, "Fears for the Contras," *Washington Post,* May 21, 1986; "President Rejects Kemp Request to Fire Envoy Habib," *Washington Times,* May 24, 1986, p.1; Joanne Omang, "Habib Called Wrong, Imprecise, in Letter on U.S. Latin Policy," *Washington Post,* May 24, 1986; telephone interview with Habib, November 1987.
34. Goodfellow, *op. cit.,* p. 152.
35. Leiken testimony before the Senate Foreign Relations Committee, April 1, 1982; interview with Cameron, Washington, D.C., September 1987; also Michael Massing, "Contra Aides," *Mother Jones,* October 1987, pp. 23–26, 40–43.
36. Edward Cody, "Contras' Leaders Again Divided by Rivalry Between Politicians, Fighters," *Washington Post,* September 26, 1986, pp. A29, 35.
37. Telephone interview with Leiken, May 1987; interview with Cameron, *op. cit.*; Cameron memo to Channell, July 1, 1986, released by ICH, September 1987.
38. Telephone interview with McCurdy, December 1987.
39. Telephone interview with a senior Honduran official, September 1987.

40. Paragraphs quoted are 230, 241.
41. Telephone interview with Ferch, July 1986.
42. Shultz testimony, ICH, July 23, 1987, p. 16/1.
43. Source for this explanation of U.S. goals is an interview with a Central American diplomat, October 1986.
44. Interview with Hamrick, Rutherfordton, N.C., October 1986.
45. Gregory Selzer, interview with Canales, *Barricada*, October 9, 1986; Andrés Oppenheimer, "We Were Tired, Hungry, Hasenfus' Captors Say," *Miami Herald*, November 2, 1987, p. 30a.
46. ICR, p. 289.
47. ICR, p. 259.
48. McFarlane testimony, ICH, May 11, 1987, a.m., pp. 1/1–8/1; Robert Timburg, "McFarlane Calls Contras 'Inept Bottlers and Clerks,' " *Baltimore Sun*, May 8, 1987, p. 1.
49. ICR, p. 383.
50. The account that follows of the drafting of the Wright-Reagan plan and the negotiations in Guatemala is based on the following sources: interviews with Costa Rican ambassador Guido Fernández, Washington, D.C., August, October, November 1987; Manuel Cordero and Sofia Clark of the Nicaraguan embassy, Washington, D.C., November 1987; Wilson Morris, aide to Wright, Washington, D.C., November 1987; Philip Habib, telephone, August, November 1987; Elliott Abrams, Washington, D.C., October, November 1987; a senior U.S. official, Washington, D.C., October, November 1987; Costa Rican foreign minister Rodrigo Madrigal Nieto, Washington, D.C., September 1987; telephone interviews with a senior U.S. diplomat, January 1988; Honduran diplomatic sources, September, November 1987; Loeffler, January 1988.
51. Interview with Arias, San José, June 1985; Arias press conference San José, reported on FBIS wire, March 14; Julia Preston, "Oscar Arias, Defiantly," *Washington Post*, October 30, 1987, pp. D1, 9; Tower, pp. C11–C13; ICR, pp. 76–79.
52. Telephone interview with a Honduran diplomat, September 1987; interview with Victor Hugo Tinoco, Washington, D.C., November 1987.
53. The discussion that follows of U.S. policy following the Guatemala negotiations is based on interviews with Abrams, Washington, D.C., October, November, December 1987; telephone interviews with Habib, August, November 1987, and Loeffler, January 1988; and talk with an administration official, January 1988.
54. Interview with Walker, Washington, D.C., August 1987.
55. John Goshko, "Diplomacy by Wright, Ortega Hit," *Washington Post*, November 15, 1987, p. 1.
56. Interviews with Major Roger Miranda Bengoechea, Washington, D.C., December 1987; Tinoco, *op. cit.*; and Undersecretary of State Michael Armacost, December 1987. Interview with Yuriy Pavlov, head of the Latin American Department in the Soviet Foreign Ministry, reported in Roy Gutman, "Soviet: U.S. Distorts Nicaraguan Proposal," *Newsday*, February 29, 1988, p. 12.

Epilogue

1. Susan Rasky, "As truce chances developed, contras built private channel to Democrats," *New York Times*, March 26, 1988, p. 5.

APPENDIX I:
U.S. PROPOSAL AT
MANZANILLO (REVISED)

(This proposal was presented orally by Ambassador Harry Shlaudeman at the fourth meeting on August 15–16, 1984, and in writing at the fifth session, September 5–6. This copy was obtained from diplomatic sources and is an unofficial translation from the Spanish.)

TIMETABLE OF RECIPROCAL UNILATERAL MEASURES

Three stages at 30–60–90 days
A. Advisers

STAGE	NICARAGUA	OTHER CENTRAL AMERICAN STATES AND U.S.
30 days	Withdrawal of one third of Cuban and Soviet personnel.	U.S. military presence in Central America takes Nicaraguan actions into consideration in each stage.
60 days	Withdrawal of a second third of Cuban and Soviet personnel.	The U.S. military presence continues to take into consideration the action of Nicaragua at each stage.
90 days	Withdrawal of the last third of all Cuban and Soviet bloc military and security personnel.	The military presence of the U.S. has taken into consideration Nicaraguan action in each stage.

B. Support of Insurgencies

STAGE	NICARAGUA	OTHER CENTRAL AMERICAN STATES AND U.S.
30 days	Nicaragua closes down command and communications of FMLN. Circumvention and evasion not permitted.	The anti-Sandinistas agree not to mine or attack the harbors (of Nicaragua) or petroleum storage places.
60 days	Nicaragua closes down FMLN training centers.	Anti-Sandinistas and government of Nicaragua agree to a cease-fire in 90 days.

378

90 days	Withdrawal of all FMLN and FDR personnel from Nicaragua. FMLN/FDR political activities will not be permitted in Nicaragua. An end to foreign logistics support of FMLN/FDR.	ARDE/FDN will leave Costa Rica/ Honduras. Political activities of these groups are not permitted in Costa Rica/Honduras. An end to external logistics support for ARDE/FDN.
Final	ARDE/FDN will have been incorporated into the political process in Nicaragua and receive no foreign support.	FMLN/FDR will have been incorporated into the political process in El Salvador and will not be receiving foreign support.

C. Levels of Arms and Forces

STAGE	NICARAGUA	OTHER CENTRAL AMERICAN STATES AND U.S.
30 days	Public statement not to introduce new offensive arms. Exchange of inventories of arms and forces. Negotiations are requested among Central Americans.	Public statement not to introduce new offensive arms. Exchange of inventories of arms and forces. The U.S. will give prior notice of its participation in joint exercises and will invite foreign observers.
60 days	An end to the construction of military airports. An agreement is reached on maximum limits of balanced levels of arms and forces.	An end to the construction of military airports. An agreement is reached on maximum limits of balanced levels of arms and forces. U.S. presence and exercises to reflect the advances made.
90 days	Agreement on the timetable of the implementation of the above-mentioned phases (refers to accord mentioned in second stage). First phase on maximum limits on arms and forces has been put into practice.	Agreement on the timetable of the implementation of the above-mentioned phases. The U.S. presence and exercises are readjusted to reflect the advances made.
Final	Continuation of the putting into practice of agreements on levels of arms and forces.	Same.

D. Democracy

STAGE	NICARAGUA	OTHER CENTRAL AMERICAN STATES AND U.S.
30 days	Nicaragua invites all political tendencies to run in elections, thus restoring political rights, equal and fair access to the media.	El Salvador invites the opposition to run in the March 1985 elections; it offers security guarantees.

60 days	Election campaign period. All political rights are respected, security is guaranteed. There is amnesty for anyone wishing to participate peacefully.	Same for El Salvador.
90 days	Free and fair democratic elections are held.	Same for El Salvador.
Final	Elections are held guaranteeing free and fair democratic participation by all political tendencies. Democratic structures and rights will have been institutionalized.	Same for El Salvador.

E. Economic Cooperation

STAGE	NICARAGUA	OTHER CENTRAL AMERICAN STATES AND U.S.
30 days	An attempt will be made to form economic integration and cooperation with the rest of Central America.	U.S. will take steps to implement the Caribbean Basin Initiative in Nicaragua, promoting Central American integration and cooperation. Approval of the Jackson Plan.
60 days	Concrete points pending study.	U.S. will ask Nicaragua to participate in the CBI and Central American Development Organization under normal terms and conditions.
90 days	Concrete points pending study.	U.S. will increase its sugar quota for region including Nicaragua. Renegotiation of the debt will be permitted in accordance with the Club of Paris. Favorable consideration for loans to Nicaragua from the IADB and the World Bank.
Final	Renewal of economic integration and cooperation.	Economic cooperation and integration. U.S. will grant Nicaragua normal market access as well as access to the benefits of the Central American Development Organization.

F. Verification

STAGE	NICARAGUA	OTHER CENTRAL AMERICAN STATES AND U.S.
30 days	Nicaragua will suggest an on-site inspection of the departure of Cuban and Soviet bloc personnel, FMLN Command & Control centers and agreement on not introducing offensive arms.	Honduras/El Salvador/Costa Rica invite on-site inspection of all joint combined exercises. The U.S. and the Central American states agree not to introduce new offensive arms systems. The U.S. will intensify unilateral verification through technical means and will offer assistance in on-site efforts.
60 days	Observation of elections will verify fulfillment. The government of Nicaragua will suggest that on-site inventories of potential supply networks and of emplacement of military facilities be made by an international body on mutual agreement. Verification of the first stage will continue.	El Salvador, Honduras and Costa Rica will suggest that on-site verification of inventories, potential of guerrilla supply networks and emplacements of military facilities be made by an international body on mutual agreement. Verification of the first stage will continue.
90 days	Continuation of verification by an international body on mutual agreement. Negotiation of verification and control commission with Contadora.	Continuation of verification by an international body on mutual agreement. Negotiation of verification and control commission with Contadora.
Final	Full cooperation according to systems established for political questions and security within framework of Contadora.	Full cooperation according to systems established for political questions and security within framework of Contadora.

APPENDIX II:
SANDINISTA PROPOSAL AT MANZANILLO (REVISED)

(This proposal was presented in writing by Deputy Foreign Minister Victor Hugo Tinoco at the seventh meeting on October 30–31, 1984. This copy was obtained from diplomatic sources and is an unofficial translation from the Spanish.)

RECIPROCAL COMMITMENTS BY 30-DAY STAGES, WHICH THE UNITED STATES AND NICARAGUA WOULD BE OBLIGED TO FULFILL

A. Direct or Indirect Extraregional Military Presence

STAGES	U.S.	NICARAGUA
First Stage	The U.S. suspends its maneuvers in Central America. The U.S. will negotiate no new schools or North American military bases in countries bordering Nicaragua.	Nicaragua prohibits any international maneuver on its territory.
Second Stage	[left blank in original]	[left blank in original]
Third Stage	The U.S. dismantles its military schools, bases and installations in Honduras, Costa Rica and El Salvador. U.S. withdraws those advisers who carry out operational and training functions in the countries bordering Nicaragua. The U.S. draws up a registry and control of advisers who carry out technical functions as stipulated in the Revised Contadora Act.	Nicaragua proscribes foreign schools, bases and installations on its territory. Nicaragua withdraws those advisers who carry out operational and training functions as stipulated in the Revised Contadora Act.

B. Direct or Indirect Support for Insurgencies

STAGES	U.S.	NICARAGUA
30 days	Cessation of all logistical and financial support to the mercenary forces. Cessation of the arms traffic that is carried out with substantial North American support. Closing down and dismantlement of the diverse facilities such as organizational and recruitment networks, propaganda activities, etc., that exist in U.S. territory. Dismantlement of air, naval and land bases in countries bordering on Nicaragua which provide support for counterrevolutionary actions carried out by mercenary forces against Nicaragua. Closing of the command, communications and radio broadcasting centers used by the counterrevolutionaries in Honduras and Costa Rica. Dismantlement of all counterrevolutionary camps in Honduras and Costa Rica.	Elimination of arms traffic that may exist, destined to individuals, organizations, irregular forces or armed bands that are attempting to destabilize the governments of the region. Exercising of strict vigilance within its borders to prevent its territory from being used to carry out any sort of armed action against a neighboring state. Abstaining, should this be the case, from lending support of whatever type to individuals or groups that plan the destabilization of other governments as well as impeding the utilization of its territory for such ends.

C. Levels of Arms and Forces

U.S.	NICARAGUA
The U.S. commits itself to respect and not to violate the agreements that Nicaragua and the Central American countries reach within the Revised Act of Contadora.	Nicaragua together with the Central American countries and within the framework of the Revised Act of Contadora will commit itself not to introduce designated arms systems, to suspend the acquisition of such matériel as may be determined, to draw up required inventories, to establish limitations on the diverse types of armaments as well as limitations on numbers of troops and other personnel in conformity to the established timetable as defined in the Revised Act of Contadora.

D. Economic Cooperation

U.S.	NICARAGUA
Ceases boycott by the U.S. against Nicaragua in the international financial	Nicaragua publicly recognizes the positive change in the economic policy

organizations. The U.S. lifts restrictions and permits Nicaragua to the North American market. The U.S. supports the economic resolutions contained and defined in the Revised Act of Contadora.

of the North American administration. Nicaragua supports the economic resolutions contained and defined in the Revised Act of Contadora.

E. Verification

For both parties, the U.S. and Nicaragua, and for all of the stages.

1. With respect to agreements reached in any of the dialogue and negotiation, whether bilateral or multilateral, it is indispensable that these be subject to mechanisms of verification and control. 2. With reference to agreements within the Contadora framework, the respective commission of verification and control that this organizes will be charged with this task.

APPENDIX III:
PRE-ELECTION AGREEMENT
BETWEEN GOVERNMENT
AND OPPOSITION

(This is the draft agreement prepared by Comandante Bayardo Arce between the Frente Sandinista de Liberación Nacional, FSLN, and the Coordinadora Democrática Nicaragüense, CDN, during the occasion of the Socialist International Bureau meeting in Rio de Janeiro, October 1–2, 1984. Source: confidential minutes of the Socialist International. Translated from the Spanish original by the Socialist International.)

1. The *Coordinadora* agrees to register today 1 October and to participate in the electoral process.
2. The *Coordinadora* will request the leaders of the groups which have taken up arms against the Sandinista Revolutionary Government to keep their promise to suspend hostilities, and its candidate, Arturo Cruz, will take the necessary steps. In this connection they would be required to: a. Order a cease-fire prior to 10 October; b. Withdraw outside Nicaraguan territory to Costa Rica and Honduras and hand themselves over to Nicaraguan or Contadora authorities by 25 October at the latest.
3. The FSLN, if pacification is achieved by 25 October, will make provision for a postponement of the elections until 13 January.
4. The FSLN will meet this commitment even if some of the groups which have taken up arms against the Sandinista Revolutionary Government do not agree to a cessation of hostilities, provided that these are not the groups headed by Adolfo Calero and Eden Pastora (FDN and FRS).
5. If pacification is not achieved and the FSLN is thus prevented from postponing the elections, the *Coordinadora* shall have the option of reconsidering its participation in the voting on 4 November.
6. Therefore, in order to facilitate participation in the electoral process and for the *Coordinadora* to make up for the broadcasting time which it has not been allowed on the state television and radio networks, the FSLN is to make provision for the *Coordinadora* to be granted one-and-a-half hours per week of television coverage and a similar apportionment for radio time, and other participating parties will be allowed up to 45 minutes per week of television time and a similar apportionment for radio time.
7. Equally, the FSLN will guarantee that the rights already granted by the laws of Nicaragua to the registered parties, and other requests by the *Coordinadora*, including the Conservative Party of Nicaragua, are fully granted. (See attached Appendix.)
8. The Socialist International, for its part, will form a committee whose aim will be to act with the governments of the United States, the Contadora countries, Honduras and Costa Rica, so that all take appropriate steps to contribute toward peace in Nicaragua and to discourage any possibility of the continuation of violence. The Socialist International will also try to contribute directly with a

view to the suspension of hostilities on the part of those groups which have taken up arms against the Sandinista Revolutionary Government.

APPENDIX

Minimum conditions for a democratic election process in Nicaragua

1. Complete freedom of the spoken and written press and equal use for all political parties of the Sandinista state television network. This includes the freedom to buy time in the spoken, televised and written communication media, as well as an obligation on the part of these forms of media to give priority to the political parties during the election campaign. The Junta Government will issue appropriate decrees for the due implementation of the following measures:

A. Television
The use of television in equal conditions with the government party. This includes advertising, opinion programs, messages and political programs.

B. Radio
1. The immediate reopening of the news programs which were closed with effect from 22 March 1982.
2. The provision of radio time with national coverage, on both private and state stations, the latter being the most powerful.
3. Not to permit at any time a reduction in power during the transmission of our programs nor any interference therewith.
4. Not to resort to the practice of disabling the radio and TV channels at times when the political party programs go on the air.

C. Press
1. Free distribution and sale of the written means of social communication.
2. Guarantees of nonprohibition of reading of the independent means of communication on posters, in state offices, military installations, universities and colleges and in public offices.
3. Free inflows and distributions of newspapers, magazines, books, bills, posters or transfer processes published or printed abroad.
4. Free introduction into the country of all the necessary printing materials for the political election process, as well as the expeditious delivery of the same, whether donated or purchased.
5. Supplies of exchange for all newspapers and radio and TV channels in equal conditions.

D. All the means of social communication to which we have referred must not be submitted to prior censorship, save as related to military matters and national security.

E. Freedom of political organization and mobilization throughout national territory, both individual and collective. This involves the following:
1. The free contracting of all types of urban and rural transport.
2. Freedom of assembly both indoors and in squares, streets, stadiums, roads, properties and land both public and private.
3. Absolute guarantee that no political gathering will be hindered by the organization of shock forces or paramilitary forces belonging to other political

parties. The police and the armed forces must contribute toward the proper carrying out and development of the electoral process.

4. Throughout the day of the election there will be no free movement of mass transport and state vehicles with the exception of special cases such as ambulances, transport of wounded persons, etc.

5. Inspection by all the parties of the registers of voters and a special day for the registration of those citizens who have not already done so. A copy of the official records of the vote-counting process, duly signed, from each voting table, for the lawyer representing each party or alliance participating in the elections. The lawyers shall be entitled to speak and to note on the official records their observations in each vote acceptance committee and to guarantee a fair counting process.

6. The location of the election boxes far from the quarters and houses of the Sandinista Defense Committees, state offices and any coalition or party organization, as well as the absence of all propaganda and political pressure in the voting establishments during the day of the election.

7. Not to impose any obstacles and to allow free access to the country to the special guests of each organization comprising the Nicaraguan Democratic Coordinating Alliance.

8. Formal commitment on the part of the Government Junta for National Reconstruction, the Sandinista Front for National Liberation and the Sandinista Armed Forces vis-à-vis the governments of the Contadora group to respect the results of the elections.

9. All parties participating in the elections will be permitted to visit and speak at state companies and public offices during rest periods or in political classes and seminars during working hours. At the same time, there will be allowed in these same centers, the free circulation and reading of all material distributed within national territory relating to the political campaign. The authorities of these institutions undertake not to take reprisals of any kind whatsoever against any person expressing sympathy and support for any political party or coalition.

INDEX